"I used to worry about "Big Brother" and how much big government knows about its citizens—but I was wrong—government is way too disorganized. I now have a much greater concern about the likes of Google—and what they know—because they are far more organized."

—*Anonymous*

SEVEN TRENDS

THAT WILL TRANSFORM LOCAL GOVERNMENT THROUGH TECHNOLOGY

Alan R. Shark

Published by **Public Technology Institute** • Alexandria, Virginia

Library of Congress Cataloging – Publication – Data

Shark, Alan R.
Seven Trends That Will Transform Government Through Technology

ISBN-13: 978-1470046026
ISBN-10: 1470046024

1. Chief Information Officers. 2. Information Technology-Management. 3. Leadership. I. Title

Public Technology Institute
1420 Prince Street, 2nd Floor
Alexandria, Virginia 22314
www.pti.org

The Public Technology Institute (PTI) serves as the national voice for technology development and dissemination within local government across the United States.

Created in 1971 *by* and *for* city and county governments to address the many technology issues that impact government services at the local level, PTI continues today to actively support local government technology executives and their staffs, chief appointed officials, and local elected officials through technology research, education, executive level consulting services, and national awards and recognition programs.

A non-profit 501(c)3 organization, PTI offers online training, publications and books, and conferences designed for the local government technologist; conducts topical surveys; and creates partnerships between local government, private industry, and the federal government to ensure that local governments have access to the latest and most effective technology solutions and practices. PTI partners with leading national media and academic institutions to showcase local government technology issues and success stories.

To raise the stature of the CIO/IT executive within government, PTI has created the CIO "Thought Leadership" book series. Recent books produced as part of this series include "CIO Leadership for Cities and Counties: Emerging Trends and Practices" and "CIO Leadership for State Governments: Emerging Trends and Practices" (published in collaboration with the National Association of State CIOs.)

PTI also maintains a Certified Government CIO certificate program. In partnership with Rutgers University's School of Public Affairs and Administration (SPAA), PTI is working to bridge the gap between theory and practice through enhanced training and professional development certification for current local government CIOs and those technology officials aspiring to become CIOs.

For more information, visit www.pti.org.

PREFACE

Just as historians and archeologists try to interpret Egyptian hieroglyphics, similarly, experts in the future may look back at the last two centuries' worth of PowerPoint presentations and ask, "What were they thinking?" That is because most recent history largely has been reduced to lists and sentences, a few graphics, and inadequate explanations!

This book is a result of delivering a talk—with many PowerPoints—a few hundred times over a three-year period. While the number of trends never changed (because the cover had already been designed) the categories and subcategories have changed many times over. At the conclusion of one of my interactive presentations, someone asked for a copy of my PowerPoint presentation. However, a week later that same person sent me a list of questions about what the various slides really meant. She said it all made sense while she was in the room, however, when looking back, the presentation's logic began to disappear, so it was suggested that I write a narrative. That led to this book.

I have been fortunate and blessed with having a number of significant positions over the past decade, including serving as the executive director of the Public Technology Institute and as a professor at Rutgers University. This rich experience has allowed me to meet, observe, and listen to so many public managers, elected officials, students, and technology leaders, who have shared their views regarding technology, leadership, and change in local government. From years of giving keynote speeches, sitting on panels, teaching graduate students, writing articles, and moderating discussion groups, I have developed a collection of notes. It is with this thought in mind that I can only take credit for synthesizing and laying out the trends in what I hope is a logical and easy-to-digest format that is designed to engage the reader.

ACKNOWLEDGEMENTS

This book was designed for easy reading and intentionally leaves out citations that often can serve as speed bumps to the flow of the reading and absorption process. Rest assured, key references and suggested resources can be found at the end of the book, and any numbers, calculations, or figures have reference points and can be supplied happily by request. Keep in mind that many of the facts and figures will likely have changed since the book's printing. It should be pointed out that technology is changing in every field of endeavor, yet the focus of this book is on information technology (IT).

As with any book, this one is the result of a team process. I am forever grateful to Lindsay Isaacs, who served as copy editor. In addition, as importantly, I am so very pleased to have had Sally Hoffmaster create the cover design and layout the entire manuscript. You will note that cartoons have been added as a way of highlighting certain points and at the same time providing some levity to an otherwise serious subject. All cartoons are copyrighted and are displayed with permission.

Thanks and appreciation also go to Ronda Mosley, PTI's Assistant Executive Director for Research and Government Services, who supplied much of the green IT copy as well as information in the energy assurance section. Her timely nudging helped ensure that these topics were rightfully included.

I also wish to acknowledge PTI's Chairman, Brian O'Neill, who is serving his ninth term as Councilman for the City of Philadelphia, and Marc Holzer, Dean of Rutgers University School of Public Affairs & Administration, for their encouragement and continued support.

TABLE OF CONTENTS

INTRODUCTION

Seven Trends

To best appreciate and understand trends of any type, it is important to view them in a proper context. While the technology evolution has been somewhat constant, with each technological advancement building upon the next, each of the seven trends has occurred within the first 10 years of the 21st century.

As our nation was celebrating the turn of the century, no one could have imagined that just a few months later, America would come under attack on September 11, 2001, by a new type of enemy, who literally turned one of our own and prized technologies against ourselves. Indeed, as they greeted the turn of the century, local government leaders across the globe were largely fixated on television news and watched each passing time zone with delight. The reason was the fretful Y2K dilemma. Decades earlier, no one had contemplated the inherent limitation in the internal clocks that are found in just about every computerized device in the world. None were geared toward changing the cumulative clock to go beyond the year 1999. People feared the power grid would go out, elevators would stop, airplanes would crash, and bank ATMs would fail. Y2K happily yielded no doomsday scenarios as many had predicted.

Yes, the turn of the century saw the once-dominant America Online (AOL) about to release its newest download for dial-up—download version 6.0—replacing the rather buggy 5.0 that didn't work very well with Windows XP. By the turn of the century, cell phone penetration reached 12% of the population, and 51% of U.S. homes had computers—but only 41.5% had Internet access. Most Americans still enjoyed standard TVs and clunky computer monitors. It would be another five years before everyone began dumping their old monitors for the new flat-screen variety. It would take another three or four years for MySpace, YouTube, Facebook, and Twitter to emerge. The iPhone didn't come to market until 2007, and the iPad didn't appear until 2010.

The speed with which technological change is occurring is no less than dazzling. Every day, we read about new and improved applications. Years ago, a generation of adults happily moved from rotary dial phones to push button phones and then found themselves untethered from corded phones as they migrated to cordless phones. Early adapters were proud to show off their "mobile car phones" as they embraced the very first cell phones that were referred to as "bag phones" because they were bulky cell phones in a bag. They required either a rather heavy and hefty battery, or the power would come from a car's power adapter socket, once called a "cigarette lighter." The antenna was either a magnetically mounted roof antenna or installed on the rear glass windshield.

Today, our cell phones are truly portable and can perform thousands of applications because they are nothing less than rather powerful computers. When Apple introduced the first iPhone in 2007, the world was delighted, while the traditional phone manufacturers were in shock. Yes, history was made: It was a computer company that built the iPhone, which turned out to be a very smart cell phone. In 2007, there were less than 500 applications (apps) when the iPhone was introduced, and today there are well over 450,000 iPhone apps. With the advent of the competing Android mobile operating system, there are now more than 250,000 Android-compatible apps, and that will shortly double within a few years. There are simply no dumb phones out there anymore—just some are much, much smarter.

Like the evolution of the mobile phone, computers have steadily grown in complexity and features. In 2009, portable laptops outsold desktop PCs. In addition, in 2010, text and other data services surpassed voice communications. Computers also have shrunk in size thanks to miniaturization. With every new model, computers become lighter, smarter, and more powerful, with more brilliant graphics. Computers of old allowed us to process and store information; they now enable us to better visualize and to interact—and even better—to create content.

We have all heard that it took 30 years to reach the milestone of having 10 million people purchase TVs. Yet, in April 2010, the first Apple iPad sold 3 million units in just 80 days and then went on to sell 4.5 million in the next quarter. By the time this book goes to press, even more spectacular records will have been broken.

While a bit slow to grasp the possibilities, city and county government leaders began to realize they needed to update their thinking and look at technology as a set of tools that would enable them to better carry out their responsibilities and, thus, the term "e-government" was born. The innovations of voice, data, and video have finally come together, and have brought us the reality and benefits of convergence of the three. The journey into the digital world is still unfolding, and we have accepted a common language of what is referred to as “Internet protocol” or IP. Only with today’s lightning-fast relative connectivity, we find ourselves inextricably linked together in an increasingly virtually connected society.

Given the amazing amount of technological change in every discipline, many of the trends described in this book will have come and gone—only to be replaced by the new and improved. This is indeed good news for those in the publishing world. Like a great movie, this book promises many updated additions and sequels to stay ahead of the exponential change that affects us all.

So, what is the true purpose of this book? The answer lies with the notion of perspective. To understand change, we need to have a sense of perspective. Hopefully then, this book not only will provide a sense of perspective, but at the same time build a sense of urgency for actions and policies that can help public managers and citizens navigate a better and more secure future.

"They're encyclopedias, Timmy. . . they're an early form of **Google**."

Many may find the seven trends set out in this book to be self-evident; however, in my experience, not everyone appreciates the interdependency of the trends. Should you have any lingering doubts about their relationship to one another, just turn to the last chapter and it should become crystal clear.

So, why focus on local governments? With every government turning to websites and apps to interact with citizens, why not cover all levels of government? In a sense, this book does apply to all levels of government; however, there are more than 70,000 local governments, and the public first identifies with government at the local level. As public opinion for government has plummeted due mostly to the perception of the federal government, local governments by comparison have always fared much better when separated out as a distinct category. The origins of e-government and technology experimentation have been deeply rooted at the local government level, where it has been proven time and time again that innovation is born at the local government level.

The technologies and trends described herein will both impact and change how local governments operate and interact with citizens like never before. Moreover, with every improvement, there is another enhancement just around the corner. Technology innovation has been ingrained in the American way of life, and as citizens, we use it every day to make life more manageable, to communicate with our families and co-workers, and to search and process new information from all parts of the globe. We turn to technology for shopping and entertainment, too. We transact our orders and subscriptions online, view and hear news and entertainment services through our new devices, and pay bills and voice our opinions as never before. We share pictures and videos, and take part in actually creating information and content. We play games with ourselves or with others across the globe. Businesses entice us with new offers and services. Local governments are catching on, and their citizens over time will expect nothing less. However, this book goes well beyond e-government and takes a look at the most important challenges local governments face today, as well as new technology opportunities that lie ahead.

Simply put, the seven trends that will transform local government through technology are all about rethinking resources (budgets, technology and staff), forms of leadership and championship, and service delivery methods; understanding our technology infrastructure, citizen engagement and expectations; governing and sharing resources; and finally, protecting our networks, as well as energy assurance and efficiency. As you will see, each one of these seven trends, while presented as separate chapters, is inextricably tied to one another.

TREND ONE

Rethinking Technology and Government: Saving Green and Being Green

TREND ONE

Rethinking Technology and Government: Saving Green and Being Green

Doing *Much* More with *Much* Less

This chapter was written in the depths of what many have called the *Great* (and long-lasting) *Recession of 2008.* Well over 564,000 local government employees have lost their jobs, and technology departments have not been exempt. Unlike the federal government, local governments can't print money, thus there are greater legal pressures to balance their budgets. With housing values dropping to record lows, so has the corresponding property tax income. With more people out of work and with less money being spent, sales tax revenue has been down. In fact, all revenue (tax) sources are down. Further, with businesses of all sizes cutting back (or standing still), local governments still have much to do by way of providing essential services, but they have much fewer resources with which to do so. Unfortunately, doing much more with much less is not a sustainable strategy.

Numerous technology-related projects have been placed on hold, or technology managers have been instructed to find less expensive alternatives. The climate for increased fiscal accountability has led to new requirements for cost-benefit justification. For example, a county that had a policy to update all of its PCs every three years has changed its policy to update most PCs or laptops in four or five years. More than one city has moved much of its data storage operations to a third-party vendor, now referred to as cloud services. Some local agencies have pooled their requirements together, thereby increasing their bargaining power. A county out West has outsourced its entire IT department, while another has outsourced its police and fire operations.

When there are economic woes, despite painful choices, local government officials become very creative. Yet, saving money for short-term gains does not always lead to longer-term solutions. Indeed, many IT experts have argued against across-the-board budget cuts, where IT budgets are cut as any other department or division. They argue that in times of economic uncertainty, it is better to invest more in technology, not less. Most experts agree that IT budgets cannot be treated as other government components because most technologies—when properly applied—save money both in terms of time and labor. Computers and mobile devices, software, or cloud services do not require fringe benefits or expensive retirement plans, and they take up much less space than employees.

The need to upgrade software, replace worn hardware components, improve system security, and train key staff has not gone away, but how we plan for and justify them has changed. We can no longer rely on anecdotal references and past policies as guiding principles. Not too long ago, purchasing decisions were made on the recommendation of someone, usually an IT director, who was a trusted source, and the only rationalization might have been that if the other city or county had it, we should, too. Today, technology leaders are required to develop business plans with stated return on investment (ROI) rationales and strategies.

Unlike other governmental program cuts, technology expenditures need to be viewed differently. Sure, cuts can be made; however, just like with physical infrastructure, at some point technology must be restored and replaced. Ideally, public managers should not cut IT budgets without also creating some form of replenishment fund. In technology, delaying or postponing replenishments or upgrading systems is creating a huge liability and could severely impact critical systems with disastrous consequences that grow with each passing day. Moreover, technology equipment (hardware and software) has a much shorter life expectancy than a building that was designed to last 100 years but with some retrofitting could last another 100. Our new technologies are fragile, and when they show their age, it is usually in the form of a serious system-wide failure that could spell disaster for elected officials and IT managers alike, and more importantly, could seriously affect the safety and security of citizens.

The Consumerization of Technology

The consumerization of technology is essentially the transference of once-sophisticated and expensive technology into affordable consumer-friendly technology. As more employees have their own high-powered communication devices and expect to use them at work, local government IT departments must adjust their operations. The advantages of allowing government employees to use their personal devices at work include zero end-user equipment costs, speed in informational flow and response, interactive responsiveness, high-level situational awareness, and hopefully, increased trust with the public. A number of other benefits include:

- Improved government employee morale,
- Less or no need to carry two devices,
- Employees may take greater care because they "own" the device,
- Improved business functionality,
- Local and state governments save money,
- More efficient use of equipment,
- Less truck rolls for a growing mobile workforce, and
- Less need and dependence for central IT support.

This trend has far-reaching implications for technology in local government. Employees who have had to carry two devices generally welcome the opportunity to choose one they own, and they usually can obtain them significantly faster than going through any government procurement process. When support service is required, most mobile devices come with 24/7 assistance. This trend is not limited to mobile devices. For example, sophisticated GIS systems that once sat on desktops or mainframes can be accessed via the cloud with their own support systems at affordable rates. All the updates and software modifications are performed at the service-provider location.

We all know the term BYOB (bring your own bottle); however, we now are seeing things like BYOD (bring your own device) or BYOT (bring your own technology). The four main driving forces for this trend are: web 2.0/social media, cloud-based solutions, mobile device breakthrough, and the rise of applications (apps). Of course, the main characteristics are powerful devices, stable platforms, abundance of apps, ease-of-use, feature-rich, user-configurable, relatively inexpensive, and off-the-shelf convenience.

Consumerization of technology has some challenges, too, such as increased security risks, need for support, lack of IT control and standardization, lack of in-person training, greater risk of device or information theft, and quite possibly, diminished vendor support. For those reasons, many jurisdictions continue to ignore or prohibit the use of personal devices, but others are either experimenting or embracing the use of multiple mobile platforms and devices. For example, the City of Raleigh, North Carolina, has a policy called "Managed Diversity." It is a concept first started by Gartner that allows IT organizations to both maintain a level of standardization for support efficiency while also supporting the growing diversity of end-point devices that knowledge workers are bringing into the workplace.

This trend will only grow as the next generation of workers, the Millennials, enters the workforce with a longer history of using personal communication devices. It is estimated that by 2020, Millennials will be 45% of the workforce. This is a group that is used to independent action and is known to be technology independent. This is a group where mobility is second nature, and is looked upon as being on the forefront of social engagement and collaboration. The Millennials will have profound implications for rethinking technology and local government.

Re-thinking Infrastructure: Computers Don't Rust

Many are concerned that as budgets are cut, technology infrastructure funding will be delayed or postponed indefinitely. After all, computers rarely show outward signs of age. They do not rust like bridges and other physical infrastructure like roads and highways that over time clearly show wear. The public is well aware of poor streets and roads. The information highway is largely invisible and carries a great liability when not properly maintained.

As we increasingly depend on telecommunication-based services, both wired and wireless, citizens are at the mercy of government oversight or government neglect. Unlike the private sector, whose businesses depend on satisfied customers, local governments have different operational models where it is easier to postpone system upgrades and replacements. So, while technology equipment rarely displays signs of rust, it does age, and ultimately it will fail.

In 2009, citizens in Montgomery County, Maryland, found themselves in a traffic nightmare where a normal 20-minute commute turned into 3.5 hours for many. Citizens were frustrated and outraged. The county's traffic signals were completely out of sync. Apparently, a 30-year-old computer controller simply failed without warning. Because the manufacturer went out of business many years ago, it took several days of traffic hell to find a stopgap replacement part from a supplier who happened to have it. The county traffic officials were well aware of the aging equipment and for a number of mundane reasons kept putting off its replacement even though it had been repeatedly flagged. Just-one-more-year-type thinking can be all it takes for a piece of equipment to fail.

Does New Technology Really Save Money?

There has always been a debate over the question, "Do new technologies really save money?" This is a question often asked, and the answer quite simply is, "They can if they are planned properly." The problem is that the savings might not occur right away, and in some cases they may be difficult to measure.

Government technology managers and citizens want to believe that by spending money on technology they will save money through greater automation and other efficiencies of scale. Information technology (IT) managers like to refer to spending as investments. They view spending on new equipment and e-government services as investing for the near future while acknowledging the payback might be realized in three to five years, perhaps more.

Investing in technology becomes quite a challenge as extreme pressure builds to spend less, and when IT managers do spend money on technology, there is the expectation that the results will be immediate. At the same time, the most vocal members of the public expect greater conveniences through online services and automated systems that reduce manual labor-intensive routines. There appears to be a value clash among those who want more from their local governments and others who want less government spending and, ironically, at all costs.

How we pay for technology is quite another challenge. Often, perhaps too often, equipment purchases are added to the capital budget, and useful equipment life is stretched out over many years into the future. Other purchases are leased or paid for out of general operating funds. Some jurisdictions have special funds just for technology purchases. Until recently, there have been inconsistent rules and guidelines, but the economic woes have helped to create greater standards and guidelines for purchasing, especially technology procurement.

As we shall see throughout this book, adversity can spawn innovation. Today, there are many new and promising choices when it comes to IT.

What's the Difference Between an Expense and an Investment?

Politically, a positive justification for a purchase uses the term "investment," while the negative or opposing term "expense" is used to voice uncertainty or opposition. Surely, everything spent is an expense. In the IT environment, managers are being challenged to justify their budgets as never before. This has led to the positive development where technology managers need to develop business plans and ROI reports that clearly point out the benefits and timelines for realizing efficiencies and savings. In the recent past, IT spending went largely unchecked without performance metrics. Therefore, an IT investment is an honest term when correctly applied to realistic assumptions of inputs, outputs, and performance measurement criteria where there is a definable benefit in the end.

The more difficult debate is whether a technology application is considered an expense or an investment—or perhaps a little of both? Studies have shown that technology can streamline operations, reduce staff, reduce errors, and save time. Unfortunately, there are usually large expenses for start-up, training and development before the application goes mainstream. Such costs should be highlighted and explained as part of the cost of the operation; they should not be ignored, hidden or buried. When such "details" are omitted or not mentioned, inevitably someone finds them, and then credibility is an uphill struggle.

When cities and counties are challenged to do more with less, technology investments can help meet their challenges. A city out West finds itself with four geospatial information systems (GIS) and databases. It is costly and ineffective to maintain all of the different databases and keep up with updates, training and more. By spending a little more upfront and creating an enterprise GIS system that serves many layers of interest, the city would have a more comprehensive solution. But here, the answer may lie more in leadership than in technology. Everyone is for standards and conformity—just as long as they are theirs! Technology leadership needs to come from the highest levels of management to best ensure that the technology enterprise is well coordinated and integrated, and waste is minimized.

People often forget that even the smallest cities and counties have business lines that require IT support of some kind. More often than not, cities and counties have at least 100—and more likely 200 plus—business lines, each requiring some form of technology and support. The challenge for IT professionals and public managers alike is to ask, "Is information technology a cost center or an expense center?" If it is an expense center where it is treated as any other department, then it will appear as a large expense. If, on the other hand, it is a cost center, then IT can charge much of its operations out to the various departments it supports. Regardless of how IT is accounted for, everything is changing, and business support decisions and cost-justification tools are leading the way.

Despite the economic climate, there is some encouraging news regarding the cost of technology, and that has to do with new options. This book also will look at what it means to save money by employing green polices. We will look at IT consolidation, new forms of software as a service, new forms of governance, leadership, and regional cooperation. Certainly, the entire book could focus on doing more with less or go into much greater detail about how to save money by using more IT, but that could be a lot less interesting. Nevertheless, this book will have an undercurrent of realized efficiencies, and new ways and methods to save money and actually get much more out much of less.

Why Can't Cloud Computing Be the Total Cure?

Today, the term "cloud computing" is used to describe just about everything where the actual computers or services are located somewhere else and often managed by another entity—be it another government entity or commercial service. The largest cloud services are offered by companies such as Microsoft, Google and Amazon, to name a few. Cloud computing with its advantages and disadvantages will be fully discussed later in this book. Suffice it to say that being responsible for business functions and technology no longer means having to own the entire infrastructure. You can still own the data and processes, but not necessarily the hardware or software. One might manage a system that meets all one's operational standards and requirements yet is supplied through a private vendor physically located elsewhere.

"Are you sure our data is secure on the cloud? I just saw my spreadsheet on the weather channel!"

The concept of having external processing power, storage and retrieval of data, or the actual system functionality located and maintained by another party is in itself revolutionary. In the "good old days" where money and resources were more plentiful, it would have been near impossible to visualize cloud computing, let alone implement it. This is a remarkable trend that will grow as certainly as the overall definition. However, with every advance, there is always a countervailing force. Simply throwing systems, applications, and data into the cloud does not in any way remove the governmental entity from being responsible for the data and system security and integrity. In case of failure, the response cannot be "they" failed us. That is why redundancy and multi-path backups are even more essential. Nevertheless, cloud-based solutions are a very significant trend and will be covered in chapter three.

What about Staff? The Challenges

Even the best technologies require great staff to implement, manage, and oversee projects. When technology is discussed, public managers often overlook the impact on staff, who may not adapt well to changes or automation generally. There is ample evidence pointing to the fact that even the best of systems can fail if the human factor is not considered. This requires ongoing training and positive reward programs. Technology is no longer just about IT staff; in today's environment, it involves just about everybody one way or another.

Many reports suggest that somewhere between 3 million and 4 million public workers will be retiring within the next few years. Those who stand to gain from finding new private sector positions may come from the public technology sector. Add to this dilemma the current deficit-minded environment in which many are reporting problems with current technology staff, and we are beginning to see in many local governments across the country variations of the following:

- Poor morale,
- Reduced performance and commitment,
- Increased turnover,
- Inability to attract new talent,

- Increased technology infrastructure failures, and
- Increased retirements and knowledge drain.

We know that poor morale can lead to poor performance, and when you consider the responsibilities technology staff have in terms of running critical systems, the concern is more than justified. Local governments also know that technology managers can more easily find higher paying positions in the private sector.

The performance issue is also a human issue, which can impact an entire governmental entity when morale is low. Technology workers complain that they are not appreciated, not understood, and underpaid when compared to the private sector. Technology workers point out that they are not receiving the support they deserve, and one-size-fits-all solutions like across-the-board budget cuts help contribute to that perception. Many of the cuts are real and painful, and have resulted in increased workloads because of reduced staff, but they also have reduced or cut the following:

- technology research and information service subscriptions,
- training funds,
- opportunities to obtain or maintain certifications,
- travel to professional meetings and conferences, and
- funds for new equipment, such as laptops, smartphone devices, tablet computers, etc.

What about Staff? The Opportunities

Attrition also can be a blessing in that it can provide an opportunity to resize departments and re-staff with candidates with newer cutting-edge skills. This all comes at a time when there has been a greater need for highly motivated technology managers to keep our systems up and running and, as importantly, secure. There may be new opportunities with the large number of retiring employees from all levels of government. Many people I have spoken to really don't want to completely retire, which is a great opportunity for struggling local governments. There will be new opportunities for experienced IT managers

"He's not in today. You can send an email, leave a comment on his blog, tweet him, leave a voice mail message or contact him on Facebook. I can't take a message. That's above my pay scale."

who may be very happy to work part-time, on shared positions, or other creative employment schemes.

Job Sharing

Job sharing has been shown to be a creative solution when funds are limited and the need for talent is great. With the expected retirement boom, it will be easier to fill particle lots with different skills that save money and provide for a wider variety of expertise. Job sharing also can be used for current staff who might appreciate the flexibility to tend to other interests or family matters.

Professional Development

The need for professional development is only getting stronger, and it is also viewed as a means of providing an employment benefit. If the right programs are chosen, the impact to the government can be critical. That would be especially true with security and leadership training.

Four-day Week

One would have thought that the impetus for a modified work week would have come from a human resource department. In fact, most of the best examples come from the IT enterprise, or IT departments were at least major players in planning the arrangements. Motivations for moving in this direction range from greater employee happiness (especially when salary and fringe benefits were reduced or cut), improved energy efficiency in reduced physical plant use, less pollution from employees driving to work, improved traffic flows as congestion is reduced, and as a means to attract new employees in a changing work environment. A four-day week means that workers work the same amount of hours—except over four days instead of five. Technology staffs played the key leadership role in making sure that every system was supported in the varying business lines that governments manage.

Telework

The federal government encourages telework and operates under the Telework Act of 2010 (www.telework.gov). Cities and counties have moved more cautiously, concerned that local government workers are closer to the citizens, and they worry about public perceptions of teleworking.

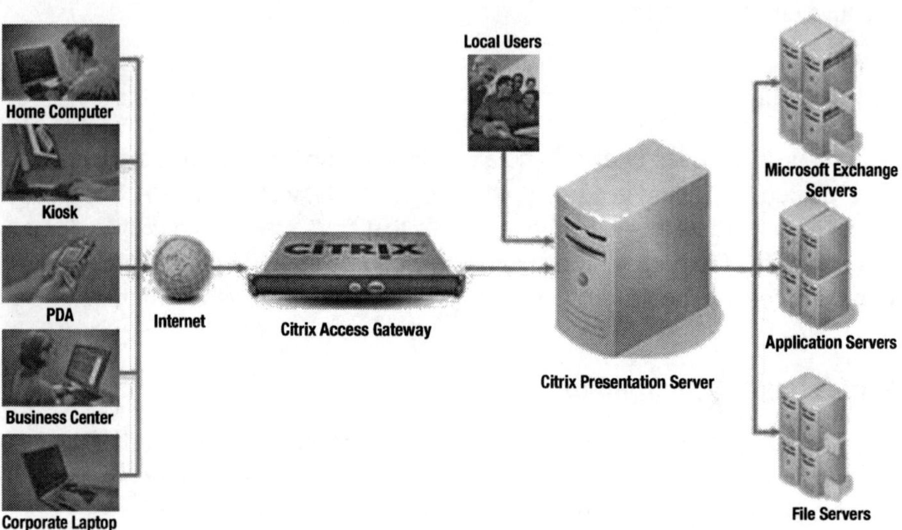

Many government organizations have begun using telework systems like Citrix's "GoToMyPC," which allows a worker to work from just about anywhere as if he or she were sitting at his or her own desk in the office. Using other Citrix tools, the remote connection is secure, empowering local government workers who choose or need to work from a remote location or home office. Telework is far more than a mere convenience to an employee. It is considered an essential component for disaster planning and can save governments money while keeping employees off the roads.

Today one can be almost anywhere and work as if you are in the office.

Staff Retraining

In an ever-changing technology environment, it is important for staff to have access to a retraining program that can transform them into employees the government values instead of employees that supervisors wish would retire. Not everyone can or is willing to learn new skills, but that alone should not be an excuse for not trying. When retraining works, the city or county is not only gaining by having someone be more productive, it is strengthening the organization by retaining the knowledge that may have walked out the door.

Managing Expectations

When it comes to technology support in the public sector, elected leaders need to recognize how important technology plays in just about everything a local government does, including public safety, utilities, health services, communications, transportation, education, and economic development. Technology is more than a simple expense line item because it supports just about every business function that a local government deploys. The issue of managing expectations is important because technology in the local government environment is not as well understood and is viewed by some citizens as more of a luxury than a necessity. Often people express a desire to return to the "good ole days" and ask, "Why can't we simply go back to a simpler time?" Technology often lacks dedicated elected leaders as well as other high-ranking public managers as champions. The most successful city and county governments have enlightened leaders who gladly serve as champions, help shape technology policies, and thus manage realistic expectations from among their citizens as well as with employees.

Common Myths and Realities of IT: Efficiency, Effectiveness, and Equity

Whatever governments do by way of providing programs and services, they are usually justified on the basis of whether it is efficient, effective, and, more recently, equitable. Listed below are many common myths and realities regarding IT that help illustrate how IT has been so poorly understood in its entirety.

1. **IT is all about hardware/software.** Information technology is much more than just hardware and software—it's about people, processes, and demonstrating productivity over a prescribed period of time. IT also must address solutions to problems, and the benefits should be apparent.

2. **Hardware/software failures tend to be infrastructure issues perhaps multiplied by inadequate preparation.** While no one would disagree that inadequate preparation contributes to failures, it usually begins much earlier through poor planning, inadequate system specification, poor oversight, poor budgeting, vendor short-comings, and lack of overall leadership. Failure is more often a failure in leadership than anything to do with technology. Often the technology provider/vendor over-promises, but in the end, it's still about leadership, and sound program and project management.

3. **New systems will solve all our problems.** This is more a wish than a realistic expectation. Failure to fully understand a problem can lead to a solution that is worse than the original problem. Technology—be it software or hardware—is simply a tool. Like any tool, it can be misused or worse if it is not well understood. Leadership and training and learning from others through best practices are the best ways to mitigate some of the risks associated with inflated expectations.

4. **A new system doesn't fix broken processes.** On the surface, this statement would appear to be true. But when we speak of systems, we need to think of the entire system with all of its sub-processes. Not all processes involve technology. Many critical processes involve people and past practices. Broken processes can be fixed with new systems just as long as there is a sharp focus on what a successful solution would look like conceptually and operationally. This needs to be adequately addressed and tested well before moving to a new system.

5. **New systems help uncover broken/flawed processes.** This statement is largely true. Usually, the decision to move to a new system is based on an older system either not being adequately supported, or because it is no longer efficient or cannot meet the new demands that have been realized over time. To be successful in developing a new system, there must be a lot of time devoted to rethinking the entire system in terms of seeing if there are new opportunities that were not present. By diagramming out system processes, one can more clearly see how a new system will solve problems and correct for flawed operations uncovered in the planning process.

6. **Inadequate training/documentation of old system.** By and large, local governments have done a poor job in the area of knowledge management. Systems that should have been replaced years ago have been kept alive by dedicated and well-meaning staff who were able to find innovative ways to keep things running longer. This is often done in times of "emergencies" when there is simply no time to sit down and document. While this may have saved monies in the short run, this practice can lead to more costly solutions later on when someone will try to decipher the old system, which can be more expensive in the longer run due to the extra time needed to plan for a new system and system migration from the old to the new.

   Inadequate training, often the result of disproportionate across-the-board budget cuts can lead to disproportionate failures. Technology is largely a critical support function. Less training can lead to fewer efficiencies and poor system performance.

7. **New systems will make us more efficient.** This is not necessarily true, as new systems can only make us more efficient if there is adequate planning and testing. The local government landscape is littered with the debris from well-intentioned systems that never provided the results as promised. The overriding factor is always leadership over technology.

8. **Technology alone cannot bridge the digital divide between the connected and the unconnected.** Technology can help as a tool, but there are many key factors that have to be addressed first as will be discussed later in the book.

9. **Technology expenditures will realize a quick payback.** Technology, whether it is labeled an expense or an investment, may not always yield a quick monetary payback. Some applications and technologies are services the public cherishes, and there may be little financial return other than a citizen happiness factor. Citizens may want smarter bus stops with signs alerting them to when the next bus will be approaching. Because public transportation is already heavily subsidized, the public may tend to ride a bus with signage, but there may be zero savings.

   Another example comes from a top 10 city where aging computers systems were taking a toll, resulting in lower performance and costly repairs. The city was asked to "invest" more than $5 million to make long-needed upgrades and purchase new equipment and software. The technology department requesting the funds never did promise any immediate savings. In fact, IT leaders remained silent on this issue while it was largely understood that failing to upgrade would cause greater immediate harm as opposed to greater immediate savings.

Performance Measurement

Given the increased public scrutiny into how public monies are spent, there is now a greater need for the deployment of performance measurement tools. Whether it is a balanced scorecard, ROI analysis, performance metrics, or dashboard performance alerts, technology managers must adapt to the basic business practices that have been used successfully by the corporate community for many years.

While many states and local governments have been experimenting with online performance measurement techniques, the federal government has created some very cool applications and is way out in front on this subject. As with local governments, one can now view how well various federal projects are doing by way of performance measures. Not surprisingly, technology is one of the eight main categories from which to search.

Performance measurement, of course, depends on a sound and fair methodology, and requires a lot of data. Local governments are very good at collecting data but fall quite short in effectively using it and, indeed, sharing data with other units.

With all the progress that has been made in performance management, most is still agency-focused. In the book "Listening to the Public," we are reminded by excellent examples how agency measurement criteria can be widely different than what the public may expect. For example, a garbage department might boast of the metric tons of refuse it has collected in a given period of time. In this instance, the public is more interested whether garbage was picked up on time—or at all—in their neighborhood. Public works might boast of the miles of streets that have been repaved, while the public is more concerned about the quality of or smoothness of the streets. A department may boast of how many restaurants were cited for sanitary violations, but the public is more interested in seeing online what the violation were for and when the restaurants were re-opened and re-inspected. With so many new tools in hand, many—certainly not all—citizens want to learn more about how well their governments are performing, yet they want the information in ways that make sense to them.

In today's environment, where we are dazzled by new and improved displays, everyone is looking for performance management dashboards. Just as geographic information systems (GIS) have improved decision making and enhanced strategic planning, today's new performance management dashboards have dramatically improved performance management reporting. Visually speaking, performance management dashboards help managers at various levels "see" the progress of projects and programs, as well as general operations all on one page. Through the use of colors, pie charts and bar graphs, public managers can drive their organizations as they would a sophisticated car or airplane. Perhaps one could say that this is a trend within a trend, but the bottom line here is that these tools are designed to be more than simply attractive. They are designed to be always-on tools that, with the proper updated inputs, one can use to better manage the technology enterprise and quickly see where the trouble spots may lie. The trend today is to have great dashboards, but most fall short by not having the means or methodology to analyze data.

Unions and Performance

Employee unions have been a challenge to local government leaders because all too often they seek across-the-board, one-size-fits-all parity with one another. This becomes problematic when public managers are trying to create more flexible organizations. Unions seek collective bargaining rights for their members, better wages and benefits, improved working conditions, and the right to file and resolve grievances. Local government leaders often find it easier to “give-in” rather than have an open fight in public.

In today’s environment, local government technology enterprise requires greater flexibility, not rigidity. Performance can be measured by technology and for technology, and before public managers give in too easily, increased performance should be rewarded whether it is a union environment or not. If unions seek more, then it is equally appropriate to seek more in terms of performance, and governments should view this is in a very positive way.

It may be instructive to note that though union negotiations, Volkswagen of Germany agreed to halt e-mail messages during non-working hours. While it’s too early to see if this type of change in policy might come to the United States, it is nonetheless one of the first examples of how labor relations may view technology in terms of looking for what they regard as “quality of life issues”, in the context of collective bargaining agreements.

From Information Technology (IT) to Information Services (IS)?

Rethinking IT in government requires a fresh new look at just about everything a local government does, from leadership to matching or aligning all the business lines with technology solutions. Traditional information technology (IT) naturally has a techno-centric bias and, hence, paradigm. In the world of IT, technology has been supported by a centralized department or division. With the shift in technology resources as well as the technology itself, many thought leaders believe there will be a shift of focus from “information technology” to “information services.” The service model is actually a paradigm that was prevalent just a decade ago. Under the service model, the focus is on actively looking for ways to better support the enterprise.

Green IT and Beyond

Rethinking technology must include green IT from the point of view of sustainability as well as saving money. Once considered just a feel-good exercise, green IT has become mainstream, and it means saving money as well as the environment. Local governments are taking the lead by setting examples in equipment purchases, equipment use, and equipment disposal.

And of course if you're feeling patriotic today, we have here a new line of PCs produced by the federal government.

When it comes to equipment purchases, local governments are becoming smarter. Aside from looking for lower prices, they are changing policies so that PCs and laptops are being refreshed at a slower pace and in more innovative ways. Instead of a blanket refresh every three or four years, some PCs and laptops can wait an additional year or more, while others will receive newer systems based on actual need sooner than later. Today, there is an increased emphasis on choosing energy-efficient equipment, such as Energy Star-certified servers, and turning to virtualization when possible instead of purchasing more servers.

In terms of equipment use, local governments are more actively promoting policies that call for more energy-efficient settings on devices as well as shutting down non-critical equipment when not in use. This is also an area where virtualization plays a leading role in replacing energy-consuming PCs and servers.

Disposal of aging equipment is another area where local governments are taking the lead. Some of the equipment is being recycled or donated to needy organizations. In some cases, because of security concerns, hard drives have been removed, but nonetheless, the equipment still has value.

"My fear is we'll invest all of our time, money and resources to go green, then someone will sue us for discriminating against red and blue."

Most importantly, local governments have policies aimed at ensuring that old equipment is not merely dumped into a landfill and is disposed of properly, with minimum harm to the environment.

Local governments also have been on the forefront of alternative fuels for municipal fleets and buses. They are building LEED-certified buildings that are smart and energy efficient, and we all know about local government efforts to encourage paper and plastic recycling.

In looking at the role of local governments, we can see how this plays out in greater detail.

1. **Recycling and Re-use**

   One of the biggest social, environmental, and economical issues facing our communities is the generation and disposal of waste. In 2006, Americans generated about 251 million tons of waste. So, what did we do with all of it? Where did it go? There are three main paths that our waste takes when it leaves our hands: disposed in a landfill, recovered (through recycling and composting), or burned to capture energy.

   Recycling presents not only an effective way to reduce our waste, but also to reduce our energy consumption and greenhouse gas emissions.

Materials that are usually sent to sit in a landfill are instead diverted to materials recovery facilities where they are cleaned, separated, and manufactured into useful products and commodities. These recycled products then re-enter the market where governments, businesses, and citizens can purchase and use them.

Fast Facts about Recycling and Re-use

- In 2006, Americans generated about 251 million tons of trash and recycled 82 million tons of materials (32.5% recycling rate). Recycling 82 million tons of solid waste saved the energy equivalent of more than 10 billion gallons of gasoline. The 82 million tons of waste that were recycled also led to a 49.7 million metric-ton reduction in carbon emissions, which is equivalent to removing 39.4 million passenger cars from the road each year.
- In 2006, the recycling rate for aluminum was 36%, including 45% of all aluminum beverage cans. Recycling just 1 ton of aluminum cans conserves more than 207 million BTUs, the equivalent of 36 barrels of oil or 1,655 gallons of gasoline.
- From 1990 to 2006, the total volume of waste going to landfills dropped by 4 million tons, from 142.3 million to 138.2 million.
- Paper and paper products represent the largest portion of our waste stream. In 2008, paper accounted for about 77 million tons of all materials in the solid waste stream, and Americans recycled more than half of that total (56% recovery rate). In 2009, the recovery rate for paper rose to 63.4% of all paper consumed in the United States. Every ton of recycled mixed paper can save the energy equivalent of 185 gallons of gas.

2. LED Lighting/Lighting Efficiency

Lighting affects every aspect of our daily lives. Different levels and qualities of lighting can affect our comfort, health, safety, and mood. Representing about 19% of the total electricity consumed in 2007 for both the commercial and residential sectors, lighting presents us with some of the biggest opportunities for improving energy efficiency through retrofits and technological developments. The Department of Energy estimates that using new lighting technologies can help reduce lighting energy use in homes by 50–75%.

Fast Facts about Lighting

- Residential lighting consumption was about 215 billion kWh in 2007, equal to about 15% of all electricity consumption. About 311 billion kWh was consumed for lighting by the commercial sector, equal to about 23% of commercial sector electricity consumption.
- The U.S. Department of Energy estimates that rapid adoption of LED lighting in the United States over the next 20 years can:
  - Deliver monetary savings of about $265 billion,
  - Avoid 40 new power plants, and
  - Reduce lighting electricity demand by 33% by 2027.
- Energy Star-qualified LED lighting uses at least 75% less energy than incandescent lighting and lasts about 35 to 50 times longer (two to five times longer than fluorescent lighting).
- LEDs last up to 10 times as long as compact fluorescent light bulbs (CFLs).
- When used in battery-powered applications, LEDs use only 2-10 watts of electricity and will extend battery life 10 to 15 times longer than standard incandescent bulbs.
- Many cities in the United States are replacing their incandescent traffic lights with LED arrays because the electricity costs can be reduced by 80% or more.

3. Smart Buildings

Typically, buildings are designed and constructed in a very segregated way. Each system in a building (HVAC, lighting, telephone/data, etc.) is designed and installed by a specialist with expertise in that specific area of building operation. Each of those systems is then operated separately within the constructed building. More recently, the concept of “smart” or “intelligent’ building design has become a priority for many building owners, developers, architects, and engineers. Smart buildings involve the integration (rather than segregation) of the multiple technology systems commonly found in all buildings and the implementation of advanced IT technologies to create a “communication network” of sorts between the systems.

For example, a building may have its lighting controls integrated with the sun blind controls, so that the dimming of lights in a room will trigger the raising or lowering of sun blinds to allow more or less natural light. Another example is the integration of the security system with the fire alarm system. If the fire alarm is activated in an area, it may trigger the security system to focus on that area for closer monitoring. There are many reasons to implement these smart technologies into our buildings, such as the realization of energy and cost savings, functionality, and increased efficiency in management of the buildings.

Fast Facts about Smart Buildings

» In a study conducted by the Continental Automated Building Association, first costs for integrated systems were 56% less than non-integrated systems.

» Annual operating and maintenance costs for an integrated system are 82% less than for a non-integrated system.

» Integrated systems save 10% of utility costs compared with energy costs for non-integrated systems.

» Smart building technologies can lead to an annual savings in maintenance, repair, and replacement of $0.20/square foot, and a utility cost savings of $0.16/square foot. In a 100,000-square-foot building, that would equate to an annual savings of $20,000 in maintenance, repair, and replacement, and $16,000 in utility costs.

4. Zoning and Land Use Development

Land use planning has become even more important in recent years because of population growth and expanding urban development. Zoning, a local government prerogative, is a tool used by government officials and city planners to determine the size and function of buildings, the location of buildings, and development density. The first zoning resolution was established in the United States by New York City in 1916. Zoning requirements can cover anything from height to setback of individual buildings, from the amount of trees to be left untouched to the size of a property's parking lot.

As trends in population numbers, demographics, and technology shift, so does the need for new and improved zoning regulations. Needless to say, zoning practices have changed tremendously since 1916, and the idea of smart development has come to the forefront of many city planning strategies. The U.S. Environmental Protection Agency's (EPA's) Smart Growth Program is one of the more prominent development tactics used in sustainable urban design. According to EPA, the "program helps communities improve their development practices and get the type of development they want." Through the promotion of 10 guiding principles, the Smart Growth Program offers local, state, and national experts information on creating stronger stakeholder collaboration, promoting diverse housing options, making neighborhoods more walkable, preserving open space, and providing residents with transportation choices. Development using smart growth principles (or other types of smart development strategies) can help save water and energy, and preserve land while leaving residents healthier and happier.

Fast Facts about Zoning and Land Use Development

» A 2000 study found that compact development in New Jersey would produce 40% less water pollution than more dispersed development patterns.

» A 2005 Seattle study found that residents of neighborhoods where land uses were mixed and streets are better connected, making non-auto travel easier and more convenient, traveled 26% fewer vehicle miles than residents of neighborhoods that were dispersed and less connected.

» Residents living in communities using smart growth principles drive as little as one-fifth as much as their counterparts in conventional sprawl developments.

» Using smart growth principles could help cut greenhouse gas emissions by about 595 million metric tons in 10 years, or 10% of total U.S. emissions.

» Over the next 10 years, if all new residential construction in the United States were built using smart growth principles, the economic benefit would exceed $2 trillion.

» The Minneapolis-St. Paul Metropolitan Council found that by using smart growth techniques, "the region overall could save $3 billion...94% [of which] would come from local communities saving money on roads and sewers."

5. Green Buildings

The built environment has a vast impact on the natural environment, human health, and the economy. In the United States, buildings account for:

- 39% of total energy use,
- 68% of total electricity consumption,
- 38% of carbon dioxide emissions, and
- 12% of total water consumption.

The significant amounts of resources used and pollution produced by buildings calls for more efficient use of the built environment, and building more sustainably has become a popular strategy. Green building, also known as sustainable or high-performance building, is the practice of creating and using healthier and more resource-efficient models of construction, renovation, operation, maintenance, and demolition. This practice expands and complements the classical building design concerns of economy, utility, durability, and comfort. Green buildings are designed to reduce the overall impact of the built environment on human health and the natural environment by:

- Efficiently using energy, water, and other resources;
- Protecting occupant health and improving employee productivity; and
- Reducing waste, pollution, and environmental degradation.

For example, green buildings may incorporate sustainable materials in their construction (e.g., materials that are reused, recycled, or made from renewable resources); create healthy indoor environments with minimal pollutants (e.g., reduced product emissions); and/or feature landscaping that reduces water use (e.g., by using native plants that survive without extra watering). By adopting green building strategies, both economic and environmental performance can be maximized.

Fast Facts about Green Building

» Buildings accounted for 38.9 percent of total U.S. energy consumption in 2005. Residential buildings accounted for 53.7 percent of that total, while commercial buildings accounted for the other 46.3 percent.

» Buildings accounted for 72 percent of total U.S. electricity consumption in 2006, and that number will rise to 75% by 2025. About half (51 percent) of that total was attributed to residential building use, while 49 percent was attributed to commercial building use.

» On average, Americans spend about 90 percent or more of their time indoors. Indoor levels of pollutants may be two to five times higher, and occasionally more than 100 times higher, than outdoor levels.

» The overall green building market (both non-residential and residential) is likely to more than double from today's $36 billion–$49 billion to $96 billion–$140 billion by 2013.

» Green building will support 7.9 million U.S. jobs and pump $554 million into the American economy over the next four years (2009-2013).

» In comparison to the average commercial building, green buildings:

- consume 26% less energy,
- have 13% lower maintenance costs,
- have 27% higher occupant satisfaction, and
- have 33% less greenhouse gas emissions.

6. **Sustainable Fleet Management**
Fleet vehicles are groups of motor vehicles (cars, vans, and trucks) owned or leased by a business or government agency, rather than by an individual or family. Typical examples of fleet vehicles are those that are operated by car rental companies; taxicab companies; delivery services; refuse haulers; airports; school, transit, and shuttle bus companies; and police enforcement. Fleet management can include a range of functions, such as vehicle financing, vehicle maintenance, vehicle tracking and diagnostics, driver management, fuel management, and health and safety management.

A growing number of organizations and government agencies are moving toward sustainable or green fleet management. Because fleet vehicles consume large amounts of fuel and emit polluting greenhouse gas emissions, green fleet management can serve as an opportunity for organizations to save on operating costs and reduce the ecological footprint of operating the fleet. Several options are available to meet this target, such as using alternative fuels and advanced vehicles. Existing diesel fleets can be converted to biodiesel, which use a cleaner form of fuel and produce lower greenhouse gas emissions. Other alternative fuel vehicles include electric, hybrid electric, and natural gas vehicles.

Fast Facts about Sustainable Fleet Management

- In 2008, the transportation sector used 28 quads of energy, which is 28% of total U.S. energy use. Nearly all of the energy consumed in this sector is petroleum (95%), with small amounts of renewable fuels (3%), and natural gas (2%).
- President Obama recently announced that the federal government will lead by example in replacing older cars in the federal fleet with fuel-efficient hybrids and plug-in hybrid electric vehicles, reducing its dependence on foreign oil as well as cutting carbon dioxide and other pollution. President Obama signed the Executive Order in October 2009, calling on agencies to cut the federal government's fleet petroleum use by 30% by 2020.
- With close to 9 million vehicles, commercial fleets–comprised of both light and heavy vehicles–account for about 4% of the vehicles in the United States today.
- Organizations interested in implementing more sustainable fleet management can access a collection of tools, database searches, calculators, and interactive maps available on the U.S. Department of Energy's Alternative Fuels and Advanced Vehicles Data Center Web site: http://www.afdc.energy.gov/afdc/applications.html.

7. **Green Data Centers**
Data centers are facilities that primarily contain electronic equipment used for data processing and storage, as well as communications networking. They have become integral to the functioning of business, communications, academic, and governmental systems, and provide computing functions for the daily operation of top U.S. economic, scientific, and technological organizations. These data centers consume large amounts of energy to run and maintain their computer systems, servers, and associated high-performance components. However, to protect and maintain these systems, data centers also use energy-intensive air conditioning systems, fire suppression systems, backup power supplies, Internet connections, and high-security systems. This demand for data centers is driven by many factors, such as:

- The increased use of electronic transactions in financial services, such as online banking and electronic stock trading;
- The growing use of Internet communication and entertainment;
- The shift to electronic medical records for healthcare;
- The growth in global commerce and services; and
- The adoption of satellite navigation and electronic shipment tracking in transportation.

8. **Net-Zero Buildings**
According to the U.S. Green Building Council, buildings account for 39% of the total energy use, 68% of total electricity consumption, and 38% of total carbon dioxide emissions in the country. Going one step further than the green building concept is the idea of "zero energy buildings" or "net-zero energy buildings." These terms refer to the idea that buildings can generate as much energy as they consume. The first goal of net-zero energy design is to maximize the efficiency of the building's energy systems. Then, the remaining energy needs of the building are met through on-site power generation. The U.S. Department of Energy recently launched the Net-Zero Energy Commercial

Fast Facts about Green Data Centers

» The energy used by the nation's servers and data centers is significant. This sector consumed about 61 billion kilowatt-hours (kWh) in 2006 (1.5% of total electricity consumption) for a total electricity cost of about $4.5 billion. This is more than the electricity consumed by the nation's color televisions and similar to the amount of electricity consumed by 5.8 million average U.S. households (or 5% of the total housing stock).

» Federal servers and data centers alone account for about 6 billion kWh (10%) of this electricity use, for a total electricity cost of approximately $450 million annually.

» The energy use of the nation's servers and data centers in 2006 is estimated to be more than double the electricity that was consumed in 2000.

» One type of server, the volume server, was responsible for 68% of the electricity consumed by IT equipment in data centers in 2006. The energy used by this type of server more than doubled from 2000 to 2006, which was the largest increase among different types of servers.

» The power and cooling infrastructure that supports IT equipment in data centers also uses significant energy, accounting for 50% of the total consumption of data centers.

» Among the different types of data centers, 38% of electricity use is attributable to the nation's largest (i.e., enterprise-class) and most rapidly growing data centers.

» There is significant potential for energy-efficiency improvements in data centers. Existing technologies and design strategies have been shown to reduce the energy use of a typical server by 25 percent or more.

» Implementing best energy-management practices–including energy benchmarking and continuous monitoring–in existing data centers, and consolidating applications from many servers to one server could reduce current data center energy use by around 20%.

Building Initiative to help support the development of technologies and policies for the creation of net-zero energy buildings. The goal of the program (launched in 2008) is to make net-zero energy buildings marketable by 2025. The program will seek to create public and private partnerships, foster advanced research, and provide resources to builders, owners, contractors, engineers, and architects.

Fast Facts about Net-Zero Buildings

- » In 2010, the Department of Energy awarded $20.2 million dollars to the Oak Ridge National Laboratory and $15.9 million to the Lawrence Berkeley National Laboratory for net-zero energy building research.
- » There are already net-zero energy commercial buildings operating across the nation, including in Hawaii, California, Wisconsin, Ohio, and Minnesota.

Cities and counties are requiring new city and county buildings to be certified by the Leadership in Energy and Environmental Design (LEED) system, an internationally recognized green building certification system. Developed by the U.S. Green Building Council (USGBC) in March 2000, LEED provides building owners and operators with a framework for identifying and implementing practical and measurable green building design, construction, operations, and maintenance solutions.

LEED promotes sustainable building and development practices through a suite of rating systems that recognize projects that implement strategies for better environmental and health performance. The LEED rating systems are developed through an open, consensus-based process led by LEED committees, diverse groups of volunteers representing a cross-section of the building and construction industry. Once thought to be limited to businesses only, LEED certification has been warmly embraced by local governments.

"Any of these people would add greatly to our corporate diversity and prove we're serious about going green."

Agile Government Organizations

The discussion on rethinking technology cannot be complete without mention of an evolving term called "agile organizations." The term "agile" used to refer to a method of software development. In today's environment where we tend to be always looking for new terms to describe contemporary trends, "agile" now describes organizations that are designed to be flexible and ever-adapting, where systems are in place to adapt to rapid change. This is a rather new trend unto itself, as governments have traditionally been known for their self-perpetuating systems, silos, and bureaucracies. A high-level government official referred to silos as "Cylinders of Excellence." Now, given the new realities of public financing of public systems, there has never been a greater need for improved flexibility and functionality in government organizations.

Agile organizations can take many forms. They can focus on staffing and governance, or they can look at far-reaching policies, such as telework, or even the physical structure of the office place. As in the private sector, many new "spaces" are being created with flexibility in mind, eliminating traditional physical walls and replacing traditional offices with open and structural flexibility. Collaboration is encouraged, and agile organizations require openness, flexibility, and a nurturing environment. Agile organizations require a new paradigm for leadership at all levels of public management.

TREND TWO

Technology Leadership: Who Decides?

Trend Two

Technology Leadership: Who Decides?

With today's new devices come such terms as BYOD, "bring your own device," or even BYOT, "bring your own technology." These relatively new terms help illustrate an amazing shift from total central IT control and suggest a more democratic form of IT thinking and governance. As a result, IT leadership needs to change and adapt.

IT Governance: Centralization and Consolidation

IT governance is one the hottest topics of discussion these days. The topic is all about organization structure and decision rights: who ultimately decides? A city manager once stated that when he had to replace a purchasing officer or a chief financial officer, he knew exactly what to look for. Yet, when he needed to hire a chief technology manager, he was at a loss. He said, "So many speak a different language, and I'm not sure what I should be looking for. Should I be looking for a fixer, a leader, a strategist, or all of the above?"

Historically, most IT functions had their origins in the accounting and finance offices in business and government departments 25 or more years ago. Technology took hold with the advent of payroll processing, time sheets, and program budgets. Today, it is estimated that 20% of IT managers are still reporting through a high-level finance manager.

It was not too long ago that every departmental function had its own technology staff that consisted of one person or more. Application-specific tasks were left to each department or division. However, when data systems and network operations became more centralized, mostly for reasons of greater scale and efficiency, the question of who supports what and who pays for what became an issue—and still remains an issue in many places. Every day, we hear stories about a senior manager who should have known better, who decided to purchase a particular device or application for his or her operations without any realistic comprehension of how and who would support it. Who provides the immediate and ongoing training? Who does the updating? Who is responsible for securing the system? Who does one call when there is a problem? How well does the system or application integrate with other systems? To what extent is there duplication elsewhere? Might the new service or application also serve other departments, thus spreading the cost over a larger group?

In some cases, vendors may have overstated what they could do or underestimated the local government's true internal capabilities. In any event, purchasing equipment and new software-based systems requires a great deal of planning, integration, and training. In our ever-evolving technology-dependent world, systems need to be purchased with an eye toward spreading the cost across a larger number of government entities.

With everyone believing their "mission-critical" application is the most important application in the universe, when they don't get immediate support from the outside group assigned to provide help, they go ballistic. One medium-sized city was beset with the challenge of dealing with four

separately owned and operated geospatial information systems (GIS). Each department recognized both the advantage and need to integrate all the databases and informational layers into one solid, robust system. At the same time, each "owner" voiced the need for the others to integrate the other systems in theirs! Moreover, no one from above, including the city manager, wanted to intervene. This is where higher-level IT leadership and trust is required.

CIO Relevance

Not too long ago, the head of a technology department might be called something like "director of information technology" or "director of management information systems." The departments generally played a support role in making certain that the main network computers were operating and supporting the enterprise. Some local governments continue with this type of model.

However, as the complexity of technology has evolved, so too have technology job requirements, position descriptions, titles, and functions. There has been an evolutionary trend toward the many new skills required for the technology leader who resides at the top of any public organization. This trend addresses the issue of qualifications regarding what best constitutes a technology executive regardless of title. Aside from the evolving new skills sets comes the issue of where should this person be located within the organization chart, and why?

Just as the concept of having a high-level technology executive was taking hold, some now are beginning to rethink the relevance of the position. Clearly someone needs to be in charge of a city's or county's IT infrastructure even if the current trend is to once again decentralize IT functions. Of course, there is no one model that will solve or address all problems and situations; technology management depends on the locality, its history, current needs and resources, and goals. It is safe to say, however, that cities and counties are upgrading the top technology position when the opportunity presents itself because of the complex expectations in an ever-growing technology landscape.

The chief information officer (CIO) or chief technology officer (CTO) each have classic definitions, yet, their titles have become almost interchangeable. From here on, we will use the term CIO to symbolize the chief technology strategist. From this vantage point, the CIO must wear a number of hats, be people-oriented yet technically grounded, and speak many "languages," almost simultaneously.

To be successful, today's CIO must first be a leader, not a dictator. He or she must be a technologist, not a technician; be a business-minded person, not close-minded; be a financier, not an accountant; be proactive, not reactive; have vision; and finally, be a diplomat, not a politician. These distinctions can be significant. Leadership requires a variety of skills, especially people skills that require developing trusted relationships inside as well as outside of the IT area. A recent survey of CIOs across the United States showed that a majority of CIOs see themselves as having to spend up to 20% of their time building and maintaining relationships with other senior managers. Entirely too many technology managers spend a huge amount of time putting out fires, or what they refer to as "break-fix" and not enough time developing strategic plans and enterprise visions.

Possessing strong leadership skills is essential. The new CIO must know how technology can work best, as well as have the people skills to keep things humming. When it comes to the business side, one cannot solely focus on budgets and reports that are filed away and never read. I have nothing against accountants, but their role is generally that of a historian. A finance-oriented person looks at the many options that exist for funding and moves forward, making decisions with skill and acknowledged risk. Being proactive suggests that the CIO must develop a vision for the future, not merely sit around and wait for the phone to ring or an e-mail or text message to arrive. On the political side, one cannot be a politician that simply tells people what they want to hear; one must be able to tell people in delicate terms what they need to know.

The successful CIO needs to be able to speak interchangeably on different levels of communications to different levels of people—from the highly technical to the elected leader. Deeper and more detailed communication skills are required for technology managers, who need to be able to convey information convincingly to senior managers and quickly and clearly to elected officials. Each group has different needs for information.

Being a CIO today is perhaps similar to being a symphony conductor, where you come to the podium with your own specialty, and recruit, place, train, mentor, and orchestrate a sense of human and technological harmony throughout the enterprise.

"NOT ANOTHER UNFINISHED SYMPHONY....!"

Recognizing the need for more training and development for the next generation of technology leaders at the local level, three universities offer CIO certification programs to help build the profession—just as has been done for city attorneys, city managers, chief financial officers, and purchasing officers. The programs have much in common and have formed a consortium, with the Public Technology Institute (PTI) serving as the coordinating hub. Each of the programs calls for 240 contact hours, leaving each institution to decide just how the time is allocated. The University of North Carolina's Center for Public Technology has trademarked CGCIO™ (Certified Government Chief Technology Officer) for exclusive use among the consortium members and was the first to offer such a program. The second institution to offer such a program was the Florida Institute of Government ,which is affiliated with Florida State University. The third institution is Rutgers University School of Public Affairs & Administration with PTI as its primary partner.

One thing is clear: there is a growing need for a new professional class of CIO. Moreover, with the record number of retirements that are expected to occur in the next several years, the need for new, highly skilled CIOs will only become more critical.

Because innovation has never been more valued than it is today, it makes sense to view the CIO as the chief innovation officer and an invaluable leader serving the entire enterprise. In the end, everyone tends to agree, it's more about leadership and vision than technology and solutions. This becomes especially important as more city and county employees are developing applications separate and apart from the purview of the CIO as well as the central network. If the CIO isn't careful, he or she will be completely by-passed over time.

Need for high-level champions

After studying the needs and challenges CIOs have faced over the past seven years, one realizes the importance of having supportive champions involved in technology decision making. Whether the champion is a CFO, mayor, chief of staff, assistant city manager, or commissioner, the most successful technology managers usually have support from a higher authority.

Of course, the opposite can occur when a city manager takes little interest in technology innovation. A city manager from a West Coast city once told me, "I want to be last when it comes to adopting new technology solutions." Apparently, he had been burned several times in the past and had developed a strong mistrust of new technology and the change that accompanies it. Perhaps the most unfortunate outcome was the negative impact on staff at all levels. In fact, it was in this same city where staff complained that there were four different GIS systems that needed to be merged into one, but there was no leadership or champion anywhere on the horizon.

A key question always seems to surface when discussing the need for champions: Should there be a technology committee? If yes, then who might lead a technology committee? Should it be a mayor or a senior public administrator? Having an active technology committee can provide a forum that is inclusive rather than exclusive. Because technology systems cut across so many traditional department and division boundaries, having a group that meets regularly can help in the strategic planning and visioning process. The group can assist in setting priorities and look for opportunities for greater collaboration.

There is a need in today's environment for external champions of technology, too. If none exists, perhaps a public-private technology advisory group should be created. Such a group might comprise business leaders, a representative from the chamber of commerce, and other politically neutral citizens who are knowledgeable about IT. The group could be a useful place to bounce ideas and experiment with new concepts and applications.

Strategic Planning

Strategic planning is a critical element in the technology enterprise. When asked how many IT departments have a written strategic plan, an overwhelming majority say that while they would like to have one, they lack the time to create one.

There are essentially two types of strategic plans. The first is a plan that is internal to the IT department or division. An internal plan can be helpful in ensuring how the department operates, and provides a clear picture of the levels of reporting relationships and authority as well as department priorities. The second type of strategic plan focuses on the needs and requirements of the entire governmental enterprise. It is here where the technology department seeks alignment with overall city or county requirements and needs.

Perhaps in the end, the most important planning document is the budget plan itself. It is here that priorities already have been addressed, and it is here where the city and county is committed to placing its resources. The most successful strategic plans, in one way or another, link to a budget document.

Leading Innovation

Ideally, the CIO is the one to lead the innovation challenge, as long as that person is well connected to all the business lines of a governmental enterprise. However, one of the top three complaints from CIOs is the lack of time or resources that enable them to be innovators. Someone has to be able to contemplate the possible risks and rewards of technology initiatives, and match business needs and requirements with available technology solutions. CIOs always must be scanning for newer solutions and learn from others' best practices, and they should make time to pursue continuing education and maintain their certifications and competencies.

The Case for a CIO at the Table

Far more controversial than a title is the level of responsibility of the CIO and the position's reporting relationships. Many observers of technology governance argue that given the complexities and risks of today's technology, the CIO should report to and be situated at the cabinet level. This means that when the mayor, city council or county commissioners meet, the CIO should be present, too. When the cabinet meets, the CIO should also have a seat at the table. The more the CIO knows about what is being discussed and planned, the more effective he or she can be. That also will provide a greater opportunity to become acquainted with other high-level decision-makers and to form strategic relationships that can lead to better teamwork, communication, and productivity.

Centralization, Decentralization, Consolidation

The terms centralization, decentralization, and consolidation have varying definitions depending on how they are applied. Given today's severe economic realities, many governmental jurisdictions are centralizing and consolidating their operations at the same time. There is an irony here in that many of the newer technologies cater to individuals through individual applications. Therefore, while it probably makes sense to consolidate network and storage systems, IT departments may want to push back from supporting just about everything considered "technology." After all, many of the newer government workers are quite familiar with today's workforce-related technologies. Public managers along with IT leaders must look at their respective organizations from a holistic point of view. There is a need today as never before to reduce waste, redundancy, and inefficiency.

Today's technology leaders must view their missions as not only supporting the enterprise where they can but also seeking out ways to get more out of less. Such expectations must be met with the appropriate decision-making authority, which includes titles and positions that give them the undisputed power to actually lead.

Technology Enterprise

Some people joke that the initials CIO stand for "career is over" and that the term enterprise resource planning (ERP) really means "enhanced retirement program." Both puns share a common thread, which is increased leadership, responsibility, and visibility, plus added risk that goes along with added responsibilities. At a training class for new CIOs, I recall one of the speakers, a seasoned CIO nearing retirement, who said his success was due to him never being found. He loved working in the background and bragged about often hiding and not being located. That might have worked for him in the past, but in today's environment, it is quite the opposite.

Today, ERP undertakings carry a heavy weight, and the expectations are so much higher than before. ERP is something that everyone appears to look forward to, and most support the goals and objectives of looking at the entire enterprise and seeking system-wide solutions. Unfortunately, there are many devils buried in the details. Agencies, divisions, and departments that start out supporting ERP often find themselves arguing for exceptions to the plans down the road. Arguments may include wanting to preserve current business practices, resisting any changes to processes or reporting requirements. Rather than take a bold, hard look at how to live with a new system and the changes it will bring, managers often fight to preserve the status quo. Such behavior will not only lead to serious delays, it will likely cost more money

"I USED TO FETCH THE NEWSPAPER. NOW I JUST ACCESS IT ONLINE AND PRINT IT UP."

because of the need to write exception code. In the end, the more deviations to the new system norm, the more it will depart from what ERP is supposed to achieve.

The main purpose for mentioning ERP here is to restate the need for high-level technology leadership and champions. When it comes to ERP, this is no place for "lone rangers" or weak leaders.

TREND THREE

Cloud-based Solutions

TREND THREE

Cloud-based Solutions

Before we can focus our thinking above the clouds, we need to look below the clouds to see where things stand between the traditional network of yesterday and the contemporary network that is emerging. We know that information systems had their origins within the financial processes of accounting, payroll, and human resource record management. Computer access was limited not only on a need-to-know basis, but also the data center was usually physically located far from other governmental business units.

Computers and the concept of networking grew out of early word processing systems, in which a bunch of rather clumsy, green-screened monitors, called "dumb terminals," were connected to a central computer mainframe where the word processing applications resided. At the risk of oversimplification, as cost and technology changed, the individual PC was born, and we began to purchase software applications for each unit. The intelligence of the central

"You should have been here back in the old days before cloud computing."

network was shared with the local intelligence of the desktop PC. We evolved into a distributed system, where mainframes would do the heavy processing, overall storage and back-ups. Individual PCs were both connected and independent. Over the years, laptops would overtake desktop PCs in popularity, and now we have smartphones and tablets added to the mix.

Shift is Happening

The fast-paced growth of different systems—often within the same jurisdiction—went unchecked until recently. With budget cuts related to dramatic shortfalls in revenues, cities and counties have had to re-examine the entire enterprise. While certainly not a typical-size city, New York recently consolidated 50 data centers from among 40 city agencies into one new center. The city claims that the move will save $100 million. This type of system consolidation is taking place all across the country in cities, counties, and states. The federal government also announced it will cut 800 data centers across the country, which amounts to a 40% cut among its existing centers.

In addition to centralizing data centers, many local and state governments are adopting virtualized systems. In the not-too-distant past, nearly every application required its own physical "box" or server. Today, virtual servers are near commonplace throughout the enterprise. A virtual system is really a software version of a hardware operating system. This allows for multiple "boxes" to be located on one central sever, thus reducing hardware costs and related operating expenses, including less power consumption. With the advent of virtual systems, a main server could house a number of different operating systems each with its own application and all sharing one common hardware infrastructure.

Google is taking an approach that takes us ahead by taking us back in time by building laptops that are little more than "dumb terminals" that become fully functional once they are attached to a wired or wireless broadband network. Microsoft is now offering its entire office software suite in a cloud-based subscription service, which ensures that every user is always up-to-date when signing on, and makes it easier to maintain and support each unit.

Microsoft, Google, and few others have developed applications that reside either in the cloud or in a central on-premise network that allows for greater efficiencies. When it comes to business applications such as word processing, spreadsheets, and more, imagine the savings of not having to equip each device with its own licensed physical software packages and applications. Also, imagine the frustration when, for whatever reason, there is interrupted, limited, or no broadband connectivity.

In the Clouds

The IT director was livid; after all, he had just opened a brand new, state-of-the-art green data center. Then, he read a letter written by a prominent elected council member asking why the city was not placing its entire network operations in the cloud, and thus saving millions of dollars over a short amount of time. The IT director was frustrated because when he responded to the letter stating that there would be no immediate savings because of the sunken costs of the new data center, the council member shot back, saying, "You are just trying to protect your job and staff!"

The meaning of the term "cloud computing" changes faster than the weather. There are two common features of cloud computing and cloud-based applications: one is the geographic location of the cloud is typically off site, and the other is the idea that someone else will manage the data or process.

This reminds me of a story that I used to tell about my experiences with cloud computing. I start by saying that I "came out of the closest" in 2005, a year after coming to PTI and serving as its fourth CEO since its founding in 1972. Now that gets the audience's attention. Of course, what I was referring to was a bunch of servers all located in a crowded closet with a makeshift air conditioner ported to an overhead duct vent. On one corner sat a finance server, because there was a time when it was a best practice to have a financial records server physically independent of any other device. Then there was an e-mail server, a voice mail server, a webserver, and finally a network server. Add to all this, a membership database system that was located as part of the network server. Finally, we had a physical back-up system that required that someone periodically take a back-up tape to another, hopefully safe location.

To make matters worse, the PTI headquarters was located at the time just a few blocks from the White House (a known terrorist target) and unrelated to that, the aging building was prone to electrical spikes and outages. Some of the critical servers, such as the network server, had uninterrupted power sources (UPS), but they were limited to a few hours of back-up power at best.

Cloud computing in 2005 was basically nonexistent, but the concept of "managed services" was beginning to gain acceptance. Eventually, managed services would be referred to as software as a service (SaaS), which describes an outside solution provider who hosts and/or manages a particular function or service. Taking advantage of the "new" technology, we moved and converted the membership database system to an external, cloud-based system. Aside from having our membership system hosted on a far superior and stable platform, we not only saved money, we could now access the data from just about anywhere in the world as long as we had Internet connectivity. We no longer had to be concerned about internal data back-ups, software patches or power faults because that was all included in our contract. We paid for exactly what we needed, and the system was scalable, too. If we needed features or additional storage, we would pay for more, and if we needed less, then we would pay less.

The next to go was the webserver, and the savings were immediate and substantial. We were able to pay for the space we used. No longer did we have to continue to purchase larger and larger drives, each time trying to plan ahead for growth.

"My boyfriend and I aren't ready to move in together, but we've started keeping our data on the same cloud."

The next server to go was the e-mail server. Here, too, the savings was immediate, and we received far better service than ever before. The remaining two servers (phone and voicemail) are soon to go into the cloud and will be combined virtually.

This is a simple but key example of reviewing what systems and services you have and preparing a business case for each available option. PTI may be a small organization, however, the thought process is similar, whether it be from the perspective of a small or large government operation.

Today, cloud computing takes many forms, and has advantages and remaining challenges. There are at least eight definitions or classifications of cloud computing:

1. **Software as a Service**—a particular software application is provided by another resource at another location.

2. **Platform as a Service**—a particular hardware platform is provided by another resource at another location.

3. **Infrastructure as a Service**—a broader range of technology systems and infrastructure are hosted by another resource at another location.

4. **Storage as a Service**—records (text or video) are stored remotely and managed by an outside resource.

5. **Private Cloud**—usually refers to a fee-based cloud operated by a private company.

6. **Public Cloud**—usually refers to a government data processing operation open to other government entities usually for a fee. Some public clouds have nothing to do with governments on any level; they simply exist to share in convenience, risk, and cost—much like a cooperative.

7. **Hybrid Cloud**—a mixture of applications and other external resources in addition to in-house capabilities.

8. **Government Cloud**—a cloud system operated by one or more governmental entities and is not open to any other business or to the public.

State and local governments have been at the forefront of cloud computing operations. For example, most states use a single private vendor to handle their hunting and fishing licenses, and all transaction are performed online. Cities and counties use specialized cloud-based software for parks and recreation registrations, where citizens can pay for certain events, reserve a sports or picnic field, or reserve a camping ground location online. One of the best examples of cities and counties turning to the cloud's software as a service (SaaS) is hosted e-mail. In the simplest of explanations, one IT manager claimed that cloud computing was like renting or paying for a service as you go. Whatever the definition or practical example, cloud computing is both growing in complexity yet is very much here to stay.

Cloud computing raises as many questions as proposed solutions. The entire concept, when applied, is a total transformation in the way local governments have traditionally operated. In 2008, CIOs at a PTI forum stated that there was no way they would let their data reside on someone else's system or computer. In 2011, a similar group, seeing the savings and advantages said, "Show me the way!"

Cloud computing met with such a high degree of skepticism because of many factors, not the least of which was security, data integrity, data protection and back-up, two-way data migration, and legal considerations. One question often asked is, "Can a locality legally take both critical and confidential information and place it in the hands of another party?" The answer depends on what laws the jurisdiction must operate under as well as how the requirement for privacy and security would be met. Will the data be encrypted, and to what level? Can data be retrieved under various scenarios? What would happen if the cloud-solution company fails or goes out of business? How will the data be moved or returned if the service turns out to be unsatisfactory? How adequate are the company's data and power back-up systems? Where are the company's severs physically located; somewhere in the U.S.A.? What is the financial health of the company?

In some cases, states and large counties have developed private governmental clouds. Yet, as solid an approach as that may sound, the very same questions still must be addressed. Government entities have been known to have security issues at least as serious as that of private companies. In April 2011, the State of Texas reported that personal data from approximately 3.5 million residents was inadvertently left open to anyone to see, thus making it one of the largest state or local government data breaches ever. This was not about a technological mistake—it was human carelessness.

Aside from the technical and legal perspective, there is a strong leadership and management side to this argument, too. Many CIOs have said that they believe that protecting public records is their inherent responsibility and something they were sworn to protect. They would not like to see this major responsibility stripped away. Others expressed privately the concern that they would have less power, less staff to manage, and perhaps their job would someday be outsourced. As mentioned earlier, the CIO could become the "chief cloud officer" or "chief contracting officer for technology."

Under closer review, more than a few conceded that a third party might actually provide a more secure environment than that of a local government on its own. Depending on the remote server's location, it might be safer than a city or county system located in an earthquake-prone area, or an area that gets frequent tornadoes, hurricanes, or flooding. Add to those arguments that budgets have never been tighter, and what may have seemed impossible in the past has now become quite plausible moving into the present. Those who have taken a step in the cloud arena generally have been very pleased with moving their e-mail services and/or data back-up or storage requirements as a start.

Distance and Ownership

Local government CIOs who have placed certain applications in the cloud have not lost their jobs or their perceived value to the enterprise; indeed, they have become stronger and have been looked upon as innovators. A CIO in the Southwest told a group that ever since placing a number of data applications in the cloud, he has received greater accountability from the outside company. He went on to say, "In the past, if an issue arose—say at 2:30 a.m.—there was a 50/50 chance that a city staff person would respond. Now, if under that same scenario a company is contractually obligated to provide 24/7 care, it works." So cloud computing, when done properly, can provide greater staff flexibility and accountability, and in some cases, better service.

Today, companies like Microsoft, Google, Amazon, IBM, Rackspace, HP, Lockheed Martin, and many others are actively looking to convert city and county government operations to the cloud in one form or another. They offer guarantees and provide assurances for data integrity in all forms, and have made ease-of-use data migration a reality. They offer improved continuity of services, reduced capital expenditures to the local government, a very high degree of operational reliability, and scalability. Scalability is all about only paying for what you use or need at the present, and being able to adjust that as needs change. Operational expenses can be greatly reduced, and local governments can benefit by being "device independent."

With all the stated advantages and guarantees, there still remains certain unease when one considers all the possible "what-ifs?" That is especially true given all the increased threats to our nation's technology infrastructure. This is where the "hybrid cloud" can make the most sense. In a hybrid cloud, an organization may manage some applications in-house and some externally in a private cloud, or it could be a series of clouds coupled with internally managed systems. In some cases, a hybrid cloud might provide a lot of added security through redundancy.

As one CIO said, "I can now focus more attention on the big picture and partially remove myself from being a glorified network administrator." Cloud computing can provide the emerging CIO leader with more time to devote toward strategic planning on how to best support the enterprise with new technologies and procedures. The shift from *owning* the infrastructure to *managing* the infrastructure is a major advance in how we govern government systems. In a fast-paced and ever-changing environment, CIOs need greater flexibility in staffing, to better serve local governments' ongoing need for greater efficiencies.

One thing is clear, cloud computing is a game-changer when it comes to IT governance. The notion that to fully manage a computer network requires that the technology infrastructure be owned and operated and placed within proximity to a local government is no longer true. The best advantage of cloud computing is that data management can take place just about anywhere regardless of the actual physical location of the data source or service. Distance, too, has its advantages because data centers can be located in safer areas. Cloud computing, with all its advantages, is vulnerable to two basic enabling factors: reliable electricity and broadband. For without one or the other, any advantage of cloud computing is lost.

At the Starting Line

Few completely dismiss the operational advantages of cloud-based solutions. The more perplexing problem is where does one start? Looking at best practices, it appears the best place to start is with basic independent applications, such as e-mail, webhosting, or saving unstructured data. However, even before one gets to planning for cloud-based solutions, one must take stock of what they have and examine current and future computing capacity, where the equipment stands in terms of lifecycle management, and the scale of staff support. A locality that has a relatively new data center may find that it has plenty of capacity and perhaps should be offering excess capacity to other neighboring jurisdictions, thus serving as a cloud solution for others.

A sound internal analysis might begin with not only looking at every application and IT function, but how well the current servers are used. We know that data centers are designed for growth, and there is usually a lot of excess capacity. So, starting with servers, determine how well they are being used. Second, most successful IT managers have maximized their investments through virtualization, where virtual software acts as if it were a self-contained and

free-standing server—even with different programs and/or operating systems. If it is found that the servers have been optimized, the next move may be to seek ways to consolidate operations. Some have merged local data centers into regional data centers. Still others have reconfigured their data processing operations into a dynamic mix of different locations and perhaps with some outsourced or SaaS services. The point here is that there are endless solutions, some in the cloud and some on premise; it simply takes time to develop the appropriate business strategy. It appears from best practices that the more time spent on sound business planning, the greater the results.

Storm Clouds

In its "Cloud First" initiative, the federal government issued a call for more data center consolidation and cloud services from all agencies. IT managers must be prepared for the unthinkable, such as system failures in the cloud. The cost of service disruption can be huge in terms of real dollars as well as the political cost. On August 25, 2010, the Commonwealth of Virginia experienced a colossal failure in its then-newly christened data center located just outside Richmond and operated by Northrup Grumman. The disruption affected 13% of Virginia's file servers and 26 out of 89 executive branch agencies, 16 of which reported financial effects from the outage. The Department of Motor Vehicles was hit especially hard as it found itself unable to process driver's licenses or ID cards at its 74 customer service centers. The public was outraged, and more than 3,000 citizens had to have their license pictures retaken. When the system was restored, staff had to work on weekends and holidays to catch up.

A year later, a report found the data center operator had not followed best practices and did not respond appropriately when replacing hardware that had failed. So, the question then becomes, how can one prepare for the unthinkable, human failure? The answer is redundancy and closer monitoring of all systems.

On April 21, 2011, Amazon experienced an outage that shook the IT world because so many had believed the claims that the "cloud never goes down." Also in 2011, Microsoft, venturing into cloud services for colleges, local governments, and small businesses, also succumbed to a cloud failure that lasted nearly half of a day. It happened again in September 2011 when the company's Office 365, Hotmail, Skydive, and other various services went down throughout the world for a few hours. Likewise, Google Docs was offline for about 30 minutes during the same week. What do employees do while waiting to do their business? Who does one call, and would they be given better information about when a system may be up at a local IT operation or a distant cloud? Will employees have some sort of backup for their files and programs? Or will they be totally beholden to the cloud for everything, which could mean that if the cloud is down, so is the entire operation?

When clouds fail, it affects more customers than if a small city data center fails. It's like reading about a small commercial airliner crash as opposed to a jumbo jet—the larger the impact, the larger the headlines. Yet, if you are an unfortunate passenger, the effect is the same. As bad as cloud failures may appear, they are still relatively rare, and we must remember in-house systems have had their share of failures and local hard-drive crashes.

The bottom line is that small or large cloud infrastructure can fail. Yet, with that in mind, there are workable solutions. As Rich Miler, writing for dataccenterknowledge.com puts it, "...the difference is that cloud deployments offer new options for managing redundancy and routing around failures when they happen."

Cloud Computing and Risk Management (Mitigating Risk)

Sure, cloud computing and software as a service is increasingly becoming popular with local governments. The upside is that both offer fewer daily operational worries because the responsibility shifts to the provider. The downside is that some of the companies may not have the same exacting standards needed for security and reliability. It also remains to be seen how these service providers will perform under various market conditions. What happens if a company goes out of business? How is the data returned? In what format? In what timeframe? What are the security precautions taken by the service providers, and what is their guaranteed "up time"? Where are backups stored? How is system redundancy built in?

Cloud computing must be viewed through the lens of risk management. Depending on the importance and critical nature of data and online services, more contingency planning is an absolute must and should be included in any ROI comparison between in-house systems and cloud-based systems. Cloud-based services need not be an all-or-nothing proposition. Many local governments are very happy with placing some data and operations in the cloud while maintaining critical or sensitive operations in-house. Unstructured data is a good place to start in terms of cloud solutions. Next, e-mail systems and servers can follow. The question is no longer "why?" but "how?"

As remarkable as cloud computing is and will be in the near future, this chapter is surprisingly short. The reason is simple. Aside from noting a significant trend and successful examples, cloud computing intersects with every other trend and chapter in this manuscript, and is still unfolding. Cloud computing is about rethinking the enterprise piece by piece as well as function by function. It is about IT leadership, strategic planning and network security. Cloud computing is about having reliable broadband and technology infrastructure. Finally, cloud computing is very involved with social networking and citizen engagement because the overwhelming number of those applications reside in somebody's cloud.

TREND FOUR

Broadband: The life-blood of E-government and M-government

TREND FOUR

Broadband: The Life-blood of E-government and M-government

The fourth trend involves the growth and impact of broadband, which permeates just about every facet of American life. It makes not only the Internet possible, but also all other forms of communication and what we now regard as electronic necessities. A mayor of a small-sized city once commented at a PTI conference, "I really don't give a hoot about broadband. All we want is fast, always-on Internet connectivity!" Today, such a comment deserves a sympathetic chuckle.

The term "broadband" is a confusing term unto itself. Is broadband limited to cables and wires, or can broadband be wireless, too? The answer is that it can be either or both. In a sadly memorable U.S. Senate hearing, the late former Senator Ted Stevens, who was then-chairman of the all-powerful Senate Committee on Commerce Science and Transportation, was immortalized on YouTube as he struggled to define broadband during a Senate Commerce Committee debate on net neutrality. He stumbled here and there, but referred to the Internet as "a series of tubes." Even the most prominent policymakers have struggled with the terms "broadband" and the "Internet."

Thanks to the expansion of broadband use, cable and mobile wireless carriers now focus their marketing campaigns on what they provide by way of business efficiencies and entertainment features, such as texting, movies, games, or social media applications. Rarely do we see any mention about call quality. As much as modern society has come to depend on broadband infrastructure, so too has the corresponding need for city and county governments to use and promote the many benefits of broadband. Moreover, broadband is no longer a luxury, it is now an essential part of just about every mode of communications found today, which includes voice, data, and video.

Broadband has become as critical as electricity and water in modern society. Because of the confluence of digitization of just about all forms of media, we can view full-length, high-definition (HD) movies on computers with the same quality as can be found in cable or satellite TV. Tablet devices can now stream movies and, in some cases, live TV, too. None of that would be possible without broadband. While many are drawn to broadband for social entertainment value, there is even more innovation in the fields of education, medicine, public safety, government business applications, and personal and homeland security.

It used to be that a company looking to build a factory or office building would consider transportation infrastructure as a major criteria for locating a new facility. With the growth of other forms of reliable transportation, the focus shifted toward the availability of a stable workforce. That evolved into an educated workforce. At a conference of high-level CEOs, I asked them about the importance of broadband, and the answer was startling: strong broadband had become the No. 1 criteria when choosing a location for a new facility. With broadband, one can easily stay connected with an educated workforce anywhere in the world. They voiced concern that without broadband they would be economically isolated and noncompetitive.

Once upon a time, broadband was defined by the federal government as having the capability to transmit 250 kilobits per second (kbps) either up or down stream. By today's standards, that cannot be considered broadband. There was a time when most offices and homes accessed the Internet via a modem connected to a phone line. It took a few minutes to get connected, and each time you were logged on, it was called a "session." When you were done, you would log off, and the connection would be gone. It was inconceivable at the time that we would soon have the capacity to have an always-on connection.

On August 6, 2011, the Internet celebrated its 20th anniversary. Now, those annoying dial-up sounds have been replaced with blazing fast, always-on silent connections. Indeed, the term "login" is becoming an outdated term, too, because we are always connected one way or another. Today, instant Internet access has become commonplace, allowing for a new round of technological innovation.

When it comes to Internet use, in 2011, Netflix accounted for up to 30% of downstream Internet traffic during peak times. With competition growing from Amazon, Hulu, and others, movie viewing alone may account for at least 50% of peak Internet traffic in the very near future. This is only the beginning as more bandwidth-hungry devices and services emerge. Spectrum is limited and finite, and much more needs to be done to get more resources out of what is allocated today.

Local governments and businesses realize that as more citizens use the latest technologies, they will want to transact and/or engage with other users. According to October 2010 estimates from the International Telecommunication Union (ITU), there are more than 2 billion people on the Internet worldwide. By the end of 2010, there was a 77.4% Internet penetration rate in North America. Eight trillion text messages will have been sent in 2011. There were 5.3 billion mobile subscriptions by the end of 2010, which is equivalent to 77% of the world's population. In 2011, it was reported that there were more mobile devices than people in the United States.

Mobile devices—whether they are standard or smart devices—are leading the way to more broadband use. They serve as our personal communication

Mobile Device Features

Over 500,000 iOS apps and 400,000 Android apps as of February 2012

- Address book
- Air traffic control monitor
- AM/FM/Internet radio
- Answering machine
- Appointment calendar
- Banking (deposits, statements, and bill pay)
- Barcode reader
- Bio-hazard detector
- Blood pressure monitor
- Book reader
- Calculator
- Calendar (multiple years)
- Caller ID
- Camera–still
- Camera–video (HD)
- Clock/world clock
- Computer
- Currency converter
- Diabetes monitor
- E-mail
- Enterprise apps
- Flashlight
- Foreign language translator/converter
- Games (3-D)
- GPS tracking/mapping/directions
- IM (Instant messaging)
- Level (carpentry tool)
- Magazine
- Maps
- Movies
- MP3 player
- News, weather, traffic report alerts
- Newspaper
- Note pad
- Phone
- Picture viewer
- Police scanner
- Recording machine/tape recorder
- Slide show
- Smart cards (transportation)
- Smart payments (RFID, AFC)
- Speakerphone
- Spreadsheet
- Stocks, market performance, and portfolio management
- Stopwatch
- Timer
- Tip calculator
- TV and cable viewer
- TV guide
- TV/cable remote
- Vanity mirror screen
- Video clips
- Video conferencing
- Video editing
- Voice recognition
- VoIP
- Walkie-talkie
- Web browser
- Wi-Fi
- Wireless modem
- Word processor

devices and our lifeline to others. It used to be that having a car was top priority no matter how poor one found themselves. Today, the mobile device is the most cherished device—even more so than a car or fine watch.

When we talk about wireless broadband, we often neglect the role that wired broadband plays. In fact, it has always played a major role in providing the network capabilities often called "back-haul" that connects all the millions of cell sites to the network and Internet. When it comes to fixed cable, fiber is considered the ultimate conduit for carrying huge amounts of data over microscopic stands of glass. There is simply no other form of reliable conduit that can do so much to move such vast amounts of data traffic. Fiber, however, can be expensive to build out and is especially challenging because it requires tearing up streets and roads to lay the fiber cable.

At a recent conference, I spoke of my amazement that more communities reviewing new construction permits did not insist that fiber cable conduits be required as part of the permit approval process. After the presentation, an executive from a major wireless provider came up and respectfully disagreed with my suggestion. He said that the major wireless companies will shift away from fiber and that the new 4G Wireless LTE standard would replace fiber to the home. This statement reminded me of a discussion I had in class where I asked in a rather negative tone, "Do any of you still carry a radio around with you?" The class responded with an "are you nuts?" look. I then asked how many owned a cell phone and had it with them. Of course, there was a 100% positive response. That is when I said, "Did you know that your device is actually a radio?" I then went on to explain that a radio is dependent on the electromagnetic field called radio spectrum, and that it is subject to weather, geography, and other forms of potential interference.

Sidebar: Did you know that an Apple ATT iPhone has multiple "radios" inside? Consider Bluetooth, GSM frequency bands, 2G Bands, Wi-Fi frequency bands, GEO-location Chip radio device, plus international frequency bands.

Returning to the previous discussion regarding wireless companies' shift away from fiber to Long Term Evolution (LTE), raises a lot of questions about quality of service bandwidth limitations, potential for interference, congestion, and capacity. No doubt, building out new systems with wireless infrastructure instead of fiber is purely an economic decision. Fiber is expensive when compared to wireless infrastructure. There are no streets or roads to tear up, and based on the fiber cabling to the home, the excess or unused capacity far exceeds the demand.

But haven't we been wrong before in trying to estimate demand into the future? The laugh-out-loud FCC standard (22 kilobytes up or down) that remained on the books longer than even the FCC would have liked was due to the uncertainty of what would be an appropriate measure of broadband in the 21st century. Everyone knew that the outdated definition that was in the regulations was wrong; it was replacing it that was the problem, and even the newest one will most likely require adjustments along the way. In the end, however, it might not make economic sense to lay fiber by any single company without direct government support. Yet, every day developers build new homes and offices, and not laying fiber conduit is irresponsible and a sorely missed opportunity. There is simply no other (at least today) technology that has as many features and as much capacity as fiber. Wireless systems simply can't compete against fiber—except on mobility and cost. As other nations continue to work with local governments in building out fiber networks, the United States will fall much further behind and lose even more of its competitiveness in business, education, health, and science.

As broadband becomes increasingly important to everyday life, what is the government's role in ensuring a healthy, reliable, and affordable infrastructure? It is also important to note that there are many in this country who firmly believe that free-market principles should govern—not government at any level, in any way.

From E-government to M-government and Beyond

Broadband is the power behind e-government and m-government initiatives. E-government is rooted in the automation of internal systems aimed at making government more effective and efficient. The "e" stood for electronic, and "m" stands for mobile. As more people became "connected," the notion of serving people through the Internet became the new frontier. Today, e-government is near-seamlessly integrated into just about all government functionality. M-government is growing rapidly throughout the world, and the mobile device is where government now is aiming its resources.

For less than $10, just about anyone with a smart phone can purchase a credit reader that attaches to the mobile device, thus allowing them to capture credit card information on the spot. At the same time, local governments continue to struggle with such off-the shelf consumer solutions.

What is E-government?

• Always open (24-hour city hall) • Locality neutral • Faster transactions • No lines • Saves government money • Citizen satisfaction • Business satisfaction • Improved security applications • Accessibility (can be almost anywhere) • Language options • Greater citizen participation

---

E-government (Passive/Informative)

- Citizen access to information
- Government functions and services
- Directory and directions to parks and community centers
- Pictures of key staff and elected leaders
- Calendar of city-sponsored events and activities
- Property information
- Citizen services
- Job postings
- Phone and staff directories
- Meeting notices
- Statistics of city
- Tourist information

e-Government (Transactional)

- License renewal and payment
- Payment of parking tickets, fines
- Registration for functions
- Interactive job applications
- Online permits, business licenses, court documents
- Online purchase orders, bid documents
- Sales tax collection
- Distance learning
- Webcasting of city/county meetings
- Communications with local leaders
- Links to other key sites (airport, transportation, hotels)

E-government (Passive/Informative)

- Digital Democracy
- Respond to proposed rules and regulations
- View comments/pleadings
- Vote on certain issues (see results)
- View and participate in live meetings
- View streaming video of past meetings

Today, government agencies at all levels are directing their services through websites and mobile apps. A few years ago, the Internal Revenue Service (IRS) announced that it would no longer mail IRS forms to all citizens, and now it has a mobile app for tax information. Electronic submission of forms and payments of all types is common and encouraged—so much so that there are sometimes financial penalties for simply going to an office to speak with someone. "Go online, and get it online" is the new mantra. Those who have purchased U.S. Savings Bonds at banks since 1935 will no longer be able to do so as of January 2012; they can only be purchased online. This is but another example where agencies at all levels of government are trying to shift more and more operations online both as a convenience (to some) and to save money.

Former federal CIO Vivek Kundra tells the story that while sitting in a coffee shop, he was watching all the people pass by with their smartphones, and it occurred to him that average citizens had greater functionality in their hands than government workers had at their desks. So, if broadband is so necessary, what is the appropriate role for government? Are local governments following or leading, or simply observing?

Local Government Mobility

- Accessibility
- Crime prevention/reporting
- Economic development
- E-health
- E-procurement
- E-voting
- I-witness news
- Local government information
- Mobile field workforce
- Mobile payment systems
- Public opinion
- Smart parking meters (wired and wireless)
- Social equity
- Telework
- Traffic reporting/cameras
- Transportation smart cards, (RFID, AFC chips)
- Travel information
- Weather and disaster alerts and notifications
- Web 2.0 and 3.0 citizen communications and engagement

What is M-government?

M-government is simply a term to describe how government is providing information and services to mobile devices of all types. Mobile phone subscriptions now outnumber Internet connections in both developed and developing countries, and mobile cellular is becoming the most rapidly adopted technology in history, and the most popular and widespread personal technology in the world. Access to mobile networks is available to 90% of the world's population and to 80% of the population living in rural areas, according to ITU World Telecommunications Indicators database. By the end of 2010, there were an estimated 5.3 billion mobile cellular phone subscribers, including 940 million subscriptions to 3G services.

Given the unparalleled advancement of mobile communication technologies, governments are turning to m-government to realize the value of mobile technologies for responsive governance and measurable improvements to social and economic development, public service delivery, operational efficiencies, and active citizen engagement. The interoperability of mobile applications, which support quick access to integrated data and location-based services, paves the way for innovative public sector governance

"Everyone in the office is getting a netbook. Little screens make our problems look smaller!"

models—also called mobile governance or m-governance—based on the use of mobile technology in support of public services and information delivery.

There is also a growing belief that m-government may ultimately lessen the gap of those without broadband at home. The Pew Internet and Family Life Project reports that in 2011 nearly one-third of Americans do not have broadband at home. The reasons for that include that they do not see the benefits of broadband, do not have access to it, or cannot afford it. At the same time, it appears that even the poorest of Americans have some sort of mobile device.

Does the Nation Need a Broadband Plan? (We Actually Have One!)

Does the nation need a broadband plan? One might respond with the question, "Does a city need stoplights?"

One reason for the need for a national broadband plan is to make sure that there is ample spectrum available for broadband growth and to promote other forms of spectrum efficiencies, because our nation's spectrum is finite. What we have must be used efficiently and in the public interest. We simply cannot have 50 different plans for spectrum use; that would be akin to each state regulating its own airspace for air traffic control. We also need rules and regulations that address the need for interoperability across state and local jurisdictions. We would not tolerate a cellphone that only worked in one location.

As the federal government was struggling to find ways to reinvigorate the declining economy, the American Recovery and Reinvestment Act was passed by Congress in 2009. A staggering $7.2 billion dollars was allocated for broadband projects across the country. The overall plan addressed two broad categories: programs that were aimed at creating demand for broadband through education, training, and demonstration projects; and projects that focused on supply or infrastructure for increased capacity and availability. The investment represented a move that many considered political expediency that superseded logical planning.

A year later, as the monies were being awarded, Congress empowered the Federal Communications Commission (FCC) to develop a National Broadband Plan. The National Broadband Plan does an excellent job of describing the necessity for broadband in just about every major category of government and civil life and at all levels. It is a plan worth reading and makes a number of excellent well-documented points, but unfortunately there was no money allocated for implementing any of the recommendations. That would be up to Congress to provide later, if ever. Imagine spending $7.2 billion dollars on broadband projects and then having a real plan one year later. As a result, the federal government plays a key regulatory role at the very least, and yet, much is still left to the marketplace to decide.

Local governments have responsibilities, too. They are the ones who approve zoning requests for new cell site towers. This has often been a rather contentious issue with local governments, though now there are many ways to disguise cell sites. Zoning polices could be changed to require all new construction request to include a requirement to build fiber conduits.

As large broadband customers, cities and counties also are consumer advocates. Local governments have been most concerned about making

A special cell site in Scottsdale, AZ

sure that certain segments of the population have some form of access to the Internet. Targeted Internet services can be placed in senior homes, libraries, recreation centers, housing authority locations, as well as government buildings. Local governments can help with promoting sound and unbiased consumer information in their communities about broadband availability and coverage, pricing, and affordability.

National Broadband Plan's Elements

- Economic opportunity
- Education
- Healthcare
- Energy and environment
- Government performance
- Civic engagement
- Public safety

SOURCE: WWW.BROADBAND.GOV/PLAN/

Broadband as a Utility?

Some have argued that broadband should be treated as a utility, just like water and electricity. We know our society is more dependent on electricity than ever before, and just as electricity is regulated by government given its significance to daily life and national security, broadband is similar.

There was an interesting story going around the Internet that captured a glimpse of the past where arguments were being made against public ownership of an electric "lighting" utility. The news account appeared in the Richmond Times-Dispatch on October 24, 1905. Owners of an electric plant in default argued that there would be no economic incentive for any investor if the city were to build and operate its own electric lighting plant. Indeed, in a letter written in opposition to the proposed municipal lighting plant, it said, "Electricity is not in any sense a necessity, and under no conditions is it universally used by the people of a community. It is a luxury enjoyed by a small proportion of the members of any municipality, and yet if the plant be owned and operated by the city, the burden of such ownership and operation would be borne by all the people through taxation." The author of the letter goes on to say, "...electric light is not a necessity for every member of the community."

At that time, people had no idea how electric power would evolve—especially beyond lighting of streets. The concept of an "electric lighting plant" in that day saw lighting as the main and only application. That, of course, preceded electric trains, washing machines, electric heat, radios, and TVs.

Many of the same arguments have been used recently to try to persuade public policy makers from owning and/or operating their own broadband systems in what has been called "muni broadband." Governments have been looked upon as the provider of last resort, and broadband is becoming an essential element in everyone's daily life.

In 2005, broadband coverage in the United States was inconsistent and spotty. The need for municipal broadband was growing faster than providers could build the required infrastructure. Wi-Fi, high-speed wireless Internet initially designed for in-home/office use, was being adopted to operate outdoors, too. Corpus Christi, Texas, was the first city to build out a viable Wi-Fi system for meter reading, public safety applications, and more. The city, with the help of PTI and the technology community, came up with 20 proof-of-concept applications. Other cities began building and using Wi-Fi systems of their own. "Wars" began that pitted local governments against wired and wireless broadband providers. Local governments intended to build Wi-Fi systems that the public could use and then use the commercial proceeds to build out the networks for city or county applications. Private providers thought that was unfair.

The contentious issue of municipalities building out their systems led straight to state legislatures, which began to ban such initiatives. In the end, it was private enterprise that nearly killed muni broadband. A struggling dial-up Internet company named Earthlink began signing up deals to purchase and operate muni broadband systems. Unfortunately, the money ran out, and Earthlink was forced to liquidate, leaving many disappointed public officials. Today, Corpus Christi, almost a victim of the Earthlink plans, continues to operate a highly successful internal Wi-Fi system for city applications.

In 2011, 20 states had laws that severely restrict or ban municipalities from operating broadband systems for the public.

Local governments can and have shaped telecom policy at the local level. The following are some ways that they can play a significant role.

Muni Rationale

- Economic development
- Keep business and citizens happy
- Lessen the digital divide
- Powerful internal management functionality
- Visible extension of e-government
- Improved citizen connectivity
- Greater citizen communications
- Competition will drive down prices and improve services, offerings, and choices.
- Provide broadband coverage where none exists
- Is part of today's civic infrastructure responsibilities

The Cable and Phone Companies' Rationale

- Leave it to private enterprise.
- Government has no business being in business.
- Why should telecom companies invest millions when governments will become competitors?
- It's against the law, and if it isn't, we will pass laws.
- Taxpayer money should not be used.
- Public networks reduce incentives to build out costly systems.
- Local governments are largely incompetent in these matters.
- Local governments will have a monopoly or unfair advantage over private enterprise.

Government as Prime User or Anchor Tenant

In communities of all sizes, the government is often the largest user of services, including basic telephony, broadband, video, data, and mobile broadband. For good reason, most municipalities still own, operate, and maintain their own public safety radio systems, and some do the same for their data systems. Even though a municipality may appear to wield great power, there usually is zero competition among private providers and, therefore, nowhere else to go. Local governments can, however, hold back on services and seek alternative solutions.

In one Maryland city near Washington, D.C., county employees complain that after 3:00 p.m., broadband at their workstations gets frustratingly slow. Why is that? It appears they are located near a few schools, and when they let out, students log on. Most people fail to realize that every broadband system, wired or wireless is essentially a shared system. The greater the load, the less there is to go around.

In addition, if there is an emergency, how will governments be able to respond if public systems are shut down and are overwhelmed? This has happened during weather emergencies, and it happened during September 11, 2001, during the terrorist attacks in New York and Washington, D.C. If there were ever an argument for operating and maintaining a municipal network, emergency communications tops the list.

Government as Consumer Advocate

Local governments can play a key role in serving as an honest broker of what's available where and at what cost. Too often, citizens have only a website to ponder or a brochure to read. Studies have shown that advertised speeds are not always available. Local governments can post the latest coverage maps and information from citizens reporting how well their provider is doing. Because many broadband providers operate in a near-monopoly environment, local governments can serve as an advocate for customers experiencing problems that remain unresolved through their own efforts.

Government as Rule Maker

Although most broadband policy is left to regulatory agencies, such as the FCC and the National Telecommunications and Information Administration

(NTIA), and Congress, policy making at the local level can be significant. Local governments play a critical role in zoning for new cell sites, approving building permits, providing tax incentives or zoning variances for providing greater services, and building infrastructure. Cities also can provide policies and incentives for broadband training and adoption in key government-controlled facilities, or provide grants to nonprofits working in this area. Governments also can provide policies and facilities that encourage telework.

Government as Policy Maker

Local governments have been experimenting with two main policy-related features, each requiring a good deal of broadband. The first feature has been to experiment with the workweek, in particular with a four-day workweek. This change in schedule requires that more broadband applications will need to be available for longer periods of time and will have to be monitored by someone remotely on days that an office may be closed. Routine systems have been further automated so many in-person functions can now be taken care of via a self-service kiosk, computer, or mobile device.

The second area is government employee telework. Most local governments offering telework do so in two broad categories: one day or more per week, or for some employees, permanent telework from a remote location or home. Finally, governments can offer remote location facilities to non-government employees so they can be more productive—especially in terms of emergencies. They also can provide tax incentives to keep workers using telework off the roads.

Fiber to the Core

For many decades to come, fiber will be the conduit of choice. Fiber has the capacity to carry over 1.5 million simultaneous conversations or messages on a single cable. Wireless broadband carriers rely on fiber to provide reliable, high-capacity backhaul, which connects everything to the carrier and the Internet. However, fiber is expensive to deploy and currently exists as a patchwork with many holes in coverage. Equipment manufacturers and service providers often complain that their mobile devices and applications suffer from America's patchwork of broadband. This might be likened to high-speed rail. In the United States, where few high-speed rail trains operate, they operate at less than half the speed of European and Asian railroads. It's not the trains themselves that provide the limitation, it's the inadequate patchwork of aging rail infrastructure. Broadband is like the rails that allow trains to pass, and the trains are like the mobile devices that can do more but are limited by the amount of available broadband.

Government's Leadership Role in Addressing the Digital Divide or Gap

As broadband adoption grows among nearly all segments of the population, there still exists a widening divide among the "haves" and "have-nots." While poverty certainly plays into the divide or gap, as some prefer to call it, the gap also includes seniors and those who come from different cultures where trust is limited or the Internet is not well understood. We know, for example, that there are members of our society that prefer not to use credit cards and prefer to pay for things in cash. In Virginia, as in most states, where no one looks forward to visiting their motor vehicles department, they charge a $5 administration fee for those who renew their license plates in person instead of online. Therefore, it can be said that fees can be a tax on the very poorest and needy.

Local governments and other public institutions have done well in providing online resources and training in libraries, senior homes, and community centers, and they must continue this work. Some estimate that 19% to 23% of the population does not have either access, interest, or the ability to go online. As this trend continues, the gap will only widen, so if not government, then who will help address the gap?

Government's Role Using Video Technology: Video as the Killer App?

Nowhere is there greater evidence of the need and advantage for broadband than video conferencing. Hardly a day goes by when a new study is announced extolling the time- and money-saving virtues of video conferencing. Those who have iPhones, iPads, iPods, or a Mac computer enjoy video conferencing between users using "Face Time." Others have many other video conferencing options such as Skype, Viber, or ooVoo.

Local governments use internal video conferencing to save time and money in hosting video arraignment proceedings, and department and division meetings, to name a few. The time it takes to travel to a meeting, plus the expense of fuel, and wear and tear on a vehicle, makes video conferencing a great alternative. With broadband speeds getting faster and more reliable, video cameras are becoming more powerful and shrinking in size.

Cisco Systems has coined the term "telepresence" to describe a higher level of video conferencing, where both audio and video are broadcast with such clarity you can almost feel the presence of others at one or more locations. This system includes a board or conference room that allows participants to see and hear one another in multiple locations in high definition. It is as close as one can get to actually being in the same room with one another.

The familiar Verizon spokesperson who for years asked the question, "Can you hear me know?" may have a new gig. This time the same spokesperson might be saying, "Can you see me now?"

As more citizens begin to adopt video as they have voice and text communications, there may be a growing expectation that they may expect to actually see the person to whom they are calling at City Hall. When I shared this possible future scenario with a large group of local government employees, they gasped and said in near unison—"no way!" Local governments have usually followed the trends set by corporate America when it comes to the use of technology as it interacts with consumers. The tax preparation people at H&R Block have launched a new service called H&R Block Live, where a customer can chat with a live advisor, perhaps setting the stage for other to emulate.

There is another side to the video feature: security. Whether it is a traffic camera known as a "red light or speeding camera" or surveillance cameras, public safety officials have placed hundreds if not thousands of cameras throughout large cities to help reduce crime or to better monitor property and people. Cameras—especially wireless high definition cameras—require a great deal of bandwidth to operate. Local governments maintain hundreds of thousands of cameras to monitor traffic, prevent crime, monitor ports, airports, and other transportation facilities. They also monitor buildings, water treatment plants, and waterways.

Video will be the "killer app" for years to come, and display technology will continue to evolve into lighter, brighter, clearer, and even flexible fold-up displays. Less than a few generations from now, people will look at the present generation and will be unable to comprehend how people for years could "talk" with someone on a device and appear complacent with simply two-way voice. They will wonder how we could possibly talk into a device without seeing the person or persons at the other end!

The Consumerization of Broadband Devices

Apple icon Steve Jobs said that the tablet was not designed to replace the PC, but to free people from it. He said he saw the PC as a truck where heavy lifting was not always needed. Not everyone shares that vision, and it appears the competitive forces will hasten a mobile tablet device with the power of a full-powered laptop. There are already a few such devices on the market now. Rapid shifts in evolving innovation create new opportunities from which to build upon the "last generation," even if that last generation is only a few months old. Technology leaders report that many elected leaders of cities and counties are demanding that they get tablets and do away with laptops.

United Airlines, while experimenting with the iPad tablet, announced in a public statement that each pilot would receive one. United leaders believe each iPad would replace roughly 38 pounds of operating manuals and charts and that, by making planes lighter, the iPads would help save 326,000 gallons of jet fuel and 12,000 sheets of paper per pilot. Not to be outdone, American Airlines announced the same type of program.

This same type of cost benefit analysis using broadband device technologies provides similar opportunities for government innovation and applications. Internal applications have been developed to allow local government field staff to have online forms, charts, building permits, architectural drawings, zoning variances, fire code enforcement, and restaurant safety checklists, to name just a few. Mobile field workers have as much power and resources as if they were back in their offices at their desks.

Meanwhile, once the purview of public safety and private security companies, Wi-Fi surveillance cameras with built-in microphones can be purchased for a modest price. Anyone can install the technology and use a broadband-connected laptop, desktop PC, smartphone or tablet to view a room or series of rooms or other locations with a simple touch of a button from wherever one is located. People can check on kids, pets, or property from just about anywhere.

It used to be said that the citizen had the power of the vote. We can now add to that the power to create and obtain information and communicate as never before through e-mails, blogs, websites, and social media. Broadband is the underlying foundation on which social and civic networking depends.

TREND FIVE

Social and Civic Media

TREND FIVE

Social and Civic Media

According to the Pew Internet & Family Life Project, 65% of online adults used social networking sites in 2011. That is quite a jump over previous years. A slightly earlier study found that 71% of online adults use video-sharing sites. It has been said that Facebook, given its active member population of 800 million, would be considered the world's third largest nation based on population.

Social media is changing constantly.

SOURCE: WORDLE

In 2004, MySpace, the first web-based social network site, was all the rage. It was designed primarily for college students wanting to "connect" with one another. Today, it has faded from its moments of glory and it is barely alive as a company. Many observers are quick to point out that today's social media winners might be tomorrow's "road-kill" as new forms of social media platforms emerge.

In 2010, YouTube celebrated its fifth anniversary. As of this writing, YouTube enjoys more than 2 billion page views daily, where 24 hours of video are downloaded every minute. More video is uploaded in 60 days than all three major networks created in 60 years. It would take 500 years to view everything that was uploaded to YouTube during its first five years, watching 24 hours a day, seven days a week.

Twitter, which recently celebrated its first five years since it began in July 2006, has an estimated 280 million accounts, with 140 million "tweets" sent each day. Once source states that Twitter posts approximately 350 billion tweets each day worldwide.

Skype, the personal video conferencing service claims 300 million minutes of video calls globally a day, which is a 900% increase since 2007. They also claim that in the United States alone, during Sunday mornings some 30 million users are logged in on average.

Before 2004, social media had not taken hold. Since then, advances in website technologies, and the increase of Internet and broadband penetration, have served as the digital fertilizer that provided the necessary ingredients for social media to emerge and evolve. Just five years ago, who would have thought that millions of people worldwide would be heavily involved in sending messages limited to just 140 characters as in Twitter? The latest research shows that 13–33% of those who use text messaging prefer texting to voice conversations. Each new platform and improvement creates new opportunities for innovation in social media. Looking back in time, we seemed to skip over Web 1.0, as many navigated the Web for the first time and were happy to just get online and send an e-mail. Web.2.0 is a term that has been used for several years now, and while the term itself has not changed, the concept has evolved and continues to adjust every day. Some common characteristics include:

- Interactive
- Web-based
- Browser-based

- Intuitive
- Content sharing
- Content development by users
- Collaboration tools
- Interactive games
- Applications
- Mobile applications

Web 2.0 includes elements such as searching, linking, authoring, podcasting, blogging and social networking, creating content, and sharing. All of that is wholly dependent on a vibrant and open information data system called the Internet. Katie Couric at a recent commencement address at Boston University said, "The beauty of Web 2.0 is that everyone has a voice, and the negative to that is everyone has a voice!" On the later point, she was referring to the fact that we see so much civil discord and uncivil behavior, and quite frankly, ignorance. Put another way, social media holds the promise of instant intelligence, but in reality, it's more like instant ignorance.

Today, there are more than 2 billion people on the Internet worldwide. By the close of 2010, there was a 77.4% Internet penetration rate in North America. Web 2.0 and civic/social media technologies can be used as dynamic tools for informing the public about issues affecting the community, encouraging collaboration for improved communications and service delivery, and engaging the public in government decision-making.

While social networking is only a derivative of Web 2.0, the two terms are most often used synonymously. Social media goes far beyond the traditional web-site, and instead of providing mostly one-way information, it provides a way to connect emotionally, where content can be created by just about anyone and shared. Collectively, people spend more than 700 billion minutes per month on social media.

With the growth of Web 2.0 and social media, in the state and local government setting, public managers are challenged as never before and find themselves totally "exposed" to an uncertain, yet demanding, public. The challenge ahead is not only to figure out how best to embrace the new web-centricity in one's personal life, but to figure out how the enormous power, pitfalls, and possibilities can be better integrated in one's professional life. When it comes to government websites and mobile applications, much time is required for planning, experimentation, exploration, careful navigation, as well as fully addressing new media policies and procedures.

Today's city or town hall may look the same from the outside, but the way we connect with government and one another have forever changed. The Internet and its emerging social media sites and tools have helped change the landscape and focus on a new and unchartered cyber landscape where boundaries and interests are no longer bound by mere physical structure.

Moreover, local government websites are in a constant state of improvement in terms of providing information, improving navigation, and offering more opportunities to complete certain transactions online. In a few short years, we have moved from merely posting information to transacting information, to allowing citizens to react to certain events and measures, to actually seeking two-way citizen engagement.

Not everyone agrees on what citizen engagement means. To some, it means to provide citizens with the opportunity to comment on specific issues. Others see it quite differently where interactivity and content development is both encouraged and processed. For example, a police chief from a small jurisdiction in the Midwest was complaining that some younger residents, wanting to helpful, were sending in pictures from auto accidents and fires. He was upset that they were upset that the police and fire dispatch departments had no way to capture and process the photographs and, therefore, they were not helpful at all. This is an example of a growing disconnect between how technology is used and will increasingly be used by citizens. If government agencies want to engage citizens, they need to be able to interact with the devices citizens are most comfortable using.

As stated earlier, when it comes to devices, the cell phone has emerged as a very smart device that is truly nothing less than a feature-rich pocket computer in which the phone is simply an application. According to Pew Internet & Family Life Project, 35% of U.S. adults own a smartphone of some kind, and one-quarter of smartphone owners say that their phone is where they do most of their online browsing. New tablet devices, such as the iPad2, with their rich user interface simply make it easier to get and respond to information with larger high-definition screens and no external pointing device or cumbersome keyboards. New pocket cameras are on the market that not only take great shots, they record the time and date, latitude and longitude, which has the potential to take the concept of]\neighborhood watch to entirely new levels. Engagement, then, is more interactive than transparency, with citizens having the ability to actually produce content.

MIKE KEEFE, THE DENVER POST & INTOON.COM

Social media is geared toward civic engagement, and we are now seeing the start of an emerging civic engagement ecosystem in cyberspace. Used effectively, Web 2.0 and civic/social media encourage citizens to take a more active role in local and state government. They provide a platform to streamline government communications and services through knowledge bases, access to networked resources, real-time data communications and reporting, wireless access, multi-media delivery, integrated self-service options, location-based services and cross-agency information sharing.

State and local governments have evolved along with their citizens from e-government to m-government and have moved away from a web-centric model to a more multi-channel approach. While websites continue to serve an invaluable purpose of providing key information and offering online services and payments, governments are now moving to mobile devices—be it a smartphone, a laptop, or a tablet—as another way to reach and engage citizens.

Mobile applications (apps) are a relatively new channel of communication. They may exist and operate entirely outside a local government operation and website. They might take the form of a stand-alone application or one that is fully integrated into a local government's communications center. Gartner predicts that by 2013 mobile phones will overtake PCs as the most common web access device. Add to this prediction that smartphone growth is expected to have double-digit growth in the years to come—coupled with the explosive growth of tablet devices—and apps will overtake websites. A study by Flurry found iOS and Android apps surpassed 1 billion downloads in the final week of 2011. In addition, according to the analyst firm Berg, 98 billion apps will be downloaded in 2015.

Public managers are increasingly looking for new ways to engage the public as a means of improving communications and restoring trust. We know, for example, that at the end of 2010, there were 302,947,098 mobile phones, or 97.4% penetration. The research firm Nielson predicted that 2011 would be the year when smartphone penetration would surpass regular mobile phones. However, that prediction was offered before the unexpected and explosive growth of the iPad and other tablets that emerged. With iPad2 and other tablet growth, website developers are being forced to rethink their website designs and functionality to best accommodate the new mobile device medium. Location-based social media applications will present new and exciting opportunities for citizens and local governments.

With all the growth in local government outreach using social/civic media comes many disappointments. In 2010, the Public Technology Institute (PTI) conducted a national survey directed to those who manage their social media applications, asking about how they were using the largely built-in user metrics. In the past, if a local government were to send out a flyer, the best they could report was the amount of paper printed and possibly a secondary reader percentage. New social and civic media, by comparison, normally has built-in measurement capabilities.

Today, when a local government sends a message, it can know not only how many people it sent it to but whether the message was actually delivered or returned, opened or not, for how long, and how long recipients spent on a particular page. The PTI survey revealed that a large majority of managers did not use social media metrics because of three stated reasons:

- They claimed to be too busy and didn't have the time,
- They claimed that it was too complicated and lacked the proper training, and
- They claimed their supervisors did not care or never asked about social media metrics.

That is a sharp departure from what one generally finds in the business sector, where data is mined every second, and decisions are made on having relevant and near-immediate information about people, consumers, trends, and habits. Local governments will have a lot of catching up to do in this area of data analysis and interpretation. Cities and counties collect tons of data, but a small fraction by comparison is used in databases to make sound decisions and share with other agencies—and even the public.

Apple, which revolutionized the smartphone with the iPhone and surprised even the most optimistic critic with the iPad in 2010, has enjoyed enormous success with its Apps Store, where one can browse through more than 455,000 apps for the iPhone and more than 100,000 apps for the iPad. One can now browse a category appropriately named Government 2.0. Even outside the Apple App Store, apps have been developed by and for local governments that allow citizens to report potholes, animal control issues, graffiti, lighting issues, crimes or accidents, and much more. The new apps allow pictures to be submitted with the latitude and longitude, exact time, and device owner information. Because apps are usually completely separate from a website, there are greater opportunities for innovation and experimentation.

State and local government leaders and managers are challenged as never before to seek out new and better ways to engage and interact with the public they serve. With a greater than 97% penetration rate of mobile devices, which are becoming smarter with each new model, government leaders must understand and adequately address how the citizens they serve prefer to be engaged. At the same time, these same managers must always be aware of those in the population who either cannot afford or choose to opt out of communication technology.

Web 2.0 and civic/social media depends on citizens and governments alike having reliable access to affordable broadband in our homes and offices. The Federal Communications Commission's (FCC) National Broadband Plan for America includes seven major categories, one of which is "Broadband and Civic Engagement." Here, the plan highlights four key areas:

1. Release more government data online in open and accessible formats to enable the public to more actively participate in the civic life of their communities and their democracy, and hold their government accountable.

2. Expand public media's use of digital online platforms and create a 21st century digital national archive to empower people with information on broadband-enabled platforms.

3. Increase opportunities for citizens to participate in the civic life of their local communities and to engage their government through social media and broadband-enabled tools, like smartphones, as well as open platforms and innovative partnerships.

4. Leverage broadband-based technologies to modernize delivery of government services and enhance democratic processes, and ensure that they are accessible to all Americans.

While most applaud this report as a significant first step, much (if not all) of the actual recommendations were focused on the federal government and what its agencies should and must do to better engage the public through broadband technology. There is nothing preventing local governments from adopting many of the key principals, as they are, after all, closest to their citizens. The good news is they have been doing so long before the report was published.

Budget woes always bring about new or enhanced forms of innovation. While text is here to stay, video and graphic interfaces have become the new norm. Even before "the Great Recession of 2009," advances in technology were making peer-to-peer video conferencing a preferred method for instant meetings.

So, how can governments at all levels best prepare and respond? This remains an open-ended question that public managers at all levels must address with both strategy and action.

Civic Media and News Reporting

As mentioned earlier, most citizens received news about government largely from the print media; however, there is a diminishing role for "print" newspapers, as we have known them. Today, we find an ever-growing trend away from traditional printed newspapers where circulation continues to decline, yet online readership continues to grow. We know that overall print media circulation is down 35% and declining an average 7% a year. Traditional newspapers are thinner, printed less often (in some cases), and with less staff. According to The New York Times, "The reality facing American newspaper publishers continues to look stark, as figures released Monday show deep circulation declines, with average weekday sales down almost 9 percent since last year."

The overwhelming majority of Americans (92%) use multiple platforms to get their daily news, according to a survey conducted jointly by the Pew Research Center's Internet & American Life Project and Project for Excellence in Journalism (2010). And, according to the Pew Research Center's Project for Excellence in Journalism "The State of the News Media 2011, An Annual Report on American Journalism," more than 26%, or one out of four, Americans now get their news delivered to their smartphones—many instead of their front door—and no doubt, that number will continue to rise. Perhaps not surprisingly, the study also found that the Internet has become the third most popular news source. Local television has certainly become less local and more regional and national with even less time devoted to local government, except for scandals, budget cost overruns, and crime.

During the steady decline in print journalism, some have expressed fear in what they see as a decline in literacy and critical thinking. There is also a growing concentration of media ownership that can have the effect of taking a small news story in one locality and highlight it in such a way that the significance is distorted or perhaps blown out of proportion based on dramatic elements and video. Just as bad, some stories that used to receive coverage have disappeared. Finally, daily *news* has transformed into daily *views*.

Citizens are not just reading news online, they are contributing to it. According to the Pew Internet & Family Study "Understanding the Participatory News Consumer" (2010), 37% of Internet users have contributed to the creation of news, commented about it, or disseminated it via postings on social media sites like Facebook or Twitter.

Local governments realize they can no longer rely on traditional media to reach the public. They are developing innovative channels to broadcast their messages through various new media applications, and they have done an exceptional job. Many jurisdictions now offer citizens the choice of having specific news and information feeds sent directly to a laptop, home computer, mobile device, etc. Citizens can choose to receive public safety alerts, weather and traffic bulletins, or meeting notices. Local governments using new media delivery systems can better control their own need to send out timely and accurate news and information with greater frequency and detail.

Social & Civic Media Implications for Public Safety

Nowhere has social and civic media gained greater importance than public safety applications. One of the hallmarks of social media is the ability for just about anyone to either create something positive or, in some cases, create havoc. Cybercrime is growing both faster and more dangerous with every

"It used to be we were the first responders!"

SIOBHAN DUNCAN

passing day. Social media has become an innocent carrier, and despite all the good, it can carry misleading and inaccurate news, information, malware, and theft. It was reported on national news that a family posted a detailed itinerary of their weekend trip and came home to find their house had been completely robbed. Apparently, someone had read the posting and knew the house would be vacant. It must also be pointed out there are many upsides, where local authorities are actively monitoring social media sites to gain intelligence on gang, drug activities, or sexual offenders.

Public safety and social media can be reduced to three overall categories: fighting crime, both traditional and cyber; getting the word out or broadcasting critical information to the public; and figuring out ways to use existing resources to encourage the public to send in critical information, including pictures or video.

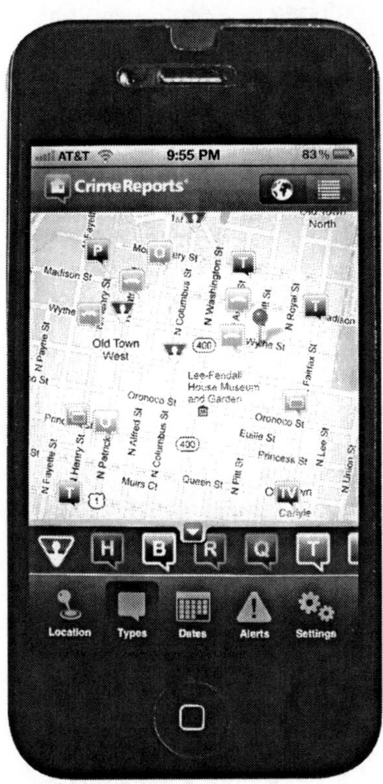

CRIMEREPORTS®

Now, high-definition (HD) video and sound is being introduced that is so life-like that people in other locations can't believe they are not in the same room. The next generation of video cameras will be smaller, lighter, and more powerful in every way. New still cameras can take HD video and can easily be connected to the Internet as well as big screen TVs. Citizens will have forward- and backward-facing higher-resolution cameras that will enable greater peer-to-peer and group-to-group communications. Moreover, just as word processing programs allowed almost anyone to be a publisher, new easy-to-use video processor programs allow almost anyone to be a movie producer.

As with any technology, always a dark side or vulnerability needs to be understood. Just two days before the 10th anniversary of the September 11, 2001, terrorist attacks, followers of an NBC

News Twitter feed were told, "Breaking News! Ground Zero has just been attacked. Flight 5736 has crashed into the site. More news as the story develops." Another tweet followed that stated this was not a joke; reporters were rushing to the scene. As it turned out, to the horror of NBC News officials, their Twitter account had been hacked (hijacked might be a better word for it). The news outlet regained control of the account in about 40 minutes. However, for the 112,000 followers, there was much concern, and we know that stories build upon stories, and complete panic could have ensued. NBC Nightly News apologized to the public for three consecutive nights on its national newscast.

One can never be too careful in protecting and monitoring social media accounts. The NBC News Twitter account hacking was considered a "prank" by the proclaimed organizers, and similar pranks are just as likely to affect local governments as respected businesses. They not only compromise trust, they might be used as diversionary tactics by someone or a group with far worse intentions.

Flash Mobs, Swatting, and Gangs

There have been other disturbing examples of people using social media for "swatting" and "Flash Mobs." Swatting is a term used to describe a situation where someone or groups of individuals e-mail, call, or post an erroneous claim that a particular house or building is being held by hostages. In such cases, a SWAT Team is dispatched, and not only is there a good chance an innocent person may be harmed by the public safety response, it takes special resources away from a place where they may really be needed.

Flash mobs are groups that are called upon to gather at a particular location in a specific point in time. Flash mobs have assembled for snowball fights in parks or to stand completely still in a city's major train station. Public safety officials have been monitoring such activities when they can, but there have been recent accounts where flash mobs have turned into unlawful acts. Groups are dispatched via a social media platform and enter stores, overwhelming staff and stealing everything in sight.

Gangs have found social media to be a convenient tool for communicating among their members, so public safety officials have assigned personnel to monitor gang activity via social media. Social media is always evolving, and new uses are being tried every day—some very good and others very bad. Public safety will be in catch-up mode for years to come.

The Rise of the Public

What are the implications for local governments? As the private sector is poised to capitalize on the evolving social media revolution, the public will expect no less from their government. Already the news media is encouraging everyone to be "I reporters" and upload their video clips as stories unfold. Often the first to a scene are amateurs clicking and posting away long before anyone from the media arrives.

Public safety communication officers are beginning to think about new training for their dispatchers, who will soon be viewing emergencies from the field in real-time and in HD. They are concerned that many dispatchers may be unprepared for the potential shock of seeing blood and trauma in ways that could be disturbing, shocking, and far more stressful than a phone conversation.

The new media provides many good opportunities for enhancing communications:

- Streamlined and common communications platform
- Multi-point accessible knowledge bases
- Networked resources
- Real-time data communications and reporting
- Wireless access (multiple paths)
- Multi-media delivery
- Integrated self-service options
- Location-based services
- Cross-agency information sharing
- Potential for improved citizen trust and engagement

With the potential for greater citizen input, the benefits of social media in the context of public safety really begin to emerge. For example, there is the potential for greater intelligent systems dispersed among a wider population and geographic area(s), mobility and multiple feeds in real-time, and superior technology. One public safety officer commented that many of the built-in cameras found in today's cellphones have better resolution than many the older fixed surveillance cameras. There are literally thousands, if not millions, of people that have camera phones.

What's more, the public wants to be more involved in making their neighborhoods safer, and they are happily turning to social media to do that. In a recent meeting at police headquarters in the "City of Brotherly Love," Philadelphia, it was reported that four recent murders had been solved through the posting of pictures of possible suspects on social media sites. Working with local police, social media is taking neighborhood watch and community policing to higher levels than ever before. Today, many cities have adopted their own apps that help the general public not only better visualize crime, but encourage citizens to report things that they see or hear.

From

IF YOU SEE SOMETHING, SAY SOMETHING.

BE SUSPICIOUS OF ANYTHING UNATTENDED.

Tell a cop, an MTA employee or call 1-888-NYC-SAFE.

To

IF YOU SEE SOMETHING—*SEND* SOMETHING!

If You See Something, Send Something

In every airport and train station, there are signs and recorded messages reminding citizens that if they see something suspicious, they should say something to an authority as soon as possible. However, a police captain at a public safety forum where I was speaking, said, "Why can't these young folks just stop sending us pictures of stuff—can't they understand we have no way of receiving and acting upon social media?" My response was somewhat muted, but I responded by saying, "You may have that as an excuse for today, but it will not hold for tomorrow." Often, in today's world, the first to reach the scene of a crime, accident, plane crash, etc., has a smartphone, and they instinctively take and send pictures. Every local and major news outlet encourages this practice. CNN was the first to coin the term "I-Reporter." When a rare and large earthquake hit the mid-Atlantic region in August 2011, CNN was reporting the event in detail about 20 minutes before local governments began to send out brief messages informing a public of what they already knew before any "official" announcement.

According to a survey conducted by the American Red Cross, more Americans are using social media in times of emergencies. The study also revealed that most Americans who use social media feel they should receive timely assistance from local governments and national response agencies when they post messages in social media. The same people responding to the survey also indicated they still relied on 911 for emergency situations. Nevertheless, 911 is for inbound communications, and the interesting finding was the high expectation of actually receiving information in times of emergencies. It should be noted that the study was focused on citizens using social media, which does not account for the nearly one-third of Americans who do not spend time on the Internet.

IT Governance in a Public Safety Setting

The traditional boundaries that have existed between public safety IT and a municipality have become further galvanized. The human firewalls that exist serve as an invisible speed bump that clouds up cooperation and improved coordination. This reminds me of a chief of a police force who unilaterally decided to ditch the department's BlackBerrys in favor of a new smartphone for the force. The municipal IT staff was only notified after the contract was signed, yet they were expected to provide support, training and a secure server. Needless to say, that did not go over very well; however, examples like that occur each and every day.

Sound IT governance planning is essential to maintain a vibrant and secure set of systems. Social media is no exception, and everyone involved needs to be part of the planning process that includes equipment and software certification, understanding who is in charge of what, and what new skill-sets are needed. As some have said, Web 2.0 is not a wave of the future, but a tidal wave in the making, especially when it comes to public safety.

Public safety has been very effective in using outbound citizen notifications and information that includes Twitter, Facebook, YouTube, Reverse 911™, RSS feeds, special apps, and regular municipal websites. The challenge is how to assimilate incoming communications—photos, videos, text messages, e-mails, or all of them combined. Fortunately, there is technology available that can monitor aggregate messages, and there are artificial intelligence systems that can "scan" and "monitor" all inbound communications and create a real-time situational report about what is happening and where.

Social & Civic Media for Addressing the Digital Divide and Knowledge Gap

The Pew Internet and Family Life Project reports that 2% of American adults say they have a disability or illness that makes it either hard or impossible for them to use the Internet. Consequently, Americans living with disabilities are less likely than other adults to use the Internet. At the same time, there have been many advances in technology that can address some of the needs for access and accessibility. For example, those who are vision impaired can have their computer screens adjusted for larger type. A completely blind person can have access to an electronic Braille pad that allows them to "read" what is on the screen. Just as TV provides for captioning, many Internet sites provide for IP-Relay, which functions much like closed captioning, except on a computer screen. A person with a hearing challenge can have louder speakers or text-to-voice programs.

When we hear politicians talk about the digital divide, they are usually referring to the poor who lack either or all of the "three A's:" affordability, accessibility, and availability. Studies have confirmed over the years the fact that Internet penetration is highest at the upper income levels of society and, of course, the opposite is true with those less fortunate. People without Internet connectivity have less access to government services, as well as employment, health information, social services, and benefit information.

Only government can attempt to counter the gap with programs and services aimed at bringing the "have-nots" to the Internet through training, public facilities, and partnerships with other governmental entities and private businesses. The idea that many state and local governments still charge a fee for showing up to a government building for a service instead of going online is misguided and hurts the very people who need help the most.

This reminds me of a panel discussion where a Harvard professor with a background in process engineering argued that for government to further cut costs, it should limit hours of on-site operations. He said that the longer lines or fewer days of operations would prevent senior citizens and others from showing up in person. He pointed out the cost to service a citizen who shows up in person is much higher than completing the same transaction online. My response was rather heated, and I argued that such a forced play is absolutely unfair and causes many citizens great hardship. There are many reasons why certain segments of our population prefer or feel they have no choice but to show up in person.

Anonymous, Anonymity, Gossip, and Rumors

At the time of this writing, a group calling itself "Anonymous" has taken credit for hacking into a number of business and government websites. As the name implies, this is a group that operates anonymously. The group is skilled and is considered dangerous, and eventually the leaders will be caught and prosecuted, but they will only be replaced with another self-styled hacking group.

Anonymous rumors and pseudo names have unfortunately been somewhat normal in U.S. political affairs. What has changed is that social media makes it that much harder to ascertain just who somebody really is. For local government officials, simply contending with what appears to be anonymous postings, false rumors and unfounded gossip, can have an extremely negative impact on social order and stability. The environment for the need for trust is as strong as the abundance of distrust one strives to displace. This paradox cannot be ignored, and there has never been a greater time for the need for local governments to establish trust. The need extends to how local governments provide adequate, timely, and truthful information. The term "citizen engagement" needs to become operationalized from a "sounds-good concept" to a meaningful and visible process.

While it may appear that people can manipulate ways to appear anonymous, today's technology also can track and expose those who truly abuse such ruses. It is particularly important to place a burden on those who make public postings, and require respectful language and some form of opinion ownership.

Without appropriate safeguards and policies, local governments may find themselves drowning in a sea of cyber-anarchy. We know that government derives its legitimacy when grounded on trust.

TREND SIX

Shared Services: Consolidate, Coordinate, Cooperate

TREND SIX

Shared Services: Consolidate, Coordinate, Cooperate

Although shared services lately have been receiving greater attention, and governments are pursuing them with a new sense of urgency because of budgetary woes, they are not really new, and the arrangements have never been easy. For example, the Maryland-National Capital Park and Planning Commission was established in 1927 and is one of the oldest planning commissions in the United States. The original concept was to share and coordinate the planning process between two adjoining counties. Until recently, there has been a war of cultures between the technology infrastructures of both counties, and service cooperation and system sharing was somewhat superficial in spite of the organization's historic mandate.

Another early example was the formation of council of governments throughout the largest metropolitan areas in the United States. These coordinating agencies with varying degrees of power, served as a mechanism to tie together an otherwise patchwork of disparate transportation systems into more cohesive regional systems.

Shared services also involve the way we think about equipment, too. It wasn't too long ago that employees expected and wanted their own printers, computers and laptops, and software packages. Attempts to make employees share equipment and software were met with comments accusing any agent of change as engaging in "techno-socialism," and the sky would fall, and worse! Faced with the reality of even scarcer resources, most employees acknowledge the need for efficiency and even enjoy fast, feature-rich group printers, even if they have to walk down the hall.

The United States is comprised of 50 state governments, 3,141 counties, 19,492 municipalities, and 16,519 townships. There are also a significant number of independent districts that could be added to the mix, which would bring the total count of local governments to more than 40,000. Each has an elected body, an administrative body, a police force, a fire department, and in some form or fashion a technology infrastructure. Not much has changed in local government structure over the past 200 years, except the government head count has both grown and contracted based on prevailing financial and political conditions.

If we take the State of Florida as an example, there are more than 400 cities, towns, and villages located in 67 counties. As the recessionary forces have wreaked havoc in the state—with one in five houses in some form of foreclosure and a state legislature that has capped the ability of local governments to raise revenues through property taxes—shared services have started to make more and more sense to local leaders.

For every county, there is a county government with its own technology infrastructure, which includes data processing and data storage facilities, as well as various business operations. The figure below illustrates some typical local government services.

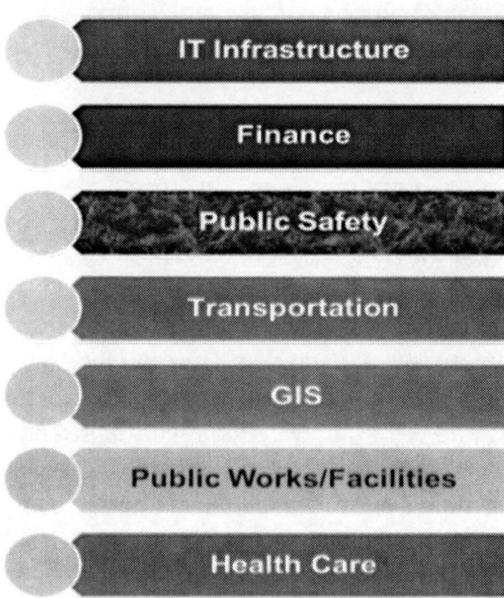

Not only does each county contain many cities within its geographic boundaries, there are quite a few totally separate governmental entities that lie within cities and counties. The figure below shows a list of just some of the other governmental entities.

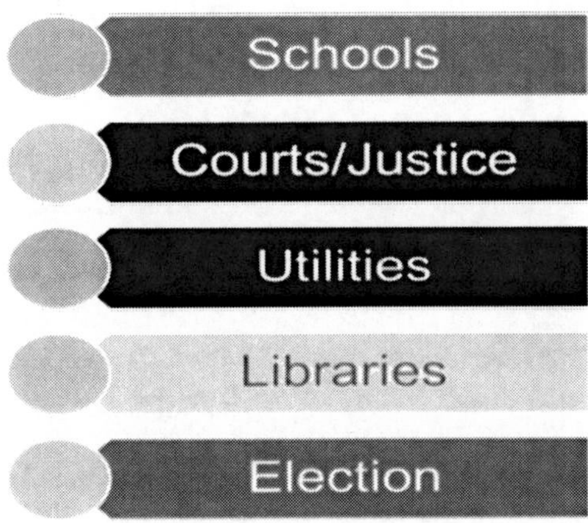

As one might imagine, each of these entities depends on some type of technology support and infrastructure. Until the economic downturn, most of the various entities never met or communicated among one another. There was no reason to. Of course, that is quickly changing as local governments of all types are seeking ways to collaborate, share or leverage their expertise or technology resources and services.

A large Midwestern county with a new data center was seeking to share its excess capacity with nearby cities. A New England city was promoting its state-of-the-art data center to its neighboring cities, too. In Iowa, a few rural cites were exploring ways they could share in a traveling CIO in an arrangement similar to a traveling nurse. None of the jurisdictions could afford a full-time technical staff person, but collectively their ideas made sense.

Depending on what level of responsibility one has, the terms "shared services" and "regionalism" are not necessarily the same, but both are very important.

"Sure we can share services with you—
as long as you follow our rules!"

When one thinks of regional approaches, the very term suggests some form of geographic boundaries where the traditional boundaries are subjected to new thinking and new governance approaches. The best examples would be regional data centers, regional emergency communications systems, and regional transportation systems. Regionalism also can signify a heightened sense of cooperation, coordination, and strategic planning.

In today's environment, we know that the placement of a data center is contingent on many critical factors, and being close to any particular governmental entity is about last on any list of considerations. Plain and simple, data centers can be placed anywhere that is safe and where there is reliable power and broadband connectivity. Most data centers are built with plenty of room to expand over time. Therefore, in practice, most data centers operate well below their peak capacity and almost always have excess capacity to take on additional applications or new clients. Pooling together resources lightens the load for every participant and can provide additional financial resources among a larger group.

Regional communication systems might include regional dispatch systems, call centers, or 311 centers. Most citizens calling in about an emergency really don't care about traditional geographic boundaries. All they want is someone to answer and respond quickly. Many localities already have taken a regional approach in sharing call centers and radio frequencies. It no longer makes economic sense for every locality to fully staff their own call centers and purchase and maintain their own equipment.

Transportation systems pioneered the regional approach several decades ago for sound economic reasons. Today, with new smart signs and electronic payment systems, citizens are benefiting by having uniform payment cards and coordinated schedules, thus providing for a rather seamless transportation system. What's more, new technologies have provided better and faster payment systems, GIS and GPS mapping that lead to improved citizen/customer satisfaction.

State Pressure

In some localities, even the dire economic climate has not spurned planning and communications with other technology enterprises. The State of Michigan has developed a unique carrot-and-stick approach. Local governments eligible for state support must adhere to three initiatives, one of which requires the local jurisdictions to demonstrate that they are sharing services with at least one other local government. As this book was going to press, the State of Michigan announced a new $2.5 million innovation fund for collaborative IT projects.

NGOs and other Nonprofits

Nongovernmental organizations (NGOs) as well as a handful of nonprofit state associations have provided a good degree of leadership in helping out member cities and counties. The Texas Association of Counties (TAC) created the County Information Resources Agency (CIRA) to provide central, cooperative and coordinated assistance and services to members in all matters relating to information resources and technologies. The group aims to increase efficiencies and improve the quality, reliability, and interoperability of their information resources, technologies, and services. Among the many services available include:

1. **CountyConnect Data Integration Service:** allows the sharing of data between otherwise incompatible systems. The service can be used by all county offices to share various types of information with local, state, and federal government entities.

2. **Domain Name Registration:** enables CIRA to register, file, and maintain a county's domain name.

3. **Electronic Payment Services:** provides reliable electronic payment services to increase county collections. With this centralized service, counties can reap clear benefits by opting to accept electronic payments for fines, fees, taxes, permits, and other payments. This service also meets all state and federal legal requirements, and is payment card industry (PCI) compliant.

4. **E-mail:** offers secure e-mail to elected county officials and county employees in CIRA member counties using their correct domain names.

5. **Public Notification System:** provides a Public Notification System, which allows members to broadcast information to large groups of pre-determined individuals without triggering spam filters or overloading system. The Public Notification System can be used to send everything from courthouse news to emergency information.

6. **Websites:** a free, standard website for CIRA members. If CIRA hosts the domain name, it will also host the county-designed standard website for free.

CIRA is simply an example of what a state association can provide. Most small counties could not possibly offer those services without the collective help of an association.

The Florida Local Government Information Systems Association (FLGISA) and the North Carolina Local Government Information Systems Association (NCLGISA) are two good examples of state associations that are helping cities and counties with technology leadership as well as providing the opportunities for shared services. FLGISA is an organization for CIOs, IT managers, and technology decision-makers from the state's local government agencies. The mission is to "assist local government technology leaders in providing the best possible service in the most cost-efficient way to our customers, the citizens of

Florida." FLGISA is closely associated with Florida State University's Florida Institute for Government. NCLGISA is quite similar to FLGISA and is closely associated with The University of North Carolina's School of Government's Center for Public Technology. It hosts one of the largest and most successful conferences for technology staff and leaders. Both associations, working with their respective institutions of higher learning, offer certification programs for technology leaders.

Another example would be in Colorado, where the Statewide Internet Portal Authority (SIPA) was created in 2004 by an act of the Colorado State Legislature to provide efficient and effective e-government services to eligible government entities and citizens through the use of modern business practices and innovative technology solutions. Eligible entities include state and local governments and school districts.

Some of the many innovative services provided by SIPA include:

Content Management System: SIPA has selected and provides for a special content management system that localities can use to manage content on their own websites. As is often the case, many localities lack the knowledge, talent, or budget to pursue developing a content management system on their own. Instead of each city and county creating its own CMS at its own expense, SIPA offers an extremely efficient collective solution.

Transaction Payment Engine: The secure Transaction Payment Engine (TPE) works smoothly with state and local financial processes. Using this service, an entity can accept online payments via credit card or electronic checks. The system processes and stores payments and is fully payment card industry (PCI) compliant. It provides faster transactions, which translates into faster payments to each entity, and users can research transactions. Many smaller entities have struggled on their own trying to be PCI compliant. By using the TPE, entities have a great solution that might not be possible on their own.

Public-private Partnerships

In 2005, the State of Alabama Department of Homeland Security lacked a comprehensive state-wide geographic information system (GIS). When a series of tornadoes struck the state, there was almost no ability to view before and after maps that would be useful in determining the extent of damage in any given area. The state, along with a small but innovative group of counties, teamed up with Google Maps and began planning for a shared state-wide GIS. In August 2006, Virtual Alabama began operating. By 2010, Virtual Alabama had more than 28,000 users, representing more than 1,500 agencies and the best imagery available from all 67 Alabama counties loaded into the program.

The greatest challenge was to get each county to cooperate and *share* their maps and data layers so that they could be stitched together into one comprehensive system. Many of the 67 counties were reluctant, asking, "Why should we take the time to help the state and the other counties? We are happy with what we have, and we are too busy! What are the benefits of sharing?" It took three years, but the collective state-wide GIS system has earned numerous awards for innovation.

The comprehensive system has many uses, including:

- Common operational picture
- Emergency evacuation routing
- Situational awareness/understanding
- Vehicle and asset tracking
- Critical infrastructure mapping
- Student density
- Identification of assets and vulnerabilities
- Visualization of risks
- Plume modeling and real-time sensor feeds
- Implementation of protective measures during events
- Damage assessment

The Virtual Alabama Project is just one good example of what can happen when local leaders get together and develop a shared solution in which everyone benefits.

Public-private partnerships can be described in different ways. As another example, an unincorporated city in Fulton County, Georgia, found itself in a financial crisis. It incorporated in 2005 after gaining state approval and today claims to have outsourced everything except public safety and fire/EMS. According to city leaders, they now have a surplus, and residents couldn't be happier. The city essentially contracted out the management and coordination of services to one company, which hired numerous subcontractors for various services.

Politically, the term "public-private partnership" has a more positive ring to it than "outsourcing," which is very much the same idea. Public-private partnerships might also include sharing in revenue through the deployment and use of red-light and speeding cameras, or perhaps automated parking meters.

Regardless of the label, local governments are actively seeking ways to control costs while trying to maintain services. As attractive as it might sound, there are certainly some potential drawbacks. Jobs will most likely be lost along with fringe benefits that normally would benefit a local community through employee spending. There is constant need for contract oversight, and there have been some reported cases of underperformance and, worse, failure to deliver.

The City of Corpus Christi, Texas, which enjoys a national reputation for innovation, was contemplating outsourcing a number of IT functions. Before moving ahead, city leaders conducted an outside study and review by a well-respected company, and found that it would actually cost the city more by doing so. The bottom line is that there needs to be a careful business analysis to help determine true cost benefits.

Councils of Governments

According to the National Association of Regional Councils (NARC), there are more than 385 Metropolitan Planning Organizations (MPOs) and approximately 5,000 councils of governments. Initially formed to better facilitate coordination of transportation systems, they have moved into newer areas of coordination such as regional planning, environmental and energy issues, as well as emergency communications. Recently, they have begun to examine regional technology approaches and services.

NARC supports its membership by advocating and representing their interests on national issues with the U.S. Congress and the Executive Branch. The function of the regional council and the MPO has been shaped by changing dynamics in federal, state and local government relations, and the recognition that the region is the arena in which local governments must work together to address challenges—social, economic, workforce, transportation, emergency preparedness, environmental and others. Additionally, regional councils and MPOs often are called upon to deliver various federal, state programs that require a regional approach, such as transportation or comprehensive planning, services for the elderly, and clearinghouse functions.

Regional councils and MPOs have learned to be entrepreneurial because of shifts in priorities for federal funds. These organizations are experienced collaborators, adept at bringing people together and getting results. States are relying more on these organizations as vehicles for engaging local governments and delivering programs.

Consolidate, Coordinate, Cooperate

On the technology front, city and county governments are creating regional data centers, regional communications systems, and shared systems, and they are finding ways to do more with less through operational consolidation of services and equipment. The newest trend to take hold is where cities and counties are teaming up with other local agencies such as schools, libraries, and in some cases, the private sector. In 1999, the County of San Diego outsourced its entire IT department.

San Carlos city officials facing a severe budget shortfall took an innovative approach to cost cutting. They evaluated all their operations and arrived at a set of creative options. They decided they could no longer afford to maintain their own police force, so they outsourced their police department to the local sheriff's operations. When they began to examine their fire department the reverse made more sense. The City ultimately decided to re-establish a city fire department managed by neighboring Redwood City where thy already enjoyed a shared service relationship. They also found they could save money by providing recreation services to another city.

The shared and contract services project in San Carlos has been a huge success where they went from a structural deficit to a $400,000 surplus in the first year.

As pointed out earlier, economic disasters can often lead to positive innovation and benefits to the taxpaying public.

Most people view the concept of shared services as a positive direction. Unfortunately, working out the details often leads to frustration and dismay. Take, for example, a city and school district whose leaders believed they could save money by having the city mow the school's lawns instead of having a school district do one part and the city the other. No one imagined the "turf battles" that ensued. It turns out the school staff believed that their standards of cutting lawns, which included a different blade height and mowing frequency, were higher than the city's, and that ultimately became the deal-breaker.

SIOBHAN DUNCAN

Turf Wars

From a technology viewpoint, the ingredients are now in place that can provide a new paradigm for moving ahead to reach new levels of scale and efficiency. Broadband availability and accessibility continues to increase while the traditional concept of having to own and manage equipment has shifted to shared services and cloud-based solutions. Like the earlier example of everyone once having their own printer, does every city and county require its own data center, its very own networks, and separate communications systems? Does physical location matter anymore, except for the need for disaster planning and recovery? The answer to these trends and questions sets the stage for a completely new way of looking at reining in the growing costs of technology and at the same time provide greater control and security.

In another example using technology to help solve consolidation problems, the Municipality of Gouldborgsund, Denmark, a city which was organized into six administrative districts, found itself having to find a dramatic way to cut operating costs while somehow maintaining citizen services. Each of the six regional offices were expensive to maintain and were geographically separated by great distances. Their solution was to create a “Video-Operated Citizen

COURTESY OF CISCO

Municipality of Guldborgsund, DK

Service," and in the first phase closed half of the regional offices and replaced them with video stations where citizens, using telepresence video equipment, could conduct business as if they were in a government office

Technology and the broadband revolution have made it possible to both think and act differently. The only remaining worry is the ongoing need for energy assurance—as we shall see in the seventh trend.

Can Sharing Go Too Far?

The State CIO from Utah was quoted in Public Sector CIO Magazine saying that he questioned the need for 50 separate systems that do essentially the same thing. He was referring to the states' aging technology infrastructure. From a pure efficiency point of view, one could conclude that many, if not all, of the 50 state services could be combined into a series of central networks. This argument should not be confused with those who advocate doing away with small townships and cities as being politically inefficient. The argument here is about technology support and infrastructure. Perhaps there would be one center for motor vehicles and another for unemployment services. While this might sound attractive to some, where do consolidation and cloud services stop? That would be akin to saying that our nation should have one airline, one healthcare company, and one mobile phone provider.

There is, however, a set of sound reasons for not going too far in centralizing resources. The first reason is the U.S. Constitution, which reserves the rights of states as the primary and preferred provider of services. Secondly, redundancy is good. It provides greater protection on a geographical basis, which certainly comes in handy in times of emergencies. Thirdly, innovation and experimentation occurs at the local level. The greatest advances almost always start from the bottom up. Without a rich population of potential users, innovation would not exist.

TREND SEVEN

Protecting the Enterprise: Power, Grid, Network and Cyber Security

Trend Seven

Protecting the Enterprise: Power, Grid, Network and Cyber Security

With so much at stake and with our increasing dependence on energy use, energy assurance, network and cyber security becomes both a new trend as well as an ongoing challenge, and that is protecting our society as we know it! We grew up with the notion that all we needed to survive was air, water, food, and shelter. In our modern world, we must now add energy to the mix. Many of us will also recall Maslow's hierarchy of need, which addressed man's quest for self-actualization. He used a pyramid to show the hierarchy, as displayed below.

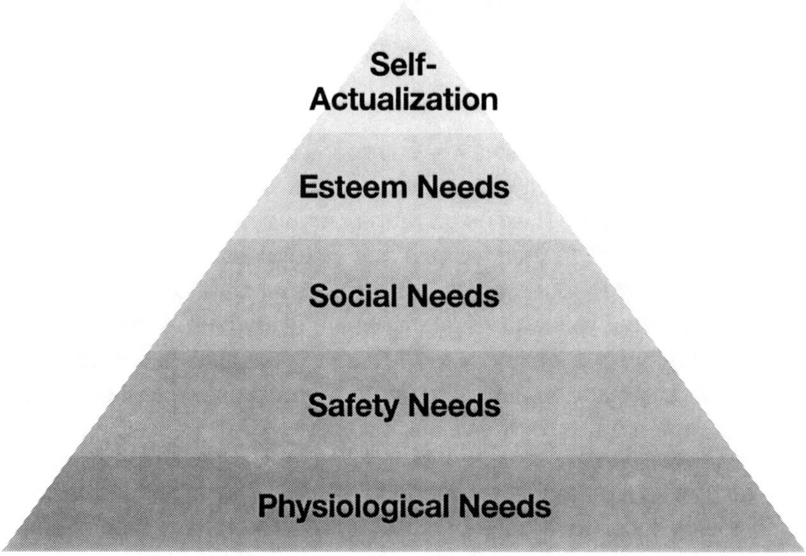

Maslow's Hierarchy of Need

This model was developed in 1943, and not even Maslow would have envisioned the impact 21st century technology would have on our daily lives and how it could affect self-actualization in ways never contemplated. It was during a technology and public management class that I somewhat jokingly toyed with a complementary pyramid that I lightheartedly called "Shark's Hierarchy of 21st Century Realization." This model actually takes self-actualization for granted and adds to the layer implications for contemporary society, where energy and the Internet are critical to not only self-actualization, but survival in a modern world.

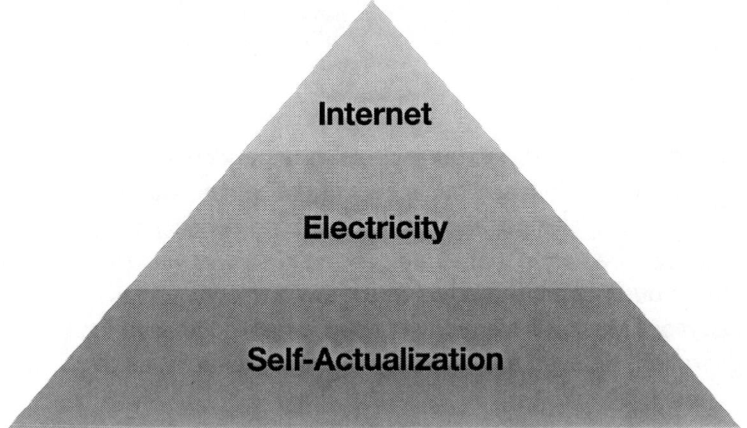

Shark's Hierarchy of Twenty-First Century Realization

In that same class, we discussed what happens when the electric grid goes down for a few hours versus a few days, versus a longer duration. The students first expressed concerns about hair dryers not working and possibly not being able to recharge their laptops and cellphones. The discussion progressed to rotting food, no lights, no heat or air-conditioning. We discussed the loss of our monetary system, where everything is being purchased using plastic or mobile devices. Then, the discussion turned to civil disobedience, rioting and looting, and finally the collapse of civil society, depending on the duration of the power outage.

Local governments are the first responders in times of emergencies. When it comes to energy, local governments must be prepared for any type of emergency—tornado, hurricane, earthquake, forest or brush fire, flooding, mudslide, pipeline or infrastructure breakdown—as well as extraordinary storms or enemy attack. Most entities have developed continuity of operations (COOP) plans, however in most cases, the focus of the plans is on succession of power of key individuals to keep things running. Such plans usually lack consideration of the loss of power as an energy crisis when people and governments are trying to figure out what to do when the lights go out. When there are power disruptions, it is not merely an inconvenience, it poses serious consequences for all forms of transportation, banking, retailing, food supplies, gas stations, public health, public safety communications, and schools, to name a few.

Local governments are on the front lines of virtually all energy emergencies. Experts agree that these governments are going to be faced with an ever-increasing number of energy-related emergencies. The reasons for the rise in these numbers are at least three-fold:

1. aging energy infrastructure,
2. aging energy systems are not matched to the complicated demand profile of today's user, and
3. all-hazard events are increasing in number, severity, and length.

Supporting those points are the following facts:

- The average generating plant was built in 1964 using 1959 technology, and more than one-fifth of U.S. power plants are more than 50 years old.
- On any given day, more than 500,000 U.S. customers are without power for two hours or more.
- Today's high-voltage transmission lines were designed before planners even considered security measures or imagined that electricity would be sold across state lines, therefore, the lines are subject to overloading and blackouts.
- Line losses have increased from 5 to 10 percent since the 1980s, placing a little-recognized $12 billion "tax" on consumers that didn't exist 20 years ago.

- Most of the equipment that guides the flow of electricity dates back to the 1960s and 1970s. Real-time tracking of disturbances and interruptions does not, and cannot, occur in most places; the information is usually relayed 30 seconds after the fact.
- Smart, "self-healing" power grids that anticipate problems before they happen are non-existent. While the technology needed to make the power grid smarter is available, due to a number of factors, including overwhelming costs and varying utility regulations across state lines, these technologies are years away from implementation. So, blackouts and power outages are not only likely to happen in the future, they are guaranteed.

Energy interdependencies are increasing in complexity, and the economic stakes are huge. A May 2007 Scientific American article noted that the estimated cost from all U.S. electrical outages ranges from $70 to $120 billion per year. It is no longer simply about keeping the lights on at the local factory or the corner drug store. It is about keeping Internet businesses accessible to consumers, ensuring that high-tech factories have guaranteed back-up power, and guaranteeing that the banking and financial industries have reliable, around-the-clock power. Literally, billions of dollars are at stake. Therefore, energy assurance planning requires careful thought and preparation.

Energy assurance planning has evolved from the relatively simple state energy office petroleum shortage analysis and scenario responses in the 1970s, to state public utility commission electricity and natural gas supply reliability analysis and planning in the 1980s and 1990s, to government-wide energy analysis and planning since September 11, 2001. Emergency preparedness and the quality of a response to interrupted energy depend largely on the first responder's energy supply. Local governments are the first responders, so energy supply and energy back-up systems are crucial.

In 2011, an employee was performing a routine maintenance procedure when somehow his actions tripped the substation located a few miles north of Yuma, Arizona. This action led to a massive chain reaction that in 11 short minutes led to the worst blackout in Southern California's history, which is now referred to as the Great Southwest Blackout of 2011. The same blackout affected western Arizona and northern Mexico, too. It took 10 hours before power began to be restored to some areas, and full power was not restored for up to 24 hours in some locations. Nearly a year later investigators are still looking into why so many fail-safe procedures failed to work. There was no evidence that the cause was intentional or from a foreign cyber source, so the cause remains a great mystery. Such experiences serve as a strong wake-up call for local governments to be prepared for the absolute unexpected, including fail-safe systems that can turn out not to be fail-safe at all—or promised smart-grid technology that turns out not to be very smart.

Just a few short years ago, the State of Texas experienced a series of hurricanes that caused havoc throughout the state's electrical system. The state was forced to coordinate rolling blackouts, which was a last-resort measure. State officials felt they did a great job given the circumstances, but most of the local governments didn't quite share the state's enthusiasm. For reasons not explained, the local CIOs were never notified about the frequency and/or duration of any rolling blackout. The local CIOs were frustrated by literally being kept in the dark, which made it nearly impossible to plan. First, what should they tell their internal and external customers regarding the extent of the problem? Second, should they shut down their systems in an orderly fashion? Third, what emergency power back-up plans should be initiated? Fourth, what was public safety supposed to do? Fifth, and finally, what should local governments be telling the banks, gas stations, schools, and other critical infrastructure leaders?

Energy assurance planning is back on the forefront of local government agendas for a number of very compelling reasons:

- Substantially higher energy prices outstripping the ability of many local governments to deliver basic services;
- Hurricane Katrina and the documented disarray and loss of life that resulted from the lack of adequate energy planning;
- Major "economy-freezing" electrical outages in the northeastern U.S.;
- Unusually severe weather and associated heavy flooding throughout the U.S. in recent years;
- Concerns about how to address possible climate change and the accompanying emphasis on minimizing carbon use at the local government level;

- Drinking water and wastewater treatment plant service issues arising from knocked-out power supplies and failed back-up systems;

- A coordinated outreach effort by key federal agencies to educate local governments about local and regional energy assurance planning benefits;

- A national trend toward more sustainable planning and development, including calls for much more green building, energy efficiency, and renewable energy development; and

- Sustainability—preparing for numerous hazards through energy assurance planning will move government toward sustainability goals. Linking energy assurance planning with sustainability efforts can be a crucial link in capturing the hearts and imagination of city and county leaders and the general public. Folding energy assurance plans into sustainability planning increases the likelihood that key buildings, transportation, utility, public infrastructure, and industrial-related issues are addressed.

There are dozens of other contributing factors for the renewed interest in energy assurance, but those are the most salient. Energy assurance is about building resilience and redundancy into energy systems, so cities, counties, regions, and citizens can survive without help for three days... or longer if necessary. Cities and counties would be wise to carefully examine links in their energy systems and see where they are most vulnerable, and then build redundancies into those areas. It involves saving lives and maintaining economic competitiveness.

Start with a few simple questions, such as how do energy assurance plans relate to other energy-related initiatives under way, and how do those plans complement, or contradict, other energy-related initiatives? The answer is that an energy assurance plan fits neatly into most any other energy initiative under way. It is often better to piggyback an existing initiative than to start a new initiative; consider adding an energy assurance component to any existing energy plan.

Energy assurance is also about guaranteeing citizens that reliable services (power cannot be guaranteed) will be there when they are needed. It is about assuring citizens that planning for energy emergencies is occurring while partners are engaged. Energy assurance generally involves three key areas:

- critical infrastructure protection (CIP);
- security issues; and
- emergency preparedness.

When we think of mission-critical functions, we must consider:

- Hospitals;
- Public service entities, including emergency operations centers, critical government facilities, and Red Cross facilities;
- Communications with emergency responders, including police and fire, telecommunications and the media;
- Water and sewage facilities;
- Transportation infrastructure;
- Gas supply utilities;
- Electric company facilities;
- Prisons;
- Other essential entities, such as schools, nursing homes, and critical care facilities; and
- Others as designated in coordination with government and the emergency operation centers.

Energy assurance covers the source and continuity of power in our nation. As critical as energy assurance is, one must also be aware and proactive in protecting our networks and system operations.

Finally, energy assurance is also about communications between government agencies at all levels as well as with the public. The public needs to know not only what is going on, it needs to know what to do and for how long. As stated earlier, our society has become increasingly interdependent and connected, with power serving as the essential force required for modern living.

Protecting Everything—Network and Cyber Security

While energy assurance focuses on the sources and distribution of power, network security is about protecting data and data systems. Regardless of where the applications and data reside, protecting data is of paramount importance to all levels of government whose foundations are rooted in citizen trust.

There is no local government responsibility more critical than network security. It's a responsibility that simply cannot be delegated. This topic alone could easily fill an entire book, but, given the changing nature of network security and all its threats, that same book would need to be updated so often as to make a print copy impractical. This chapter will highlight the basics of network security from the perspective of high-level management and oversight.

Last year, reported data breaches increased 47%, according to the nonprofit group the Theft Resource Center. Moreover, the Federal Trade Commission (FTC) received more than 800,000 consumer fraud and identity theft complaints where consumers reported losses from fraud of more than $1.2 billion. Today's networks are constantly under attack, and some local governments report receiving more than 20,000 serious threats a day on average, with more than 50% coming from foreign nations. Security threats from the "outside" are increasing in frequency and sophistication, but there is also an alarming trend that some of the greatest threats are coming from "within." This is one chapter were the key importance lies at the end with discussion questions. It is not the questions, but the answers that will determine where you are in securing your network.

Before going further, it is important to review and understand the types of data that are collected, processed, validated, indexed, archived, and stored. Most local governments have at least 200 or more business lines of operations. The figure to the right lists some of the typical government functions.

Given the amount of sensitive data that is collected and stored, it is imperative that this information is not only protected, but the free flow of information is not

Typical Government Functions

- Budget and Administration
- Community Affairs
- Corrections (Prisons)
- Education (State Systems)
- Emergency Management (EMT)
- Environmental Protection
- Employment Services
- Health Systems and Human Services
- Highways and Maintenance
- Insurance Administration
- Licensing (Vehicles, registration, titles)
- Justice and Courts Systems
- Lottery
- Parks and Recreation
- Pension Systems
- Public Safety (Police and Emergency)
- State Judicial Systems
- Social Services
- Transportation
- Taxation
- Vital Health Records
- Voter Registration

compromised. Because critical public safety information plays a significant role in local government systems, it must be able to operate under almost any type of emergency. To protect and support local government networks, the need for sound polices and prevention systems is critical. One must also understand and recognize the types of threats that network managers encounter. Not too long ago, it was acceptable to have a system rating of 99% up time. Now, applications demand a minimum up time of 99.9%, and network engineers will argue that there is a huge difference between the two.

Sidebar: A system that claims to be up 99% each month actually equates to being down 7 hours and 26 minutes, while a system that claims a monthly uptime average of 99.9% equates to 44 minutes and 38 seconds of downtime. Unless you can certify 100%, there will always be some downtime for routine maintenance. See www.easyuptimecal.com.

When it comes to network threats, there are essentially four major areas that are interrelated but require separate strategies. They are:

1. Network security,
2. Web security,
3. E-mail security, and
4. Mobile workforce security. There are also external threats and internal threats—the latter being the most troublesome.

The network could be viewed as the hub of all activities. Therefore, protecting the hub requires a multi-layer approach to security, where the network is protected with smart firewalls, intrusion protection systems, secure and encrypted virtual private networks (VPN), and updated and secure user validation. The Internet is increasingly becoming the dominant source of two-way communication between cities and counties and the public they

"The new hidden cameras will allow us to see if anyone is violating our privacy policy by reading someone else's email."

serve. Web security includes virus protection, content filtering and spyware protection. E-mail security includes virus protection, phishing protection, and spam protection. The mobile environment includes remote systems, such as satellite offices or workers at home or in the field. Wireless communications also would be included, where workers have laptops, portable storage devices, and personal digital assistants (PDAs) or smartphones. The mobile environment requires the same protections as the other forms, except in the mobile environment, there is less control of the devices themselves. And in the wireless arena, special precautions need to address encryption and remote monitoring.

Today's modern systems employ sophisticated network and traffic monitoring devices that help data managers see exactly how the network is functioning at any given point in time. Others employ ongoing vulnerability scanner or penetration tests. Policies must be continually updated, and training of employees must be part of any sound security plan.

When it comes to employees accessing government systems, most adhere to the triple "A's:" Access, Authentication, and Authorization. Some favor the three "D's:" Deter, Detect, Defend. Some localities issue physical devices that help in authentication. Here, the emphasis is placed on trying to control who has permission to enter a network and determining whether the person is whom he or she says they are. However, with the growth of the consumerization of technology and the widespread use of mobile devices, local governments need to be more vigilant than ever before. Another growing concern has to do with staff turnover, reduced training, and diminishing morale as a result of budget cuts.

An advantage of coming into a new local government jurisdiction provides an excellent opportunity to ask hard questions, such as what systems and policies are in place? When was the last time they were reviewed and/or modified? When was the last time there was a major network security audit carried out by a reputable independent source? What kinds of historical data has been collected that can be used to better understand trends, patterns, and possible abnormalities. Rather than wait for the next job to try this out, it might make sense for you to simply come in one day to work and pretend you are new to the enterprise and begin reviewing and asking all those questions. The answers may be scary because you perhaps thought all was well, but most would trade scary answers any time for the opportunity to prevent a catastrophe.

Keeping employees up to date with the latest information is also essential to the success of any written policy. The need for ongoing training and education needs to be a continuous process of written guidelines, updates, and hands-on demonstrations. Some will argue there is simply no time; experts will argue that it is necessary and time well spent.

Examples of User Training and Education:

- Data classification—public and non-public data
- Rules for adding "unauthorized" content or programs
- Rules for file sharing
- Rules for social networking websites—dos and don'ts
- Files, backups and storage of data and how to ensure copies of your data
- Ethics and computer misuse
- Wireless communications technologies and security
- Rules for creation of passwords and changing passwords regularly
- Using the Internet—explanations of "phishing," "spyware" and other vulnerabilities.
- Uses of e-mail—when to avoid e-mail and attachments
- Physical security
- Rules for laptop data protection and encryption
- Providing users with lists of the most frequently asked questions

Phishing and other Tactics

There have been numerous documented instances where a public official has been tricked into believing an e-mail message is real when, in fact, it is a ruse to help extract critical information, such as passwords and other sensitive information. Phishing schemes have extracted millions of dollars from unwitting public managers and citizens alike. Phishing schemes are effective because they appear to be authentic e-mails from trusted sources. The trend toward tricking individuals will not go away and will only get worse. There are a number of good online and in-person programs designed to educate workers about the perils of phishing: what to look for and how to avoid being scammed. The bottom line here is that we can no longer simply rely on a central IT staff to protect us with the latest antivirus or malware software. Employees must be trained periodically and be encouraged to take greater responsibility for their actions.

The Difference between Network Security and Cyber Security?

A recent Bloomberg Business Week cover had the headline "Cyber Warfare Has Begun" with a lead story regarding the fast-growing crisis. When Leon Panetta was testifying before the Senate Intelligence Committee before beginning his term as the new Secretary of Defense, he spoke about the need for greater vigilance regarding our nation's technology infrastructure and systems, and warned of a possible "Cyber-Pearl Harbor" attack in the not-too-distant future. The Director of National Intelligence testified at the same meeting that there are some 60,000 new malicious threats identified each day.

Cyber security shares much the same focus as network security but in a larger context. Cyber warfare and defense focuses on the protection of our nation's technology infrastructure and is most concerned about enemies trying to bring down essential governmental operations and related utilities, such as water and electricity. In essence, the wars of tomorrow may well be found with computers attacking computers. Cybercrime is also a growing concern to public officials, as governments must cooperate and fight it so that it does not disrupt business, markets, personal, and government operations.

Not too long ago, most networks were relatively insulated from the outside environment. Today, with so many employees with network access and with an increasing number of public interfaces (due to enhanced e-government services), networks face an increased threat because of increased exposure. With the growing use of videos and other forms of social media, network capacity and bandwidth issues will emerge. How can today's networks manage the predicted and dramatic increase in the need for more bandwidth?

Certainly, network use will grow dramatically. Early in the Obama presidency, the president and his staff learned first-hand what happens when a huge group of citizens tries to go to the White House website as directed by the president himself, who had asked for input on his proposed policies. The result was the White House e-mail system crashed and was knocked out for several days. The White House system was simply unprepared for the overwhelming traffic—both legitimate and illegitimate.

"Wahoo! I'm rich. Someone in Nigeria left me 50 million dollars."

Threats begin with people. The first line of defense is sound policies, followed by well-trained staff, followed by state-of-the-art detection and prevention systems. The fast-growing mobile workforce is growing in complexity. A police chief in a mid-sized western city, with the best of intentions, purchased new PDAs for his entire force without the input from the technology manager or anyone outside of the police department. Unfortunately, the new devices lacked known security features, was not supported by the city's network or IT staff, and required a time-consuming workaround for security, backups, and more. All too often, departments make computer equipment or software application purchases without the knowledge or consent of IT security officials. Only when they turn for post-purchase help for support do people realize the need for better purchasing policies, greater security integration, and oversight.

More local government employees are accessing applications from their homes or on the road. But, how secure are wireless communications? In addition, peer-to-peer networking is becoming commonplace. How adequate are authentication protocols and encryption systems to protect both the data communications and entry into the network itself?

Malware: Denial of Service, Botnets and more....

According to the anti-malware company Kaspersky Labs, in 2007, two pieces of malware were released online every two minutes, however, in 2011, one piece of malware was released online every two seconds. Experts believe this upward trend will continue as long as it is deemed profitable by the high-tech criminal elements. While we know where malware is largely coming from in terms of countries throughout the world, we must also recognize that there are people intent on bringing down systems for either political or anarchistic intentions as opposed to monetary gains.

The list of external dangers continues to grow both in frequency and sophistication. Even well-educated people get duped every day and are tricked into turning over sensitive data, including passwords and bank account records. In simpler times, we just had to worry about computer viruses, then spam, then phishing, and identity theft. Now, we see some of the same categories manifesting into monster applications. Added to the list, we worry about "botnets" and "denial of service requests."

A botnet, as its name implies, is a jargon term for a collection of software robots, or bots, that run autonomously and automatically, and are controlled by someone with malicious intentions. According to PC Magazine, "A botnet is a large number of compromised computers that are used to create and send spam or viruses or flood a network with messages as a denial of service attack. The computer is compromised via a Trojan that often works by opening an Internet Relay Chat (IRC) channel that waits for commands from the person in control of the botnet. There is a thriving botnet business selling lists of compromised computers to hackers and spammers."

Denial of service, unlike a virus or worm, can cause severe damage to databases. A denial of service attack interrupts network service for some period of time and attempts to prevent legitimate users from accessing information or services. By targeting your computer and its network connection, or the computers and network of the sites you are trying to use, an attacker may be able to prevent you from accessing e-mail, websites, online accounts (banking, etc.), or other services that rely on the affected computer. Here, the network is flooded with information.

When you type a URL for a particular website into your browser, you are sending a request to that site's computer server to view the page. The server can only process a certain number of requests at once, so if an attacker overloads the server with requests, it can't process your request. This is a huge problem that has shut down many well-known websites from some very well-recognized companies. Although there very few examples of local governments being attacked by denial of service threats, the principals are the same, and one must be prepared just the same. Because these types of attacks are almost impossible to prevent, network system engineers have developed secondary sites for just such an emergency. There are also procedures for minimizing risks and damage.

There are at least six areas of threats, and a surprising number may be found and growing within the enterprise itself.

On any day, a local government might encounter...

- **Denial of service**–an incident where an organization is deprived of the services of a resource
- **Social engineering attacks**–the use of influence and persuasion to deceive someone into believing you are someone you are not
- **Phishing attempts**–an attempt to acquire sensitive information, such as usernames or passwords, by masquerading as a trustworthy entity in an electronic communication
- **Pharming attempts**–an activity where criminals redirect users from a legitimate website to a fraudulent one where credit card numbers or bank accounts are requested to commit identity theft
- **Data leakage (intentional/non-intentional)**–non-intentional could be a back door into your network where data can be removed; intentional can be data theft from within
- **Insider threats**–deliberate malicious activity committed by an employee; malevolent intent from within.

There is a rising threat coming from malevolent intent from employees within the enterprise. Here, local government employees could be the greatest threat. Employees, after all, have access to sensitive data, including financial data and personal information. Embezzlement is not uncommon, and without checks and balances, crimes could go undetected for some time. However, malicious intent mostly comes from employees who are unhappy with their supervisors, the department or agency, or angry with the government itself. Not too long ago, an IT staff member held the entire city of San Francisco network operations at bay because he was angered in not receiving a pay raise. He changed all the passwords, withheld them in a standoff, was put in jail, and only then offered them to the mayor. No security system or policy can ignore threats from the inside, and there is growing evidence in the private sector to warn of this growing danger, as well.

Social Media or Web 2.0 Applications and Temptations

New media holds the promise of bringing people together into various social networks and interest groups. With benefits come threats, as well. Employees may be lured by clever e-mail into reveal sensitive data or passwords if they leave their guard down while online. They also might be lured into opening attachments, visiting websites, or opening "reports of interest" that might contain Trojans, spybots, or other security threats.

More people are sharing files, which also opens opportunities for unintentional consequences, because the files might carry various security threats unknown to the sender or recipient. Peer-to-peer networking through social networking sites has become a common routine for many, but it can become a gateway for unexpected intrusions.

Budget cuts. With the pressure for local governments to reduce costs, there could be greater staff turnover, with exiting employees taking invaluable knowledge with them. Budget reductions usually lead to less travel, training, and perhaps system updates and monitoring systems. Finally, remaining staff are often asked to perform more, and there is a risk of not always being able to do the job as they normally would—leaving room for carelessness and costly mistakes. It is amazing how local governments don't always view network operations as something that is as essential as public safety and critical communications.

Mobile workforce. There is an increased danger of losing laptops, PDAs, cell phones, USB thumb drives, and other mobile devices and the data they may contain. Downloads of funny video clips, music, or amusing pictures can contain embedded network threats once introduced into a system. The mobile environment and wireless environment requires strong VPN authentication, strong passwords, security manageability, encryption, and remote-kill capabilities, which allow a network administrator to delete all data remotely on a laptop or PDA when it is online.

Common Security Myths (Employees)

"I don't have anything anyone would ever want." This is a serious breach in understanding. It may be true the employee has nothing of value, but bad guys and botnets alike are constantly searching for points of entry into the main system. Once they find a weakness, like a password or code, they can use your system like someone would use a back door.

"I have the best antivirus software installed." Once upon a time, this might have been true; however, there are thousands of new threats launched every day. Experts warn that virus protection is but one element in a secure network, and it requires constant updating with the latest defensive definitions. Most experts advise to use more than one virus protection program, too. There are many security suites available that are designed to guard against phishing, worms, malware, and Trojan horses, to name a few.

"I don't use Windows, so I'm safe." There is growing evidence that no system is safe from harmful malware. Often, simply going to a website can infect a device, and we are seeing some malicious software being imbedded in pictures that are being shared from device to device. Even if your system is not infected, it may still be a carrier of malware to other systems you may be communicating with.

"My network has a great firewall, so I am safe." This would be like saying the Titanic was unsinkable during its maiden voyage. Firewalls are important, but in today's environment where there are multiple points of entry, firewalls are just one line of defense.

"I only visit safe sites, so I'm okay." Visiting certified safe sites is a good practice, but even "safe sites" have been known to pass along malware at times. So, keeping up-to-date protection programs with multiple layers is the best defense.

"My network administrator is the one in charge of my data." Best practices prescribe that each individual should be responsible for his or her data. Many still have important files stored on local drives where network administrators have no access. Some folks continue to store data on unencrypted USB drives, and add to that the advent of smartphones and smart tablets, there is no way a centralized system can be responsible for all data and files.

"I have had my password for years, and nothing has ever happened." Password protection is like the master key to your front door. With so much at risk, one cannot be too careful with passwords. Many public managers still find employees with passwords written on notes pasted on their monitors or underneath their keyboards. The days when a four-digit combination would

SIOBHAN DUNCAN

"No worries, I keep all the necessary passcodes pasted to my monitor so I don't lose them!"

suffice are gone; today, the minimum password should be at least eight characters with a capital letter or two, and at least one number. It can take just two hours to find a password with just four digits compared to eight days for an eight-character password.

Common Misperceptions about Securing Public Sector Data

Citizens and elected leaders often have their own views on public data and security, too. A well-known politician confided in me that he has no patience for "fancy passwords" and claims he was always forgetting them anyway! I know of some CIOs who privately admit that they do not regularly backup their personal computers, and some have stated that they are too busy to worry about complicated, hard-to-remember passwords. This isn't as much a technology issue as it is a human nature issue, which requires real solutions. One cannot ignore the serious implications of weak passwords and ones that are not periodically changed. The following are a few misperceptions expressed by citizens.

"Taxpayer money funds our operation, and therefore, we have the rights to all the data." While taxpayer money may have funded an operation, the public does not have a right to any data—unless the law specifically permits it. At the same time, local governments are beginning to share data—which was once private and held sacred—with the public as a means to better engage citizens and renew a sense of trust. Such information may include budget information, planning documents, maps, positions, and resolutions. Many local governments have added interactive features, too. Some offer photo-sharing and other kinds of information-sharing. Of course, this all means that local government websites will need to install higher levels of security to provide greater safeguards to websites' integrity.

"No one cares about our information." As mentioned earlier, there are literally millions of automated botnets that scour the Internet seeking weak or soft spots from which to capture information, passwords, codes, secret documents, or worse.

"Data security is an IT function." One cannot overstate the need to ensure that everyone is made aware that data and system integrity is everyone's responsibility.

Strategies for Success

Don't forget the human factors. The human factor plays a very significant and growing role in network and cyber security. Many worry about internal threats from within more than external attacks. People need to be treated more as people and not machines. Public managers need the resources to provide training and to make sure that staff are kept up to date with the latest trends and best practices. Also, senior staff must always be vigilant regarding disgruntled employees.

Don't forget the whole is the sum of its parts. The term "data systems" implies that there are many parts that make up a system. Any weakness found in any one part can cause an entire system to fail.

Plan for internal and external attacks. Like fire drills, public managers should insist on drills to better prepare for the "what-ifs" that can occur.

Work with HR and legal. Because there have been a number of cases where public workers have caused security breaches either intentionally or not, policies must be up to date and managers must be equipped to handle disciplinary actions like offenses that lead to immediate firings. Do you have a solid policy on passcodes, document storage, backups, keys, etc.?

Authentication, Authorization, and Accounting (AAA) network security. Security experts are always reminding us of the three A's. Although aimed mostly at IT managers, it is important that everyone be aware of the larger environment in which such decisions are made.

Confidentiality, Integrity, and Availability (CIA). Another term of terms that help guide thinking toward how we view and treat data.

Test, Improve, Monitor, Secure (TIMS). Some people love acronyms or other ways to remember sequences or key words—even passwords. To an IT manager, these are self-evident. The one thing often overlooked is the need for network audits to be conducted periodically. The best are conducted by an outside firm that specializes in data and system protections. Just as public entities are required to conduct outside financial audits, the need is as strong for someone to assess and certify that a given network meets or exceeds security requirements.

Policy Considerations

One might be surprised to learn how inadequate many local governments policies, rules, and regulations are pertaining to network and cyber security. The following list is a good example of what should be included. It is not meant to be the definitive end-all list but one that highlights some of the more popular issues.

- Frequency of password changes
- Type of secure passwords
- Encryption of files and records
- Access to files and records (in office and remote)
- Citizen privacy protection
- When workers leave (what happens to passwords, entry codes, e-mail, local data files, etc.)
- Laptop and portable storage policies
- Portable device policies
- Back-up policies
- Portable device cut-off and destroy systems
- Blocked Internet sites
- Policy on social network sites
- Security training policies
- Security clearances (by whom and criteria)
- Network security audits (by whom and frequency)

Network operations and security also must take into consideration procedures for keeping systems operational during storms, power outages, and other physical threats to network operations. It used to be completely adequate to have back-up electrical support for up to 72 hours. Nowadays, experts are recommending power back-up systems that can operate for much longer periods of time. Individual employee and agency files and data require not only routine backups, but also redundant systems in case one system fails. Many local governments use remote storage systems, and in some cases have relationships with other jurisdictions to store and retrieve critical data in case of emergencies.

Experts agree that we can never let our guard down. Every network must have a strategy for prevention, intervention, and restoration. Terry Takai, former CIO to the states of Michigan and California and current CIO for the U.S. Department of Defense, recently told an audience that she plans to use cloud-based applications cautiously and will keep highly sensitive data services in-house.

Identity Management

Another area of growing concern is identity management. In much simpler times people knew everyone they worked with and didn't require building passes and special ID cards to gain entrance. There was also a time when people actually printed their social security numbers on their personal checks as a way of proving who they were. Our population will double by the year 2050 and has grown steadily over the years. What's more, our demographics are changing in just about every measure. Because so much is now placed on the Internet and within other networked systems, there is a greater need to be able to determine if people are who they say they are. This is extremely important not only for national security purposes, but for financially sound reasons. For example, the states in 2011 unveiled a new computer database that allows them to check for fraud in medical claims and prescription drugs. Local governments have a tremendous responsibility to protect identities of their residents as well as to authenticate identities. As our population grows, so too does our ability to tell one another apart, and we are becoming a nation of strangers. Identity management is a new and growing trend that will help state and local governments provide greater personal security.

Forms of identity

- Certificate of Birth
- Social Security Number
- Drivers License
- Passport\Voter Registration Card
- Fingerprints
- Retinal Display
- Facial Recognition
- Voice recognition

Behind each form of identity authentication lies a series of technologies aimed at ensuring one's true identity to prevent fraud or criminal activity. This area will surely grow in the next several years as public managers and law enforcement officials struggle to stay one step ahead of those who try to abuse the systems that are in place. Identity management is critical in maintaining trust at all levels government and, as importantly, maintaining trust with citizens.

President Obama once said to a group of reporters discussing identity management that at some point in time it might make sense to revisit the sanctity of Social Security numbers, which were never intended to serve as a national ID. Indeed, the closest thing we have at the moment is a state driver's license. What the President said was truly thought-provoking when he lamented that someday we might see ourselves with IP addresses as new forms of ID.

The Seven Trends—Closing Thoughts

No matter how isolated a city or county may find itself geographically, our society has never been more interconnected virtually. There is hardly any city or county that is not connected to the Internet, where our interdependence grows exponentially. A student once asked in a class, "Why can't we simply elect to disengage from the larger networks as a means of protection?" The answer is that while in theory you could, you would also be shutting yourself off from not only emails, but also critical updates and information. Even if one could find a way to maintain a true isolated network, someone would find a way—with a thumb-drive, software upgrade, or a complex and targeted hack—to get in. With every solution, there is a new hack.

As guardians of today's networks, local governments have a far greater responsibility to protect their citizens as never before. It was bad enough when a decade ago a flood or natural disaster (recall Hurricane Katrina) could wipe out citizen records, or a local data center could have a crash requiring back-up tapes to restore lost or damaged data. Today, however, the risk and complexity has gone up tenfold. At the same time, local governments are faced with fewer resources and aging infrastructure. They have cut desperately needed training and development of staff. Memberships have been completely cut or drastically reduced with travel; often with misguided across-the-board cuts.

Our dependence on technology is growing with each passing improvement. In 2011, there were two great examples. The first involved a catastrophic system failure in which millions found their coveted BlackBerry mobile devices—long known for their secure networks—were not receiving any e-mails. Millions of users across the globe found themselves uncomfortably "disconnected," to say the least, as the global outage lasted for over 24 hours.

The second example took place at the Denver Marriott on New Years' Eve 2012, when a computer glitch caused all the plastic room keys to stop working. Over 300 guests could not return to their rooms from midnight to about 3:00 a.m. as hotel personnel attempted to fix the problem.

We are told that our smartphones and devices will soon replace our keys, credit cards, and ID cards. One can only imagine the frustration that will erupt when such systems fail both individually and collectively. Our growing interconnectedness through technology can be a blessing when it works and a curse when it fails.

The seven trends fit together as tightly as a jigsaw puzzle. We have to think about technology very differently in terms of what we want to accomplish, how to do it, and how we must manage expectations. We must focus and refocus on leadership and governance as to who decides and how. Cloud computing offers governments a wonderful opportunity to rethink how data is processed. We must also keep in mind that data processing is becoming overtaken by knowledge management—and while related, they are very different. Cloud computing, when properly embraced, offers many new possibilities, and yet if it is not managed very carefully, one could easily be worse off. Broadband is the lifeblood for the Internet and the connected society we have become. Without it, like electricity, our society simply cannot exist because we have no orderly way to re-engineer backward mapping to restore our society to a different time and place.

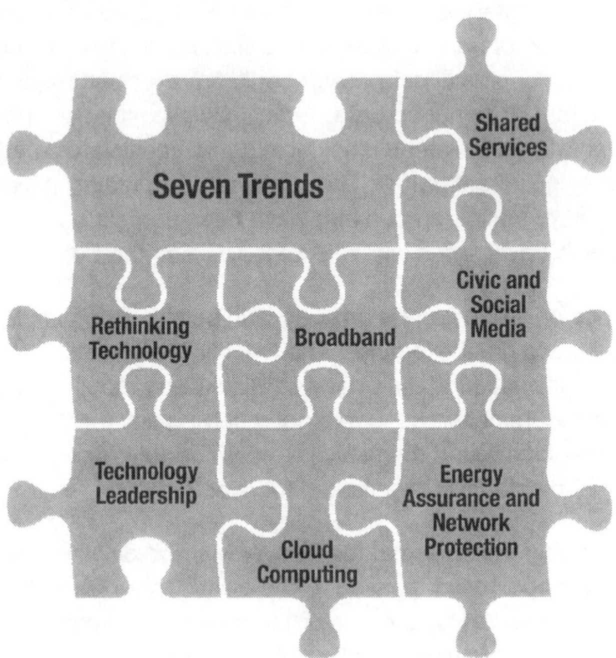

Social media will continue to evolve and serve as societal glue that holds us together, and I dare guess in ways we have yet to contemplate. But with video as one major "killer app" along with GIS, we will see a lot more of the good and, unfortunately, the bad. Finally, the very society that we know and love depends on our ability to protect what we build, and that is why energy assurance and network security is so critical to plan for and practice.

Yes, the pieces do fit together and rather tightly, and with all the change that is coming our way, one can only hope that the value of this book, which captures a critical moment in time, will provide some ideas and a call to action that will help ensure a positive and secure future through understanding and mastering technology. Failure to invest and reinvest in equipment, infrastructure, and staff can negatively impact the very fibers of our tightly connected society.

This is as true when it comes to technology leadership in public management as it is with enlightened elected leaders. The new technology paradigm blends and weaves many forms of digital threads that connect us in ways never imagined. Technology also can be used or misused and has the potential of reversing trust into mistrust, convenience into inconvenience, and civic action into societal chaos. Today, we live in a highly interconnected digital world, yet our laws are inadequately analog—very outdated. There is no doubt there is a growing awareness and that we must remain ever vigilant and master technology before it masters us. Put another way, failure to lead will lead to failure to govern.

DESTINATIONS AND RESOURCES

General Resources for Information on Technology for State and Local Government

American City & County Magazine: www.americancityandcounty.com

Government Technology Magazine: www.govtech.com

National Association for State CIOs (NASCIO): www.nascio.org

Public Technology Institute (PTI) www.pti.org

Chapter 1

Allen S. (2009). Human Resource Management: Selecting and Maintaining Great Staff. In A. R. Shark (Ed.), *CIO Leadership for City and County Governments—Emerging Trends and Practices,* (pp.235-245). Washington, DC: PTI

Cleverley, M. and Clarke, C. The Greening of IT and Local Government. In A. R. Shark (Ed.), *CIO Leadership for City and County Governments—Emerging Trends and Practices,* (pp.205-213).Washington, DC: PTI

Energy Star: www.energystar.gov/index.cfm?c=tools_resources.bus_energy_management_tools_resources

http://www.energystar.gov/ia/partners/prod_development/downloads/EPA_Report_Exec_Summary_Final.pdf (accessed April 2010).

http://www.energystar.gov/ia/partners/prod_development/downloads/EPA_Report_Exec_Summary_Final.pdf (accessed April 2010).

http://www.energystar.gov/ia/partners/prod_development/downloads/EPA_Report_Exec_Summary_Final.pdf

http://www.pti.org/index.php/ptiee1/inside/705/

Purcell, C. (2011). 2020 Vision. In A. R. Shark (Ed.), *CIO Leadership for State Governments—Emerging Trends and Practices,* (pp.3-16). Alexandria, VA: PTI

Rutgers University, Public Performance Measurement and Reporting Network: www.ppmrn.net

Shark, A. R. (2010) Social Media/Web 3.0 in the Public Sector: How to Measure Performance and Gather Business Intelligence. In A. R. Shark and S. Toporkoff (Eds.), *Beyond eGovernment-Measuring Performance—A Global Perspective* (pp. 1-12) Washington, DC: PTI

Tufts, S. (2011) Measuring Technology Investment Success and Impact. In A. R. Shark (Ed.), *CIO Leadership for State Governments—Emerging Trends and Practices,* (pp.215- 223). Alexandria, VA: PTI

U.S. Government Telework Policies and Resources: www.telwork.com

U.S. Environmental Protection Agency–U.S. Department of Energy, "ENERGY STAR: Partner Resources," EPA Report to Congress on Server and Data Center Energy Efficiency (Executive Summary), August 2, 2007

U.S. Environmental Protection Agency–U.S. Department of Energy, "ENERGY STAR: Partner Resources," EPA Report to Congress on Server and Data Center Energy Efficiency (Executive Summary), August 2, 2007

Chapter Two

Beaird J. and Massey L. (2009) IT Governance, in Shark A. R., (ed.), *CIO Leadership for Cities & Counties—Emerging Trends and Practices* (pp. 43- 52). Washington, DC: PTI

Dearstyne, B. (2009) Chief Information Officers: Leading Through Challenges and Change, in Shark A. R., (ed.), *CIO Leadership for Cities & Counties—Emerging Trends and Practices* (pp. 23-34. Washington, DC: PTI

Jacknis, N. (2009) Transformation of the Local Government CTO/CIO, in Shark A. R., (ed.), *CIO Leadership for Cities & Counties—Emerging Trends and Practices* (pp. 35-42) Washington, DC: PTI

Khanna, G. Restructuring the Operations of Government: The New Frontier–Thoughts for the Next Generation (2011) in Shark A. R., (ed.), *CIO Leadership for State Governments—Emerging Trends and Practices* (pp. 27-35). Alexandria, VA: PTI

McKinney R. (2009) IT Consolidation: Tearing Down the Silos, in Shark A. R., (ed.), *CIO Leadership for Cities & Counties—Emerging Trends and Practices* (pp. 53-65) Washington, DC: PTI

Rujan, A. (2009) Information Technology Governance, in Shark A. R., (ed.), *CIO Leadership for Cities & Counties—Emerging Trends and Practices* (pp. 67-77) Washington, DC: PTI

Chapter Three

25 Point Plan to Reform Federal IT: http://www.cio.gov/documents/25-point-implementation-plan-to-reform-federal%20it.pdf

Cleverley, M. (2009) Cloud Computing, in Shark A. R. (ed.), *CIO Leadership for Cities and Counties—Emerging Trends and Practices* (pp. 181-187) Washington, DC: PTI

Federal Cloud Computing Strategy: http://www.cio.gov/Documents/Vivek-Kundra-Federal-Cloud-Computing-Strategy-02142011.pdf

National Association of State CIOs, Cloud Publications: http://www.nascio.org/publications/

Pew Internet, Cloud Computing: http://www.pewinternet.org/topics/Cloud-Computing.aspx

State & Local Cloud Commission Report: http://www.techamericafoundation.org/cloud2-slg

The White House: http://www.whitehouse.gov/blog/Streaming-at-100-In-the-Cloud/

Chapter Four

Best Muni Broadband (Jim Baller) news push: list@baller.com

FCC Broadband Report: http://www.broadband.gov/

Pew Internet, Broadband: http://www.pewinternet.org/topics/Broadband.aspx

Pew Internet, Internet: http://www.pewinternet.org/topics/Future-of-the-Internet.aspx

Pew Internet, Mobile: http://www.pewinternet.org/topics/Mobile.aspx

Shark A. R., Cable S. (Eds.) (2011) *M-Government—Mobile Technologies for Responsive Government and Connected Societies*, Geneva: OECD/ITU

Chapter Five

Cohn, B. (2005) *Listening to the Public—Adding the Voices of the People to Government Performance Measurement and Reporting,* New York: Fund for the City of New York

Cutting edge social media blog: http://www.briansolis.com/

Pew Internet, Digital Divide: http://www.pewinternet.org/topics/Digital-Divide.aspx

Pew Internet, Web 2.0: http://www.pewinternet.org/topics/Web-20.aspx

Shark A. R. and Cable S. (2011) *Civic Media in Action—Emerging Trends and Practices,* Alexandria, VA: PTI

Shark A. R. (2011) Turning Citizen Enragement into Citizen Engagement: Managing Expectations with Web 2.0 and Social Media (pp. 155-168) in *Transforming American Governance—Rebooting the Town Square,* Balutis A., Buss T., Dwight I. (eds.), Armonk, New York: M.E. Sharpe

Solis, B. (2011) Engage—*The Complete Guide for Brands and Businesses to Build, Cultivate, and Measure Success in the New Web,* Hoboken, NJ: John Wiley & Sons

Solis, B. (2012) *The End of Business as Usual,* Hoboken, NJ: John Wiley & Sons

Chapter Six

Colorado Portal Authority: http://www.colorado.gov/SIPA

County Information Resource Center, TX: http://www.cira.state.tx.us/assoc/cms

Florida Local Government Information Systems Association: http://www.flgisa.org/

Holzer H. and Fry J. (2011) Shared Services and Municipal Consolidation—A Critical Analysis, PTI, Alexandria, VA

Leidner A., (2009). A CIO Perspective on Integrating Geo-Information Systems into IT, in Shark, A. R. (Ed.) *CIO Leadership for Cities and Counties—Emerging Trends & Practices,* (pp139-148), Alexandria, VA: PTI

National Association for Regional Councils: http://www.narc.org/

North Carolina Government Information Systems Association: http://www.nclgisa.org/

Virtual Alabama: https://virtual.alabama.gov/

Chapter Seven

Local Government Energy Assurance Guidelines, (2009) Public Technology Institute, Alexandria, VA

Local Government Energy Assurance Guidelines, Version 2.0, (2011) Public Technology Institute, Alexandria, VA

Local Government Energy Assurance Planning: http://energyassurance.us/

Lohormann, D (2008) *Virtual Integrity: Faithfully Navigating the Brave New Web,* Grand Rapids, MI: Brazos Press

NASCIO Report (2011) *State Cyber Security Resource Guide: Awareness, Education, and Training Initiatives,* http://www.nascio.org/publications/

Shark, A. R., (2009) Network Operations and Security, in Shark A. R.,(ed.), *CIO Leadership for Cities & Counties—Emerging Trends and Practices,* (pp. 149-154) PTI: Washington, DC: PTI

U.S. Department of Energy, Energy Assurance Newsletter: http://www.oe.netl.doe.gov/ead.aspx

U.S. Department of Energy, State & Local: http://energy.gov/public-services/state-local

CPSIA information can be obtained
at www.ICGtesting.com
Printed in the USA
LVOW10s1548040118
561822LV00012B/1191/P

9 781470 046026

THE FIRST TURKISH REPUBLIC

A Case Study in National Development

Richard D. Robinson

HARVARD UNIVERSITY PRESS
Cambridge, Massachusetts
1965

Second Printing

Distributed in Great Britain by Oxford University Press, London

Publication of this volume has been aided by a grant from the Ford Foundation.

Library of Congress Catalog Card Number 63–17210

Printed in the United States of America

To Beth, who shared my life in Turkey

PREFACE

In these comments on the emergence of modern Turkey, I do not attempt a complete chronology of events or an exhaustive encyclopedia of fact, though admittedly such would be useful. Rather, I seek what insight the Turkish historical microcosm adds to our understanding of human events. I look for meaning, relationship, cause, effect, valid generalization.

From a number of points of view, Turkey provides us valuable insight into the process of rapid social change. First, the Turks have been trying — with a startling measure of success — to make the transition from authoritarianism to liberalism with a minimum of political violence. Second, Turkey is deeply involved in explosive economic development. Third, Turkey has emerged as a modern military power. It may come as something of a surprise to hear that Americans qualified to assess Turkish military strength do so in terms that indicate that Turkey may now possess the most effective *land* force in continental non-Soviet Europe. In other words, Turkey is once again a military power with which one reckons, particularly in view of the uncertain situation in the Middle East.

It is these things that attract attention to Turkey and keep many observers vitally interested in what is happening there. One may reasonably suggest that the evolution of modern Turkey is an experimental pilot run of accelerated development under western-oriented leadership without recourse to the harsher methods of the totalitarian state. Will the experiment succeed? Frankly, we do not know. The 1960 army-inspired revolution was not reassuring.

Turkey was initially simply an object of study for me but I have gradually evolved a deep interest in the Turkish people for their own sake. I have shared too deeply the excitement of their accomplishments, the disappointment of their failures, the agony of their fears, the stimulation of their hopes, and the bitterness of their resentment against those who would deny the Turk his dignity as an individual for it to be otherwise.

For a number of reasons, the case of Turkey throws the whole problem of accelerated development into bold relief: (1) The Turks are the transmitters of an extraordinarily rich cultural heritage, an admission made only infrequently by Western books of history. For this reason, the Turks entered their period of development possessed of a highly complex society and well integrated structure of values. (2) The Turks have a long history of virtually unbroken national independence, an independence protected by an all-out, national, victorious effort following World War I. Unlike many of the Arab states, Turkey was not held captive by an imperial power. Hence, the Turks have not been preoccupied with the issue of colonialism and the redress of past wrongs, for the wrongs were redressed physically and *psychologically* by military and diplomatic victory. (3) The Turkish modernist movement has its roots in prerepublican Turkish history going back, in a significant way, at least a century. Therefore what is happening today is not simply a new foreign import, nor is it a complete break with the past. Basic social institutions remain, though their functions be somewhat modified. Indeed, there has been a deliberate attempt to build the new on the old. (4) The Turks are experienced in the art of administration; for several centuries they ruled a vast empire — and ruled well by the standards of the day. (5) The Turkish population does not press hungrily against the available natural resources of the nation; there is a margin in which to maneuver, even though it be small by Western standards. (6) Turkey has been blessed with relatively enlightened, honest, dedicated leaders since the inception of the Republic in 1923, and political violence has been infrequent and limited. (7) By dint of comparatively wise leadership and skillful diplomacy Turkey has been able to stay free of foreign military adventures, except for its deliberate — but limited — participation in the Korean War. (8) The country is relatively small, so that it avoids the enormous administrative problems inherent in the sheer size of population and vastness of geography of an India or China. (9) Of recent years, Turkey has generally supported Western foreign policy and has received in turn well over $3 billion of foreign aid, largely of United States origin.

If, even under these circumstances, the Turkish experiment in democracy and development fails, those committed to liberal political concepts are surely in trouble elsewhere. This thought merits sober reflection, for Turkey is right now afloat on a sea of troubles in a very leaky boat. And most of the holes were not punched by the Turks; it was the rough water which split the seams. One could argue that it would have been better had the Turks stayed ashore or, even now, were to put back. But as the Americans and the Russians strive to be the first in space travel whatever the cost, so the Turks have committed themselves to a catch-up pace of economic and social development whatever the cost. Anything short of such development commits the Turk to perpetual inferiority in terms of economic well-being. And, in the long run, such inferiority might well cost him his individual freedom, national independence, and human dignity. These things may not be taken lightly.

Acknowledgments

Included in some of the later chapters is material from articles written by the author for the American Universities Field Staff, *The Moslem World, World Politics, The Middle East Journal, Foreign Policy Bulletin, The New Outlook* (Tel Aviv), and the *Harvard Review.* These publications have very kindly permitted me to make use of this material.

I feel a deep sense of gratitude to the Center for Middle Eastern Studies, Harvard University, for the interest which stimulated the preparation of this book. Particularly, I owe much to Sir Hamilton Gibb, Director of the Center and to Derwood Lockard and A. J. Meyer, Associate Directors. My Turkish studies were made possible initially by Walter S. Rogers, then executive director of the Institute of Current World Affairs. To him, my debt is so great that words are inadequate. My debt is also great to Professor Fahir Iz and Dr. Howard A. Reed for their critical reading of the manuscript. And finally, I must declare my gratitude to those thousands of Turks of all walks of life who gave me hospitality over the years, answered my interminable questions, and permitted me to observe their private lives, thus making this book possible.

Richard D. Robinson

Weston, Massachusetts
1963

CONTENTS

TABLES

ILLUSTRATIONS

(Following Page 144)

THE FIRST
TURKISH REPUBLIC

— None of these new concepts, let me emphasize, conforms to the axiom that the whole is the result of its parts. On the contrary, they all conform to a new and by no means yet axiomatic assertion, namely that the *parts exist in contemplation of the whole.*

— Peter F. Drucker in *Landmarks of Tomorrow* (Harper & Brothers, New York, 1959)

Chapter I

THE YOUNG TURKS

For nearly four decades — from 1923 to mid-1960 — the Republic of Turkey maintained its national independence under relatively stable civilian government, meanwhile moving constructively and rapidly — if somewhat sporadically — in the direction of economic, social, and political modernization. It is this relative stability and sustained movement that sets Turkey apart in the Middle East, an area noted for its short-lived leaders. From the birth of the Turkish Republic in 1923 up to the military take-over in 1960 — a period of 37 years — there were no coups d'état in Ankara and only one real mob scene — that in Istanbul in 1955. And even now, after the 1960 political upheaval, change and development go on. By almost every measure, republican Turkey has realized enormous material and social progress with a minimum of blood-letting, even if one includes the 1960 riots — in which perhaps three persons were killed, almost accidentally.

Would the closing years of the last century and the first two decades of this have given a really competent contemporary observer the basis for an accurate prediction of things to come? Of this we can be certain: there was no such observer, or, if there were, he remained strangely silent. Ottoman Turkey was the "sick man of Europe," and the Great Powers were merely biding their time until the propitious moment to pick the bones with maximum benefit to themselves. There seemed little evidence of a rebirth.

The entire first quarter of the 20th century was a chaotic one for the Turks — an era in which men and governments rose and fell. Over much of Turkey there was no really effective rule. Between 1908 and the 1918 armistice there were twenty-four changes of cabinet in İstanbul.[1] In 1907, the British Embassy in Istanbul reported to London, "At the present time, the whole of the provincial administration is apparently falling into a state of a complete anarchy. Taxes have been refused; recruits have been refused. Valis (i.e., provincial governors) have been driven out, sedition has been preached almost openly."[2]

And so the great powers waited eagerly for the impending collapse, unaware that the climate for genuine reform had already been created.

A CLIMATE FOR REFORM IS CREATED

Despite the wholly unexpected resurgence of Turkish power after World War I, the extraordinary development of modern Turkey has not been a process of recent origin. There was no dramatic break in the continuity of Turkish history, only acceleration. One can, I think, quite safely say that in the absence of the reform movement of the late 18th, 19th, and early 20th centuries, a forward-oriented Turkey could not have emerged when it did. For out of this earlier era was created an intellectual climate which encouraged later and more radical moves.[3]

The intellectuals of this prerepublican era very frequently doubled as military officers, for the best *modern* education prerepublican Turkey had to offer was in the military schools. Meanwhile, European travel became common among both the bright young officers, who were sent for training, and the young intellectuals, who fled westward from the sultan's police. Understandable discontent and frustration set in among those who — by reason of education or foreign travel, or both — perceived the true reasons for the weakness of Ottoman state in its closing years, the principal ones being: (1) failure to keep pace with the West in technology; (2) weakness of national loyalties above and beyond regional, religious, and ethnic ties; (3) continued identity of church and state; (4) popular disinterest in economic pursuits other than agriculture; and (5) administrative and political corruption.

Several major points stand out from the 19th century reform effort. First, modern Western technology and political philosophy entered Turkey through the military, the initial motive being to build up national military power in the face of a series of shattering defeats by European armies, clearly the result of the latter's superior technology and organization. It is no coincidence that the leadership of all four modern Turkish revolutions — those of 1908, 1909, 1923, and 1960 — have been of a military nature.

It should also be noted that official proclamations of reform issued at various times in Ottoman Turkey[4] were not simply ceremonial rituals but in fact were surface ripples of vital currents among certain groups within Turkey. Important changes were made. Among the reforms demanded — and partially effected — were a military technology equal to that of the West, guarantee of personal security, limitation of religious authority to religious matters, control of corruption, improved education, introduction of some secular law codes, and, finally, the proclamation of a republican constitution. Under the authority of the Constitution of 1876, one parliament was in fact convened (1877).

Still, the *depth* of this early reform movement should not be exaggerated. For the most part, its impact was felt only by a limited class within the society — the urban intellectuals; the commercial group; and the administrative, political, and military leadership. It did not permeate to the grass roots level in village and small town where the vast majority of the people lived, and still do. The masses were relatively isolated from the stream of national life, indeed from any real feeling of national consciousness. Therein lay one of the many obstacles to the creation of a national state. It is significant to note that in the Ottoman state the ruling class and the ordinary Turkish village-farmer had little in common, even in language. The very words representing national loyalties were unknown in the Anatolian village. One day a new language would have to be developed.

In 1877–1878 a period of prolonged crisis for the Empire was ushered in by the Russo-Turkish War. This external threat led to the reintroduction of absolutism under Sultan Abdul Hamid II, the last of the *Tanzimat* sultans under whom Ottoman Turkey attempted to modernize in bits and pieces without really altering its basic social structure, values, or institutions, thereby introducing an impossible dualism into Ottoman life. Internal conflict became inevitable, and the longer the tension was contained, the more brittle the situation became.

Although under the new absolutism of Abdul Hamid the 1876 constitution and political freedoms were generally suspended, the process of modernization — in terms of material culture — was possibly accelerated. By reason of the very fact that the Hamidian government was authoritarian, it could force the acceptance of mechanical and material innovation without undue concern for popular opposition. But, in the end, the new technicians, the newly awakened intelligentsia, and the Western-oriented army officer — that is, the Young Turks — turned against the regime. Modern technology cannot survive in a tradition-bound society, nor can tradition-bound values live in a technologically innovating society.

The absolute rule of Sultan Abdul Hamid II was terminated by the Revolution of 1909, when the "Young Turks" came to power, and *political* reform was resumed. It is really at this point that we take up the story of Turkey's emergence into the 20th century. In so doing, one is well advised to look closely at the early years of the republic and those immediately preceding it, for modern Turkey had its real genesis in the confusion attending World War I and the psychological reaction it generated in the minds of the Turks — both the ordinary people and that of a single man, Mustafa Kemal Atatürk.

THE YOUNG TURKS ORGANIZE

The central thread linking events immediately prior to and during World War I lay in the hands of the "Young Turks," a term now idiomatic in English. The Young Turk movement had its origin in the 1860's and 1870's when the first young Turkish intellectuals left the confines of the Ottoman Empire to pursue studies in Western Europe. One can easily imagine how some of these young men, on becoming aware of Western civilization and of Western science, developed an appetite for Western learning. Smarting under the harsh governments of the Ottoman Empire, they moved westward, forming small groups as they did so and writing against the rule in Turkey.

Gradually, their activities culminated in organization, as groups of individuals of similar mind drew together. The names of some of these individuals are now renowned in modern Turkey. Namik Kemal, one of the most famous of these Young Turks, is reputed to have been the first man of real literary ability to give Turkish nationalism artistic expression. He is the first to have used in literature such terms as *vatan* (fatherland), *hürriyet* (freedom), *meşrutiyet* (constitutional government), and the like. These were strange terms to contemporary Turks.[5]

In the latter years of the 19th century, a small revolutionary society was founded within the imperial military school in Istanbul. This society had as its principal purpose the overthrow of the sultan — but not of the sultanate as an institution. Soon the movement spread to other government schools in the city. By the mid-1890's, the group began expanding, and a number of prominent men joined. A steady trickle of members went off to Europe as life became either unpleasant or dangerous for them in the Ottoman Empire. Many of these individuals lived in Paris, and it was there that the core of the Young Turk group gathered to agitate against Ottoman rule. A variety of periodicals was published by this group and distributed through the foreign post offices in Turkey which operated within the framework of the extraterritorial rights enjoyed by the foreign communities in the Empire. The Young Turks were aided and abetted in their cause by Armenian, Kurdish, and other revolutionary groups, which were equally interested in overthrowing the Turkish sultan, though perhaps for different reasons. The constant propaganda barrage thrown up by these disaffected Ottomans generated substantial publicity and ill will generally against the Ottoman Turkish regime, particularly against the person of Sultan Abdul Hamid II.

It was in 1902 that the First Congress of Ottoman Liberals met in Paris. (Note that they called themselves "Ottomans," not Turks.) The Congress plotted the overthrow of Hamid, and indeed there was an abortive attempt in 1903 to do so. Very little came of this premature move other than to alert the sultan and excite him to even more energetic efforts to protect himself and the institutions of the caliphate and sultanate.

It is revealing that by this time Kemal, along with many others, was participating actively in the subversive movement against the regime which, by 1900, was well under way both inside and outside the Ottoman Empire. Kemal is credited with having taken perhaps the first steps in creating a *military* organization committed to overthrowing the sultan, a group known as the Fatherland and Freedom Society. Soon it was submerged in the larger Ottoman Society of Liberty, headquartered in Salonica, center of subversion. In a relatively short time it was difficult to find a Turkish officer in all of European Turkey who was not pledged to overthrow the government he served — obviously, a highly explosive situation. The sultan became alarmed, although there was very little he could do at this point; the game was too far played out. There now existed a large, organized military body within the empire committed to destroy the regime and an articulate revolutionary movement abroad — the Committee of Union and Progress, some members of which were now returning to participate in the impending revolt. From September 1907 on, the two groups were united under the single banner of the Committee of Union and

Progress, which came to have a strong military flavor. The second Congress of Ottoman liberals, meeting in Paris in December 1907, committed the movement to the overthrow of Sultan Abdul Hamid II, by violence if necessary.

The immediate causes for unrest against the sultan are of interest; they were not entirely of an ideological nature. The sultan, understandably dubious of his officers' loyalty, began withholding authority from his commanders while extending his intolerable espionage system to the army. Army pay was constantly in arrears, and nearly all enlisted men were serving well over their stipulated terms of duty completely unnoticed. Meanwhile, army officers began to have increased contact with the personnel of European military missions as they appeared upon Hamid's bidding in his desperate attempt to modernize the Ottoman forces and stave off collapse of Ottoman sovereignty. Laid on top of ideological commitments, these more mundane issues added up to substantial unrest among the military, particularly the leadership.

Finally, during 1906 and 1907 a series of army mutinies broke out for the reasons cited above. So numerous were these incidents that, when the 1908 revolution really got under way, the British Embassy in Istanbul sent a dispatch to its Foreign Office reporting that it was just another in a long line of mutinies. Later, it belatedly admitted, "We have greatly underestimated the strength of the force at the disposal of the Committee [of Union and Progress]." [6]

THE REVOLUTIONS OF 1908 AND 1909

The Young Turk-sponsored Revolution of 1908 erupted in Salonica when Army units stationed there openly demanded restoration of the 1876 Constitution, long since suspended. The sultan reacted by sending a royal emissary to placate the Salonica group; however, the emissary was shot, at which time various Third Army Corps officers fled to the Macedonian mountains. In the group was a junior officer named Enver, a man destined for leadership in the political hierarchy. These refugee officers began organizing groups of irregulars in the Macedonian mountains. The sultan, now alarmed for his own safety, felt compelled to reinstate, by royal proclamation, the Constitution of 1876. This event took place on July 23, 1908 — a development causing great disappointment to the revolutionaries, for by this act the sultan temporarily managed to save his position.

The 1908 Revolution was thus over, and the empire allegedly went wild with joy. A tremendous wave of emotional fervor swept the empire, with Greeks, Armenians, Turks, and Jews reportedly embracing one another in happy harmony. It was apparently expected that an entire new era was beginning. This assessment was, unfortunately, quite wrong; the new era was not destined to begin for at least another decade, despite the fact that the 1908 Revolution heralded a change of administration.

In 1908 the Committee of Union and Progress was still not strong enough organizationally to take over effective control of government. It was particularly weak in Istanbul itself, where the Committee had been so harassed by the sultan's spies. Also, the sultan was moderately successful in making it appear that the idea of reinstituting the 1876 Constitution had been his own. Despite years of uninspired rule, he still — as the caliph-sultan or the padishah — commanded the veneration of the vast majority of the people. In fact, the Committee of Union and Progress had not dared speak out among the common soldiers against the sultan himself because of the religious significance of his office.

The sultan played his new role of constitutional monarch to unexpected and disappointing perfection. He even expressed a wish, which was not gratified, to become president of the Committee of Union and Progress. He opened the new parliament in person, greeted the deputies — most of whom were Committee members — with well-chosen words, and received an impressive ovation while passing on his way to and from the session. The president of the new parliament was Ahmet Riza, one of the veteran Young Turks, but the Committee was content to remain behind the scenes as a shadow government. Suddenly, on April 13, 1909, the new government was overthrown by a mutiny of the Istanbul garrison. It appears likely that this act was stimulated by the sultan himself, who had been secretly disseminating propaganda to the effect that the Union and Progress movement was directed against the Sheria (the religious law) and against the very authority of the Ottoman state. Consequently, the movement was subversive not only to the person of the sultan, but to the institution of the Ottoman sultanate and to Islam itself. The Macedonian army again played a key role by marching on Istanbul and seizing control. Although the chief of staff of this force was Kemal, the hero of the day was Enver, who overshadowed all other men for the next few years. It had been he who had first proclaimed the insurrection against the sultan in Salonica in 1908 and helped persuade the Third Army Corps to march on Istanbul in 1909.[7]

In the first session of the reconvened parliament, a *fetva* — or religious pronouncement — of the *Sheikh-ul-*

Islam — the chief religious official of the empire — was read, declaring that the sultan had forfeited his position. His disposition was voted unanimously, and his brother, Mohammed V, was named to succeed him. The new sultan declared, while taking his oath, "I shall not swerve one iota from the will and the aspirations of the nation." This was new language for a sovereign of the Ottoman royal house. Meanwhile, Abdul Hamid was dispatched to Salonica, where he remained in exile as a state prisoner. He remained a prisoner in Salonica until the Greeks took over the city during the course of the Balkan War. He was returned to Istanbul by the Germans and in 1915 removed to the interior. He died in Istanbul on February 10, 1918.

THE YOUNG TURKS IN POWER

Although the 1909 Revolution placed the Young Turks in political control — which they retained, with but a brief interruption in 1912–1913, until the 1918 Armistice — still they hesitated to lay the foundations for a new state; they sensed that they lacked support from a large enough part of the population to push through any fundamental reform. Religious law still dominated, and the *millet* system continued — that system whereby various religious and national minorities had access to their own national or religious courts of justice. These majorities could not be expected, of course, to conform to Islamic law. Some lesser reforms were announced, but the Young Turks refused to abandon their idea of empire. Maintenance of the Ottoman Empire — that Middle Eastern conglomerate of states and races — remained a fixation despite the rise of nationalism in the Middle East and the Balkans and despite the inability of the Istanbul government to defend the empire against external forces. As one writer observed: "To prove successful the Young Turkish revolution needed ten years of peace, and instead it got 12 years of war." [8] It was at this point, 1911, that Italy attacked the Ottoman Empire in North Africa. In 1912, the Balkan League was formed against Turkey, and later that year she was attacked from the Balkans by Greece, Bulgaria, Montenegro, and Serbia in one of the few instances in which these states were allied. In the ensuing fighting, the Turkish army was completely routed from Macedonia, and Turkey lost the greater part of Thrace.

Ottoman forces then experienced a series of military disasters under the leadership of Enver, surely one of the most unfortunate generals in history. Enver also encountered political difficulties. The Young Turk government was split into two schools: one sought a democratic, decentralized empire to be obtained by peaceful means, and the second, military in composition, favored centralized authority and alliances with the Great Powers. A struggle for power within the governing group ensued, which ended finally in January 1913 when Enver Pasha, a professional soldier, and two others — Talat and Cemal — seized power in a coup d'état. Enver, 32 years old at the time, was the central figure and soon succeeded in elevating himself to virtual dictator.

Talat was a 39-year-old post office official who had been secretly active in the Committee since 1900. As a member of Parliament from Edirne, he had been elected deputy chairman of Parliament in 1909. Cemal, age 41, was an army general who had supported the Committee. Significantly, all three men were relatively young, came from or near Istanbul, and two of them had graduated from the military academy in Istanbul.

Perhaps Enver's most important decision while at the

head of the government was to commit the Ottoman Empire to the cause of the Central Powers on the eve of World War I. Thereupon, the empire entered what was to be its final struggle.

Just why Enver made his decision in favor of the Central Powers is a disputed subject, but it is no secret that the final blow was a decision by Winston Churchill, then First Lord of the Admiralty, to requisition two Ottoman naval vessels which were under construction in England. Germany immediately reacted by announcing that it would make up the loss. Within hours, the Ottoman Empire had joined the cause of the Central Powers. One cannot assume that the Ottoman Empire would have sought an association with the Allies had Churchill been a little more generous, but that this decision at that particular moment was fraught with emotional consequences in Turkey was apparent. The Turks went to war.[9]

Other than the rout of Ottoman forces on all fronts save one and their ultimate defeat, three events stand out from World War I.

First, the Western allies, in a series of secret agreements, conspired to chop up the empire and distribute the pieces among themselves with only a small fragment in Central Anatolia remaining to the Turks. Istanbul was to go to the Russians. This threatened partition of Anatolia and deliverance of Turkey's cultural center to Russia, Turkey's historic enemy, later proved to be an Allied blunder of the first order, for it created a hard core of unremitting Turkish resistance. The Allied intent was not only to carve up the Ottoman Empire — that is, the non-Turkish parts — but to seize large sections of the very heartland of Turkey — Anatolia — where the Turks themselves lived.

Second, the problem of the Armenians living in eastern Anatolia drew down much popular condemnation on the head of the Turk. Although the Armenians numbered at most not more than 40 per cent of the population in any single province save two,[10] the bulk of their numbers was concentrated in that area adjoining Russia, thereby enabling the Russian army to draw Armenian recruits out of Anatolia. The Armenian community let it be known generally that it would not support the Ottoman war effort, and, encouraged by President Wilson's principle of self-determination, moved to create an independent Armenian state. To the Ottoman authorities, these activities constituted wartime treason, and they reacted violently.[11] Most of the Armenian population was forced to flee, and large numbers perished at the hands of the Turks. These Turkish reprisals recharged the racial-religious animosity of the earlier period of Armenian troubles shortly before 1900. Though the fact does not in the least excuse Turkish behavior on this occasion, the Turks did consider the Armenian defection as treason, a stab in the back that was all the more painful because of Turkish military reverses. It was also quite clear that the Armenians reciprocated in kind, and many Turks lost their lives violently.

The third event to stand out from the war years was simply the appearance of Kemal as a national figure. His wartime exploits and the excessive Allied demands on Turkey provided the opportunity for him to gain a national stature that perhaps no other Turkish leader had enjoyed since the days of uninterrupted Ottoman military success which had ended two centuries before.[12] "No battle he directed was ever entirely lost."[13]

It was the Armistice of Mudros (October 30, 1918) that rang down the curtain on World War I for Turkey, and on the Young Turks as well, whose leaders felt obliged to flee the country two days after signing the unfortunate agreement. The conditions forced on the Turks were these:[14]

1. Severance of relations with the Central Powers
2. Immediate demobilization of all Turkish armed forces
3. The placing of all Ottoman possessions in Arabia and Africa under Allied military control
4. Opening of the Straits to Allied vessels and the occupation of all fortifications by the Allies
5. Recognition of the right of the Allies to occupy any strategic point in the event of a threat to Allied security.

Indeed, it was a black day in Turkish history — but worse was to come.

The end of World War I found a new sultan, Vahideddin or Mohammed VI, on the throne in Istanbul. The Young Turk leaders, Enver Pasha and his colleagues — the men responsible for the disastrous war — had fled. The Ottoman armies had been defeated on every front except the northeastern, where six divisions remained more or less intact and armed. Alien powers were occupying Istanbul and a number of other places. Although Russian claims to Turkish territory had been renounced by the Bolsheviks in 1917, it was apparent that the Allies — the French, British, Italians, and Greeks — had designs on a large part of Anatolia itself.

FAILURE OF THE YOUNG TURKS: AN EVALUATION

The Young Turk regime provided Turkey with a useful exposure to parliamentary government, but it did not achieve lasting and basic reform. And even the parliamentary regime degenerated into a military dictatorship. The reasons for the failure of the Young Turks lay in their inability to resolve the several conflicting currents of thought, or political objectives, inherent in the multiracial, multireligious, geographically vast Ottoman Empire.[15] The main currents of thought were these:

1. Ottomanism — the creation of a multiracial, multireligious nation encompassing much or all of the Ottoman Empire
2. Islamism — the maintenance of a state based on a common religion, Islam, and religious law
3. Pan-Turkism — the union of persons of Turkish culture or "race"
4. Turkish nationalism — the bringing together within a common national loyalty of all persons living within a given geographical area, specifically Asia Minor, within which area most persons possessed a common culture.

There were also conflicting ideas about the methods to be used in achieving political objectives: violence or nonviolence, democratic or authoritarian, conservative evolution or massive reform. In all areas, the Young Turks maintained the dualism of the earlier era: religious law and secular law, the caliphate and the constitution, the traditional and the modern.

An *Ottoman state* obviously could not rest on loyalty to a common religion or to a common race. Hence, a democratic Ottoman state would have to be secular and nonracial. If it were not, it would have to be authoritarian in political structure, and probably conservative in attitude. Otherwise, it would fly into pieces. By definition, an *Islamic state* could not be secular, nor would such a state appeal to non-Moslem peoples included in the Ottoman Empire, an estimated 11 to 15 per cent of the total. The nature of law and authority — necessarily Islamic in an Islamic state — precluded a single national entity in a multireligious state; hence, the traditional "millet" system. A *Pan-Turkish state* would have extended into central Asia, and not included Arabia, thereby encompassing a different geographical area than the Ottoman. Clearly, it was not politically realistic. A *Turkish nationalist state* would have been much smaller than an Ottoman state, for it would have been confined to Asia Minor, the area within the Ottoman Empire in which the majority identified themselves as Turks. Strangely, the most realistic political objective — the last — was never accepted by the Young Turks. They argued interminably about Ottomanism, Islamism, and Pan-Turkism, and in the end tried to ignore the conflict by accepting both the Ottoman ideal of a multiracial, multireligious federation, and the political institutions and loyalties of an Islamic state — the sultanate and the sheria. When this arrangement fell apart, as was inevitable, Enver Pasha led a move toward Turkish racialism and Pan-Turkism which finally culminated in his death in Russian Turkestan in 1922 fighting for a new Asiatic Turkish state.

With the rise of Soviet power, Pan-Turkism was simply not feasible. And a Turkish state in Asia Minor based on common race would have been against the interests of many, for the racial minorities of Kurds and Arabs were too large to be overlooked — perhaps 15 to 20 per cent of the total. In any event, the concept of Turkish race was a very vague and unappealing one to most Anatolian Turks when measured against loyalty to religion, community, or region. In short, the Young Turks under Enver, Talat, and

Cemal never resolved these many conflicts — either on the level of ends or of means — so as to make possible a united effort. Nor did they formulate any solid basis for modern Turkish nationalism except in a negative sense. They surely demonstrated beyond all doubt the unwisdom of Ottomanism, Islamism, and Pan-Turkism — the alternatives to the limited geographical concept. One of the intellectual advisors to the Young Turk leaders, Ziya Gökalp, did finally — after much mental meandering — formulate a political philosophy for a new Turkey. But his words seemed to have carried little weight at the time, possibly because he had been of so many minds at so many different times.

The importance of the Young Turks to the next act in Turkish history was their demonstration of the necessity for a change in national objectives and for sweeping political and social reform to support those objectives. The liberal Ottoman nationalist concept espoused literally by Namik Kemal and the Turkism of Ziya Gökalp's younger days ultimately blended to give form to modern Turkish political nationalism (*Turkçülük,* or sometimes *Türkiyeçilik*), a form to which Ziya Gökalp finally gave substance at the close of World War I when the fallacy of Ottomanism and the unreality of political Pan-Turkism became painfully apparent. In 1923, he wrote: "Nation is not a racial, ethnic, geographical, political, or voluntary group or association. Nation is a group composed of men and women who have gone through the same education, who have received the same acquisitions in language, religion, morality and aesthetics."[16] Note his inclusion of religion.

Initially, Gökalp placed no politically feasible geographical limit on what he conceived to be the Turkish nation.

He merely declared, "It is necessary to consider everyone a Turk." [17] It was Kemal who modified Gökalp's definition of Turkish nationalism by secularizing government and limiting Turkey's territorial claims.

Chapter II

THE NEW TURK

FOR the moment we move back in time — back to 1915 when a series of events commenced which made it possible for Kemal, the prototype of the new Turk, to emerge with the halo of a national hero, without which his rise to political power would probably have been unthinkable. And without Kemal there might not now be a Turkey. We must understand this man and the circumstances that created him.

KEMAL'S OPPORTUNITY

Despite earlier agitation against the Hamidian regime via his military committees, Kemal had been shoved aside by more plausible and glib military officers — Cemal, Enver, and others. In the 1909 Congress of the Committee of Union and Progress, Kemal had argued vigorously against direct involvement of the army in partisan politics. Once the revolution was over, he resigned from the Committee to plunge himself into a purely military career.[1]

As Moorehead has written so well in his book, *Gallipoli,*[2]

> From 1909 onward Kemal had been constantly in Enver's shadow; he took part in the revolutionary march on the capital that year, but was in the rear planning the administration of the army when Enver was rushing over the barricades. He served under Enver in the Tripoli campaign, again in the Balkan war. He was even present at Enver's triumphant entry into Adrianople. At every stage the two men quarreled, as they were inevitably bound to; for while Kemal was a

military genius, Enver must surely be judged as one of the most inept and disastrous generals who ever lived. It is not evident that Enver ever learned the first principles of warfare or ever profited by the experience of any of the appalling disasters which he so confidently planned. Through all these chaotic years it was Kemal's galling fate to take orders from this man . . . By 1913, Kemal had reached the low point in his career: he was an unemployed lieutenant colonel in Constantinople, and Enver had gone far over his head.

Kemal's rise to fame and power commenced on April 25, 1915, on the blood-soaked Gallipoli peninsula which guards the southern entrance to the Dardanelles. Kemal was 34.

It was here that the Allies launched their most famous and costly campaign against the Ottoman Empire. If the effort had been successful, some historians believe, the war might have been shortened by two years. The action began on March 18, 1915, with a naval battle at the southern end of the Black Sea Straits in which the Allies tried to force their way up the Dardanelles, a move designed to bisect Turkey and open up a line of supply and communication through to the Russians. The Allied navy failed to force a passage, and a mass landing on the Gallipoli peninsula ensued in an overland effort. The maneuver turned out to be poorly executed. The main body of troops landed on the wrong beach, thereby taking both themselves and the Turks by surprise. It happened that the nearest body of Turkish troops, a small reserve battalion, was commanded by one Lieutenant Colonel Kemal. As Moorehead wrote:

From the Allies' point of view it was one of the cruelest accidents of the campaign that this one junior commander of genius should have been at this particular spot at this moment, for otherwise the Australians and New Zealanders might well have taken Chunuk Bair [the highlands] that morning, and the battle might have been decided then and there.[3]

Moorehead continues:

> There is an air of inspired desperation about Kemal's actions this day. He even seems to have gone a little berserk at times. Instinctively he must have realized that his great chance had come, that he was either going to die here or make his name at last. He was constantly at the extreme front, helping to wheel guns into position, getting up on the skyline among the bullets, sending his men into attacks in which they had very little hope of survival. One of his orders was worded: "I don't order you to attack, I order you to die. In the time which passes until we die other troops and commanders can take our places." The soldiers got up from the ground and ran into the machine gun fire; presently the 57th Turkish regiment was demolished.[4]

— and, Moorehead might have added, the Atatürk legend was born.

Kemal kept up his fanatical attack on the Anzac beachhead all afternoon. By nightfall, the dominion troops were in a state of siege. Some months later, in the final critical engagement, General Liman von Sanders gave full command of the troops on the major front to the colonel. It was perhaps a surprising appointment for him to have made, in view of the past friction between the two men. "One can only conclude," writes Moorehead, "that Liman had long since devised Kemal's abilities, but had been prevented by Enver from promoting him. But now in this extreme crisis he could afford to ignore Enver." [5] Though the failure of the Allied landing had been sealed in August when the Turks under Kemal recaptured the heights, the Allies did not evacuate until January. After his August success, Kemal was promoted to colonel, and in December he returned to Istanbul, ill and exhausted, but a popular hero. Enver promptly dispatched him to Bulgaria as military attaché.

Early in 1916, Kemal was back on active duty on the Caucasian front, a corps commander in an army directed by Enver, as Minister of War, to undertake a "decisive blow" against the Russians, which blow was to have been one of Enver's Pan-Turanian thrusts. It proved to be a disastrous effort in which Kemal's occupation of Muş and Bitlis were the only successes, even though short-lived. One military historian commented on the venture: "The Turks had found in Mustafa Kemal a young commander of first quality who did not fail to impress the power of his personality even on a most unfriendly destiny" [6] — in this case, an impossible military objective. Even Enver was forced to recognize Kemal's ability and later that year gave him the command of an army and title of pasha.

A veteran Turkish journalist recalled a conversation with Kemal in 1917 in these words:

The real enemies of Turkey, Mustafa Kemal explained to me, were the short sighted men in power in Turkey, the leaders who had proved themselves incapable of recognizing facts and acting accordingly. The young Turk triumvirate Enver Pasha, Talat Pasha, and Cemal and their appointees, through their own lack of ability and perspective, had decided that Turkey could not save herself without foreign alliance. Losing sight of every essential of independence, they had committed Turkey to German command. All acting chiefs on Turkey's general staff and in the army were Germans. They were running Turkish participation in the war to relieve pressure on the German fronts and to reduce the already deficient and seemingly helpless Turkey to a colony. That Turkey was bleeding too much meant nothing to the Germans, except that an enfeebled Turkey would be easier prey for them.

"Our own men in high office are gamblers, staking Turkey's destiny on the turn of the single card of final German victory,"

Mustafa Kemal said. "They are not aware, at this moment, that they have lost the war, because Germany has lost the initiative and even the will to succeed." [7]

In October 1917, Allied forces split the Bulgarian army, defeated the Turkish army in Palestine, and the end was in sight. In October 1918, the last resistance of the Ottoman Empire broke with the Arabs in full revolt. Kemal, now commander of an army group in Syria, was able to reassemble some portion of the defeated Ottoman forces and, by organizing a fighting retreat, prevent headlong flight. He finally established a line of defense just north of Aleppo beyond which the British did not go. Once again, he was the single man to emerge with any sort of military reputation from a major campaign — indeed, he was the sole Turkish military leader to come out of war with increased stature. Enver Pasha, the man held personally responsible for the disastrous Ottoman defeat, had fled along with his immediate colleagues. Because of Kemal's resignation from the Committee for Union and Progress in 1909, his open scorn for Enver, and his pro-German policies, Kemal was not tarred by the same brush as were the defeated politicians and some of the other pashas.

The moment the Armistice of Mudros was signed (on October 30, 1918) and Enver Pasha had departed (two days later), a contest for power between the sultan and Kemal became inevitable; they remained as the only two potential leaders in postwar Turkey. Obviously, there was not room for both. Kemal's name had become known in every village as returning soldiers told of his exploits. Still, loyalty to the sultan-caliph was strong.

The Allied take-over of the Empire commenced. On November 13, 1918, the Allied fleet arrived in Istanbul. The British had already occupied parts of the Arabian Peninsula, and soon they were in southeastern Anatolia. (Later the French replaced the British in Anatolia and Syria.) In April 1919, the Italians landed at Antalya. The disliked foreigner was now setting foot on the sacred soil of Anatolia itself, not the Balkans or Arabia but Anatolia. Then came the final blow on May 14, 1919, when the Greeks landed in force in Izmir — a landing covered by Allied warships.

Once again, Kemal strode onto the stage in a lead role, precisely at the most propitious time and place. Early in 1919, he had been named by the sultan to undertake a unique mission. Just why he was picked for this job is still debated. The situation was this. The British and other Allied forces in Istanbul had been unable to establish effective control over Central Anatolia. In the northeast several divisions of the Ottoman army were still intact and in possession of their arms. There was much restlessness. A Society for the Defense of National Rights had appeared in the eastern provinces, and elsewhere other local resistance groups were emerging. The terms of the Mudros Armistice could not be enforced. Arms were not being surrendered. The sultan was pressured by the Allied authorities into sending a high-ranking army officer to Anatolia to supervise the disarming and demobilization of what remained of the Turkish forces. Kemal was that officer, unlikely as the choice seems from some points of view.

It is true that Kemal and the sultan, as Crown Prince, had traveled together to Germany in 1917. The sultan had been impressed with Kemal and his great sense of identity with Turkey. And both detested Enver. Perhaps the sultan, having confidence in Kemal, merely hoped that Kemal might help him out of an awkward spot.[8] Others have speculated that the sultan knew full well what he did in selecting Kemal, that he knew Kemal was the only hope. Somehow this heroic figure who was so dramatically committed to the concept of Turkey-for-the-Turks might rekindle the spirit of Turkish resistance. Or perhaps the sultan was merely trying to rid himself of a man whom he feared as a rival. It was also possible that the Allies, knowing of Kemal's anti-German position during the war and feeling that only he could induce the Turkish forces to abide by the terms of the armistice, had suggested his name to the sultan.[9] Finally, Kemal himself may have maneuvered the appointment as part of a long-range conspiracy. Any one, or all, of these factors may have led to the sultan's rather surprising choice. Kemal himself observed that those who sent him to Anatolia did not realize what they were doing.[10] But whatever the reason, Kemal was appointed Inspector General of the Third Army headquartered in northeastern Turkey, with two Army corps — comprising six divisions — under his personal command. He was to report on the unsettled conditions in the interior and to take necessary measures to deal with them. His great opportunity had come. He departed at once by boat for Samsun on the Black Sea coast.

KEMAL, THE MAN

What manner of man was this who strode ashore in Samsun during Turkey's darkest hour? It depends somewhat upon who reports.

An American foreign service officer described a 1921 interview with Kemal as follows:

> . . . Upstairs Mustapha Kemal stood alone, nervously dangling conversation beads of pink coral with a blue tassel. The office was bare except for a large table and lots of chairs.

"The well-trained superior waiter," was my first thought. But even as we sat down, face to face across green baize, I changed it to, "tough customer!" He wore a slate-blue lounge suit, quite natty, with soft-collar white shirt and a black bow tie. His age was forty-one but he looked younger, with a college boy's slicked-back sandy hair. Chin small yet doughty, cheek-bones high, trim reddish mustache over a mouth that was but a line. His eyes lay in narrow slits, their straight brown brows close above the steel-blue pupils. Every feature showed non-Turkish blood, — Hellene, Jewish, Circassian; he was born at Salonika. The whole face was sensitive, subtle and mercuric rather than domineering. I felt his power of concentration, a ruthlessness with an instant grasp, but wondered — was he adolescent still, or man? . . . Below quick furtive glances, only his mouth revealed emotion-warmth if its corners upped, scorn if they drooped. I felt the least facial change to be against his will.[11]

In an article written for *McCalls,* Zsa Zsa Gabor, a confidante of Kemal shortly before his death in 1938, described her first view of him:

He stood framed in the entrance, suddenly alone: slim, gray at the temples, impeccably dressed in black tie, his shoulders back, his head up, surveying the room as if utterly indifferent to what he saw.[12]

Like almost all who described Kemal, Miss Gabor speaks of his eyes: "The pupils were so light blue as to be almost colorless; it was like looking at a blind man, yet one whose eyes pierced you through." [13] She reports that in private Kemal laughed a great deal, drank incessantly, was greatly interested in a foreigner's reactions to Turkey. Over twenty years later, she writes in obvious awe of the man. One senses that men she has known since Kemal have been measured against his stature. In fact, she admittedly married the next man who reminded her of him.

But there are many divergent views. The best-known

biography of Kemal is H. C. Armstrong's *Grey Wolf*. Armstrong refers to him as follows:

> A man born out of due season, an anachronism, a throwback to the Tartars of the Steppes, a fierce elemental force of man . . . With the mind of an Emperor, he lives in brutal royalty . . . a primitive chieftain in a morning-coat with a piece of chalk and a blackboard for his weapons.[14]

There is also the hero-worshiping stance, an attitude which has certainly permeated the thinking of the newer generations of Turks. An excerpt from a 5th grade reader used in the Turkish public schools until recently is revealing. A boy is telling his father about an experience he had at school:

> Today, who do you suppose was in my class? Atatürk. We saw him with our own eyes. We listened to his voice. He was as near to me as you . . . He remained and questioned us until night. When he came to my row in the class the room had begun to get dark and the lights had not yet been put on. From the roots of his golden hair, light issued as if his head were illuminated . . . I cannot find the words to explain the joy which his look gave. I'll probably not get another chance to see him so close in all my life. Just think, father, the Turkish world, what am I saying, all the world will not forget this man.

Suffice it to say that to most Turks 40 years or younger Kemal is a hero, adored and revered. During his time, he was both loved and feared, but never despised.

Kemal was born in 1881 in Salonica, now in Greece, the center of revolutionary activities within the Ottoman Empire. He was the son of a poor Ottoman Moslem bureaucrat, a clerk in the local customs office (who died when Kemal was 7), and his peasant wife. The family was on the edge of Ottoman respectability, at the very lowest extreme, though nonetheless identified with the ruling class.

The only way young Kemal might upgrade his position was by military or religious training. Intrigued by the former from a very early age and, despite the opposition of his mother, whom he apparently held in very high respect, he entered a military school as a 12-year-old youth. He was a brilliant, if unruly and unpopular, student and rose rapidly through the echelons of military education up to and including military staff school. He learned French and became well versed in Western political concepts, as did many young Ottoman officers of the day.

A point to remember about this man is that he had no distinguished forebears, a handicap in Ottoman Turkey; there was no distinction in the family which would aid and abet his career. Apparently, he never accepted the values of the ruling class, although he identified socially with it. His attempt to participate in Ottoman high society is a rather tragic, pathetic story and surely not without its psychological scars. Although handsome and elegant of dress, he did not possess the easy social graces characteristic of the Ottoman elite, a fact which seemed to irritate him. At times, when he tried to imitate its ways, he was mocked and became furious and sullen. Indeed, perhaps this self-contained fury and resentment was typical of his early career, during the time when his true genius was not recognized nor given an opportunity for expression.[15] And the fact that from age 7 he had no father may well have contributed to his feelings of resentment and irritation toward traditional society and led to his later efforts to introduce different institutions and values, an act of a creative personality.[16]

The military dominated Kemal's early life, and there was no question of his military genius. Despite his unpopularity, he rose rapidly. "Military genius" may be defined best in terms of five qualities: personal courage, ability to anticipate the acts of others, patience and the insight to time one's own acts for maximum effectiveness, ability to feint convincingly in many different directions without disclosing one's actual objective, and ability to assess objectively and accurately the relative strength of opposing forces. Kemal's courage, to which the legends surrounding his name give substance, was founded probably on an overdeveloped self-confidence and smoldering scorn for dilettantes and politicians. He was a man of strong conviction, decisive action, and impatient with indecision. During his earlier years, he was apparently inclined to state his views very emphatically on any and all occasions and, when people disagreed — as they frequently did — to go into sullen retirement. He had that supreme egoism that permitted him to say to himself, "I am right; everyone else is wrong." He must have rationalized his lonely position at times by convincing himself that most of the People would agree if only they knew the Truth. This was Kemal's period of retreatism.

Kemal had to find outlets for his energy. When he was thwarted and legitimate expression was denied for his enormous energy, and after periods of concentrated effort, he turned to drinking and to women — stories about which the Atatürk legend abounds and behind which was a very large element of truth. Only by extracurricular carousing could he contain his impatience to be about the job rather than biding his time, which he knew he must. At some point it must have come to him that he could use his military abilities with the same deadly effectiveness in political matters as he had on the battlefield. And, as he grew older, there is increasing evidence that he grew wiser in the manipulation of individuals and events and that he was much less inclined to reveal his real objective before the event. Characteristically, he was really intimate with no one, with the possible exception of Ismet Inönü who had been closely associated with him in the Caucasian and Syrian actions and who was later to become his chief civilian assistant.

As a military leader, Kemal realized perhaps more than most that the real strength of the country lay in the ordinary folk of village and small town, and this fact — or belief — he never forgot. Whenever the opportunity arose, he was fond of giving rather dramatic expression to his faith in the common man and woman of Anatolia.

There was something of a paradox in this man. On the one hand, there was the military man inclined to the authoritarian; on the other hand, the rebel against constituted authority. He had been a subversive agent under the Hamidian regime, being jailed briefly in 1904 and later absenting himself from his military duties without leave to participate in the underground movement. He had not hesitated to disagree with his military superiors. He had openly opposed Enver Pasha's war policy. He had openly opposed General Liman von Sanders, the German in command of the Turkish troops at Gallipoli. During the height of the battle, he had threatened to resign if his superiors did not fall in with his views on how to conduct the campaign. He was retained only because of his recognized military talents and ability to motivate the troops to extraordinary effort. Later, when ordered by another German commander, General Falkenhayn, to attack the British in Palestine, he had refused point-blank and resigned his commission. But eight months later he was back in command, and two months after that he had Falkenhayn's job. He was not a man to be blocked for long. Though infuriating many, he had developed a solid corps of fellow officers who believed in him — such men as Ismet, later to be Turkey's second president. On the other hand, he had many enemies — ambitious politicians, conservative religious groups, and a substantial share of the landed class.

Using the helpful insight of hindsight, it is quite clear now that Kemal understood the true ailments of Turkey and saw clearly the concept of total revolution — surely not all in one blinding flash of illumination although the concept must have developed in his mind fairly early. One might observe that in psychological terms Kemal undoubtedly possessed a vigorous "need disposition" to destroy and reform. He saw the necessity for change because he himself *needed* to see it. What distinguished him was that his personal compulsion corresponded to reality. That which he felt compelled to destroy and change was consistent with the social evolution. Further, he had the genius and opportunity that enabled him to translate need into reality.

In retrospect, Kemal's ideas — regardless of how they were derived psychologically — appear completely logical. The first axiom was the necessity for shrinking the Ottoman Empire down to a small, culturally more homogeneous and politically more viable Turkey and to renounce all imperialistic or irredentist claims, a dramatic departure from past Ottoman policy. Recall that the Ottoman Empire had stayed alive through conquest and gain at the expense of others. Its economic welfare had been a function of plunder and booty, not of internal development. Consequently, we derive the second axiom: the fortunes of Turkey must rest on internal development, not on conquest. Kemal envisioned a relatively small national state, enriching itself through internal development. A third axiom follows: internal development could rest only upon a modern, industrial, scientifically oriented society. To achieve that objective, and to do so before the Great Powers moved into the Turkish power vacuum, required a total revolution in a relatively short period of time: new values, new institutions, *a new Turk,* for which he — Kemal — was the prototype.

Kemal must have seen very clearly that technology, be it military or civilian, was but one part of a whole socio-politico-economic complex. To adopt modern technology meant social and political revolutions as well — total revolution. One suspects that Kemal's reasoning began from the point of military defense, for Turkey occupied an area long coveted by the Great Powers. He saw that a modern military establishment was impossible without modern science and industry. Most importantly, he realized that modern science and industry were impossible without a vastly revamped political and social system which would permit the human potential of Turkey to be utilized to its maximum. Illiteracy, debilitating disease, religious dogma and fatalism, the inferior position of women — all of these things must go, and go fast. The necessity for authoritarian leadership thus became clear, for many of these changes would at first be exceedingly unpopular.

It was this man who stood on the beach in Samsun on May 19, 1919 — a man of decisive action, of provoking single-mindedness, and possessing a sort of intuitive understanding of what was required. He was 38 years old.

As he gained the beach, he was told of the Greek invasion of Anatolia through Izmir which had started four days before. He must have realized immediately that this unprovoked and, according to the terms of the armistice, illegal attack might be the one thing that could fire his exhausted people to a final desperate effort to save what remained of Turkey. Again, Kemal was at the right spot.

Chapter III

KEMAL'S PROBLEM

KEMAL, in a marathon six-day speech before the 1927 Congress of the People's Party, eight years after the event, described the situation as of the day he arrived in Samsun. His account opened with the following words:[1]

Gentlemen, I landed at Samsun on the 19th of May, 1919. This was the position at that time.

The group of powers, which included the Ottoman government, had been defeated in the Great War. The Ottoman army had been crushed on every front. An armistice had been signed under severe conditions. The prolongation of the Great War had left the people exhausted and impoverished. Those who had driven the people and the country into the general conflict had fled and now cared for nothing but their own safety. Vahideddin,[2] the degenerate occupant of the throne and the Caliphate, was seeking for some despicable way to save his person and his throne, the only objects of his anxiety. The Cabinet, of which Damad Ferid Pasha[3] was the head, was weak and lacked dignity and courage. It was subservient to the rule of the Sultan alone and agreed to his every proposal that could protect its members and their sovereign.

The Army had been deprived of their arms and ammunition, and this state of affairs continued.

The Entente Powers did not consider it necessary to respect the terms of the armistice. On various pretexts, their men-of-war and various troops remained in Constantinople. The Vilayet of Adana [in south-central Turkey on the Mediterranean coast] was occupied by the French, and Urfah, Marash, and Aintab [in the southeast part of Turkey] by the English. In Adalia [Antalya] and Konia were the Italians and in

Merzifun and Samsun were the English troops. Foreign officers and officials and special agents were very active in all directions.

POWER

Kemal pondered his first moves.

The country was exhausted, having suffered an almost unbroken series of disastrous military defeats. Nonetheless, Turkey occupied an extraordinarily important geopolitical position. The passage of time, a falling-out among the Great Powers, and Turkey might gain bargaining power — as it had in the past. Local resistance groups were already forming, such as the Eastern Anatolian Society for the Defense of the National Rights. In Kemal's pocket was a royal commission. But the sultan was a virtual captive of the Allies in occupied Istanbul, and his only real means of communication with Anatolia was the telegraph system. These facts suggested certain moves if one were conspiring to achieve personal power and national independence.

For the time being, Kemal could anticipate no external assistance from any direction, with the possible exception of Russia. The Turks would have to stand or fall alone. There was some talk of an American trusteeship, but Kemal was not interested, perhaps because he realized that Western opinion was solidly against any recrudescence of Turkish power. Said the *Literary Digest* in March 1920, "If there are [any American journals] which favor continuing the Turk in Constantinople, with his record of five centuries of pillage and murder, they have not come to our attention." Meanwhile, the *New York Tribune* was calling the Turk "the pirate of the Bosporus whose hands are dripping with blood . . . [The Turks have] always been a parasite and a stench in the nostrils of civilization."[4] A Milwaukee paper declared, "The sentiment of the whole civilized world is against letting the Turk retain Constantinople. He has shown neither a desire nor a capacity for civilization; let there be no temporizing with him." [5] The *Philadelphia Inquirer* editorialized, "The Turk is incapable of reform and cannot be trusted to fulfill the promises he makes." [6] The unprovoked Greek attack against Turkey in 1919, news of which had not reached Kemal on board his vessel en route to Samsun, was supported generally by articulate American opinion. Pontificated the *Chicago Tribune,* "Only the recalcitrant and purblind Senate is responsible for depriving American soldiers of the honor conferred upon the Greeks." [7] The Greek invasion was obviously viewed as a 20th Century Crusade. In July 1919, the scholarly *Annals of the American Academy of Political Science* published an article in which the Turks were held guilty of torture "beyond the ingenuity of the inquisition; deportation of entire communities into the deserts; indiscriminate slaughter and robbery; rapings and ravishing; systematic starvation of whole villages." [8] In another respectable American journal, Kemal was called the leader of "the largest and worst brigand bands" of Anatolia.[9] Being the realist that he was, Kemal knew that he could ask no quarter from the Western Allies. They would understand only power.

DISUNITY

But how to build this power? The problems were many, not the least of which was the fundamental disunity of the country, even if one were speaking only of Anatolia.

The vast majority of the Anatolians lived in some 40,000 small, isolated villages, resting upon an economic base of subsistence grain farming and animal husbandry. Few possessed any real sense of national identity, but they did possess a deep sense of identification with Islam and of resentment of the Western infidel. Contemporary observers noted that the ordinary Turk, asked who or what he was, was inclined to answer, "I'm a Moslem" — not "I am a Turk." * An intellectual might declare, "I'm an Ottoman," but never a "Turk," a term of derision reserved for the country bumpkin. Though there was perhaps some feeling of religious identity among the common folk, in fact the population was not religiously homogenous. The division between Sunni and Shiite sects was significant and deep.

The Shiites consider that the House of Ali (son-in-law of the Prophet Mohammed and Fourth Caliph of Islam) had exclusive right to the caliphate. This involved the repudiation of the first three caliphs as usurpers and the recognition of Ali's twelve descendants — called Imams — as the true caliphs. To these twelve Imams were ascribed the qualities of sinlessness and infallibility and the authority to interpret and proclaim doctrine. "In orthodox Islam the Caliph has no such interpretive functions and cannot define doctrine; he is simply the political and religious leader of the [Islamic] Community." [10] There are a number of rather important differences between the Sunni and Shiite schools of law in regard to marriage, inheritance, and ritual.

In Anatolian Turkey Sunnis were in the majority, but the number of Shiites ran into the millions.[11] Rarely did members of the two sects intermarry, and on occasions the

* This same point was made by a Turkish writer, M. S. Karayel, in *Bozkurt*, September 1940. Kemal Karpat, in his *Turkey's Politics* (Princeton University Press, 1959), observes that in the republican era, the masses "accepted nationalism by identifying it with religion." (p. 254).

Persians had used their fellow Shiites in Ottoman Turkey as a fifth column.

Also present in Anatolia was an important ethnic minority group, the Kurds, which is currently estimated at anywhere from 2 to 4 million out of Turkey's current population of 27 million — a significant group, and certainly of equal significance in 1919. There were also sizable communities of Armenians, Greeks, Jews, Laz, Circassians, and other lesser groups.

A further divisive influence was the rough terrain and inadequacy of communication. Regional loyalties and differences tended to blot out national loyalties and similarities. And the disparity between city and village society was very great. Outside the big cities, literacy was virtually unknown. There was, of course, a severe shortage of scientific and technical skills in both town and village, but there was a regional unevenness in this regard as well which tended to pull the country apart, thereby accentuating the regionalism already described. Nomadic tribes — both Turkish and Kurdish — wandered about the eastern provinces. The Western world and its ways were virtually unknown to them. As one moved westward across the country the degree of exposure to Western development increased until at the Aegean seaboard and in Istanbul one found Western-educated intellectual groups and some penetration of alien ideas even into the countryside. But the primitive, isolated village of the Anatolian Plateau was the typical environment for the Turks upon whom Kemal must depend. The Western provinces were under foreign control.

Even yet, an estimated 70 per cent of the Turkish population identifies itself with the village.

TRADITIONAL VILLAGE SOCIETY

To get a feel for the traditional Turkish village, and therefore for Kemal's problem, one must somehow sense the environment and rhythm of life in these traditional rural communities.[12] Although we speak here in the past tense, it is only within the past decade that the pattern of Anatolian life has begun to change significantly from that described here.

Typically, the Anatolian Plateau village lay amid a seemingly vast, semiarid, semibarren steppe country. The community was semi-isolated; the roads were not true roads, merely tracks in the mud or the snow or the dust — depending upon the season. The nearest habitation lay perhaps 10 to 15 miles off. In between there was nothing but open country, barren hills, and rolling prairie. Rocky outcroppings and an occasional rugged mountain chain broke the monotony. Trees were rare and even the grasses and scrub brush struggled to sustain themselves. The winters were cold and snowy; the summers, hot and dry. The ordinary community — containing between 800 and 2,000 persons — consisted of a tight, compact cluster of homes, very frequently immediately adjoining one another. There were virtually no isolated dwellings, for villagers did not reside on their fields. Homes were constructed of rough-hewn stone or, more typically, sun-dried brick — an adobe-type construction. Adobe was preferred, for it was easier to work than rock, provided better insulation, and did not sweat in cold weather as did stone. Finally, in much of Turkey earthquakes were common, and rock walls constituted an added source of danger. Across the top of the walls — whether of rock or adobe —

were placed wooden beams, brush, and then packed earth. The latter was rolled down occasionally to keep the texture solid. A good housekeeper occasionally sprinkled salt on the roof to keep plants from growing, the roots of which would break up the solid texture of the soil and permit seepage. The chief livelihood of these people was, of course, agriculture — primarily the growing of grains and secondarily the raising of livestock, principally goats and sheep. Water was scarce, and only a few small vegetable gardens were irrigated. The principal crops — wheat, barley, and rye — subsisted on natural moisture, which even in the best of years was enough to sustain only very low yields. No fertilizers enriched the parched soils. There were a few primitive tools, but no modern machines. (The technological revolution did not really hit the Turkish village until well after World War II.) At least eight persons were required on the land to keep ten Turks alive. That is, the eight produced food for themselves and two others. (In the United States, each farmer produces enough to sustain himself and at least nine others.) Per-capita economic productivity in the village was exceedingly low, and the area of the family field was small, perhaps 8 to 12 acres, half of which lay fallow each year to accumulate nutrients for the following season. Without better draft power and better tools, the usual farm family of five or six persons could not have cultivated more land even though it had it. The standard of living was thus very low, barely above a mere subsistence level.

The sheer fact of isolation had important consequences, for isolation meant that this community lived outside of the stream of national consciousness. Communication from village to village was slow and uncertain. Communication from region to region was exceedingly difficult. Word of mouth was, of course, the most important means of communication. There was no radio in the village, no postal service. On the infrequent occasions when a villager went into the market town some 40 to 70 miles off to sell what surplus crop he might have and to buy the few simple items he needed, he might sit in the town coffee house and talk with people from other villages. Other important points of contact among villages were the small rural flour mills located wherever water was available to drive the millstones. Villagers from a number of different communities might collect at the mill and pass the time of day as they waited for the miller to grind their flour. Weddings involving families from different villages were also occasions for mixing. But communication was uncertain, and when the snow lay deep, the central Anatolian plateau was virtually devoid of movement.

However, isolation might be desirable. Some villages deliberately chose to isolate themselves unnecessarily. Not so many years ago, in a village in the mountains of south central Turkey which could be reached only by an almost impassable 20-mile "road" that required many hours to navigate even by wagon, I asked the village elders why the community showed no interest in fixing up the road so that they could get their crop into market more easily. One old man looked around and grinned at the others, shook his head, and said, "Well, you know, if we had a good road in here, we'd have all sorts of government officials coming by." There is a certain amount of wisdom reflected in that comment. Isolation provided a sort of protection against tax collector and draft official. On the other hand, isolation made a village vulnerable — vulnerable to bandits and the corrupt functionary. Indeed, the need for protection, given isolation, was undoubtedly one reason for the highly compact nature of the village.

But whatever its merits, isolation tends to make a people highly provincial, and the economic structure, regional. Villages in a given region were oriented toward the market town. Hence, one encountered striking differences in dress, manner of speech, and social custom from region to region. Village and regional loyalties superseded national loyalty, particularly when the latter was divorced from religious authority. The only break in this traditional isolation was that experienced by the men while in the army. Hence, the army was a great unifying force, perhaps one reason for the enormous prestige of the army in Turkish society.[13] The broader experience gained by men in this way perhaps gave further substance to the alleged inferiority of women, who very rarely left the environment of their birthplaces.[14] But despite the male military experience, the villager was largely sedentary, and his mental horizons tended to coincide with the geographical horizon. His world was flat and small and monotonous.

The subsistence level of living in the traditional village also had important ramifications. The importance of the individual was as a producing member of the community, regardless of sex. The woman as well as the man was fundamentally a producer, not a consumer, as tends to be the case among large numbers of her counterparts in the West. Among Turkish village women, there was no emphasis on consuming well, only on producing well. The situation surely had a great deal to do with the fact that marriages were arranged between families on an economic basis, not by the boy and girl by reason of emotional attraction. The health and strength and skills of the prospective bride were important, so likewise was the relative economic positions of the two families. The family remained the producing unit until the death of the eldest male member, at which time the sons might divide the family lands and split into separate households. But until that time, sons and their wives and children remained in the household of the sons' father, and the family land was operated as a unit. It was important to the family, then, that the new wife be a productive member — hence, the all important role of the family in arranging marriage. If individuals were permitted to make their own marriage arrangements, emotion might have governed.

Another important aspect of traditional village life was the lack of privacy, such being a result of three factors: the semi-isolation of the village, its compact nature, and its relatively small size. Under these conditions, one could get away with nothing without its being known community-wise. If one knows that his every act, twenty-four hours a day, will be known to the entire community, his behavior is likely to be more circumspect than it might otherwise be. Such was the case in a Turkish village. Significantly, village men tended to behave quite differently when visiting the market town than when in their villages. Drinking and prostitution were exceedingly rare in the village, not so in the town. The point is that in the village deviant behavior could be spotted at once, and enormous social pressure exercised to force the individual back into the accepted pattern of behavior. Even deviation of a constructive nature — useful innovation — was discouraged under these circumstances, and for several good reasons. First, innovation was noted immediately. Second, society and environment bore too close a relationship to permit innovation. The adjustment had been too finely worked out through centuries of trial and error correlation. Innovation could throw the whole system out of adjustment. It was dangerous to experiment. Error could be disastrous; the margin was too small.

This close interrelationship between individual and environment also related to the security provided the individual by traditional village society, a security inherent in relating oneself in a known way to society and environment. In such a well-adapted subsistence economy there was little room for experiment, for deviation from accepted ways. If an individual followed the accepted, he could probably stay alive; if he did not, survival was not at all certain. Here was fundamental wisdom.

The very philosophy of these people was perhaps an adaptation to the environment. Their interpretation of Islam, a folk Islam, differed in some instances quite markedly from the orthodox Islam of the elite. At the village level, religion was highly fatalistic, highly traditional, and associated with massive superstition. There was little room for independent religious thought. Such was not so true of the urban-dwelling religious intelligentsia, for in the city were religious schools wherein theological exploration was taking place — slowly, but exploration and innovation nonetheless. But at the village level a predeterministic philosophy dominated. Every man's fate hung about his neck — and in fact, it did. Given his subsistence level of living, the rigors of life, the unavoidable hardships, and the inability to influence one's economic position by personal effort, this predeterministic philosophy perhaps made possible a maximum of human happiness. This life was but a fleeting moment, and then one moved on to something better so long as he followed the prescribed practices. One could thus derive certain satisfaction and pleasure despite the hardships and difficulties of this life. Adverse weather — or a large family — might wipe out wealth, but not faith.

Moving over into the realm of material culture and the adaptation to environment it represented, one may cite housing as an example. Wood was scarce and expensive, so adobe brick was used. This material provided excellent insulation, which was necessary in this high steppe country where temperature variation was great. There was an interesting relationship between the use of animals for draft power and the fuel burned in village homes. The typical draft animal was the bullock or long-suffering cow. A step toward making agriculture more productive would have been the introduction of good draft horses, thereby cutting the time of cultivation by at least a third, which is important on the Anatolian plateau where the period during which a crop should be planted is limited generally to ten days or two weeks. Difficulty arose, however, from the fact that this was a treeless area. Normally, one could not afford to burn wood for fuel; dried dung was burned instead.[15] Horses did not provide a good fuel, so if horses were substituted for cattle, one was immediately confronted with a difficult problem. One must have fuel. Not only was the climate a rigorous one but there were certain foods — particularly bread — which required heat in the preparation. There is another relevant point: on very cold winter days when the fuel supply was short (a normal situation), animals were brought into the household to provide warmth. Villagers preferred a bullock to the horse, for it generated substantially greater warmth. Granted, this claim was not, to my knowledge, ever put to scientific test, but it is nonetheless true that it is still cited by villagers as a serious obstacle to the substitution of the horse for the bullock or cow. After all, what people *believe* to be true is often more important than objective fact. (One might add that even on a cold winter day it is possible to keep quite comfortable in an adobe home alongside a pair of bullocks.)

Clothing represented another adaptation to environment. Because the villages had little wood, they possessed virtually no furniture; one sat on the floor — hence, the baggy type of trousers worn by both men and women. If one sat on the floor, loosely fitting garments were more comfortable than our more tightly-fitted Western type of dress. Furthermore, in cold weather one simply stuffed the baggy trousers full of leaves, rags or what have you to gain additional insulation.

All these things fit the facts of the physical environment. One might add that certain village practices were *scientifically* sound. For instance, many villagers still wear a heavy band around the middle part of their bodies in all seasons. Doctors working in Turkish villages claim that maintaining a constant temperature around the middle part of the body is probably one of the best home preventives against a variety of stomach and intestinal infections. A basic item of the popular diet has long been yogurt. The milk which goes into yogurt must be boiled, so as to clear it of unwanted bacteria. If not, one simply brews sour milk, not yogurt, for yogurt is in effect a pure culture of a particular bacillus, which is introduced into the pure milk by adding a bit from the last brew. As a matter of fact, villagers rarely drink unboiled milk, and one hears uneducated villagers associate unboiled milk with sickness. There is also a great interest in water in this semiarid country. It is entirely possible that these people have actually developed a highly discriminating taste for water. Sometimes, they go miles out of their way to drink from a particularly good spring where the water is reported to be particularly tasty. The uninitiated Westerner is unable to discern any difference in taste, which fact leads one to suspect that in some instances the Turkish villager may be able to taste pollution where the alien cannot. In Anatolia, one is occasionally warned away from springs with the words, "Don't drink there; you'll get ill. The water tastes bad." Such a development of taste would not be the first example of extraordinary development of a sensory perception. Many village practices are related to good health, practices which perhaps were developed through trial and error association over centuries of experience. Here, then, is another element of security. One has faith in the traditional: it works, the new might not. There is no reason to believe that these attitudes are of recent origin.

Apart from these elements of security, there was an informal social security system operating in these rural communities. The extended family groups within the village tended to be interrelated, and within each group the individual had a well-defined place. A few years ago a visitor in a back country village asked whether there were any outsiders residing there. Two families were so designated, although it developed that they had lived in the community for two generations. They were still deemed outsiders because they were not related closely to one of the two or three main family groups forming the village, the so-called *kabile* (or in some areas, *sulale*), which was defined as a patrilineal group to the depth of two or three generations. The membership of a *kabile* was known. The men of a given *kabile* might pass their idle hours together, and on certain issues a *kabile* would fight as a unit. Within this structure, the individual was taken care of. He would not be allowed to starve or die of exposure. The individual would be provided for in time of crisis by his immediate family, by his *kabile,* or by the village if need be. There was a very real element of security here.[16]

The word *kabile* is also said to mean, in the Kurdish context, "medium tribe" as compared with *asayir* or "great tribe" and *taife* or "small tribe." *Asayir* are subdivided into *kabile* and *taife*.[17] It may be that the term *kabile* is used by communities that were nomadic until relatively recently, *sulale* by others.

One author, in speaking of preindustrial society, has written:

> . . . The physical elements were the main source of his sorrows as of his joy. Religion was the source of his consolation and of his terrors. One of the chief offices of the priest was not only to reconcile man with his gods, but also to influence the forces of nature in his favor. Floods, famines, fires, crop failures, earthquakes, the majestic immensity of the heavens and the overpowering violence of storms, all drove home the lesson that, by comparison, he was pygmy grudgingly permitted a brief life, a fleeting smile, and then oblivion.
>
> In these circumstances, the social organism was an instrument forged by man to hold in check the forces of nature. It was as much a tool evolved in the struggle for existence as the hoe with which he tilled the fields or the weapon with which he hunted wild animals or other men. The individual and society were not only inseparable from each other but it would never occur to him that it could be otherwise. Exile was death, physical and spiritual. Between him and the terrors of nature stood only his tribe, his clan, his small society. Inside it he was warm, comforted and to some extent safe. Outside, he was nothing.[18]

This statement accurately describes the bond between individual and village in the traditional Anatolian setting.

Another element, which again made for individual security, was the high degree of social harmony existing in traditional Turkish village society. The concept of role conflict is useful in pointing up this attribute. In American society, the individual participates in a wide range of activities and organizations. He is asked to give his money or time, or both, to a variety of institutions and activities. He has conflicting obligations running out in many directions because he identifies himself with many groups, all with somewhat different goals. In the traditional Turkish village, the situation was quite different. There were few institutions demanding an individual's loyalty. There was the immediate family, the *kabile,* and the village itself. A man felt loyalty to the village; he might fight to defend it. For instance, if the land of one villager were in danger of being taken over by someone in another village, the villagers might meet en masse in battle. There was also loyalty to Islam and possibly to a particular religious sect. Of only very recent origin is loyalty to a political state, but this attachment as something distinct was not felt in the older, traditional community where religion and state were considered as one. Even recently, when asked what choice they would make if the state required one course of action and their religion a conflicting one, villagers were unable to answer. The situation was such an unthinkable one, they were incapable of imagining it. Lerner reports in a study of Turkish society, "The consistent incapacity to link oneself to the outer world underlay most of the regularly recurring differences among respondents (i.e., modernists, transitionalists, and traditionalists) . . . The most satisfactory way of accounting for these differences was the personality variable of empathy," which Lerner found very low among traditionalist groups in Turkey.[19]

There was a feeling of loyalty to the head of the empire — the sultan-caliph — by reason of his religious status. Within the traditional village, there were no formal voluntary social organizations. The web of an individual's responsibilities and obligations was remarkably simple and well defined. All possible conflict between loyalties to family and village and religion had been long since resolved through religiously sanctioned formulas. There were few calls for individual decisions of any importance, religious law and custom having been worked out in great detail. When a situation involving possible conflict of loyalty arose, the individual followed certain prescribed paths of action. He was not called upon to make an individual decision. This manner of behavior induced a mentality quite different from that prevailing in American society, for instance, where the individual is caught daily in a web of conflicting loyalties demanding individual decision.

One might suggest that this traditionalizing of decision-making had much to do with the relative inability of the villager to empathize, that is, to identify himself with new aspects of his environment, to project himself into new or imaginary situations, or to enlarge his own identity by attributing to himself desirable attributes of something or somebody else.[20] All conceivable situations of conflict and tension had been defined and systematically resolved. Also, the physical and psychic immobility of the individual in this land-bound, illiterate, isolated, poor and status-bound society was such as to make an ability to empathize dysfunctional. If the shepherd could really have imagined himself as the general of an army, he would have been much less resigned to his hard, lonely fate among the hills than he was. As Lerner reports, posing such a role-playing situation to the shepherd was likely to get the response, "My God! How can you say such a thing?" [21]

The traditional Turkish village was, of course, overwhelmingly illiterate. There were very few literate men, virtually no literate women. The few rural literates who did exist were either religious or administrative officials of some sort. The fact of illiteracy had important consequences. In the first place, memory was vastly more important than in a literate society. Wisdom could only come about through the accumulation of either one's own remembered experience or that recounted by others and remembered. There were no short cuts by substituting book learning or note taking for remembered experience. Consequently, knowledge tended to be associated with age, and hence, great prestige for age was to be expected. Surely, there was considerable validity in the relationship between illiteracy and patriarchal authoritarianism.

Literacy was often used merely as a tool for memorization, for example, memorization of the Koran. As a matter of fact, education itself tended to be equated with religious education. The very word for education had a religious connotation about it, and also a connotation of rote memorization. The educated villager was one who could quote the Koran at great length, and secondly, might also claim to read it. This grass roots association between formal education and rote memorization was one of long standing, and one difficult to break even as new secular education began to enter the picture in the 1930's.

The religious influence in village life has been mentioned in several contexts. Perhaps the overriding philosophy of fatalism and predeterminism of folk Islam was in part a rationalization of the rigors of the environment and the inability of the individual to control the environment effectively so as to improve his lot in life. After all, thanks to the operation of Islamic law, by which a family's land was broken up into small fragments and distributed to designated heirs, a family could be reduced from riches to rags in a single generation if it were so unfortunate as to beget many sons. As an example: assume that a man died leaving a wife, two sons, two daughters, a father, a brother, and a first cousin. The brother and first cousin received nothing; the first was excluded by the father (also by the son) and the cousin, by the mother. Shares to the others would be: 3/31 to the wife, 4/31 to the father, 4/31 to each of the two daughters, and 8/31 to each of the two sons. Although the foregoing was the division according to sophisticated Hanefi law, the actual practice in many Turkish villages was to exclude the daughters entirely. There seems to have been a regional difference in this regard.

The head of a household could not dispose of more than one-third of his property by will, and in fact wills were virtually unknown in the traditional village. During the era of Ottoman ascendancy, even the landed noble class did not hold land in perpetuity; real estate generally reverted to the state upon the death of the title holder. One owned only the right to use land. Not until later, when the central power could no longer control, did a landed aristocracy appear in the true sense of the word.[22]

Private ownership — that is, *family*-ownership or use — of property was another important aspect of traditional village society. There was very little communal activity of an economic nature. Surely the most important factor in determining the status of a given individual or family was the ownership of (or right to use) land and secondarily, the ownership of animals. (The only real challenge to status established on such a basis was religious learning, piety, and military exploit.) Because a family could be reduced in wealth very quickly, the traditional society was in a certain sense an open society. Generally speaking, there was no landed aristocracy in the interior rural areas. (An aristocracy by blood was virtually unknown in most of Anatolia until very late, although in some cases large land-wealthy families were able to maintain their power. For the most part they did not live in the villages; they identified themselves with the towns. And for reasons already explained, most of the landed aristocracy was far removed from the seat of central power in Istanbul.) There was, therefore, good reason for this emphasis on the *private* ownership of land, for land was in fact the only meaningful wealth of the Turk, the only form of wealth that could assure a living. It gave a person security of life despite war, economic crisis, unemployment, currency debasement, inflation. The land was still there; one could still eat. Without effective law and order, without adequate security of the market place, without enforceable commercial codes, all forms of wealth that were not themselves capable of sustaining life were of low value.

As already suggested, the individual villager existed primarily as a member of the extended family unit. Traditionally, what the eldest male member of a Turkish family group said was law, though not without prior discussion, for the family council was likewise part of Turkish tradition. But finally, after everybody — that is, the men — had spoken their pieces, the eldest male member articulated the consensus and further discussion was unwelcome. The village tended to fall into a similar pattern in that there was an all-male council of village elders on which the heads of the most important families sat. The elder having the highest prestige — generally by reason of landed wealth — acted as the village leader or headman. The council concerned itself with resolving personal disputes and keeping the peace, employing a village watchman, herdsman, and religious leader, determining water rights, and deceiving agents of the central government.

There were several reasons for this authoritarian organization. First, there was the disinclination to break up the family land holdings so long as the central family authority still existed, that is, so long as the father was living; fragmentation of land was something to be avoided. Further reasons were the high labor requirement at certain points in the agricultural cycle and the occupational specialization as between men and women. The labor requirement in Anatolian agriculture, given dry-grain farming and no machines, was very great in certain seasons of the year, which fact meant that it was to the economic advantage of a household to operate all the land it possessed as a unit as long as possible. The authoritarian nature of the village likewise had something to do with the isolation of the village and the constant threat of crisis or emergency implicit in that isolation. The fact of subsistence living also carried a constant threat of insufficiency. One suspects that there was a close relationship between these conditions and the authoritarian nature of rural society of Turkey.

Another important point was the social segregation of the sexes in a Turkish village community. This situation arose out of the belief that women were inherently inferior to men in intellectual capacity, wisdom, and morality. The very word used for woman in the Turkish village, *eksik,* meant something which was lacking or deficient. Not so long ago in a central Turkish village a school was opened for the first time. One village girl enrolled. Everyone seemed to find her effort vastly amusing; she could not be expected to compete intellectually with the boys. As a matter of fact, she did not do too well, all of which tended to drive home the point. Traditionally, village women accepted this assessment of their capabilities. They had been conditioned by society to assume their inferiority; they had no reason to doubt it.

Although rationalized in religious terms, this belief in female inferiority perhaps had some functional basis in the social structure, for instance in the institution of marriage. We have said that a woman's value lay chiefly in her productive capacity, both in terms of her immediate labor and in producing additional labor. If a family household were going to lose a productive member, it naturally wished to be compensated. And this was precisely what happened when a marriage was arranged between two Turkish village families. Because the bride moved into her husband's family household, his family compensated the family of the girl for the loss, in that a bride price was paid. Women accepted this type of barter, because they were taught to accept unquestioningly the authority of the family and the fact of their own inferiority. (Of recent years, due to increased use of machines and growing pressure of population, large families are often more of an encumbrance than a help. Their labor is no longer needed. Still the practice of bride price continues, with much hardship, even though its economic justification is no longer as compelling.) The bride price had a further function of making divorce or separation difficult and hence, the family more stable. Under Islamic law it was exceedingly easy for the husband to divorce his wife. But under the bride price system remarriage by the man necessitated the payment of another bride price. His family was not likely to look kindly upon this unnecessary drain upon its limited resources. Also, at the time of marriage, the girl's family donated a substantial dowry of household goods which the bride took with her to her husband's household. If her husband divorced her, his family was obliged to return the dowry. The girl's family would, of course, likewise resist a divorce, because in such event the family was theoretically required to return the bride price. Her family would have much leverage in this regard if the separation had been initiated by the wife, for in the village there was no place for her to go except to return to her father's household. Otherwise, she became an outcast and, in the end, would probably have to leave the village — which was unthinkable.

In fact, by reason of the extended family household and the segregation of the sexes within that household, man and wife infrequently fell out by reason of social incompatibility. Social compatibility in the Western sense was not expected as an integral part of marriage. The man spent his idle hours with other men, the wife, with other women. Given the expense attending a village wedding and the importance of the extended family as an economic *unit,* it was important that divorce or separation be held to a minimum — *family* interests were very directly involved, not only those of the man and wife. Hence, we can deduce one reason for the social segregation of men and women in the traditional village. And the whole structure of relationships was, of course, supported by Islamic law, which fact made change difficult even long after the structure ceased to have relevance to the facts of Anatolian village life. In several ways, then, the institution of marriage itself was in a very real sense an adaptation — an adaptation to economic realities.

In recent years, as the village began to rise off the subsistence level, as improved communication made the villagers increasingly aware of Western society, and as village women began to realize that they were not intellectually and spiritually man's inferior, the traditional system of marriage began to break down. One measure of such change has been the increased number of elopements reported in the villages. Up until very recently the concept of romantic love — the emotional attraction between two persons — was not permitted to play a large part in the arrangement of marriages. There was a curious paradox here, for the folklore of Turkey was full of poetry picturing romantic love, an emotion which seemed to bear such little relevance to traditional practices. One wandering folk minstrel told me some years ago that people think and talk about that which they have least — an explanation which left me somewhat less than satisfied.[23] Perhaps a better explanation is that the concept of romantic love is part of Persian mysticism, which meant that the romantic love in Turkish folk literature was really a portrayal of an ideal that was impossible to obtain, specifically identity or union with Allah, with God. Perhaps that is what the minstrel was saying. One should add that the harsh facts of marriage in the traditional village were often tempered by the fact that prospective bride and groom frequently knew one another, and their reaction to the proposed match was taken into consideration by their respective families, particularly on the girl's side, although it would rarely have occurred to her to act contrary to her father's will in any event.

All of these elements of traditional village society added up to an enormously stable, tradition-bound and highly conservative community, one exceedingly resistant to change on any level. The satisfactory resolution of conflict made it unlikely that any significant number of deviant personalities would appear. Children felt that the roles and attitudes of their parents were satisfying, and thus they offered little resistance to the assumption of identical roles and attitudes. The system was stable and self-perpetuating.

Thus it was that Kemal would have to launch his resistance-reform movement on the basis of a society whose fundamental units — family and village — were illiberal and reactionary in the sense that *individual* decision counted for little and innovation was considered dangerous. The individual existed as a member of a group, though up to the point of decision by family or village elders he might express an opinion. Everywhere, women were far behind men in opportunity and accomplishment. Their activities, their values, and even their language differed from those of male society. At the same time this was, in a way, an open society — at least, the male half. The folklore was full of beggars and poor village boys who rose to high position, and there was just enough reality in this concept of upward mobility (for example, in the merit system of the Ottoman army and bureaucracy, particularly in the Janissary corps) to give it some force as an ideal.

(The Janissary corps refers to an elite body (created in 1362) of trained, professional soldiers and administrators forcibly recruited as children from non-Moslem groups, converted to Islam, and trained at state expense to the limits of their abilities. The most talented achieved high office, although in a sense they remained "slaves" of the sultan. Ottoman historian Paul Wittek observed in lecture,[24] "By the 16th Century, we can say without any hesitation that the Turkish state was run by non-Turks." Initially prohibited from marriage and promoted on the basis of loyalty and merit, the corps slowly degenerated into a corrupt, self-perpetuating body disinclined to take the field in any military engagement. As such, it became a factor in the decline of Ottoman power and an active agent against change and reform, even mutinying against the sultan on occasions. The corps was finally liquidated by Sultan Mohammed II in 1826.[25])

The traditional village was a society in which the pattern of mutual assistance within kinship groups was strong. These facts of traditional life lent some support for the growth of a more dynamic, liberal society, though perhaps structured quite differently from what we know.

TRADITIONAL TOWN SOCIETY

Kemal's problem was not limited to traditional village society; there was also the provincial town, which in many respects was even more resistant to change than the village. The small town was of signal importance to Kemal, for it constituted the link between any *national* leadership and the mass of people — the villagers. The Turkey of 1919, judging by the 1927 census (the first of republican Turkey), included fifty-two towns with a population of 10,000 persons or more and five cities (Bursa, Adana, Izmir, Ankara, Istanbul).[26]

A town was socially and functionally distinct from the village. Socially, it was very much more complicated. Inhabitants were not interrelated, although typically three or four large landowning families dominated town society life. The landed wealth of many of these families had its origin in grants of land from the sultan, so loyalty to the sultan represented a vested interest. Functionally, a town was differentiated into a number of distinct groups: government administrators, military officers, craftsmen, merchants, landowners, professional persons (that is, lawyers, doctors, teachers), religious functionaries, soldiers, and laborers. For reasons already discussed — specifically, greater physical mobility and exposure to Western learning — the military officer and professional groups tended to be more of an *avant garde* culturally than the rest. Here was the growth ring on the provincial level, some of whom had earlier associated themselves with the Committee for Union and Progress before its advent to power. Those engaged in crafts and commerce were tightly organized into guilds and associations of religious as well as economic significance. Heavily influenced by religious leaders and economically based on the status quo, these groups were resistant to social change. They tended to block national economic integration, for they feared outside competition and the challenge to their authority inherent in that competition. Their conservatism was supported by the larger landowners and religious leaders, who likewise gained authority and prestige in the relative isolation of the provincial town.

Together, this small town "middle class" provided the hard core of reaction to Kemal's later social innovations. It was their women, for example, who were kept behind shuttered windows and permitted to venture into public only behind a veil and cloaked in the all-encompassing, shapeless black gown, the *çarşaf*. It was this group which supported some of the more fanatic of the religious sects. The status of this middle class derived from traditional relationships which had been solidified by religious sanction and behind which stood the awesome authority of the sultan-caliph. And Kemal was soon to be declared an outlaw by that sultan-caliph.

The craftsmen, despite their religiously significant *esnaf* or guilds, were perhaps the most vulnerable to change, for by 1919 there was already some awareness of, and an interest in, technological innovation, particularly by those already skilled in the use of modern devices, such as in communications. Laborers, on the other hand, tended to be ex-villagers who were simply biding their time until they could amass the means of returning to the very much more satisfying surrounding of their home village. Few conceived of themselves as permanent town dwellers.

Generally, Kemal could anticipate an effort on the part of most town dwellers to cling to traditional values and social structure and to regard their position as a buffer between national authority and village society. Any effort by a national leader to short-circuit this hierarchy of authority by appealing directly to the masses would be deeply resented. One Turkish scholar could still observe as of 1960, "The town is the cradle of dogmatism, of ossified Islamic concepts, which make it an almost invulnerable fortress of conservatism." [27] Something of the relationship between town and village is contained in this comment:

> The villager has some relative or close friend, often a storekeeper, in a nearby town. He will get in touch with one of them and seek advice, especially the latter, every time he comes into town for shopping or for government business, or whenever he has to make an important decision.[28]

Resistance could be anticipated to any reform movement that would move the townsman out of this key role. Later, Kemal was to be confronted by many local insurrections against his revolutionary regime, often incited by town dwellers. Even during the War of Independence against the Greeks, Kemal faced opposition from those who refused to recognize his authority to command in the absence of a valid commission from the sultan.

One of Turkey's leading novelists of the republican era, Yakup Kadri Karaosmanoğlu, wrote of the resistance in Anatolia to Kemal's national struggle in his novel *Yaban* (Istanbul: Remzi Kitabevi, 1945). His hero vigorously condemns the readiness of the religious officials and wealthy to cooperate with the enemy (that is, the Greeks). The following gives the flavor of the volume:

> What do I see? Anatolia. This is the place which breeds and raises the *müftü*'s [local religious officials] who teach the enemy, the town aristocrats who pillage their neighbors' possessions and seize all, the loose women who embrace army deserters, the spurious religious devotees who collapse of syphilis, the white bearded preachers who pursue boys at the mosque fountain. Here is crushed the head of Turkish youth which are filled with so many ideas and hopes . . . Here, many of those who protected the defenders of the fatherland facing the enemy have been stabbed in the back with a dagger. Here, how many times was the road to national independence blocked? (p. 95)

AN EVALUATION

In the Turkey of 1919, one thus moved in several different worlds. This was not one nation, it was many: Ottoman and Moslem, Sunni and Shiite, Turkish and non-Turkish, male and female, city and village. Other than the dubious ties of religion and region, there were no common allegiances to which the people responded, except perhaps at the very top to the person of the *padishah,* a term used reverently for the sultan himself. Herein lay one reason why it was so difficult to abolish the sultanate: it was the symbol that held many diverse groups together in common loyalty. But there was one powerful negative force that could generate and direct enormous collective energy — a Christian invasion of Anatolia. Perhaps Kemal was not too unhappy over the news of the Greek invasion through Izmir which greeted him at Samsun.

Still other problems must have plagued Kemal's mind.

Economically, the country seemed in hopeless condition. There was, in 1919, virtually no modern industry, except a very few foreign-owned plants and utilities in the Istanbul and Izmir areas — largely in the Allied-controlled areas. In agriculture, almost no machinery was used, and farming practices followed the same cycle that had prevailed for many centuries. The economic basis for a modern state was plainly not visible. And worse, the people were held within the grip of highly traditional and fatalistic religions, whatever the sectarian differences in theology and ritual might be. But there is a relevant point to be made here. Fatalism or predestinationism can have two effects: it may spur a rising people to enormous effort because of conviction in their manifest destiny to become superior; or in the face of reverses, the same philosophy may provide rationalization for resignation to defeat and inactivity. There is nothing anyone can do about the course of events. It is Allah's will.

Therefore, in virtually all respects except their loyalty to a sultan-caliph, their misery, and their rancor against

Christian invaders, Kemal faced a divided population, and one sunk in preindustrial poverty, enervated by religiously justified resignation, and exhausted by seven years of war.

Chapter IV

THE ATATÜRK REVOLUTION

If Kemal were to lead a national movement, first against the Greeks and then to achieve massive reform, he would have to move carefully—one step at a time. He dared not alarm people unduly by talking about future reforms. At the moment, he would concentrate on the immediate threat, the Greek invasion.[1]

KEMAL'S RISE TO POWER

To consolidate his personal power position, clearly he must accomplish several things. The record leads one to believe that Kemal was quite conscious of these and moved deliberately toward their fulfillment:

1. The personal allegiance of the top military commanders and key civilian administrators in Anatolia for a renewed national struggle
2. Control of a united Society for the Defense of the National Rights and other local resistance movements
3. Control of the telegraph system, thereby breaking the sultan's link with Anatolia and assuring his own ability to communicate with the country
4. A dramatic declaration of national aims to attract popular support
5. The reorganization and rearming of troops loyal to his cause
6. Victory in battle against the Greeks.

To carry off such a program successfully, he must pose as a loyal subject of the sultan-caliph carrying out the true desires of the captive monarch who was no longer able to protect the national sovereignty, to act in the national interest, or even to communicate with his people. At the same time, Kemal must so phrase the national aims in the struggle against the Greeks as to make it awkward for the sultan and his government to oppose them openly. But in the end, Kemal felt certain that the Allies would leave no choice to the Istanbul government — that is, to the cabinet of Damad Ferid Pasha. Kemal would then identify the regime as one dominated by traitors and cowards. By thus discrediting the cabinet and appealing directly to the throne, he would demonstrate that the sultan himself was a traitor to the national will in refusing to support the Nationalists. Meanwhile, telegraphic communication between Istanbul and Anatolia would be interrupted. Kemal would still avoid very carefully any hint that he was designing to destroy the ruling institution itself and replace it with a secular government headed by a president — himself. And so he proceeded, step by step, as though he were completely concerned with the immediate problem — the Greek invasion of Anatolia. Doubts as to his ultimate intent expressed by more thoughtful Turks were shunted aside.

Kemal himself claimed later that before leaving Istanbul in 1919 he had resolved to create a new Turkish state — without a sultan-caliph. He likewise admitted deliberate deceit on this score.[2]

One Turkish historian reports that Kemal told Generals Cevat and Fevzi that he was going to Anatolia to establish a "National Administration."[3] Some scholars have questioned the contention that Kemal had conceived of any grand plan as I have suggested here. Rather, they claim, he merely took advantage of opportunities as they presented themselves. It is my opinion that this latter view explains too little and requires the introduction of too many fortuitous happenings.

His uncontested national stature, his demonstrated military leadership, his unyielding nature, and his irresistible persuasiveness enabled Kemal to achieve his first three objectives within weeks of his Samsun landing. Several of the top military commanders, convinced of Kemal's loyalty to the national interests and to the sovereign, joined him in a general call for a united resistance movement.[4] Key among them were two military friends, Generals Ali Fuat Cebesoy and Kâzim Karabekir, who, as army corps commanders in Ankara and Erzurum, respectively, had already created a hospitable climate for a resistance movement. Shortly thereafter, the sultan ordered his arrest, but his personal ties with key commanders held fast. With their support, he was elected chairman of the Eastern Anatolian Society for Defense of the National Rights. Civilian leaders very wisely fell into line, though not until after dangerous opposition in several important areas had been met and overcome. Kemal narrowly missed arrest on at least one occasion. It was probably true that "by and large . . . the civilian support of the early Kemalist movement came from former Unionist politicians and other local notables rather than from local representatives of central authority."[5] Fortunately, most telegraph operators seem to have supported the Nationalist cause from an early date, thereby giving Kemal control over the all important telegraph network.[6] A call for national unity was issued to local resistance groups. Without unity there was obviously no hope, and Kemal was the only rallying point.

The initial statement of national aims was issued from the schoolroom in Erzurum where Kemal and his fellow conspirators in the Eastern Anatolian Society for the Defense of the National Rights met during July 1919. The essence of its resolutions, as later summarized by Kemal, was as follows:[7]

1. The entire country within its national frontiers is an undivided whole. (The frontiers were those implied in the Armistice of Mudros, namely Asia Minor and Istanbul.)
2. In event of the Ottoman Empire's being split up, the nation is to resist unanimously any attempt at occupation or interference by foreigners.
3. Should the government (i.e., that in Istanbul) be incapable of protecting the independence of the nation and the integrity of the country, a provisional government shall be formed for the purpose of safeguarding these aims. This government shall be elected by the national congress [to be called by the Nationalists in Sivas later that year] and, if it should not be sitting at that time, the executive committee shall proceed to elect it.
4. The chief object is to consolidate the national forces into a ruling factor and to establish the will of the nation as the sovereign power.
5. No privileges which could impair our political sovereignty or our social equilibrium shall be granted to the Christian elements.
6. No mandate or protectorate shall be accepted.
7. Everything possible shall be done to secure an im-

mediate meeting of the National Assembly and to establish its control over the proceedings of government.

This last was a reference to the body created under authority of the Constitution of 1876. The sultan, under the eyes of the Allies, was hardly in a position to espouse these aims. Hence, there would ensue a move to form a provisional government elsewhere. And then events would start moving in Kemal's favor, providing the sultan did not join the Nationalists. Kemal must have thought these things through, otherwise the long series of timely "opportunities" becomes inexplicable — opportunities which led in a direct line to the consolidation of Kemal's personal power, to the destruction of the sultanate and caliphate, and to the creation of a republic.

Because the Erzurum session had been of a regional nature, the next step was to secure support for these aims in a meeting of national character. Meanwhile, the Istanbul government declared the entire proceedings unconstitutional and illegal and ordered local authorities to prevent the convening of a national meeting, which was scheduled for September in Sivas. Kemal later confessed, "We chose Ferid Pasha's cabinet alone as our target and pretended that we knew nothing about the complicity of the *Padishah* [i.e., in the effort to prevent the Sivas meeting and to arrest the Nationalist leaders]. Our theory was that the Sovereign had been deceived by the Cabinet and that he himself was in total ignorance of what was really going on." [8] This language is revealing, for by it Kemal admitted to deliberate deceit in respect to his ultimate object. While reaffirming his loyalty to the sultan, Kemal maneuvered so as to make the sultan's position untenable.

The Sivas Congress, officially known as the Assembly

for Defense of the Rights of Anatolia and Rumelia, confirmed the objectives stated in Erzurum now as a national pact[9] and founded a permanent organization under the same name, but known alternately as the Representative Committee of the Sivas Congress, with Kemal as president. The Congress demanded the resignation of Damid Ferid Pasha's cabinet in Istanbul and the convening of the Chamber of Deputies. As anticipated, nothing happened, and the Nationalists severed telegraphic communication with Istanbul, thereby isolating the Istanbul government. Nonetheless, shortly thereafter, a new cabinet (under Ali Riza Pasha) was formed which agreed to the Nationalist demands. Plans were made for elections and the convening of a national assembly in Istanbul. Kemal moved to Ankara and awaited developments, feeling certain that the sultan, under Allied pressure, would have to move against the Assembly, dominated as it would be by aroused Nationalist partisans. The sultan would thus play into Kemal's hands. The Nationalists, winning a large majority in the ensuing elections, assembled in Istanbul to sit in the National Assembly, which was called to order on January 20, 1920. The Nationalist deputies promptly voted to proclaim the statement known as *the* National Pact, which had been drafted initially in Erzurum and rephrased in Sivas. Its main provisions:[10]

1. The destinies of the predominately Arab portions of the Ottoman Empire, plus Western Thrace, should be settled by free vote. The remaining portions inhabited by an Ottoman-Moslem majority (with the exception of Kars, Aradahan and Batum, where another plebiscite might be necessary) formed a whole and did not admit of division

2. Freedom of commerce in the Black Sea Straits was to be permitted so long as the security of Istanbul was maintained
3. Rights of minorities should be assured ("in the belief that Moslem minorities in neighboring countries would have the benefit of the same rights")
4. Turkey should be completely free and independent.

The Allies reacted by placing Istanbul under formal military occupation and exiling all of the Nationalist leaders they could find. The sultan's brother-in-law, Damid Ferid Pasha, was renamed Grand Vizier. He promptly declared the Nationalists to be outlaws, enemies of the sultan, and the *sheikh-ul-Islam* added a powerful propaganda weapon by proclaiming a *fetva* — an interpretation of religious law — on the issue, which likewise condemned the Nationalists.[11]

Thanks to the extreme demands of the Allies and the timidity of the sultan, Kemal was now in a position of power, though not uncontested as both pro-sultan, religiously motivated forces and the Greeks were pressing hard. It was a state of national emergency.

Those assembly members still at large made their way to Ankara where on April 23, 1920, the Grand National Assembly of Turkey convened and elected Kemal as its president. The assembly, at Kemal's bidding, proclaimed:[12]

> The founding of a government is absolutely necessary . . . The real authority is the national will. There is no power superior to the Grand National Assembly. The Assembly embraces both the executive and legislative functions.

Most assuredly with tongue in cheek, Kemal added, "As soon as the Sultan-Caliph is delivered from all pressure and coercion he will take his place within the legislative principles which will be determined by the Assembly." [13] There had been some disquieting rumors that Kemal had been thinking of a republic, with himself as president. (Somehow it escaped most that a republic had already been proclaimed; all that was needed was the name.) He was able to dominate the situation probably only because of the state of national emergency and the fact that many of his would-be rivals had been exiled by the Allies. Also, the sultan's government soon undermined its own popular appeal by signing the Treaty of Sèvres (August 1920),[14] thereby driving many of those civilian authorities and army generals who had been loyal to the sultan up to this point into the Nationalist camp.[15] By the terms of the Treaty of Sèvres, all non-Turkish territories were to be stripped away. An independent Armenia was to be created. The Straits were to be internationalized. Thrace and the Aegean islands were to be Greek. Izmir and its hinterland were to be Greek-administered for five years and then a plebiscite would be held. The Allies thus betrayed the Armistice of Mudros, and the sultan acquiesced. A few weeks before, in June, the Greek army had struck out from Izmir toward the interior. Repeatedly, the Turkish Nationalist forces had to fall back. Elsewhere, the Nationalists were harassed by local revolts,[16] apparently incited by elements supporting the sultan who claimed that Kemal was acting in an unauthorized and irreligious manner. Some of these elements were motivated by national interest, some by religious conviction, some by political ambition, some by Allied pressure and perhaps money.[17] This was the summer of 1920.

During all of these events, and contributing substantially to the worries of the Allies, the Nationalists had been smuggling arms out of Allied depots in Istanbul and elsewhere. The Nationalists had many friends within Istanbul, even in the War Ministry itself. Some military supplies had arrived from the Soviet Union. During the summer of 1919, Kemal had met a Russian general in Anatolia sent to him to offer aid. Kemal accepted the offer of arms, but not of Russian troops.[18] In September 1919, Kemal dispatched a mission to Baku to secure Russian help. This mission made contact with the Baku Communists, who from this time on "played the role of a bridge between the revolutionary proletariat of Moscow and the revolutionary movement in Turkey. Through this bridge connections were established between Moscow and Turkey."[19] In a September 1959 interview, Ismet Inönü told the author that although he had seen some Russian arms during the War for Independence, he had no precise idea as to their amount. He characterized it as small.[20]

Despite these activities, the Turks continued to give ground. The politicians in Ankara grew hysterical, and Kemal was voted full political power. It was only on that basis that he would assume direct military command in the field. Kemal's principal field commander by this time was Ismet Inönü, the man who had been his right hand on the Caucasian front in 1916 and in Arabia in 1917 and 1918. Despite enormous political pressure to mount an offensive, Kemal had used his emergency powers to shield his generals and troops from the politicians. In late August, 1921, the Greek offensive neared Ankara and the sound of heavy guns could be heard in the city. Impatiently, Kemal awaited the best moment to commit his forces to the decisive battle. Taking over field command from Ismet, Kemal himself had assumed full personal responsibility for commanding the final retreat which had brought the Greeks so terrifyingly close to Ankara. With the Greeks only 40 or 50 miles outside the capital, he finally ordered his troops to stand. The Battle of Sakarya began on August 22. By the end of the first week of September the Greeks began to weaken. In another week, they were falling back. One year later they were literally driven into the sea at Izmir, where they were evacuated by Allied ships. The date was September 9, 1922.[21]

This had been total war. Entire villages had been liquidated by the Greeks, and in revenge Greek villages had been annihilated by the Turks. Some antinationalist Turks had cooperated with the Greeks. The Nationalists had retaliated. The civilian population suffered heavily, and the war ended on a note of enormous animosity between Turk and Greek. The other allies had no stomach for an all-out war in Turkey; public opinion at home would not allow it. When the battles began to go against the Greeks, the Allies began to talk to the Nationalist government in Ankara. The first foreign power to recognize the new Turkish Nationalist government was the Soviet Union, with which a treaty was negotiated in March 1921, thereby securing Turkey's eastern frontier and releasing troops for the struggle against the Greeks. Lenin had pronounced the Turkish revolution a genuine "revolutionary movement worthy of support."[22] In October 1921, a separate agreement was reached with the French at which time the French abandoned their Armenian friends in southern Turkey, many of whom had openly supported the French occupation. In October 1922, after the Greek defeat at Izmir and a Turkish advance to the Dardanelles, British, French, and Italian representatives negotiated an agreement at Mudanya with the Turkish Nationalists. In so doing, the Allies acceded to the Turks' military objective — namely, removal of all foreign troops from Anatolia, and from Thrace up to the Maritza River, including the Straits zone and Istanbul.

After the Turkish victory in Anatolia, Turkish forces began to advance on the Dardanelles in order to effect a crossing into Thrace for eventual occupation of Thrace up to the Maritza River, including Istanbul. A British force stood in the way at Çanakkale on the Anatolian side of the Dardanelles, and a Greek army was forming in Thrace. As the Turks advanced cautiously toward the neutralized Straits zone, an Anglo-Turkish war seemed likely. Lloyd George had appealed to the Allied Powers and to the British Dominions to join in the defense of the Straits. But France and Italy refused, and, of the dominions, only Australia and New Zealand responded with interest. The upshot was that the British felt compelled to permit the Turks to walk through their lines; not a shot was fired, for the Turks advanced with weapons reversed. The failure of the British to halt the Turkish advance and the Allied capitulation to Turkish demands at Mudanya brought about a popular clamor in England and the resignation of Lloyd George.[23] The near precipitation of a war by England at Çanakkale, plus the nonparticipation of the dominions in the subsequent negotiations at Lausanne, were the immediate events leading to the Dominion Act of 1925, which in essence recognized the principle that the dominions would accept active obligations only when they had taken part in the negotiations and agreed to the results.

This so-called Armistice of Mudanya was superseded in 1923 by the Treaty of Lausanne.[24] Some have described the Treaty of Lausanne as the best treaty ever won by a defeated nation. But Turkey had never really been defeated — the Ottoman Empire, yes, but not Turkey. The

Allies had not succeeded in controlling the entire country.

At Lausanne, the Turkish delegation — headed by Ismet — willingly gave up all claims to non-Turkish territory, but insisted that all extraterritorial rights in Turkey be abolished. There were to be no reparations. The Straits were to be opened, though not fortified. In short, the Turks were to be undisputed masters of what now constitutes, with some minor exceptions, modern Turkey.

THE TRUE REVOLUTION

The country had been freed of immediate foreign threat. The uniqueness of the Turkish story is what we have come to call the Atatürk Revolution. By reason of his military victory and his organizational backing, Kemal now held effective political power. He had succeeded in at least temporarily establishing a provisional government in Ankara under various pretexts and was ready to set about a series of truly revolutionary moves.[25]

The first thing that had to be done in creating a modern secular Turkey, but which most reform leaders of the past had desisted from saying (or succeeded in doing), was the unseating of religious authority. Virtually the whole structure of the Ottoman state rested upon religious law, even though some modifications in the fields of administrative, commercial, and criminal law had been introduced in the 19th century. But governmental authority itself rested squarely on religious law, which in essence purported to be a logical extension of divinely revealed sources and practices. Islamic law, of course, went back to the Koran and Propet Mohammed. True, there had been a tremendous extension of law from the time of the earliest Islamic communities, but it was rationalized in terms of a logical extension of the divine revelations contained in the Koran and of the early practices of Mohammed and his immediate colleagues. This was no man-made law; it could not be changed by act of parliament. Granted, it could be — and was — changed, but slowly, through the consensus of the learned religious men of Islam. Later, the law was expanded from time to time through administrative practice or parliamentary act, such as the introduction of commercial law.[26] But the fundamental structure of personal law was religious, and the very authority of the state rested upon religious justification. The sultan was the head of state, and at the same time, the caliph — the recognized head of the orthodox Sunni Moslem community.[27] Obviously, in order to create a modern, progressive secular state, this whole structure had to be swept away. But Kemal moved carefully, because he knew full well the power of these age-old institutions. The inertia of tradition and religion can be very great.

In January 1921, well before the fighting was over, Kemal pressed the provisional assembly in Ankara into enacting a constitution (*Kanun-i Esasî*) which provided for popular sovereignty, a parliament as the only representative of the nation and elected by manhood suffrage, a responsible ministry, and a president with extensive power.[28] But Kemal refrained from using the word "republic," and he deliberately led many to believe that this law was only a stopgap measure until independence had been won and the sultan could be freed from Allied control.[29]

But on November 1, 1922, six weeks after the fighting ended and before the sultan in Istanbul had a chance of freeing himself from the stigma attaching to him by reason of his apparent cooperation with the Allied powers (witness his signing the disgraceful Treaty of Sèvres), Kemal moved to abolish the sultanate. His hand was forced by Allied moves to invite the sultan's government to send representatives to the peace conference in Lausanne. Kemal wished only Nationalists to be present. The principal reason he gave for eliminating the sultanate was that the incumbent sultan had been a traitor to Turkey and was no longer able to represent the will of the Turkish state. The provisional assembly in Ankara more nearly represented the people of Turkey. In fact, the Constitution enacted 21 months before had declared popular sovereignty and had invested the Assembly with all government authority. Therefore, there was no room for the sultanate although the caliphate might stay. Some objected that this was not what the "Constitutional Law" had intended. But by dint of much arguing, and some questionable parliamentary tactics in which a threat of force was implied, Kemal was able to drive his point home and persuade the Ankara assembly to do his bidding. Three weeks later, the Lausanne Conference convened, and only the Nationalists were represented. The Ankara assembly had thus gained international recognition as *the* government of Turkey.

But the caliphate remained, which meant that the two offices — caliphate and sultanate — were now divided; one had been abolished and the other retained. Kemal must have realized that popular opposition to the abolition of the caliphate, the religiously significant office, would be too great at this point to permit a direct attack.

A series of carefully-timed moves now followed, each of which was very logical when looked at from the point of view of Kemal's objective — the creation of a thoroughly modern, strong state. A Turkish republic was proclaimed.

After all, the monarchy had been removed and something had to replace it — so, enter the Republic. In fact, as already pointed out, Turkey was a republic in spirit from the day the National Assembly recognized unlimited popular sovereignty. These moves were not easily accomplished. Substantial opposition developed within the more conservative groups, both within the National Assembly in Ankara and without. It was only because Kemal had consolidated his military power and his political authority through skillful maneuver and organization that he was able to hold on. But even so, he was hesitant to use too much overt force. The rank-and-file of the army and police might not support his radical reforms. Also, Turkey was not a homogeneous country. There were many diverse groups, and it was impossible for Kemal in this short period of time to control all effectively. At best, it was difficult to gain effective control over a sprawling village agricultural society; the state of communications and the law-enforcing agencies were not such as to make control easy to accomplish. Various devices were used — the army command, the so-called tribunals of independence, a political party.

On March 3, 1924, the inevitable move came: the caliphate was abolished.[30] In a recent book of memoirs, General Kâzim Karabekir makes the undocumented claim that Kemal had entertained ambitions of making himself sultan and caliph.[31] In his famous speech of October 1927, Kemal declared, "Certain persons who wrongly believed that it was necessary, for religious and political reasons, to maintain the Caliphate proposed at the last moment when the decisions were to be taken that I should assume the office of Caliph. I immediately gave a negative reply to these men."[32] I find Karabekir's claim untenable, for such an ambition on the part of Kemal would have not only been out of character; it would have been wholly inconsistent with his behavior both before and after the abolition of the caliphate and it would render meaningless many of the things Kemal did.

The abolition of the caliphate was a blow to many Turks, and large-scale opposition on the grass roots level could be anticipated. Kemal realized that he could not do away with the caliphate without softening up various elements ahead of time. The story is that before publicly stating his case against the caliphate, Kemal called into session in a small town on the Sea of Marmara a group of the nation's leading newspaper editors. They had no advance knowledge of what the meeting was to be about; they simply knew that Kemal had requested their presence. Best they go. Anyway, it might be a good story, and it was. The journalists convened, the doors were locked, and for many hours Kemal talked. He declared that the only move making possible the emergence of a modern Turkish state and continued independence of Turkey was the abolition of the caliphate. The journalists were stunned. The debate lasted for a day and a half, and finally the last die-hard was convinced. The recollections of one of the participants of this meeting are of value in understanding what happened.[33]

This conversation, barely outlined here, but continued over many cups of Turkish coffee and hasty common meals, gave not one of us any feeling of fatigue. We were all conscious that the wheels of history were turning with an overwhelming speed in this very room. A society, medieval in its make-up and outlook in spite of superficial changes, was about to be forced, by absolutely unique methods, into the modern mold of the era of reason, and into a more balanced order than any society had been previously able to achieve. Throughout history, equally extreme changes had been made high-handedly by dictators; each change was enacted in great secrecy at first; then all publicity media were used to praise convincingly the *fait accompli.*

Mustafa Kemal did not want to dictate; he wished to persuade. The tactics we finally agreed to use were unique. We, in our newspapers, were to attack the government for not realizing the danger to the unity and stability of the country which the continuation of the khalifate constituted. We were to point out that the khalifate was obsolete from the standpoint of a modern Turkey, that the prestige attributed to it was a myth, and that the victory of the Turkish nation would not be complete without a concerted assault on the theocratic influences which blocked progress.

This plan was carried out in a marvelous spirit. We were astonished when we did not encounter the opposition and resistance anticipated. Following this concerted preparation by the press, the law to abolish the khalifate was passed on March 1, 1924; and two days later, laws for the secularization of courts and schools and the abolition of all theological seminaries (to be replaced by a theological faculty at the university) were passed as matters of course. Deportation of all members of the old imperial Ottoman dynasty caused general feelings of joy and relief.

* * * *

A barrage of publicity was fired against the departing dynasty. A sort of magical spell which had protected the palace from being seen realistically suddenly vanished . . .

* * * *

All the scandals and crimes which had been taking place, even in recent times, behind the palace walls were mercilessly divulged. The whole thing presented an abominable picture.

A further step was necessary. Veteran journalist Yalman describes what now transpired:[34]

Even after the abolition of the khalifate, a reference had been left in the constitution to Islam as the "state religion" of Turkey. Elimination of this stipulation was the final stage in Mustafa Kemal's major operation to sever the theocratic grip on public life. When the khalifate was a thing of the past, this incongruity of a state religion was discussed in a press conference. I asked Mustafa Kemal, "Why have you left recognition of a state religion in the constitution so long after a regime based on free reason and full tolerance seems well established?"

"Why don't you attack me in your paper for not being radical and consistent in my acts?" he challenged me.

"I don't feel that it is a proper subject for discussion in a newspaper."

"The moment that you feel it is proper to make this a subject of public discussion, you may rest assured that the provision to which you rightly object will be taken out of our constitution."

As a matter of fact, this last stage of the operation was performed in the constitutional changes of April 15, 1928, so that a regime of secularism in Turkey became complete.

We get a glimpse into the secret of Kemal's success here — patience, timing, singleness of purpose, accurate assessment of persons.

Meanwhile, the entire legal system of the country was shifted from a religious to a secular basis. The basis for such change had been laid with the proclamation of a republic in 1923 and adoption of a republican constitution in 1924. This was a man-made constitution, enacted by the parliament in Ankara without mention of any religious authority (except that Islam remained the state religion). As the basis of national law in a secular state, the constitution defined very generally the rights and obligations of the citizens and the organization of government. In 1926, Western codes of law — civil, criminal, and commercial — were enacted to replace the *sheria*. The test was whether the people could — or would —

shift their loyalties from a divinely ordained authority to one resting on mere popular sovereignty and social contract.[35]

Apart from the secularization of authority, Kemal attempted to achieve a more homogeneous population — racially, culturally, and emotionally. An early move in this direction was the exchange of population with Greece, which eliminated from Turkey a very large share of its Greek ethnic minority, though a substantial community remained in Istanbul.[36] Most of the Armenian minority had already been eliminated.[37] The Arab minority was small, for the Arab lands were gone. The Kurds posed a somewhat more difficult problem, for there were periodic Kurdish revolts up to 1937. The Kurds were Moslem, so there was no religious difference between Turk and Kurd. Even the Shiite-Sunni split crossed the ethnic line. During the 1920's, and indeed part of the 1930's, the principal challenge was simply the maintenance of law and order in the Kurdish areas as the Turks tried to contain the Kurdish nationalist movement. Later, through forced resettlement and education, the back of Kurdish resistance was broken, and today it is probably safe to say that most Kurds are by and large loyal to Turkey.

Part of this general move to create greater unity was the legislation secularizing education, suppressing all religious orders, and forbidding individuals to wear religiously significant clothing. The wearing of religious garb — whether Moslem, Christian, or Hebrew was limited to the highest religious officials of each community (Moslem, Armenian, Greek Orthodox, Hebrew, etc.). The fez, the curious tasseled headgear of the male Moslem, was forbidden. Of the substitution of the hat for the fez, one contemporary observer noted:[38]

In 1925, the fez was abolished. I remember very well the early days at the International College in Smyrna, now Izmir, when one of the students went out on the campus, not in the town but just on the campus, wearing a hat. The whole city was excited. The implication was that to take off the fez and wear a hat was a sign of giving up one's religion. I've been told that one of the most learned men in Turkey never wore a hat and that when he left his library at night, he bundled up his head with a bandage as though he had a terrible toothache. To observers he was obviously in no condition to wear a hat.

But greater homogeneity of race and culture alone was not enough to create new loyalties. Into the situation had to be thrust a positive emotional element, something that would draw and hold popular loyalty. Geographical and political nationalism was the device to which Kemal turned. All the paraphernalia of a nation-state were created — emblems, music, patriotic holidays, statues, and monuments. But it was a race against time. On the one hand, religious activities were held down by police force; on the other, all the instruments under state control were used to create a feeling of political nationalism — sometimes confused with religion, sometimes with race — but still, something very different from either. There was a deliberate and sustained effort to weld together a Turkish nation. History itself was rewritten under Kemal's order, a history calculated to inculcate pride in the ordinary Turk, pride in being a Turk. He was no longer the "terrible Turk," he was the purveyor of a great pre-Islamic civilization in central Asia and, later, a great Islamic civilization in the Middle East which far surpassed the contemporary West in power and the arts. Indeed, the Turk had much in which to take pride. The new historians went beyond the strict compass of truth, although given the circumstances perhaps they were justified in doing so. The Turks were pictured as the creators of the world's first great civilization, the inventors of the first written language of literary value. Though these claims were undoubted exaggerations, it is true that the Turkish language is an antique one and that the Turks are an ancient people who created organized states in central Asia many centuries before their rise to power in the Middle East.[39] Unfortunately, these efforts had produced a strong chauvinistic overtone. An attitude of "Turkey for the Turks" came to dominate the thinking of many, and life in Turkey for foreigners was not always pleasant during the 1920's, 1930's, and early 1940's.

In any event, secular education with a strong nationalist character was thrust into the vacuum left by the abolition of religious influence. In 1924, Kemal invited John Dewey to visit Turkey to study its educational problem and to recommend how the government might best proceed. But even Dewey did not foresee the possibility of, or need for, Kemal's most dramatic reform — the change of the written script (which had been Arabic) to a simple Latin alphabet.[40]

The entire cultural heritage of a people is upset, of course, by a change in the form of writing, but Kemal felt that the advantages outweighed the disadvantages. In the first place, the new nationalist tendencies tended to favor a distinctly Turkish system of writing. The move was in part a nationalistic one. Secondly, the old script was of religious significance. Arabic was the language of the Holy Koran. So the move was also part of the sustained effort to de-emphasize everything religious. Thirdly, the leadership wanted to cut the youth off from the traditional literature, which was overwhelmingly religious, and force the new Turks to read the new national literature of history, science, and technology. And finally, most important of all perhaps, the simplification of the writing system was designed to bring literacy within the grasp of the masses. Overnight, in 1928, the entire country became momentarily illiterate as the old Arabic script was banned from all publications and official communications. Kemal set the pace by touring the country with blackboard and chalk teaching the new alphabet. Words were spelled phonetically. The time and effort required to become literate were radically reduced, and literacy became a reality to many thousands of people. In 1927, only 10 per cent of the Turkish population over the age of 5 was literate. The 1955 figure was 40 per cent. The educational effort had been expanded to include the adults as well. So-called People's Houses sprang up in town after town to constitute local cultural centers. The vehicle for their organization and support was Kemal's Republican Peoples Party, under whose protective mantle the more progressive elements in the provincial towns moved into positions of leadership.

One can discern several threads running all through these early reforms. There was the concerted effort to unseat religious authority and to de-emphasize everything religious. There was the deliberate drive to eliminate divisive influences and symbols and to create a new Turkish political and geographic nationalism. (In 1938 it became illegal to form any society based on religion, race, region, or class.)[41] And, finally, there was the effort to make more effective use of the human and physical resources of the country. There was a sustained push to spread enlightenment and new skills among the people. Women became the legal equals of men, though true equality had to be won — it could not be given. Public health became a matter of national concern, and a start toward the acceptance of modern hygiene and medicine was made. Only by patience, careful timing, political manipulation, persuasion, and occasional use of force were these things accomplished, for even Kemal's great stature was not enough, of itself, to counter the massive resistance that greeted many of these moves. For example, apparently he felt unable to legislate against the wearing of the veil.

Of the effort to make better use of the physical resources of the country, with which the next chapter deals, suffice it to say here that Kemal saw economic development as the foundation of both national defense and social evolution. But just as clearly, he veered away from setting down any ideology. His economic policy — and political as well — was one of expediency. Indeed, the avoidance of a well-defined ideology has been of enormous help to Turkey, for in its absence the Turks could shift gears without an emotional political crisis. They could and did move from nationalistic isolation to international cooperation, from economic liberalism to socialism and back to a mixed economy, and from dictatorship to democracy and back to a controlled democracy — all as the leadership felt that the circumstances demanded. The leaders were not hampered by an ideology which could not be shed after changing circumstances had divorced it from reality.

AN EVALUATION

Politically, Kemal acted very much as a dictator, though certainly not of the modern, totalitarian stamp, in that there continued to be a substantial area of private enterprise and public discussion. Secret police did not terrorize the public, nor were concentration camps important features. Kemal's power rested initially on the army and the Society for the Defense of the Rights of Anatolia and Rumelia. During the War for Independence, he was voted emergency powers by the National Assembly sitting in Ankara. A law on treason was enacted which created summary courts designed to enforce national "security" and empowered to pass the death sentence in cases of "disloyalty." In 1923, the People's Party was founded with Kemal at its head. In 1925, ostensibly to deal with the Kurdish uprising, the Law for the Restoration of Order was passed reactivating two extraordinary "Tribunals of Independence."

But it was no blood bath. One authority reports:[42]

> Reported executions were thirteen for an attempt on Atatürk's life, twenty-eight in a dervish uprising to restore the sheriat law, and not more than ten others. There were, however, more deaths later in a military suppression of Kurd uprising near the eastern border of Turkey.

Despite the fact that the Turkey of the 1920's and 1930's was a one-party state under authoritarian rule, there was room for difference of opinion at certain levels. Violent arguments occasionally erupted in the National Assembly and in the press, arguments directed against Kemal's policies. Not infrequently he answered these accusations personally within the Assembly or used his prime minister, Ismet, to do so, thereby shielding himself. In 1930, Kemal deliberately encouraged an opposition political party to form. It became apparent very quickly, however, that this new second party was a rallying point for elements which, for reasons of sincere conviction or personal gain, wished to jettison many of the basic reforms — secular law, the Latin alphabet, even the republic itself. The body politic was still illiterate, poor, provincial, uneasy. Sensing the drift of events, Kemal moved to squelch the opposition that he himself had created. One wonders whether he really believed that a start toward a multiparty system was practical at this juncture. Perhaps he was proving to some of his critics the danger in lifting political controls or maybe he was merely smoking out into the open some of his more dangerous opponents. One cannot be sure.[43] But one thing is certain, the experiment was ended, and the regime quickly reverted to single-party authoritarianism.

It is quite clear that the members of the Grand National Assembly during Kemal's regime were far better educated than their constituents, were not inclined to identify closely with the districts they represented, and very frequently had been public employees — in government, the military, or in education. They were what one scholar has called the "national-intellectual," as opposed to the local leader. To a significant extent, the sweep of Turkish politics — even up to the present — can be explained in terms of a struggle for political security between a fairly radical national elite and the more conservative local elite, members of which were usually less well educated, less urban, more traditionalist than the former.[44] The local elite were also a much less cohesive group.

Political liberalism was impossible so long as a large part of the population — probably the vast majority — denied the very authority of a *secular* government to rule and felt no loyalty other than to religion, region, race, and community. Liberalism — democracy — would have merely meant the collapse of the whole fabric of the revolution and either reinstitution of theocracy or a general civil war — minority pitted against minority or region against region. Certainly the development of Turkey as a modern, progressive state would have been set back many, many years.

Kemal was an authoritarian ruler, but, unlike some, his record was unstained by personal corruption. There seems little doubt that he was motivated by great ideals and not merely by a desire for personal power. The ideals toward which he strove were: (1) the creation of a national political state in full possession of its sovereign powers; (2) the development of some element of national power and international stature so that Turkey might have a chance to live; (3) a steady advance to a western standard of living by marshaling the physical and human resources of the country; (4) a slow but continued movement toward more liberal political and economic institutions. Perhaps Kemal died at the right time, in 1938, for it is difficult to see the emergence of a democratic state taking place under his leadership even though he himself had this vision.

Periodically, Kemal was bitterly denounced in the West. He had thwarted Allied hopes of taking over Turkey; he had accepted aid from the Russian Bolsheviks; he had threatened large European vested interests; he had taken over control of the Black Sea Straits, a vital waterway; and he had become a dictator in a socialistically inclined state. Clearly, his was not a regime to be trusted. What most contemporary observers seemed to miss was the fact that occasionally a corrupt self-seeking elite may have to be overthrown violently, and an evolution toward a greater recognition of human dignity set in motion by authoritarian devices. If such a revolution takes hold, it probably means that the people were ready. In Turkey, the Atatürk reforms reached deeper and deeper into

Turkish society as time moved forward, not only in outward form but in the very thinking of the people. Unconsciously, the Turks were ready for change — as their ultimate acceptance of change indicated.

The great man died in 1938 after a serious illness, perhaps brought on by his periodic debauchery — for there is much in Mustafa Kemal Atatürk that one cannot admire. During these final months, there was an apparent falling-out between him and Ismet Inönü, his closest friend and chief military commander during Turkey's War for Independence. We are not quite certain of the reason for that falling-out; perhaps the crowd of hangers-on deliberately conspired to separate the two. (Or perhaps the falling-out was part of a deliberate act designed to free Ismet so as to place him in a better position to mend his political fences and assure himself of the presidency upon his mentor's death.

In a personal interview in September 1959, Ismet told the author that the falling-out had occurred over a relatively trivial matter. Ismet felt that Kemal, wittingly or not, had so undermined his position in the government that he (Ismet) had felt compelled to resign. One received the feeling from Ismet's words that he felt Kemal's position had become brittle and irrational during those last months because of Kemal's illness. Ismet happened to be the victim. In any event, Celal Bayar, destined to be Turkey's third president, replaced Inönü as Prime Minister.

Atatürk remains the great national hero — the Turkish George Washington, Thomas Jefferson, Abraham Lincoln, and Franklin Roosevelt combined in one. On anniversaries of his death, the entire Turkish press still borders its front pages with black. His body now rests in state in a great mausoleum crowning one of the hills of Ankara. Some thought this grand edifice to be an unnecessary extravagance for a poor nation such as Turkey. But as one watches the common folk come before Kemal's tomb, hat in hand, eyes full of emotion, to stand in silent reverence, there is no doubt about the value of this symbol in the continuing process of building a modern Turkish state. Atatürk is still the driving spirit behind the total and permanent revolution that continues to move inside Turkey.[45]

Chapter V

ECONOMIC DEVELOPMENT TO 1945

THE attitude of Turkey's leaders, and more recently of a good share of the Turkish people, toward economic development has been compounded of two major ingredients: an immediate demand for the wherewithal to prevent a power vacuum in Turkey and a long-run desire to catch up with the West in material well-being.

Evidence indicates that Kemal began moving toward these goals almost from the start of his regime. These two felt needs of the Turkish leaders were closely interrelated, but neither could be ignored. On the one hand, the maintenance of a large modern military establishment was dictated and on the other, a dynamic economy subject to even more rapid growth than those of the West. It was obvious to the leaders of republican Turkey that only by rapid economic advance could the nation maintain her military strength and political stability, neither of which the Turks could do without if they hoped to stay alive and in possession of their sovereign rights. Economic development was therefore made doubly difficult by the coincidental heavy military outlay. Centuries of misgovernment and foreign control had made it impossible for the human potential of Anatolia to assert itself and for the enlightenment and stimulus of the industrial and scientific revolutions to penetrate. But the idea of greatness nonetheless still lived in the hearts and minds of the people. It was this force that Kemal tapped and which today is driving the Turkish people out of their more comfortable, traditional way of life into an unknown future. It is not that the Turks en masse have consciously chosen to change; it is more as if evolutionary forces had burst in upon Anatolia and caught up the people in a mighty surge of development.

It has been observed that theoretical economists and highly trained technical men from Western Europe and North America often tend to think in a purely Marxian manner — that is, they assume that motivation for all human behavior can be understood in strict economic terms. They imply that if one provides economic opportunity the individual and society will respond in a predictable way. But in fact, one suspects, economic opportunity is but a function of the urge for "economic progress" (that is, an increase in per capita productivity and real income). And surely that urge is an attitude conditioned by historical, cultural, and environmental factors. For a variety of reasons this urge or economic incentive tends to be relatively weak in certain of the underdeveloped countries that tend likewise to be backward, Turkey among them. Here, "underdeveloped" is equated with poverty in the presence of a physical possibility for development and "backward," to a state of mind — attitudes — which have arrested the technical and scientific development of the people. Turkey has been both and, to a considerable degree, still is. In the Turkish connotation, the very word "progress" has been equated with military conquest and expansion and the benefits derived therefore, not with internal economic and social development.

The economic growth of an underdeveloped-backward country, then, rests heavily upon social and personal development. Obviously the evolution of human society moves only so fast as the mind and body of man permit. Regardless of the quantity and quality of machines which may be thrust into a given society, that society will fail to progress if its base of scientific thought and technical knowledge is inadequate, and its incentives and vitality weak. Hence, to talk in terms of long-range economic development in Turkey is ill-conceived unless close attention is likewise given the education, culture, and health of the people, factors which must inevitably condition any economic growth. In Turkish agriculture, for instance, the major bottleneck has been the painful scarcity of enlightened farmers; in industry, of skilled labor and trained management; in business, of qualified executives and effective administrators; and in society at large, of scientific thought and personal initiative.

The economic development pattern of a people is thus shaped in part by historically conditioned attitudes. By this term is meant the sum total of those traditions and customs that stem either from past interaction between environment and society or from inspired and revered leadership, become part of the mores of the society, and pass down from generation to generation through parental-child conditioning in a sort of static equilibrium. The whole structure and residue of Islamic law, for instance, with its divinely-regulated pattern of inheritance and emphasis on private property, is perhaps a case in point. Although it is extremely dangerous to generalize on the poorly understood subject of national attitudes, a partial list of Turkish attitudes bearing directly on the matter of economic development would necessarily include the concept of "manifest destiny," the association of "work" with low prestige, the absence of an hereditary aristocracy, respect for formal education, willingness to assimilate new cultural forms, a fatalistic interpretation of adversity, and great emphasis on military power and the warrior virtues.[1]

Also of undoubted importance in regulating economic change is the form of the social structure within which it moves. We have discussed previously certain aspects of the traditional society, many of which carry over into the contemporary scene. Recent research in Turkey would indicate that even yet "there is good evidence" that Turks feel considerably "less need for achievement than do comparable Americans." The author of this finding concludes that it seems unlikely that there will be any dramatic increase in achievement motivation "unless the extremely dominating role of the father undergoes some change."[2]

KEMAL'S ECONOMIC LEGACY

A proper appreciation of the genesis of the chief policies that have shaped Turkish economic development requires a short excursion into history.

In 1922, a publication of the British community in Istanbul declared, "The experience of nearly three centuries and a half has shown that without these rights . . . (the foreigner) cannot live in Turkey."[3] The rights to which reference was made were the Capitulations. From the start of the Ottoman Empire, various foreign and non-Moslem minorities living within the shadow of its rule were accorded special status. Initially, this situation was felt to be a perfectly normal one in view of the non-Moslem character of the groups concerned. Islamic law, of course, could not properly apply to these people and hence, the law of the land could not protect, judge, or punish them. In the end, however, as Ottoman authority weakened, what was originally considered something in the nature of a disability and a penalty (exclusion from Islamic jurisdiction) turned into an enviable privilege which served as the basis for oppressive commercial and industrial exploitation by foreign business interests. A foreign business house could, for instance, establish itself in the country without leave of the Ottoman government and could organize according to the laws of its own country. It was likewise largely exempt from Ottoman taxation, and its foreign personnel enjoyed inviolability of person and domicile and the jurisdiction of their own consular courts.[4]

Considerably augmenting the influence of the foreign business interests on the internal affairs of the Ottoman state was the difficult financial position in which the Ottoman sultan found himself at the close of the 19th century. Heavy borrowing from European financiers by the Ottoman government between 1854 and 1875 had given rise to a heavy public debt. Most of the funds thus raised were used for economically unproductive purposes, and virtual bankruptcy finally came after the Russo-Turkish War of 1877–1878. At the instigation of foreign bondholders, Sultan Abdul Hamid II, in December 1881, signed a decree which placed the administration of the debt in the hands of the so-called "Council of Administration of the Turkish Debt," predominantly a group of representative foreign creditors.[5] This Council was eventually ceded the right to collect and dispose of revenues derived from taxes on tobacco, salt, wines and spirits, commercial stamps, fish; from the tithes on soil, tobacco and cattle in several provinces; from railway guarantees; and finally from various taxes levied on fishing and hunting, as well as certain surtaxes.[6] The Ottoman government thereby forfeited to a considerable degree control over its financial, commercial and industrial life.

The railway guarantees were particularly onerous. To promote foreign loans for the construction of railways, the Ottoman government had guaranteed to the respective concessionaires that the gross receipts per kilometer of the rail lines concerned would come to a certain amount, depending upon the relative difficulty of construction. To secure these guarantees, the collection of various taxes in the districts through which the lines passed were put in the hands of the Council. These taxes were to make up the difference between the actual gross receipts per kilometer and the amount guaranteed, any balance to revert to the Ottoman treasury.[7]

The Lausanne Treaty (1923) abolished the capitulations system and effected a downward revision in the Ottoman debt inherited by the Turkish Republic. The old Ottoman Empire had been severed into several states, leaving Turkey only a slice of Thrace in Europe and the Anatolian Peninsula in Asia. About 65 per cent of the debt was apportioned to the embryonic republic, the balance being assigned to the other states created out of the imperial fragments. Meanwhile, Kemal's young government in Ankara expanded its area of economic control, and the Council of Administration of the Ottoman Debt was cut off from the source of most of the revenues ceded to it by the Decree of 1881 and subsequent agreements. All effort by the Council to regain these revenues failed, and so ended its effective administration. Although republican Turkey honored the Ottoman obligations assigned to it, later, by various unilateral acts, it succeeded first in suspending payments and then, in 1943, in offering a compulsory redemption of the outstanding bonds at a reduced price. Bonds not presented for redemption during the period of this offer ceased to be listed by the Turkish government as outstanding.

Further breaking the non-Turkish hold over the business and industrial life of the country was the exchange of population with Greece which commenced in 1923 and finally concluded in 1930, a process that eliminated from Turkey virtually all of the Greek population outside of Istanbul. A 1928 census of refugees in Greece reported a total of 914,300 Greeks who had emigrated from Turkey over the 1912–1923 period. Adding the total who had died or moved on in the interim, one student of the population exchange concluded that there must have been about 1.1 million Greek emigrants from Turkey prior to the establishment of the Mixed Commission in 1923 that was to implement the Convention Concerning the Exchange of Greek and Turkish Populations.[8] Under the auspices of the commission, another 189,916 Greeks (through 1925) left Turkey.[9] It is estimated that some 10,000 Turks had left Greece and moved to Turkey during the 1912–1914 period. In 1914, an estimated 115,000 Turks made the move. Under the auspices of the Mixed Commission, another 355,635 moved.[10]

Just prior to this period, Turkey's Armenian population had been reduced through fighting, Turkish reprisals, and deportation from an estimated 1.3 million to something over 100,000, thereby almost eliminating this commercially important group.[11] With these Greeks and Armenians, one might add, went a very substantial proportion of Turkey's skilled craftsmen and business and industrial know-how, although Greek and Armenian communities remained in Istanbul.

The percentage of business and commercial affairs just prior to World War I under direct foreign control was very large, which fact is revealed by statistics relating to the immediate postwar period. For example, of the 13,683 "industrial establishments" (apparently including handicraft shops) reported in 1921 as employing four or more persons, 642 were owned by foreigners.[12] "Of the several hundred [mining] concessions in force on March 31, 1920, there were 282 held by foreigners."[13] The figures shown in Table 1 purport to reflect the situation in 1914.[14] One author notes that these figures "err in neglecting the amount of investments of other nations such as Austria-Hungary, Italy, Russia, and the United States."[15] The same scholar continues, "Prior to World War [I], Turkish private funds were confined largely to two or three steamship lines and to a small share of the Public Debt.[16] Obviously excluded from these calculations was traditional and small-scale industry (for example, grain milling, construction, handicrafts, et cetera).

Table 1

Foreign Capital Invested
(1914)

Sector	*French (per cent)*	*British (per cent)*	*German (per cent)*	*Total (per cent)*
Public debt	60.31	14.36	21.31	95.98
Private enterprise	53.55	13.66	32.77	99.98
Totals	60.08	14.46	25.42	99.96

Foreign groups administered the major ports and owned outright many of the most important mines, all but 13 per cent of the rail lines, and the greater share of the larger public utilities.[17] And much of the rest was owned by Greek, Armenian, and Jewish minorities — that is, until the Armenian troubles had taken their dreadful toll and the exchange of population with Greece had been effected. It is important to note, too, that a major part of the Turkish-owned industry was state-owned even in these prerepublican days. During the 19th century, the Ottoman government had established several plants, and as of 1915, out of 264 industrial establishments, 22 were state property.[18]

Labor, largely unorganized, had been exploited mercilessly by both Turkish and foreign employers. Following the proclamation of a constitutional regime in Turkey in 1908, a rash of strikes had broken out in an effort to better working conditions. Inasmuch as these strikes caused a suspension of work in various important public utilities, the Work Suspension Law of 1909 was passed to prohibit collective action by labor and prevent workers in public service industries from setting up trade unions. The same law created a system of arbitration to solve labor disputes. As the move toward industrialization accelerated during and following World War I, the working class came to occupy a more important place in the life of the country. Nonetheless, because of the ineffectiveness of the legal measures designed to protect workers from exploitation, labor was still unable to gain more favorable conditions. The need for some sort of organization was recognized by Kemal's regime as early as 1922 when the current Minister of Economy declared, "Unless occupational organizations — for instance . . . worker's syndicates . . . are formed, and unless they consider their rights collectively, they (i.e., workers) are going to remain weak." [19] Although the worker's unions set up under the 1921 Ereğli Coal Zone

Law and the Mutual Assistance Reserve Funds of earlier dates appeared as labor organizations, these were not unions in the modern Western sense for they were primarily semiofficial vehicles for providing various types of social assistance to workers, not for collective bargaining.

In 1913, mechanized Turkish industry employed an estimated 17,000 persons in 252 establishments.[20] "Establishment," as used here, is vague, but apparently it includes only productive enterprise taking place in a factory or shop and does not include handcrafts or home industry. Although these figures were based on a count only in the major cities of western Turkey, there were very few industrial establishments located elsewhere at the time. Twenty-eight per cent of these establishments were devoted to food processing — principally milling — and another 28 per cent to textile manufacture.[21] An inventory of the major industrial plants at this time would have included: five armament works, two army supply plants (a cloth mill and a sewing establishment), seven cloth and carpet mills, several leather plants, a shoe factory, five large mining enterprises (Zonguldak coal, Ergani copper, Keçiborlu sulphur, Balya lead, and Eskişehir meerschaum), one glass plant, two ship repair yards, two vegetable oil and soap manufacturing plants, three breweries, and seven power stations.[22] The power stations produced an annual 47 million kilowatts.[23] In addition, of course, were many hundred small, semimechanized flour mills, seed presses, looms, and metalworking shops. The 4,240 kilometers of rail line linked only Istanbul, the Aegean coastal area, and the eastern Mediterranean, but did not serve central Anatolia (except Eskişehir, Afyonkarahĭsar, and Ankara), the Black Sea region, or the Eastern provinces (other than the Russian-built broad gauge line into Kars and the narrow gauge line on west to Erzurum). In 1923, less than 1,000 kilometers of good roads and 8,300 kilometers of broken-surface roads existed.[24] Despite these deficiencies in land transport, an extensive telegraph system linked many parts of the Ottoman Empire. There likewise existed a state shipping line and a private Turkish steamship company, but with a total gross tonnage of only 34,902.[25] In respect to agriculture, all one can say is that modern farm practices and equipment were virtually unknown. The village-farmer pursued his traditional ways.

During World War I and the War of Independence, a great many of these plants and facilities were either destroyed or worn out and the man power of the country weakened. Even some of the rail line had been torn up to furnish steel for munitions. In the Turkey of 1923, a country of perhaps 12.8 million persons, there were all told but 341 mechanized factories, most of them small and ill-equipped.[26] Apparently the definition of a factory used in this tabulation was any location where a stationary power machine was used for production, whatever the number of persons employed. An underdeveloped-backward, village economy, weakened by half a century of foreign control and smashed by a decade of war, was the economic legacy handed down to the Republic of Turkey, the point at which Kemal and his colleagues started trying to build a modern economy.

ÉTATISM[27]

Economic development obviously had to move with political and social reform. Otherwise dangerous stresses and strains would be set up in the body politic, a situation which could degenerate rapidly into a situation of weakness and perhaps even of deterioration. If the level of expectation of the people — encouraged by social reform, education, and improved communication — got too far out of line with the economic capability of meeting expectations, trouble could be anticipated.

Although a military man and no economist, Kemal was from the first keenly aware of the economic needs of the country. On March 1, 1922, even before the end of battle, he set forth a six-point program of economic development. His declared aims were: to resuscitate and modernize agriculture and industry, "which had been ruined and neglected by reason of European rivalry" (There is no convincing evidence that in the absence of European rivalry Turkey's agriculture and industry would have been very different. Kemal was probably making this point largely for propaganda purposes, though he himself may have believed it.) . . . "to develop the forests;" . . . "to nationalize — in accord with the ability of the State — those economic institutions and enterprises most directly concerned with the general welfare;" . . . "to exploit the mineral wealth of the country;" . . . "to protect and reinvigorate existing industry"; and "to consider protective measures for . . . new industry;" . . . "to secure the financing of the national revolution by creating . . . a balanced budget suited to the national economic structure." And in 1923, he declared, "Whatever happens, we must give primary importance to our economy in order to attain a rank worthy of our New Turkey; we live in an economic era."[28] "The New Turkish State," he added, "will not be a world conquering state. The New Turkish State will be an economic state." In 1924, he revealingly observed, "Without economic (development) a weak state cannot be saved from poverty; it cannot attain civilization, comfort, or happiness; it cannot be saved from social and political disease (deterioration) . . . There is no civilized state which does not think of its economy before its army and its fleet." [29]

By reason of the obvious inability (or unwillingness) of native capitalists to finance the purchase of foreign-owned economic enterprises in the country, even those directly concerning the general welfare, it fell to the State to buy out the foreign owners. Thus, the principle of *étatism* (state responsibility and leadership in economic matters) began to take root, its growth in the first instance being limited to establishments formerly foreign-owned and to those state enterprises inherited from Ottoman times.

Meanwhile, private Turkish capital was to create the new national industry and modern agriculture of which Kemal spoke. In 1923, the Agricultural Bank, which had been a central government institution since 1888, was organized as a joint-stock company, shares being distributed to its district offices in proportion to the investment of each. Upon Kemal's personal insistence and partial financing, the Business (*İş*) Bank was organized in 1924 as a privately owned (by public personages), but publicly controlled, popular savings bank. During its early years it was concerned primarily with improving the Zonguldak coal fields. In 1927, a law for the encouragement of private Turkish industry was promulgated by the Grand National Assembly. Under its provisions, State-owned land (up to ten hectares) required for the construction or expansion of an industrial establishment owned by Turkish citizens could be given without charge to the enterprise, so long as it satisfied certain conditions.[30] Accepted enterprises were exempted from a long list of taxes and given a 30 per cent reduction in rail and sea transport rates. The government was empowered to subsidize industrial plants up to 10 per cent of the value of their finished products, and even though imported goods were often cheaper than similar domestic products, city, provincial, and national governments were required to buy home-made commodities. And finally, those who put up an entirely new industry were awarded a 25-year monopoly. During this period, industrial enterprise enjoyed almost complete freedom from state intervention inasmuch as state and private enterprise were accorded similar treatment.[31] A number of private establishments took advantage of these provisions, though their contribution to the economy was relatively small. In 1932, 1,473 establishments employing 55,321 persons were operating under the law. In 1939, only 1,144 were covered; the number of employees is not available. Over this same period the value of production from these plants increased by 140 per cent, but wholesale prices meanwhile rose by 110 per cent. In a 1927 survey, 13,675 establishments employing four persons or more each were reported. All in all, it thus seems safe to conclude that the law induced *relatively* little *new* industrial investment.[32]

In 1929, as soon as the customs freeze imposed by the Lausanne Treaty ran out, a wall of protective tariffs was erected, but without noticeable effect. (Prior to this period, Turkey had agreed to impose an ad valorem duty of not more than 9 per cent on all imports.)

Kemal was apparently hopeful of attracting foreign capital to assist in the development of the country. In 1923, he declared, "Do not suppose that we envy foreign capital. No, our country is extensive. We require great effort and great capital. Therefore, we are always prepared to provide the necessary security to foreign capital on the condition that its profits be regulated by law."[33] But the climate was not right. The memory of the corruption, political instability, and financial defaults on the part of the Ottoman government was too fresh in the minds of foreign capitalists to encourage fresh plunges. Nor did the emergence of a militant Turkish nationalism under Kemal give foreign businessmen reassurance for the future.[34]

Apart from a private American loan in 1930, a Soviet government loan in 1934, British government loans in 1938 and 1939, and French and German loans in 1939, the financial resources utilized were Turkish public resources and those generated domestically by the new banks, to each of which was deputed the task of establishing and controlling various industries or economic activities. (Between 1924 and 1939 the combined deposits of all the national banks increased from 13 million liras to 170 million.) In spite of their limited financial resources, the Turks were, by this means, able to wipe out the foreign control of vital services and industries. This process was completed only in 1947 when the government bought out the French interests in the rail line (405 kilometers) skirting the Syrian border on the Berlin-to-Baghdad run. This move placed the entire Turkish rail net in the hands of the Turkish government for the first time.[35]

The form of Turkish étatism[36] in fact evolved out of the investment-banking structure created to develop a home-owned industry. The semipublic Business Bank has already been mentioned, so likewise has the move to make the Agricultural Bank a private institution. In 1926, this latter organization was given the task of organizing agricultural credit cooperatives on the village level, and in 1937, the Grand National Assembly enacted a measure reconstituting the Agricultural Bank as a government institution. At that time, it became — and still remains — a direct function of the central government. The capital of the bank consists of that inherited from the earlier bank, from funds gained from annual earnings, and since 1938 from annual grants made by the national government equal to 6 per cent of the yield on the land tax and ½ per cent of the national budget.

Meanwhile, in 1925, the Turkish Industry and Mining Bank was founded with government capital for the express purpose of implementing the state industrial program. This institution, the activity of which was limited to the management of existing works, was split into two concerns in 1932, the State Office of Industry and the Industrial Credit Bank of Turkey. These two once again became one in 1933 to form the Sümer Bank, an institution endowed with a financial and administrative structure designed to spark an industrial expansion. Shortly thereafter, the first industrialization plan (1934–1939) was announced.[37] Also, in 1931, the Ottoman Bank, a Turkish joint-stock company whose shares were owned by British and French nationals, was replaced as the central bank of issue by the new Central Bank of Turkey, thereby nationalizing the banking structure. Another state investment institution for mining and power development, the Eti Bank, came onto the scene in 1935.[38]

Finally, in 1937, étatism was written into the Constitution as one of the six cardinal principles of the republic. Up to this point it had, legally speaking, been only the doctrine of a party, though in the predominantly single-party administration of Kemal, this distinction was perhaps more theoretical than actual.

Aside from industry, transport, and banking, Turkish étatism likewise invaded the field of labor-management relations. An increasing necessity for the codification and enforcement of basic labor regulations was felt as industrialization moved ahead. In the absence of effective labor organization, some sort of state administrative machinery was required to prevent the previous exploitation of labor. It was here that the benevolent paternalism of étatism was most clearly exposed. Without organized pressure on the part of labor, the Public Health Law of 1930 was enacted, an act that provided for the protection of pregnant women workers, fixed minimum ages for industrial labor, established maximum hours of work, and authorized the issuance of industrial health and safety regulations. In 1933, an amendment to the Turkish Penal Code prohibited both the right to strike and that of lockout. The Public Health Law was the prelude to the first comprehensive piece of labor legislation, the Labor Law of 1936, which is still considered the basic labor code. This latter law applied to persons partly or wholly engaged in the performance of manual work in industrial undertakings where at least ten persons were normally employed (since August 1952, four or more persons under certain circumstances). It dealt with such matters as employment contracts, maximum hours of work, rest pauses, night work, public holidays, the Saturday half-holiday, protection of wages, employment of women and juveniles, health and safety, labor inspection, employment exchanges, and conciliation and arbitration. Strikes and lockouts were again prohibited, and compulsory arbitration enforced. In essence, this law provided that employer-employee relations should be arranged entirely by the State. (It was not until 1947 that legal recognition was given to the right of either employers or employees to associate freely in the formation of associations and unions.) Accompanying these developments was the growth of various forms of social security for labor

— old age, maternity, and occupational sickness and accident. Though labor was thus legally protected, the enforcement of these laws in private industry left much to be desired, a fact that convinced many Turks of the necessity for direct State participation in industry.[39]

As previously indicated, étatism could be defined simply as the intervention of the state in economic matters in the interest of more rapid economic development and the protection of the general welfare. It was an economic expedient and a responsibility of government. We have seen that at first there was no intent to cut into or discourage private enterprise. In fact, the initial tendency was in quite the opposite direction. But the bureaucratic empire-builders who saw in étatism an opportunity for personal power eventually used this state machinery as a weapon against private competition. Their major advantages were tax exemptions, low-interest public capital, state subsidies, priority in the allocation of scarce materials, first claim on foreign exchange, and state assistance in training technical personnel. Private enterprise, nonetheless, continued to grow and to compete successfully in a number of fields, one reason being that the production costs in some of the state plants were abnormally high by reason of their uneconomic (though perhaps socially profitable) sites and the many social benefits they were required to provide. Turkey's largest industry — flour milling — remained almost 100 per cent in private hands throughout, so likewise did a substantial part of the textile industry. Purely as a revenue-begetting scheme, the government established as state monopolies the production of salt, tobacco products, alcoholic beverages (other than wine), matches, and explosives. Air, rail, postal-telegraph-telephone, and the maritime passenger services likewise became government monopolies, ostensibly both for revenue purposes and to protect the public against exploitation.

In short, étatism grew as a result of the compelling need for accelerated economic development, the failure of private enterprise to maintain the desired pace, the non-availability of foreign capital, and the ambition of empire-building bureaucrats. In addition, one might cite the military orientation of the leadership which perhaps inclined it toward a policy of economic regimentation, the world-wide economic depression of the 1930's which served to establish on a global basis the failure of private enterprise, the absence of any domestic public opinion to oppose the move toward state control, the inadequacy of domestic commercial law and its enforcement, the shortage of capital and the necessity for channeling that which was available into projects of highest social return (not necessarily equated with high financial return, especially in the short-run), the authoritarian nature of the political institutions of the country, and finally the apparently impressive examples at that time of state economic control in Nazi Germany, Fascist Italy, and Soviet Russia. Étatism was thus in harmony with the historical, social, political, and economic environment of Turkey.

Though Turkish apologists for étatism claim that it never crystallized into an ideology and, hence, was always subject to change, such was not entirely the case. In 1937, étatism was written into the Constitution as a principle of the State. In 1935, Kemal had explained, "Accepting the principle of private enterprise and personal initiative, but recognizing its inability to satisfy all the requirements of a great nation and an extensive territory, the system of nationalization pursued by Turkey relies upon the principle of State control of the national economy." "But," he added, "this system is not a mere application of the ideas proposed by the 19th century socialist theorists."[40] Later, one of the principal economic thinkers for the People's Party, the party of Kemal, stated,

> The political program of the People's Party clearly defines the limits in this country between state-controlled economy and the free enterprise. While the State will deal with heavy industry, manufacture of armaments and public utilities, all other industries are open to private enterprise. We are not capitalists; we resemble the socialists. We do not believe in exploitation . . . While other countries are moving towards étatism, we have no wish to return to an 18th century economy. We believe in étatism as a means of preventing the exploitation of the workers.[41]

By this time étatism had become something very much akin to an ideology in the minds of many if one defined the term as a specific, social, economic, or political principle or program to which people cling obstinately for emotional and symbolic reasons. But the ideology had not been seized upon by the masses. Hence, it was still susceptible to change.

The outstanding features on the étatistic landscape were the large investment banks — the Sümer Bank for industrial establishments, the Eti Bank for mining and power developments, the Agricultural Bank for agriculture investment, and, in the case of monopoly industry and transport and communication, various government agencies. From the start, an important function of these enterprises was education and social development. Many were planned with the idea of regional development more in mind than immediate financial profit. Because of various price controls, social and educational functions, and inadequate accounting, it is impossible to state with any certainty whether particular state enterprises were financial successes or not. But the fact remains that in the three developmental plans (1934–1939, 1937–1942, and 1946–1950) a number of modern factories were constructed, and the economy began to creak into motion. Progressive labor legislation of a paternalistic nature was enacted simultaneously, although its application was spotty.

Various moves calculated to induce social change in the village and, coincidentally, greater agricultural production, paralleled this industrial development and must be considered as part of the general étatist policy. Specifically, these moves included an expanded farm-credit system, protective tariffs, a village school program, land distribution (to increase the number of landowners), road improvement, the introduction of a small amount of machinery, and the dispatch abroad for technical agricultural training of a few Turkish students. Until the seeds of fundamental change had been laid in Anatolian rural society and more trained agriculturalists were available, relatively little profitable investment could be made in agriculture other than in a limited number of factories which, by utilizing farm products, would increase farm income and encourage improved farm practices. The outstanding example of this process was the sugar refineries. Turkish agriculturalists insist that the general influence of these plants on farm practices in their respective areas has been very great. Also, in all three industrialization plans large chunks of capital went into the building of a modern textile industry, a move which encouraged both the expansion of the Anatolian goat and sheep population and the improvement of Turkish cotton. Not only did the increased demand for wool and cotton effect the farmer's income, but the new textile industry brought cheap, factory-woven cloth within his means. As a result, village clothing changed. During World War II, the government stepped in to increase agricultural production through the device of creating several large state farms equipped with modern machines and operated according to scientific farm practice. Though originally conceived simply as an effort to augment production at a critical time, these state farms have not been without importance as demonstration models and experimental areas in modern agriculture under Anatolian conditions.

Did étatism fail in its purpose? One unusually qualified foreign observer commented, "Although the favorable economic results of the étatist policy are plain for all to see, its disadvantages now receive greater stress than its advantages, and consequently there is a tendency, in some quarters, to claim that it has "failed!" This same person wrote:

> While sympathizing with the self-critical attitude this implies, we see here a danger of jumping to premature conclusions. In this connection we may recall Thornburg's[42] criticism of the statement that private enterprise in the early days of the Republic had "failed." "It was hardly," he says, "given a fair trial." Equally well it may be claimed that, today, public enterprise has not had a fair trial. In Turkey, it has suffered from much of the same difficulties as stifled the growth of private enterprise in the earlier period. Capital, in spite of foreign aid, is still a scarce commodity; communications, although vastly improved, are still inadequate; managerial and technical skills, despite the sending of large numbers of young men to foreign countries for training, remain in short supply; administrative skills, of a modern type, are even rarer. In these circumstances, is it correct to assume that, now that étatism has laid a basis for industrial and commercial development, the future of Turkey's industry and commerce lies in the hands of the individual entrepreneur? We suggest that it is not.[43]

AN EVALUATION

During the initial period of republican Turkish development, from 1923 to 1930, great economic inertia existed. Despite substantial investment and government-inspired prodding, little seemed to happen which could be measured statistically. In the years following 1930 a considerable number of large State industrial enterprises appeared, but it was not until after 1945 that per capita real income began to register a steady rise. In fact, if Turkish income estimates bear any relevance to reality, per capita real national income was very little higher in 1945 than in 1929, if at all.[44] The reasons for this slow improvement were doubtless varied. Most important perhaps were the heavy residue of Ottoman mentality which tended to disparage business and industrial activity, the changeless and tradition-bound nature of Anatolian village society, and the small number of educated and technically skilled persons in the country. On the economic side, the size of investment in modern capital goods was simply inadequate to boost gross national product over and above population gowth.

It was perhaps just as well that investment during this period was not greater, for because of sociological and psychological factors in Anatolian life, it would doubtless have brought very low returns. It was during these years, however, that the combined influence of extensive village and technical education programs, relatively successful control of a few major diseases, establishment of some modern industry, improved communications, and participation in the semimodern military training forced upon every able-bodied male, began to take effect. And the economy began to move. Once under way, the movement gathered momentum fairly rapidly, for it was based upon the release of tremendous pent-up human energy and long-thwarted demand for the satisfaction of certain felt needs.

Although it is true that two fundamental desires — prevention of a power vacuum and material advance to the Western level — motivated Turkey's leaders, the manner in which they gave expression to these impulses changed with the times. Turkey's unhappy experience with foreign economic exploitation in the closing years of the Ottoman Empire, the political scheming against her by the Western powers following World War I, and the inability to raise foreign loans, led the Turks at first to a policy of virtual economic isolation. Surrounded by hostile, or at least apparently untrustworthy powers, the Turks concluded that self-sufficiency in foodstuffs and basic industrial products was the answer. The ruling concept of economic development at this time emphasized the growth of that domestic industry which would render unnecessary previously vital imports, thereby making the country less vulnerable to foreign pressures. Undoubtedly, the world-wide economic crisis of the early 1930's and its depressive effect upon world trade (particularly upon the commerce of a country such as Turkey which was selling largely unprocessed agricultural and mineral products) confirmed in the minds of the Turkish leaders their already strong inclination toward a policy of economic self-sufficiency. World War II again demonstrated to the Turks the practical utility of their drive toward self-sufficiency, for the new State plants kept the country supplied with a number of vital products despite the semi-isolation of Turkey during the war years. The post-World War II world saw Turkey following a different policy — one of international economic cooperation.

Another characteristic of Turkish development was the partial divorce of two processes long thought by Western economists to be indissolubly married — industrialization and urbanization. Though the industrial labor force had increased from 5.6 per cent of the population in 1929 to perhaps 7 or 7.5 per cent in 1945, a mass rural-urban movement had not yet gotten underway by the end of World War II. There are several alternative explanations for this relative immobility of the population. From the start of modern industrialization in Turkey, that is since the mid-1930's, it was a deliberate policy of Turkey's leaders to use industry not only for production but also as an educational device and a lever for regional development. Many of the big state plants, so criticized by Western economists for being poorly located, were in fact placed in their present sites for reasons other than purely economic. It was a matter of calculated policy to prevent the creation of industrial concentrations and to hold the population in the villages and small towns. Not only were the building and administration of industrial cities both expensive and difficult, but the leaders feared the possibly politically disruptive influence of an industrial proletariat which had cut all ties with the land and had broken away from the protective stability and security of village life. With the Soviet Union so close at hand, there was occasion for concern. It was also true that the persons constituting the major source of new industrial labor, the landless or near-landless villagers, were strongly disinclined to leave the village on any permanent basis. The bachelor dormitories associated with many of the new state industrial plants of this period are clear evidence that the Turkish leaders likewise did not envisage any such permanent move out of the village. But regardless of the motives, the fact remains that Turkey built up its industrial plant with a minimum of urban development. According to the 1927 census, about 24.2 per cent of the population was living in the cities. In 1945, that percentage was almost the same. (The 1950 figure was only 25.2 per cent. These figures are distorted somewhat in favor of the village by reason of a large amount of migrant labor that continued to identify itself with the village, but which in fact resided most of the time in the cities.) Under these circumstances it is an error to judge the value of a factory to the national economy by its profit and loss statement. Calculation of its net contribution should include such factors as the cost of new housing made necessary by the plant, the training it provides, and the extent to which it stimulates other productive activity. How does one calculate the profit or loss of a school? Some of these state plants were as much technical training centers as factories.

An important factor keeping the people on the land was the relative sparseness of population in many rural areas. Not only were most rural communities initially isolated from the stream of national development by reason of poor communications and rough topography, but there was also the opportunity at hand for expanding agricultural production and hence, income, once better motive power — plus incentives — entered the village. The only limit on the amount of land a farm family could cultivate was the animal and man power it could recruit. With only oxen, the expansion of cultivation was necessarily slow. But the use of good horses alone increases the area a farm family can cultivate by perhaps two or three times, and a tractor multiplies the area many times. Until very recently, therefore, there was little economic pressure operating in the village to induce people to migrate to the cities on a permanent basis. Those who did were either farmers who worked at nonfarm jobs during the off season, the younger sons of large families, or those unfortunate few who owned little or no land.

Another feature of Turkish development was its regional unevenness, despite a deliberate effort by the government to distribute the benefits of industrialization over as wide an area as possible. With the exception of a few pockets, there still existed a continuous gradation from west to east across the country from Europeanized city dwellers to isolated seminomadic tribesmen all but untouched by modern development. The geographical contiguity of western Turkey with eastern Europe and the location of Turkey's political and intellectual capital in Istanbul on the extreme western edge of Anatolia throughout the life of the Ottoman Empire from 1453 on does much to explain this unevenness.

But still, one might have thought that the eastern wilderness would have been considered a frontier and would have drawn many of the more dynamic elements of the Turkish population in search of fortune, fame, and adventure. As a matter of fact, the reverse was the case, for there was a constant flow from all over the country into the larger cities (Istanbul, Izmir, and more recently, Ankara) of the most intelligent, the most energetic, the most ambitious, and the wealthiest. Numerically, the movement was perhaps insignificant, but not otherwise. These people came in three main groups: the scholarly inclined, who were attracted by Ankara and Istanbul Universities and who lived out the rest of their lives in the shadows of these universities; the wealthy landowners and businessmen who were drawn by the luxury and glamour of the city; and finally the MP's who—once having tasted the elixir of modern Ankara — were loath to return to their home towns, even if ultimately deprived of their parliamentary seats. It is small wonder that Ankara and Istanbul and Izmir progressed and flourished, while the rest of the country moved forward at a much more sluggish pace.

To counter this movement, the government literally forced professional people into the eastern and more remote communities. For example, the State was compelled to assign government doctors to these places in order to provide any medical facilities at all, so reluctant were private doctors to answer the challenge and see the opportunity of the frontier. Despite growing competition in the big cities, the professional man was very much disinclined to go into these areas where he might be assured of a larger income but would be deprived of most of the "fringe benefits" of life in Istanbul, Izmir, and Ankara — not the least of which was intellectual companionship. Still another attempt to reverse the trend was the policy of assigning army personnel coming from the more advanced parts of the country to the less advanced. (A very recent effort to divert the movement of local talent from the big cities of Western Turkey has been the establishment of a center of learning, Atatürk University, in Erzurum in eastern Turkey.) All along one heard a great deal in Turkey about the development of the eastern provinces, for the unevenness of the nation's development was — and is — of critical importance in that much of its unexploited natural wealth — water, minerals, and land — doubtless lies in those wild eastern highlands.

Many have made the criticism that the Turkey of Kemal and Inönü devoted entirely too little attention to agricultural development. Even as recently as 1948 there were only 1,700 tractors in the country, and the standard of living in most village communities was little better than bare subsistence. It was probably true that the overwhelming bulk of Turkey's nonmilitary investment during the Kemal and Inönü regimes went into industry and communications, and that aside from certain highly specialized crops and some agriculture-based industry (textile) little was done to improve agriculture. Possibly more might have been undertaken in the agricultural sector during this period, for instance, greater effort to replace the ox with the horse, though return on investment in agriculture during these years would have been very low indeed. Nothing could have changed village farm practices until a core of literate and mechanically knowledgeable farmers had been created. Prior to the post-World War II period, the rapid introduction of modern farm techniques and equipment would have represented largely wasted effort and investment in view of the inadequate preparation of the village-farmer for anything more complicated than his traditional routine.

Another important observation one must make about Turkish economic development of this period is that it came about not by reason of any compelling popular pressures, but rather by deliberate planning and pushing on the part of the top leadership of the country. The fundamental problem was how to create incentives toward which the mass of people would respond with greater economic effort. To touch off the process, various programs were forced upon the village and provincial town with little regard for the immediate wishes of the people involved. For instance, religious education was banned and a secular village school thrust into its place, a school built by forced labor and to which all village children were required to go (though never with anything like 100 per cent attendance). The rural teaching cadre was created out of a corps of dedicated village youth who were trained in special rural teachers' schools, the Village Institutes.[45] Road construction was accomplished in part with forced labor via the medium of a road "tax." Certain farm produce was collected forcibly. (The element of force was withdrawn from these programs shortly after World War II as democracy became a reality and public demand developed to support the further expansion of these educational and economic activities.)

The same sort of forceful policy was resorted to in the case of industrial development in that capital resources were accumulated by the device of keeping consumption down forcibly through rationing, taxation, and forced crop collections. In one instance (1942), the authoritarian regime of Ismet Inönü went so far as to impose a capital levy which, in certain instances, turned out to be confiscatory for members of ethnic minority groups and foreigners. In respect to labor, special legislation of a highly paternalistic nature both protected and regulated. The rights of Turkish labor gained were thus bestowed upon it, not won by its own effort.

Almost all of these characteristics of the Turkish development led inevitably to state domination in economic activity. It may well be that Kemal's attempt during the 1920's to depend primarily on private enterprise to lead the way in domestic economic development was too short for a fair trial and that temporary conditions during this period militated heavily against such enterprise. But the fact of the matter was that the very social and economic environment of the country was such as to make it exceedingly difficult for private enterprise to touch off Turkey's industrial and agrarian revolutions. Sensing both theoretically and practically that almost every argument was in favor of direct state participation in economic affairs, Kemal gave substance to Turkish étatism in 1934 with the First Five-Year Plan. In 1945, étatism remained a basic tenet of the Turkish republic.

Chapter VI

THE POSTWAR DECADE, 1946–1956

PRELUDE TO CHANGE

By the end of World War II, Turkey was prepared for change — politically, socially, and economically. Literacy had grown less than 10 per cent in the early 1920's to over 30 per cent (of the population over the age of six), though these figures must be taken with some reservation in that just what constituted literacy had never been clearly defined. The population was approaching 20 million, but with the percentage in the villages remaining virtually unchanged (24.9 per cent as against 23.5 per cent in 1935). Some 15,000 village schools were reported to be in operation in 1948, as contrasted with roughly 6,000 in 1938. By 1948, bank deposits were up to one billion liras, from 316 million in 1938. The labor force employed in industry had easily doubled. The State held large gold and foreign exchange stocks that had accumulated during the war years by reason of pre-emptive buying (particularly of chrome ore) by the belligerents and because of the nonavailability of imports. The country was thus in a good position to step up its investment program, roughly 30 per cent of which was necessarily in the form of imported machines, construction materials, and other commodities not produced in Turkey. True, domestic prices had risen generally by 1948 to about 400 per cent over those of the immediate prewar period. This increase was apparently the result of recurring "favorable" trade balances, the large number of men held under arms and consequent drop in production. (This factor may not have been overly important because of underemployment in agriculture and the practice of permitting a substantial number of soldiers to return home for the harvest for the few weeks each year during which their labor was really needed in the village.), an increase in money supply, a drastic increase in import duties following the devaluation of the Turkish lira in 1946, and a policy of subsidizing basic crops to a level well above world market prices. But despite these things, per capita real income was edging upward.[1]

Neither communism nor reactionary religious or racialist forces seemed to threaten Turkish society internally. Externally, the exhaustion of the great powers in a war that Turkey had all but avoided gave her a moment's breathing time. Although in 1946 she was faced with Soviet territorial demands, her security was assured by the promulgation of the Truman Doctrine and the Marshall Plan, which meant both military and economic assistance from the United States, thereby strengthening Turkey's international position and lightening Turkey's domestic investment load.

Simultaneously, President Ismet Inönü, to his eternal credit, placed the nation's welfare before personal ambition and permitted a gradual liberalization of political institutions, thus giving release to pressures that had built up under a quarter of a century of one-party rule. An opposition, later to become the Democratic Party, began to form as a splinter group from the People's Party. There had been opposition movements before, but always short-lived and never on such solid ground organizationally. From 1945 on, the Democrats worked away at the grass roots level to build a nation-wide organization. This activity became one of the most effective adult education programs in the nation's history. At the same time, the People's Party government began rethinking and redefining its economic politics. Teams of foreign experts under Marshall Plan auspices poured into the country, and, with American help, military training, which affected a large percentage of Turkey's youth, was on the way to becoming thoroughly modernized.

To the uninitiated Westerner the Turkish village might have seemed untouched by these developments, but such was not the case if one made the effort to look more closely. Below is a list of the physical changes that had occurred in one central Anatolian village by 1949:[2]

Most of the village homes reported sheet metal stoves for heating purposes; in 1932 only open braziers had been in evidence

A primary school, constructed in 1944 and staffed with a young Village Institute graduate, was operating; before there had been none

In place of the single steel plow reported in 1932, there were now between 40 and 50

The irrigated land had been increased about one-third by means of a canal constructed collectively by the village in 1946

There was general admission by the villagers that health conditions had improved. A government doctor was visiting the village several times a year to distribute free DDT, quinine, and atabrine. Malaria was all but unknown, a sharp contrast with conditions a decade before.

Instead of ten horses reported in 1932, the 1949 count was thirty, and they were preferred to the bullocks and buffalo traditionally used for plowing

One of the village fields had, in 1949, been plowed by a tractor for the first time

A bus passed close by the village once a week in 1949; none had done so before

Trucks were coming into the area for the purpose of transporting the crop to market by 1949; none had done so in 1932

All arable land had been put to the plow by 1949, whereas in 1932, considerable empty land was reported

Villagers were going more frequently into the market town, and there was general agreement that more goods were available than previously. (They commented particularly on the amount of ready-made clothing)

Adult education classes were to be started that following winter in the school

There were indications that at least some of the villagers desired to improve their living standards and saw the relationship between such improvement and better methods of production and distribution

The village mill, reported as being in ruins in 1932, was operating in 1949.

By 1947, the Agricultural Bank of Turkey had 308 branches through which it extended farm credit totaling 244 million lira ($87 million) to 1.3 million farm families (about 46 per cent of the total). Although the average farm loan of 186 lira ($67) was obviously inadequate, this was a vast improvement over the situation obtaining two decades earlier.

But despite these improvements at the village level, the cost of production on the Anatolian dry grain farm was still well above the world market price. In 1948, I made a study of the costs on a "typical" farm, assuming the most favorable conditions, and derived the price of $2.21 per bushel of wheat.[3] (The U.S. price was then $1.50.) This $2.21 price assumed the cost of labor to be the subsistence cost of living of the farm family and made no allowance for opportunity costs. Therefore, both to protect the village farmer's living standards and to encourage increase in production, the government had, since 1932, been offering subsidies on the basic cereal crops, first through the Agricultural Bank and then, from 1938 on, by means of the Office of Soil Products. In 1947, this office, which was responsible for maintaining price ceilings and price floors in respect to certain crops, established a wheat price just about double the going world price (assumes the official foreign exchange rate). That is, for every kilogram of wheat exported at the world price, the Turkish government lost an equal amount; it was selling wheat for half of what it bought it for (except in situations where Turkey exchanged wheat with bilateral trading partners for goods that would have brought a higher price on the world market than the price at which they were credited against Turkish wheat).

These subsidies were, of course, a disguised form of investment in agriculture. By 1950, the office was working through 200-odd agencies, including public grain auctions in all important farm centers, and possessed a storage capacity of some 600,000 tons, mainly at railway stations and ports.

The tax burden borne by the village farmers was light when compared to the taxes paid by business, government employees, industrial labor, and professional persons. The assessment of land for tax purposes had not been made for a decade or more, and the villager had ample opportunity to hide animals and thereby evade much of the animal tax. The road tax could be paid by means of a few days' labor in the off season. The forced collection of grain, introduced during World War II in order to maintain supplies, was discontinued in 1946. All things considered, an unduly large share of the national income was being channeled into the village in a deliberate effort to stir economic incentive. Village society was ripe for accelerated development. Change had become inevitable.

By 1947–1948, it was no longer true that Turkey was merely an agricultural country, although commerce and industry were still responsible for only 15 per cent of the national income (it had been 13 per cent in 1929), and the agricultural share still hovered around 50 per cent. Contrary to critics of the regime, these figures would indicate that agriculture and nonagricultural activity had developed apace. Such statistics should be taken only as rough approximations, however, for in the absence of firm basic data, national income statistics were necessarily constructed upon a mass of assumption. Even so, figures from one year to another were probably comparable, for they were based upon similar assumptions. But beyond that, one could not safely go.

Because of the impact of the étatist policy — both in building up state enterprise and in discouraging private enterprise — the state share in the industry of the nation became even greater. It is estimated that by 1947–1948 the following activities were 100 per cent in the hands of the State: coal mining, cellulose and paper manufacture, chemical industry, iron and steel production, all major mineral exploitations (other than chrome and lignite), mechanized processing of tobacco products, salt production, tea processing, manufacture of matches, sugar refining, production of alcohol and alcohol beverages (except wine), and the postal-telephone-telegraph systems. In addition, state enterprise was responsible for an estimated 50 per cent of the textile production, 30 per cent of the cement, 10 per cent of the brick and tile, 70 per cent of the chrome, 30 per cent of the leather, 70 per cent of the lignite, and 65 per cent of the merchant marine. Metalworking, wood processing (except matches), food processing (except sugar and most alcoholic products), wine, cotton ginning, flour milling, glass production, the construction industry, toy and furniture manufacture, and handicrafts were almost entirely in private hands.[4] Power production was, except for a few small industrial plants, a public activity. The state also owned and operated both of the broadcasting stations in service, was marketing a substantial percentage of the farm machinery sold in the country, owned close to 100 per cent of the nation's forest lands, was supplying about 5 per cent of the nation's petroleum requirements through its own retail outlets, was buying (in 1946) 20 per cent of the major field crops, was supplying most of the agricultural credit, owned all known oil reserves and oil wells, was producing about 3 per cent of the nation's cereals, owned interests in a number of "private" banks and one insurance company, and controlled all foreign exchange operations. In addition, responsible officials of the Chambers of Commerce and most "cooperatives" were government appointees, and finally, education — with a few minor exceptions — was a government monopoly.

From this list, it is obvious that the economic life of the country was controlled to an extraordinary degree by the State. But it is untrue to say that private enterprise was not moving ahead, though it did so with difficulty. In 1949, for instance, the private textile industry reported, "Private industry is not in a position to compete with the Sümer Bank trust, which is equipped with modern machinery requiring less manpower . . . and is producing at a lower cost with greater efficiency." The same report pointed out that during the war imports had decreased and as a result it had become necessary to increase local production. The government had met the situation by ordering three shifts to work 24 hours a day, including Sundays. Machinery, already badly worn, was used upon government order for seven years without interruption. During this period, machine depreciation was still carried on the books as 8 per cent of the original cost, which would have been realistic only if the working day had been the normal 8 hours. Numerous appeals by the industry to permit an increase in the depreciation rate were ignored by the government. These were only a few of many complaints which established beyond doubt that a deliberate attempt was being made by at least certain government bodies to place private enterprise in a disadvantageous position.[5] The results were as anticipated. In 1942, private enterprise had accounted for roughly 60 per cent of the cotton yarn production; in 1950 its share was only 45 per cent. The same trend could be demonstrated for the entire textile industry.[6]

In the case of labor there had been some release of government control, for early in 1947 a law was enacted permitting labor to organize. By the end of 1949, there existed 83 trade unions with 73,873 members,[7] out of a total industrial labor force of about 330,000 (includes only those establishments employing ten or more workers). The distribution of these unions was very uneven, but the heaviest concentrations were in the Istanbul area and in the Zonguldak coal fields. Elsewhere, labor organization was exceedingly limited. In December 1949, I asked Cemil Sait Barlas, who was the Minister of State at that time, if he felt that the right to strike was essential to economic development. Was not a powerful labor movement an important pressure on management to make production more efficient? His answer: "We are studying the matter, but we believe that the past view of the government is the correct one (i.e., to ban strikes). There are strikes in other countries," he continued, "because there is no adequate labor law. Because our law gives the worker everything he wants, the right to strike is unnecessary." He did not speak of the effect on management.[8]

Perhaps another still stronger argument was that it would have been difficult to grant the right to strike to labor without coincidentally awarding the right of lockout to employers. In view of the very weak financial position of the unions, it might then have been possible for the employers to destroy organized labor utterly.[9] At that time (1949), there existed at the state-owned Zonguldak coal mines a blacklist of labor "trouble-makers."[10] From time to time groups of workers had tried to bring pressure on the Zonguldak management to secure changes in working conditions. Whenever that had happened, leading members of the dissident groups had been dispersed forcibly throughout the coal mining area. In 1949, the newly organized Zonguldak Coal Miners Union engaged in no collective bargaining, nor were there any grievance committees. Workers with complaints were compelled to approach management individually. Even so, court suits brought against management were not infrequent, though no organization existed to furnish legal assistance for such worker-plaintiffs. Up to this point, labor unions had been acting largely as adjuncts of the ruling People's Party, though by the time of the 1950 general elections the nucleus for a dynamic and truly independent Turkish labor movement had appeared. Those groups that declared their desire for the right to strike — some in very emphatic tones — had most certainly been weaned from the government and were on their own.

One trouble with Turkish labor organization, then and now, was that it lacked the financial strength to become a truly independent movement. With wages at near subsistence level, it was impossible for union treasuries to accumulate adequate reserve funds to withstand pressure. Under these circumstances, the right to strike would have been more theoretical than real. Even though a worker could sue an employer for an illegal labor practice, there were no funds upon which he could draw to sustain himself and his family during the legal process. It was nonetheless true that in those cases reaching the courts the vast majority of decisions were in favor of the workers.[11] In February 1950, special courts to handle labor cases were legislated into existence and by August were actually established in eight cities. In January 1950, an amendment to the Labor Law authorized the Minister of Labor to delegate the responsibility for establishing minimum wages to local committees consisting of representatives of various official and nonofficial interest groups, including labor.[12]

Early in 1950 more energetic steps were taken to attract private foreign investment into the country. A March 1950 law authorized the Ministry of Finance "to guarantee long-term indebtedness incurred by private enterprise from foreign countries," on condition that the maximum of all such guarantees not exceed 300 million liras and that the funds be invested in enterprises contributing to the nation's economic development. The Ministry of Finance was empowered to guarantee that the necessary permission would be given for the partial or complete transfer of profits and/or capital. This law was an extension of a Council of Minister's decree on the same subject issued in May 1949, but under which exportable profits were limited to 10 per cent per year. The new law had no such limitation.

The Minister of Commerce and Economy commented to me on December 23, 1949, "We want private enterprise to come in. We have no desire to expand [state enterprise] . . . Some people say that the field in Turkey is not open to private enterprise. This is wrong . . . We are now studying all laws and regulations which give preference to Government enterprise with an eye to changing them. We rely on private enterprise. We never think of competing with it."

There were many indications that economic policy was being rethought in 1949 and 1950 prior to the general elections that were to oust the People's Party from power. Petitions from private industrialists complaining of unfair economic practices on the part of state enterprises were being given careful attention in the ministries. In the fall of 1949, the Ministry of Commerce and Economics circulated a questionnaire to 185 leading businessmen, journalists, professors, and merchants, and to all 111 Chambers of Commerce.[13] This survey was later submitted to the World Bank Economic Survey Mission to Turkey in mid-1950, a mission invited by the People's Party government in the almost certain knowledge that such a mission would advise cutting back state participation in the economic life of the nation. Early in 1950, the People's Party Government also assisted in establishing the Industrial Development Bank of Turkey for the specific purpose of recruiting capital for private business at more reasonable terms. But despite these moves, it was certainly true that the Party was split on the issue. Though one minister declared himself in favor of private enterprise, another announced in the National Assembly, "I am a member of an étatist party government. I am proud of being an étatist. We are going to see to it that the recovery works carried out in our country through étatism be even surpassed in the coming years . . . We resemble the socialists," he explained, "by not allowing the consumers to be exploited by Capital." [14]

There is some basis then for saying that economic liberalism was in the air before the Democrats came to power,[15] but one must admit that even had the People's Party Government wished to do so, it would have found it difficult to unseat the powerful industrial bureaucracy which had developed under its aegis.

By 1950, literacy was officially up to 34.5 per cent. The population was now 20.9 million, with 8.7 per cent of the labor force of 10.6 million persons employed in industry and crafts. Per capita real income had moved up to an index of 107, 1938 being the base year. In 1929, it had stood at 87. According to the 1950 census of industry, there were 98,828 industrial establishments in the country, of which 96,626 were classified as "small" (those utilizing less than 10 mechanical horsepower) and 2,202 "large" (those employing 10 or more mechanical horsepower). These plants employed 353,994 people and represented an investment amounting to 899.1 million lira, 26.9 per cent being in state-owned factories, 43.8 per cent in large private plants, and 29.3 per cent being in small private establishments.[16]

Between 1934 and 1950, land under cultivation had risen from 10.7 million hectares to 13.4 million, that is from 13.8 per cent of Turkey's total land area to 17.3 per cent. But total agricultural area, including orchards and meadows, had risen only from 72.5 per cent of the total to 74.3 per cent. The increase in crop land had been effected almost wholly at the expense of grazing land, and the *yields* of principal field crops had not risen appreciably. The production of coal, lignite, chrome, and manganese had gone up considerably over the 1934–1950 period. The seven power stations with an installed capacity of 17,322 kilowatts extant in 1913 had increased to 307 plants with 374,292 kilowatts by 1949. Starting with a paid-in capital of over 17.9 million liras in 1933, the Sümer Bank was endowed with 109.5 million by 1949. Comparable figures for the Eti Bank were 4.5 and 68.7 million. In 1949, gross public investment stood at 528.6 million with 27.5 million going into agriculture, 255 into transport, 103 into public works, 22.4 into electric power, 37.9 into industry, and 79.6 into mining. Bank deposits had risen from 197 million liras in 1937 to 1,031 million in 1950.

So it was across the board: investment, the industrial plant, foreign trade, banking activity, all had multiplied many times. But per capita real income in 1945 was up only an estimated 7 per cent over 1938. Why? The answer was compounded of many factors, but the list of the more important surely included: low incentive at the village level to produce more, the high cost of industrial production, and the delayed impact of the new investment on production. It was because a very substantial chunk of this new investment originated in American economic assistance that we now turn to that aspect of the Turkish development.

THE AMERICAN CONTRIBUTION

On February 2, 1948, Turkish Foreign Minister Necmeddin Sadak faced the National Assembly in Ankara and reported on the progress of Marshall Plan aid negotiations. Turkey had been turned down, and Sadak was doing his suave best to explain to the Assembly just why this had happened. It was true, he said, that Turkey had participated in the Marshall Plan discussion in Paris, had submitted the required information, and had requested $615 million-worth of material aid. Sadak stated that a report prepared by American experts had said this of the Turkish economic position:

> That Turkey was capable of contributing to the reconstruction of Europe
>
> That Turkey possessed sufficient gold and foreign currency for the coming 15 months
>
> That Turkey had not sustained destruction during the War (but had spent and was necessarily spending a lot of money on her army)
>
> That Turkish industry was fairly well developed, and output had increased considerably over prewar levels.

The report went on to reason that Turkey could finance her own development program. Sadak agreed with the findings as to fact, but took issue with the conclusion. He declared, "As for America's statement about Turkey — that we are in a position to pay for equipment and machinery — we have made it clear to the Americans that they are mistaken in this." [17]

Despite this initial rebuff, Turkey was admitted to the Marshall Plan a few months later, and on July 8, 1948, the Turkish parliament ratified the "Economic Cooperation Agreement between the United States of America and the Republic of Turkey." For the first three months of the Aid Program, Turkey was allocated $10 million. Meanwhile the Turkish government presented a project to Washington estimating Turkey's first-year requirement to be $85 million.[18] In the fall of 1948, a small American mission arrived in Ankara to supervise the program.

The over-all purpose of Turkey's participation initially was to increase Turkish production to a point where she could, in exchange for manufactured products, supply food and certain raw materials to Western Europe, which was then in the throes of its postwar reconstruction effort. By the end of the 1949–1950 fiscal year, American economic assistance to Turkey totaled $180 million. Major projects on which money was spent had to do with the supply of modern farm equipment, expansion of irrigation, development of the meat packing and fishing industries, modernization of the coal mines, improvement of the road and rail nets, reorganization of the steel industry, modernization of iron and chrome mines, expansion of salt and cement production, the purchase of some consumption goods (notably petroleum), and an ambitious technical assistance program. The largest of these, other than the supply of certain consumer goods, were the farm machinery, coal, and road projects.

The initial consignment of Marshall Plan tractors arrived in Istanbul in May 1949.[19] By January 1950, the Ministry of Agriculture reported 1,873 arrivals, thus making a total of 4,214 machines in the country as of that date.[20] The machinery was distributed through normal commercial channels and sold to allegedly *bona fide* farmers either for cash or on an installment basis. Eligibility for participation in the latter scheme required a letter of credit from the Agricultural Bank indicating that the potential purchaser had opened credit for 80 per cent of the value of the intended purchase, a service for which he paid 2½ per cent interest, but it was most unlikely that any farmer could secure such credit unless he were a rather large landowner.[21]

High priority was given to the development of the Zonguldak coal mines. The project called for the mechanization of underground transportation, the sinking of new shafts, provision of hoisting equipment and surface electrical and transportation facilities, construction of new coal washeries and improvement of the port of Zonguldak. The aim was to increase coal production by 38 per cent and cut back production costs by 20 per cent. By 1950, the work was proceeding on schedule.

A major effort had been launched by the Turkish government some years before to develop an adequate highway network, both to integrate the country and to lower transport costs. To assist in this work, the Turkish Ministry of Public Works obtained in 1948 the services of the U.S. Public Roads Administration (now the Bureau of Public Roads). According to the American Chief of the Highway Mission in July 1948, his group started out with five main objectives: (1) establishment of a highway laboratory and the training of the necessary Turkish technicians, (2) the outlining of a long-range plan, (3) provision of aid for current construction work, (4) the training of men to use the equipment brought into Turkey, and (5) the building of an adequate administrative organization within the Turkish government. Prior to July 1949, the road program was part of the Military Aid Program, not the Economic Cooperation Administration (ECA). Thus, the first major road construction job, the Iskenderun-Erzurum highway, was undertaken under military auspices for strategic reasons. In 1950, a 47-man mission staffed by the U.S. Bureau of Public Roads was in Turkey advising the Ministry. By this time it had helped to develop a nine-year program for the creation of an integrated 13,437-mile national highway system and an adequate organization to maintain it. Work was on schedule. In 1949, a visit to a village in central Turkey had taken me three hours by jeep to cover the twelve miles from the nearest market town. Five years later, the same trip took twenty minutes. The cost of highway transport had dropped. The social implications of the new highway system were very great. The ordinary village farmer began to go into the market town of an afternoon simply to pass the time of day, even to go to a motion picture. And the harvest began moving to market by truck.

ECA-sponsored projects in Turkey were thus well under way by mid-1950, though their full impact on production had not yet been felt.

The $477 million worth of American military aid which had been flowing into the country since 1947 had considerably relieved the pressure of Turkish state finances occasioned by the maintenance of a large military force. The annual allocation by the United States to Turkey had been stepped up from $100 million in 1947 to $233 million in 1950, increases which had the accumulative effect of freeing Turkish funds for investment in the civilian economy. It is true that Turkish military expenditures had also increased from an estimated 5.3 per cent of the national income in 1948 to 6.0 per cent in 1950, but in view of mounting Soviet pressure these figures would have been much higher in the absence of American Aid.

In short, by 1950 a number of elements had combined which could be expected to react one upon the other in such a manner as to cause rapid growth in the economy and dramatic change in the social structure. Specifically, these elements included officially inspired social change at the village level, a rethinking of economic policy (in part motivated by political considerations), some increase in per capita real income, growing confidence in the effectiveness and equity of law, some development of private enterprise, increased investment in agriculture, development of political liberalism, expansion of education, the threat of Soviet imperialism, and finally American military and economic assistance.

THE 1950 UPHEAVAL

On May 14, 1950, the unexpected happened. In Turkey's first, honest, contested, general election, the opposition Democratic Party swept into office with an impressive majority, thus upsetting 27 years of uninterrupted Republican People's Party control. Participation in the voting was high, 89 per cent of the qualified electorate. And the right to vote was limited only by age, citizenship, and sanity. What is all the more remarkable about this 1950 election was that the regime in power refused to control the election so as to assure favorable results even though it possessed the power to do so. The Army and police were loyal to it, and democratic roots were probably not deep enough to have caused serious unrest even if the election had been rigged. It appears that on the eve of the election various members of the People's Party wanted to take steps to assure the outcome, but Ismet Inönü refused; the election was both contested and honest. The Democrats were able to win 50 per cent of the village vote and a substantial majority in town and city, thereby winning generally with a 55 per cent majority. Inönü and his Republicans relinquished power without violence. The new president-elect, Celal Bayar, arrived for his inauguration by jeep, which fact seemed to represent a fundamental change in attitude. The jeep in a way symbolized the intensive grass roots campaign waged by the Democrats between 1946 and 1950. To organize effectively in 40,000 villages had not been an easy task. It could not have been accomplished with horse and donkey transport.

In the absence of Ismet Inönü, Turkish democracy might well have been delayed in its development. In his own character, in his personal reading, and in his public utterances is evidence indicating that perhaps from the very start of his administration, in late 1938, Inönü had been driving toward the eventual liberalization of the political regime. Otherwise, it becomes difficult to explain many of his words and deeds.[22] Hence, the character of the top leadership is perhaps of signal importance in explaining this unique, bloodless transition in Turkey from a single-party authoritarian regime to a multiparty democratic structure based on contested, free elections. (That political violence was to erupt ten years later does not render the event any less unusual.) Other factors inducing the change included: (1) increasing popular demand for greater participation in government by a growing middle class, (2) Turkey's signing of the Charter of the United Nations, (3) the Soviet threat and the authoritarian nature of the Soviet regime, (4) the Turkish need for Western aid and support, (5) the victory of the more liberal nations over the more authoritarian in World War II, and (6) the obvious growth of corruption within the single-party state and Inönü's personal reaction to this state of affairs. Only by the existence of a strong, vigorous opposition, could Inönü gain effective control over his own party, which by 1950 had become strongly tainted with corruption and oppression.

The Democrats had promised many things: redress of 27 years of accumulated grievances against the local administration, greater religious freedom, better roads, protection from excesses committed in the villages by the gendarmes (the rural police, in reality a branch of the army), and easier farm credit — in general, greater liberalism. Government controls of all sorts were to be loosened. At this time, the Democrats were identified as the liberal party in the true sense of the word, namely minimum government control over individual action. The Republican People's Party, on the other hand, possessed an ideology which seemed to emphasize government control and regulation, though as we have seen, the Republicans were beginning to rethink their position before bowing out of office in 1950. The Democratic leadership came from a marriage of the new middle class and the traditional, prerepublican social elite. The Republican leadership had been derived from the new military group which came into power with Kemal, plus a substantial number of intellectuals and idealists.

It has been demonstrated that even prior to the 1950 election, membership in the Grand National Assembly had begun shifting in terms of the social backgrounds of its members. Over time, the assembly changed from being primarily a national elite group (that is, strong in intellectual status but weak relative to degree of "localism," which is defined as the proportion of members representing the districts in which they were born), "oriented toward the tutelary development of the country, to being primarily an assemblage of local politicians, oriented toward more immediate local and political advantage." The newer members entering the assembly during the decade prior to 1950 reflected this change to a measurable degree.[23]

Though most certainly not an issue at the village level, where the vast majority of voters cast their ballots, economic liberalism was loudly espoused by the Democrats. Fifteen days after coming to power, President Celal Bayar declared to the new Parliament,

> The aim and essence of our economic and financial views is, on the one hand, to reduce to a minimum state interference and, on the other, to restrict the state sector in the field of economy as much as possible, and, by inspiring confidence, to encourage the development of private enterprise to the utmost. The first impact of such a program will be that only those economic activities that . . . cannot be undertaken by private enterprise will be kept for the state to operate. Such state activities will consist only of those which have the character of a public utility. According to our view, it is imperative that the field of economy belong mainly to private individuals or companies and that they operate under an economic regime founded on private ownership and personal freedom. Only when it is absolutely necessary and only in exceptional cases should the state undertake control and regulation in the economic field by participating directly in economic enter-

Mustafa Kemal Atatürk, President 1923–1938; shortly before his death

Istanbul—Bosporus waterfront

The Bosporus, from Thrace east to Anatolia; Fortress of Europe in the foreground

Cemal Gürsel, President and Prime Minister from May 1960 coup to October 1961 elections; President since then

Celal Bayar, President 1950–1960; imprisoned since 1960

Prime Minister Ismet Inönü, President 1938–1950

Prime Minister Adnan Menderes (right) and Foreign Minister Fatin Rüştü Zorlu (left), both executed in 1961

Two well-to-do Anatolian visitors

An Anatolian shepherd boy

The Anatolian village—a tight cluster of flat-roofed dwelling complexes

Minstrel Veysel Şatĭroğlu, Turkey's most famous folk minstrel

Village group pose in their Friday best

The old hoca

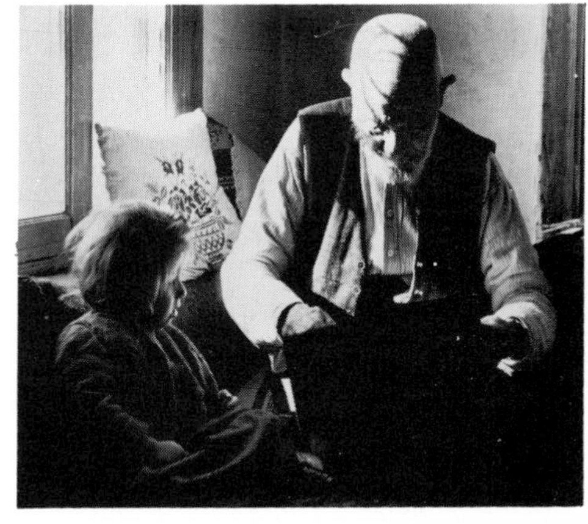

The heart of conservatism, the provincial town; showing veiled women (1953)

Town Square, Sivrihisar; Officials' Club on the left

A village school

A poor village of northeastern Turkey (1948)

President Celal Bayar during 1950 election campaign

Villagers voting in the 1950 election

prises. From now on, not only shall we [i.e., the state] avoid entering fields of enterprise other than those having a public-utility character but we intend to convert — under a specific plan and under advantageous terms and conditions — all existing state enterprises (except those of a public-utility character and those dealing with basic industries) to private enterprise . . . Our aim in the field of domestic and foreign commerce — in case interference is not forced upon us — will be to give freedom to business.[24]

Another frequent criticism made by the Democrats against the old regime was its alleged underemphasis on agricultural development. On this point, President Bayar stated,

We shall always keep in mind that agriculture constitutes the foundation of our economy. It is always necessary to take account of the fact that no government should attempt to construct a showy and expensive state administration — as was done by the former government — burdening a backward agricultural society which is still the slave of the wooden plow and oxcart. There is no avoiding the fact that such a policy has crippled the national economy. Had those who followed this road agreed with the summary presented above, not only would the agriculture of our country have developed but all branches of industrial and economic activity would have shown great progress. Acting on this plan of giving first emphasis to agriculture we shall study seriously the problems of credit, agricultural implements, farm machinery and equipment, campaigns against insect pests and plant diseases, seed improvement and general methods of bettering and perfecting agricultural techniques.[25]

In general, the new president promised maximum effort to facilitate the flow of capital — both state and private — into productive enterprises, with particular emphasis on agriculture.

There were many reasons why this change of policy should have occurred when it did, though, as already indicated, the shift was not quite as abrupt and dramatic as some observers later alleged. The presence of the ECA Mission in Ankara and its constant harping on free enterprise had had an influence, as likewise had Max Thornburg's *Turkey, an Economic Appraisal* which had appeared in 1949 and had been given considerable play in the then opposition Turkish press. But more important, the social structure of the country had changed. No longer was private enterprise without spokesmen. A new class of Turkish businessmen and merchants had appeared, and as their numbers and wealth swelled, the louder became their voice. A newly organized labor joined the chorus demanding greater freedom, including the right to strike, even at the cost of abandoning the paternalistic protection of the government, though some suspected that labor knew not what it asked. It was this new middle class which constituted the core of urban support for the Democratic Party. Within its ranks were found the free enterprise protagonists who supplied so much of the funds and energy for party organization.

In many respects, the 1950 Democratic victory represented a revolt by a materialistic, middle class against a rule by idealistic intellectuals and military-minded administrators, though one should note that much of the *leadership* of both parties — with the exception of Ismet Inönü and Celal Bayar — was recruited largely from the old ruling families of Turkey. The temporary rule by military leaders of relatively lowly origin had passed. The middle class had won the day because of the identification of its interests with those of workers, large landowners, and much of the national elite and because it was able, by dint of many months of hard work, to win 50 per cent of the village-farm vote.

GROWTH UNDER THE DEMOCRATS

By mid-1950, Turkey was on the road toward greater economic liberalism, or so everyone thought. But in fact, the 1950–1956 period was characterized by unprecedented public investment (Table 2). Gross investment — public

Table 2

Gross Public Investment
(at current prices)

Year	*Public investment via national budget (millions of TL)*	*Public investment as a per cent of total national budget*	*Total public investment (millions of TL)*	*Total gross investment, public and private (millions of TL)*	*Public investment as a per cent of total investment*
1950	180	12.3	469	1,090	43.0
1954	652	25.4	1,082	2,790	38.8
1955	910	30.0	1,538	3,180	48.4
1956	1,041	31.5	1,634	3,400	48.0

Source: Calculated from *Iktisadî Rapor, 1956* (Ankara: Türkiye Ticaret Odalarĭ, Sanayi Odalarĭ re Ticaret Borsalarĭ Birliği, 1956), p. 39; *Iktisadî Rapor,* 1959, pp. 41 and 67; *Turkey* (Paris: OEEC, 1959), pp. 20, 245.

and private — rose from an estimated 1,090 million lira in 1950 to 3,400 million in 1956, but as a percentage of gross national product the increase was but from 10.5 to 13.6 per cent. Meanwhile, over the same period, per capita real income rose by an average of 3.2 per cent per annum,[26] though the big leap forward had occurred between 1950 and 1953, when record-breaking crops were harvested. Reversion to normal weather and increasing shortage of foreign exchange — and hence, of needed imports — plus an unwillingness or inability of the government to institute adequate price and consumption controls, forced a slow-up in development. Also, almost inherent in the new semilaissezfaire economic policy was a studied disinterest in any sort of economic planning.

The general liberal policy espoused by the Democrats was extended to foreign trade. In the fall of 1950, Turkey had, upon the insistence of American advisers and its colleagues in the Organization for European Economic Co-operation, freed her imports from OEEC countries from quota restrictions to the extent of 60 per cent of the country's 1948 import level. Necmeddin Sadak, the Foreign Minister in February 1950, anticipated the problem this action would create,

> In principle, Turkey believes in the freedom of trade. The difficulties which most countries have to face in this regard, however, are far less severe than those faced by Turkey. If we are to free all our imports, we should be given long-term credits. Turkey, as an undeveloped country and in view of her present-day economy, must take into consideration the fact that her national industry is in no way on the same level as the industries of other European nations.[27]

Turkey's import surplus jumped from 62.3 million liras in 1950 to 246.4 million in 1951 and 516.0 million in 1955. On September 22, 1955, Turkey suspended all registrations of "free" import transactions. In 1953, the import surplus fell back to 382.2 million. Meanwhile, Turkey had become one of the largest debtor nations in respect to the European Payments Union, with a deficit at the end of October 1952 of $233.9 million (654.9 million lira). The Central Bank of Turkey was clearly in an insolvent position insofar as foreign exchange was concerned.

By the end of the next year, 1953, the combination of import controls and a bumper harvest of grain (which elevated Turkey to the world's fourth largest exporter of cereals) considerably improved Turkey's position. This was Turkey's moment to woo her suppliers, for optimism was high as to her immediate future. Turkey plunged forward on an enormous capital investment program, at the same time maintaining a steady increase in the supply of consumer goods. Realizing that no country would grant her the loans and credits needed to finance the import component of the investment program and to cover the purchase of necessary consumer goods, Turkish leaders adopted the policy of importing everything possible and worrying about payment later. Though eventually seriously undermining Turkish financial prestige abroad, this policy accomplished two purposes: physical possession of the needed goods and involvement of Turkey's trading partners to such an extent that they felt compelled to grant further commercial credit to help finance additional purchases abroad if they were to recoup anything of their previous "involuntary credits." Thus, Turkey took full advantage of the overoptimism about her immediate future—occasioned by a combination of extraordinarily good crops in 1950–1953 and the overselling of the progress of Turkish development by the Americans involved in the economic and military aid programs.

By October 1954, it was reliably estimated that Turkey's commercial arrears ran close to $200 million. At the same time, the Central Bank showed a deficit balance of gold and foreign exchange to the amount of 73.1 million liras. The service charge on her $297.3 million foreign debt ran $26.5 million in 1953 and $22.7 million in 1954. Turkey's commercial creditors were frantic, and by the end of 1954, in the face of steady financial deterioration caused by a reversion to subnormal weather and crops during 1954, which promptly reduced the nation to a cereal-deficit area,

Turkey was able to work out bilateral trade and payments agreements with her most important trading partners — notably Germany, France, and Great Britain.

Many talked confidently of Turkey's brilliant economic future if she could just weather the next three to five years, the period of heaviest investment. Others were less optimistic. The principal reasons for their skepticism at this point were the absence of adequate surveys of Turkey's resources (her soils, water, land, forests, fisheries, and minerals), the disinclination of the Turkish government to announce an austerity program or to take other measures to counter the growing inflation, the apparent lack of coordinated economic planning, and the preoccupation with political maneuvering on the part of top Turkish leaders — a preoccupation which was leading very rapidly, it seemed to many, toward a personal authoritarian government. Some saw this situation as simply an extension of traditional Turkish attitudes after a brief untypical interlude. And finally, few in high places were paying attention to the enormous social impact which the newly acquired farm machines were having in certain areas of the country.[28]

By the Winter of 1954–1955, villagers were obviously hiding part of the poor 1954 crop in anticipation of further dry years. Inflationary pressures were threatening dangerously. The movement of rural folk in search of work toward the cities was increasing and so, likewise, was unemployment, though neither could be measured statistically. With the exception of cotton, nuts, and chrome ore, all of which were of either questionable price and quality or both, there would be little to export until the fall of 1955. Meanwhile, through various credit arrangements, the import of 500,000 tons of wheat from the United States had been negotiated. Nonetheless, the government refused to slow down; the investment program had to be maintained or Turkey's economic—and hence, political—future would be imperiled. In short, 1954 marked the end of a series of bumper crops and of a relatively easy foreign credit market. Turkish foreign policy became more cautious and flexible. Even the possibility of a large commercial credit from the USSR was being discussed.

During this 1950–1954 period, then, a number of fundamental policies had shifted. Despite promises to the contrary, state enterprises continued to expand at a pace perhaps even more rapid than that of private enterprise, though state plants were now on a more competitive basis with private enterprise than had previously been the case, and one heard little talk of unfair government competition. The inadequacy of private enterprise to spark Turkey's explosive development was again demonstrated. Agricultural development was given much greater attention, and the problem was seen increasingly as essentially one of village education and development. Despite the anguished admonishments delivered by foreign experts, crop subsidies were continued, and the tax load on the villager was lightened. (Early in 1955, a government-sponsored project to increase the land tax was threatened with defeat in the National Assembly and withdrawn.) The construction of village roads and improved sources of drinking water was much accelerated. Farm credit facilities expanded from 336.9 million liras in 1949 to 1,172.1 in 1953. And finally, a "calculated recklessness" in investment and investment financing became official policy.

Foreign experts warned the Turks that they were trying to move too rapidly, that they should cut back and take it easy. The experts were ignored, and more and more the

Turkish government kept its plans to itself as it realized that it had few sympathizers abroad and a growing group of critics at home. The foreign expert, American included, had fallen from grace through his apparent failure to appreciate the necessities of the Turkish situation. Twenty new cement plants, ports, dams, highways, all at once? It could not be done. No country had ever moved forward so fast. In 50 to 80 years Turkey would be within the general economic range of Western Europe. That was the target. Turkish leaders insisted among themselves that in the absence of such development, Turkey would be swallowed up either by her friends — through growing dependency — or by her foes — through subversion and ultimate aggression. Turkish pride, the memory of past Ottoman-Turkish power, and the scars of more recent Great Power designs on Turkey would admit of no other logic, although Americans and others might deny it.

AN EVALUATION

What had Turkey in fact accomplished by 1956?

By almost every statistical measure, the Turkish economy had continued to move forward, though there was some question as to the realism of the statistics. And, despite an apparent drop in per capita income from the 1953 high, continued support for the ruling Democratic Party in the rural areas indicated that at least as late as mid-1956, the standard of living for most people was still forging ahead, or believed to be so. Perhaps rising cash incomes, even though decreasing in purchasing power, fooled some. But undoubtedly of greater importance in cushioning the shock of a decreased *average* real income were (1) the nonmonetary basis of much of the village economy, which provided it a measure of protection against inflation and (2) a shift in income distribution through increasing state support of commodity prices, continued tax exemption of agriculture, and a variety of other programs, all of which channeled income out of the city and into the village. The Democrats had, of course, reaffirmed their political dominance in the elections of 1954, Turkey's second, honest, contested general election. The Democrats had won an even larger popular majority (58 per cent) than in 1950, and the Opposition was reduced to but 31 parliamentary seats out of a total of 541. Indices of industrial output continued to move forward steadily over the 1948–1956 period; minerals from 100.0 to 186.5; manufactured commodities from 100.0 to 167.6; food production from 100.0 to 208.3; and the general production index from 100.0 to 184.5.

Another measure of the growth of the Turkish economy was the appearance in 1954 of 56 new corporations with a capital of 167.2 million liras. In 1950, only six new corporations with a total capital of 2.82 million liras had registered. Some observers pointed out that an inflationary situation induces heavy investment as persons and companies attempt to protect their wealth. This situation, plus increased confidence in the effectiveness of commercial law and the increased respectability of business as a career, undoubtedly operated to stimulate private investment. As a result, factory units increased from 2,335 in 1950 to 4,527 in 1954.

Notwithstanding the 1954 setback in agricultural production, there was little doubt that there had been a "normal weather" increase in production since 1948 of something between 60 and 100 per cent, with substantial increases in such cash crops as cotton, tobacco, sugar beets, and tea, as well as in the basic grain crops.[29] Power production had moved from a monthly average of 56.3 million kilowatt-hours in 1948 to 127.6 million in 1956. Several major extensions to the power-generating facilities of the country were currently under construction; there had been no slow-up. Graded and surfaced roads totaled 21,344 kilometers in 1948 and 28,717 in 1954, and the number of trucks on the roads rose from 10,596 in 1948 to 34,429 in 1956. In short, heavy investment continued in all sectors.

By 1956, some knowledge of Turkey's natural resources was being accumulated. Experts agreed that relatively little arable land lay uncultivated,[30] but they were likewise agreed that the financial return realized from much of this land could be increased substantially through diversification, rotation of crops, more timely planting, better fertilization, expansion and improvement of irrigation, more effective disease and pest control, and improved marketing practices.[31] Also, there seemed to be no physical reason why certain sections of Turkey should not develop first-rate herds of dairy and beef cattle. Ground water resources were still not adequately explored, although it appeared likely that the water table under much of Anatolia was close enough to the surface to be of economic importance. Exploratory drilling was proceeding quite rapidly.[32] Mineral exploration was still in its infancy, although Turkey appeared to be rich in a number of important minerals, chief among them being bituminous coal, subbituminous coal and lignite, iron, chromite, copper, and wolfram.[33] Two of Turkey's major iron ore reserves were practically unexploited, so likewise was Turkey's major wolfram deposit, a deposit that might possibly develop into the world's largest. Turkey possessed all of the minerals required, and in adequate quantities, to feed an alloy steel industry, which did not exist. But mineral oil, other than a small commercially important reserve in the east, was an unknown in Turkey. Serious exploration by a number of large foreign oil companies was now under way, and some petroleum geologists were optimistic about the possibilities of finding a major reserve in the country. The true extent of Turkey's forest and fisheries resources still remained uncertain.

Enough for the physical resources; what of the human resources?

The 1956 level in respect to education, health, and technical skills was still considerably below that of the peoples of the Western industrial nations. Of a population of 24.8 million, there were only 7,586 engineers and 910 architects. Nonetheless, the percentage of literacy had increased from 10.6 in 1927 to approximately 40 in 1955, during which period hundreds of schools had been constructed and staffed. This interest in mass education continued. One of the chief problems in this regard was how to induce the mass of village youth to enter secondary schools, which were by necessity located outside of the village. A parallel problem was how to induce trained teachers, even of village origin, to remain in their village assignments.[34] Although health conditions remained far from satisfactory, particularly in respect to tuberculosis, serious effort had been made to provide at least minimum public health services and to control certain of the more important diseases. Malaria, for instance, was no longer a major menace. The two-year compulsory military training, coupled with the not insignificant increase in industrial employment and mechanized farming, was producing a generation of mechanics and technicians running into the thousands. Many technical schools further augmented the nation's skills.[35] This was not to say, however, that skilled labor was in adequate supply, for Turkey's industrial expansion had kept well ahead of its supply of skills.

The increased economic activity of the country was reflected in the growing importance of organized labor. As of the end of 1956, there were reported 383 unions with a total estimated membership of 244,000. The leadership of some of these unions was impressive. Although the right to strike, as well as the lockout, was still forbidden, the Menderes administration maintained that it would eventually introduce legislation to authorize both under certain conditions.[36]

CRISIS

Unfortunately, coinciding with these hopeful developments — and, indeed, in part because of them — Turkey's foreign exchange and financial position became increasingly critical. Recurring deficit trade balances had, by mid-1956, generated commercial arrears in the neighborhood of $300 million, which taken together with investment credits of another $300 million and governmental obligations of approximately $500 million, gave Turkey a total foreign debt of well over $1 billion. Turkey's gold and foreign exchange reserves had fallen dangerously. Although the official exchange rate remained the same (2.80 liras to the dollar), the black market rate of the dollar was fluctuating between 8.00 and 10.00 liras. There was an ominous rise in most domestic prices. The absence of positive government action to reverse these trends discouraged foreign businessmen to the extent that few of those who had applied for and received the convertibility guarantee in respect to profits and capital under the Foreign Investment Encouragement Law actually invested in

Turkey. By mid-1956, only 31 foreign firms were reported as actually operating enterprises in the country, despite applications totaling several times that number.

A crisis struck at the end of 1955 as political and economic restlessness culminated in the riots of September 6 in Istanbul and Izmir (ostensibly induced by the issue of Cyprus),[37] and a subsequent political shake-up. Contributing reasons for the violence: (1) use of the Greek Orthodox Church as a political instrument by the Greek government, thus sparking latent Moslem-Christian hostilities (which were laid on top of latent Greek-Turkish national hostility); (2) the presence in Istanbul of a large, floating, unemployed, male population of village origin which sought economic gain from looting; (3) popular identification of certain Istanbul merchants of Greek ethnic extraction with hoarding, speculation, and unsavory wealth; (4) deliberate stimulation and organization of the crowds to violent ends by an unknown group. (Communists? Doubtful, none were arrested. Opposition politicians? Equally doubtful; even the government made no such charge. Prime Minister Menderes? Doubtful; the riot ran contrary to every conceivable interest of his. A group of second echelon Democrats seeking to unseat Menderes? Somewhat more likely; an effort within the party was made in December. Religious and racial fanatics? Equally likely. Possibly a combination of the last two constituted the guilty parties. In such event, criminal convictions may have been avoided because those guilty were too closely identified with the Prime Minister. An outstanding feature of the Istanbul riot: no one was killed.) In July 1961, both Menderes and Bayar were found guilty by a revolutionary tribunal of inciting the 1955 riot, but the evidence was not impressive. What was proved was that the government had planned a popular demonstration to support its position in Cyprus. A critic of the Menderes regime commented to the author in 1962, "It is now almost generally agreed that these riots were planned, organized, and started by Democratic leaders and local bosses, but developed into proportions far beyond the original plan and intention." It seems to me most likely that the demonstration was deliberately incited to unintended violence by other parties, the identity of whom still remains undisclosed. Local authorities, knowing of the government-sponsored demonstration, apparently did not know how to respond to the violence during those first few destructive hours. But there was no evidence to prove that Menderes deliberately planned the type of mass violence that in fact erupted.

Whatever the cause, this violent outbreak galvanized Menderes' opponents within his own party into political action. A showdown was created by a revolt within the Democratic Party and the appearance of a new splinter party organized by the dissidents. A 10-day cabinet crisis followed, a crisis which Menderes was able to overcome when he succeeded in forming a new cabinet December 10. Several of the more controversial ministers were dropped for the time being, and one was temporarily expelled from the party. On December 16, the National Assembly approved the program of the new Menderes government, the tenor of which indicated increased sensitivity by the administration to the needs of the Turkish economy. This was the price Menderes paid for political survival.

In agriculture, the new government announced that it would continue most of the former programs and policies, including increased farm credits, distribution of land to land-poor villagers, development of more adequate markets and price supports for farm products, import priorities for needed agricultural equipment, and the expansion of grain storage and handling facilities. The new government considered that Turkey's economic development made necessary an increase in public appropriations "for projects in the nature of investment in the tools of future production." To gain maximum benefits from such activity, the government announced its intention to draw up a plan for state investment, a plan that would take into consideration the resources and economic level of the country. The government further declared that it would encourage and activate private enterprise, eliminate all harmful intervention on the part of the state, remove all bureaucratic obstacles, exert every effort to promote the accumulation of private capital and facilitate its flow into projects of highest priority from the point of view of national economic development, balance the annual national budgets, and assure that the budgets conform to the country's economic capacity. The government also stated that it would make larger allocations of foreign exchange than in the past for the rapid elimination of critical shortages of certain consumer goods, industrial raw materials, and spare parts. The new government pledged itself to adopt every necessary measure to combat unjustifiable price increases, profiteering, and black market operations.

And so, the first half of 1956 saw the promise of vigorous measures to channel investment funds (including private) into high-priority projects, to control consumer prices and profit margins, to cut off the import of nonessential goods, to prosecute those acting contrary to the new economic measures, to curtail the flow of public funds into the capital reserves of state enterprises, to enact new tax legislation designed to encourage business and industrial expansion. The long-run effectiveness of many of these moves remained to be seen, although in the short run it appeared that the value of the lira had increased in terms of the dollar and the cost of living had fallen. Nonetheless, the foreign exchange position remained critical. The earlier policy of economic liberalism, so strongly urged by American advisers, had been all but discarded as the government leaders felt compelled to intervene more actively than ever in the economic life of the nation.

Despite heated criticism from the political opposition, the government refused to ease the situation by decelerating its investment program. So vigorous did Opposition criticism become of the moves toward greater economic control and the refusal to cut back on the rate of investment that the administration felt compelled to promote the passage of various laws to curtail Opposition activity, laws condemned by most observers as being clearly undemocratic and unconstitutional.[38] The administration, on the other hand, argued that the measures were required to stem a hostile and dishonest press and an opportunistic and irresponsible opposition, both of which were threatening the economic and financial stability of the country for partisan political purposes. The basic problem was that the vast majority of the voters still identified themselves as village farmers. Among these voters, the single, most important political issue had become the improvement of their purchasing power and the availability of certain consumer goods. This fact made it exceedingly awkward for a government to curtail consumer goods and decrease the economic advantages enjoyed by the rural population in terms of tax exemptions, crop subsidies, price control on certain popular goods, and easy credit.

And yet, both of these moves were probably necessary if the resources required to sustain current investment in other sectors of the economy were to be mustered without inducing a ruinous inflation. Unfortunately, the farm bloc was so overpowering politically that the voice of business, labor, trade, and mining interests was but a whisper in political circles. And the Opposition hesitated not at all to harass the government from all directions at once by charging too little investment, too much investment; an unduly high cost of living, inadequate farm, and labor income; and too many controls, too few controls. The government could do no right. Political tempers were aroused on both sides.

By mid-1956, then, Turkey had reached a critical turn of affairs. Many wondered whether democratic political institutions could long endure given the stress and strain of the socioeconomic situation.

Thus far we have looked at only one side of the coin, Turkey's domestic problems. During 1955 and 1956, Menderes found himself increasingly preoccupied with Turkey's foreign relations as he scurried from one capital to another. He realized, quite correctly, that the support of Turkish diplomacy was worth a great deal to the Western powers, perhaps even large-scale economic subsidy. Talk of a $300 million loan was in the air.

Chapter VII

TURKEY IN GLOBAL POLITICS

TURKISH foreign policy may change abruptly without warning or apparent reason. However, if we bear in mind how and by whom decisions are made, the relative degree of national power available, the nature of vital national interests, and the impact of historical events on the attitude of the decision-makers, and if the true context of decisions be known, Turkish foreign policy is not irrational. The problem lies in defining the context, the points of reference, for they may not be ours. In so doing, we should not merely transfer our own experience, prejudice, emotion, and values.

THE DECISION-MAKING PROCESS

The Turks have been past masters at diplomacy. A notable exception was Turkey's entry into World War I on the wrong side, an act inspired by Enver Pasha, who was in control of the Ottoman government when the war erupted. But apart from this tragic error, which later turned out to be a stroke of good fortune in that it created the preconditions necessary for the emergence of Kemal, Turkish diplomats have shown consummate skill in assessing national interests and in pursuing those interests no matter what emotional or ideological red herrings were dragged under their noses. This relative immunity to emotion and ideology in setting foreign policy has given Turkish leaders enviable latitude. Public opinion, which en masse is almost always expressed in emotional terms, is not nearly as involved in formulating foreign policy in Turkey as, say, in the United States. Indeed, the very absence of an ideological basis in Turkish society — be it Ottoman or republican — has made it possible for the leadership to shape policies to meet specific situations. Expediency governed. Turkey was committed neither to socialism, nor to democracy; hence, it was not interested in making the world safe for either. The general Turkish public — the mass of voters — is only casually concerned with foreign affairs. Certainly no Turkish government could take Turkey into an alignment with the Soviet Union overnight without considerable softening up of public opinion ahead of time. But given this vague limitation, Turkish leaders have almost unbridled freedom in matters of foreign policy. Rarely do they have to answer serious charges in parliament when a policy change is proclaimed, or subject themselves to parliamentary investigation. Certainly there has been an Opposition, and occasionally the Opposition has wished to know a little more about what Turkish foreign policy is and why, but rarely has there been any really serious challenge, certainly nothing comparable to the "Great Debate" or the "Agonizing Reappraisal" of the type to which the United States Congress periodically submits our leadership. In the United States, a major policy change must be preceded by a wooing of public opinion. Recognition of Red China would be a good example. In Turkey, such recognition could be accomplished suddenly without prior publicity and without seriously endangering the regime politically. Witness the Turkish defensive alliance with Yugoslavia, a communist power, one reason for which was that American public opinion and our anticommunist ideology would not permit a defense arrangement directly between the United States and Tito. We used Turkey as an intermediary. Prior to the Turkish-Yugoslav Pact very little warning was given to the Turkish public. Yet, there was no serious parliamentary criticism of the new relationship, which certainly could have been anticipated in the United States under similar circumstances. An ideological commitment is like a too-tightly snubbed anchor on an unattended boat. When the tide comes in, the anchor may pull the boat under. On the other hand, an anchor with enough line may save the boat when belabored by heavy seas. Or, national ideological commitment may be likened to dropping overboard an anchor that is too heavy to be pulled up as occasion demands.

TURKISH NATIONAL POWER

A nation's foreign policy — insofar as the public and leadership permit — is a function of relative national power, historical conditioning and national interest. The former is an imponderable thing, for its measure is a matter of judgment. But the accuracy of that judgment may be all important when one is maneuvering diplomatically. Hans Morgenthau, the distinguished American political scientist, lists eight elements of national power — geography, natural resources, industrial capacity, military preparedness, population, national character, national morale, and the quality of diplomacy.[1] Let us look at Turkey within the Morgenthau matrix.

Turkey lies directly at the center of an area of great conflict, both actual and potential. To the south are the Arab states; to the west, the Balkans; to the north, the Ukraine and several Soviet colonies (Bulgaria, Georgia, and Armenia) which may or may not be sources of future conflict; to the east, Iran, which by reason of her weakness and importance is a source of constant danger. In addition, of course, Turkey lies athwart the Black Sea Straits, the only seaway linking the Black Sea with the Mediterranean. And the Soviet Union is the major Black Sea power. The expenditure of over two billion U.S. dollars in military aid to Turkey in the last eighteen years and the construction of important NATO air bases on Turkish soil are clear evidence of Turkey's important *geographical position,* a position that gives Turkey bargaining power.

Though apparently potentially rich in many *natural resources,* Turkey's developed resources are not yet adequate to support a modern military action. Oil is a major problem. Given recent oil strikes, Turkey may well become a major oil-producing state, but as of 1963 it was far from self-sufficient in this regard. In 1962, it imported 3.1 million tons of petroleum and petroleum products (compared to 860,000 in 1958), which by value equaled 11.5 per cent of 1962 imports (12.8 per cent in 1958). Meanwhile it produced 508,000 tons or about one-seventh of the oil consumed.[2] The fact that comparable figures for 1958 had been 328,000 tons, or one-quarter of domestic consumption, was a measure of significant change in Turkey's oil posture. Turkey might have sufficient oil flowing out of its own wells to sustain military action, but not its civilian economy. During 1962, two new refineries were completed in Turkey. Most other important natural resources — food (with some exceptions), iron, coal, copper, wood, and the like — Turkey has in at least survival quantities. Though Turkey is now semideveloped industrially as compared to countries farther east and to the south, *Turkish industry* is wholly inadequate to support any sustained military action or to meet present investment requirements. In 1960, 52.1 per cent of Turkey's imports were construction materials, machinery, and industrial equipment. She cannot live or fight for long without these products. In respect to *military preparedness,* Turkey rates high with its 400,000-man army — if one thinks in conventional terms. Perhaps a million men could be put into the field in a matter of a few weeks. But less and less are we impressed with such figures, as the technological nature of warfare changes. Despite the fact that Turkey now possesses submarines, jets, missiles, a radar system, and perhaps even atomic weapons, replacement depends upon continued Western supply. The *population* of Turkey as of 1960 was 27.8 million. It is relatively young and vigorous, though still very short on the skills required in modern industry or a modern army. It relies heavily on the West for the import of skills, a trade figure that does not appear in the commercial statistics. Turkey has probably not yet reached the point at which her own institutions generate enough skilled persons to maintain efficient production, effective organization, and maximum military stature. Much could be said of Turkey's *national character,* that curious thread of characteristic Turkish reaction which remains more or less constant. It is a product of geographical, social, and historical conditioning, and hence changes slowly. Suffice it to say here that Turkish national character constitutes an element of strength in the modern milieu, for it is constituted of stubbornness, a tenacity of purpose, a will to fight, a social discipline, a willingness to sacrifice all in a national struggle. Perhaps the following comments by Major William E. Mayer, U.S. Army psychiatrist, about the survival rates of Turkish and American prisoners in North Korean hands are revealing:

. . . at least a third of the Americans held in captivity died in captivity. These men evidently died from diseases, from the severe conditions of living that existed in North Korea, rather than from execution or torture or anything of that nature.

Yet several hundred Turkish soldiers held under approximately identical conditions of captivity survived almost to a man . . . Close questioning of these Turks about why they survived so well and lost so few revealed that the only possible explanation was the continuance among them of an extremely strict system of military organization and discipline.

Thus, when a man became ill, a detail of soldiers was assigned to care for that man and ensure his recovery by any means possible. They often bathed, spoon-fed and cared for their sick and wounded with a tremendous degree of devotion.

Evidently, no matter how much segregation (of officers from men) the Communists attempted with the Turks, the remaining senior man invariably took command.

. . . In a disturbingly large number of instances, evidently [the Americans] did not [take care of their sick and wounded]. The reluctant conclusion must be drawn that this fact is the principal one in explaining the deaths of the hundreds of Americans who failed to survive . . . Soldiers in the most difficult early days of captivity, in a great many cases, evidently struck out for themselves, so as to speak, simply because of a failure to understand that only by a community of effort among them would the largest number survive.

. . . [This was due principally to lack of discipline], but when I talk about discipline, I am not talking about externally imposed rules, punishments and regulations. The kind of discipline that makes it possible to maintain an organized group working for the welfare of each member of this group is, and has to be, an internalized discipline on the part of each individual, a self-discipline, which can't be just an automatic, externally imposed set of values.[3]

Associated with national character is something called *national morale*, which in Turkey is generated in part by the sense of chronic emergency that permeates the scene, which in turn is a function of Turkey's geographical position and recent history. Morgenthau has said that "national morale is the degree of determination with which a nation supports the foreign policies of its government in peace or war."[4] The threat to Turkish security from Russia is real and immediate; it has been so for a long while. Hence, there is little room for divisive opinion on basic matters. The Turks are united in foreign policy. Questions may be asked, but always of a relatively superficial nature. Finally, we speak of the *quality of diplomacy*. In their flexibility, their realism, in their hard-headed pursuit of vital national interests, Turkish diplomats are second to none. Their efforts have substantially augmented Turkish national power, though sometimes pulling down on their heads charges of opportunism, supernationalism, and vacillation — witness their decision to remain a nonbelligerent in World War II until the last possible moment, February 28, 1945, thereby gaining the right to become a charter member of the United Nations.

Such an analysis leads to the conclusion that, all in all, Turkey stands as one of the foremost of the second-level powers; that is, in a regional or in the limited war context her power is to be reckoned with. By reason of the importance of the Middle Eastern region, Turkey should be accorded the same respect as a France, an Italy, or a Japan.

RESIDUE OF HISTORY

How is this Turkish power likely to be used? In seeking an answer we turn to the impact of history and an assessment of Turkey's vital interests, for it is within this context that Turkish policy decisions are made.

In the collective Turkish mind — and we do not speak

merely of the leadership now — there is a sense of greatness. The Turks were once the masters of a world empire, which was finally eclipsed only by World War I. The Ottoman Empire and its grandeur (presumed or real) still lives on in the memory of many contemporary Turks. Granted that in its final years the empire was perhaps but a shell, devoid of all real power, but nonetheless it was a name, a symbol toward which the Turk responded and in which he took enormous pride. It is frustrating to the Turk to be relegated to a second-rate power position. The frustration perhaps in large part explains Turkish sensitivity to insult and criticism, to the fact of his present dependence upon the great powers, and to exclusion from important international conferences.

A second point of historical significance is the extraordinary success the Turks have had in playing off the great powers one against the other. During the last 100 or 150 years of its life, the Ottoman Empire was weak in comparison to the Western powers. Nonetheless, by playing one nation against the other, even to the point of deceit and duplicity, the sultan's diplomats were able to maintain the territorial integrity of much of the empire. One should also bear in mind at all times when discussing Turkish foreign policy the fact that Turkey has been subjected repeatedly to propaganda attacks, exploitation, and outright aggression by the Western Christian nations. In the recent past, these nations have used Christian minorities within Turkey as weapons against Turkish authority — particularly the Greek Orthodox and Armenian communities. Though rarely articulated, the Turks feel that this difference in religion is relevant to their international relations. Not so long ago, there was a long editorial in one of Turkey's most serious newspapers on the subject of American aid. In view of Turkey's participation in the Korean War, her membership in NATO, her strategic location vis-à-vis the Soviet Union, and the importance of Western aid to her continued economic and military development, why was U.S. aid on a par (per capita wise) with that provided Iceland? the editorialist asked. Two reasons were suggested: First, most Turks were not named George, Peter, or Paul — a thinly-veiled reference to the religious difference, one of the few that have appeared in print. The second reason was the absence of any serious communist movement in Turkey. Therefore, Turkey had no leverage against the United States. What the Turkish government should do, the editorialist urged, was to take an alleged communist or two into the Cabinet. Then the Americans would become disturbed and increase their aid to Turkey.[5]

Another historical fact of significance is the recurring warfare with the Russians. Thirteen Russo-Turkish conflicts over the past four centuries have generated a full measure of hostility. The common folk of Turkey now identify communism as a form of Russianism, and hence something to be rejected. The rejection obviously rests on a different basis from that underlying American rejection of communism. Turkish-Russian hostility is now a matter of racial prejudice and animosity.

Still another point of historical importance is the long period of Ottoman domination of the Arab states and the Balkans.[6] In the declining years of Ottoman power, Turkish administration was undoubtedly bad. Consequently, it left a residue of ill will against the Turks when Ottoman rule was thrown off in the 19th and early 20th centuries. On the other hand, the long years of Turkish supremacy in these areas left the Turks with a conviction of their own superiority. The ordinary Turk is inclined to look down upon the Arab as a chap who really cannot control his own affairs in a civilized fashion. The present turmoil in the Arab world tends to confirm, in the Turkish mind, this prejudice. A vicious circle is thus established as the Arab reacts to Turkish haughtiness.

TURKISH NATIONAL INTERESTS

With these elements of national power and historical conditioning in mind, we move on to an examination of Turkish national interests and the policies devised to protect these interests. Three interests stand in primary position: (1) territorial integrity, (2) peace, and (3) continued economic and social development. The first — territorial integrity — is self-evident, though there are certain twilight zones — such as Cyprus, Mosul, Persian Azerbaijan, and Macedonia — areas in which the Turks have expressed special interest by reason of the large number of Turkish-speaking people residing within them. The Turks can be expected to react vigorously to any change in the status of these areas which might be interpreted as contrary to the interests of these "overseas Turks." The maintenance of peace is of signal importance to the Turks, for they realize full well that in any major conflict, even though the ultimate resolution be in Turkey's favor, Turkey might well become one of the initial battlefields. She stands between the Soviet Union on the one hand and the Mediterranean, Middle Eastern oil, the Suez Canal, and Africa on the other. This consideration leads us to the third vital interest — continued economic and social development. Turkish leaders believe that sustained development is a precondition for any meaningful degree of independence. Unless the issue is clearly one of life and death, Turkey cannot sacrifice her development. Becoming a battlefield might do just that if the new Turkish industry, the new ports, the new cities, the new transport system built at such enormous cost and effort were destroyed in the process.

MAIN PILLARS OF TURKISH FOREIGN POLICY

In pursuing these interests, Turkey has been following certain discernible foreign policies from the very inception of the Republic. First, *the Turks have stoutly resisted all territorial demands,* whether made by the West (as they were following World War I) or by the Russians (as they were following World War II). Insofar as the Turks are concerned, they accepted a territorial minimum after the First World War, which they defined in the National Pact of 1920. Second, *the Turks have refused, as a matter of policy, to enter into any international conferences or alliances on the basis of common religion.* For Turkey, a secular state, religion is not a valid basis for political relationship. The Turks have explicitly rejected the concept of a Pan-Islamic bloc.[7] Kemal himself was sounded out apparently at least once as to his willingness to become a new caliph, but he realistically rejected the idea on the ground that it would be an empty office; there was no power to support it.[8] Kemal was very conscious of the relationship between national power and policy. If there were inadequate power to sustain a given policy, that policy was rejected. To this date Turkey has refused to participate in any relationship with a Pan-Islamic flavor. In part, this abstention is an extension of domestic law which holds that the use of religion for political purposes is subversive to a secular state and, hence, illegal. To use religion in international politics would therefore be at odds with a clearly defined domestic policy.

Another important Turkish policy has been the disavowal of all imperialist or irredentist ventures. Ottoman Turkey lived by conquest. It relied upon the spoils of conquest to live rather than internal development. Kemal, who realistically appraised the Turkish power position, explicitly disavowed any intent to expand Turkey's territory as defined in the National Pact and over which Turkish sovereignty was recognized at Lausanne in 1923. After achievement of national sovereignty, the immediate object of Kemal's foreign policy was to stabilize all doubtful frontiers. The 1921 treaty with the USSR and the Lausanne Treaty of 1923 fixed Turkey's northeastern and western borders. Agreement on the Turkish-Iraqi border was left open, and after a bitter debate with Great Britain, the mandate power in Iraq, which almost led to war over the Mosul region, the matter was resolved in 1926 in favor of Britain and Iraq. Curiously, the abolition of the caliphate is said to have weakened significantly Turkey's claim to the oil-rich Mosul region of northern Syria. In part what had kept the Kurdish population of Mosul under Turkish influence had been the "superstitious reverence of the Kurds for the Supreme Pontiff of their religion." [9] The Iranian frontier, of lesser importance but the uncertainty of which caused some friction between the two countries, was fixed finally in a 1932 agreement with Iran.

One might add that Kemal's anti-imperialistic policy did not hinder the Turks from conspiring with the French for the take-over of the Hatay (the sanjak of Alexandretta) in 1939 from Syria. There is evidence, however, which would indicate that the Turks never regarded the ceding of the Hatay area to Syria and the mandatory power, France, as binding and final.[10] Nonetheless, the take-over was clearly contrary to the terms of the Lausanne Treaty. The Turks saw an opportunity for bargaining the French out of the Hatay region in exchange for a treaty of mutual assistance, which was important to the French in view of the impending world war. The Hatay region, wherein is located the port city of Alexandretta, now called Iskenderun, has proved to be of great importance to the Turks. It is through Iskenderun, now a NATO naval base, that Turkey's Soviet frontier defenses are supplied. Quite naturally, the Syrians have continued to condemn this French give-away of Syrian territory, which, as the mandatory power, France had no legal right to transfer. As recently as February 1960, there was a Syrian demonstration for the return of the Hatay district.[11]

Western observers have been fond of referring to Turkey's nonimperialist and nonirredentist policy. The truth of the matter is that the policy probably operates so long as it enforces Turkish interests. Kemal was well aware that Turkey had to concentrate all energy on internal development. He settled for a relatively small, relatively homogeneous Turkey, thereby considerably easing the tasks of establishing a new political authority and of internal development. During the early years, republican Turkey refrained from making overtures against anyone. In her weakness, she wished to give no cause for complaint. Other than the Hatay plum, which ripened and fell into the Turkish lap, the Turks pursued a noncommittal policy, even up to the closing months of World War II.[12] It was not until May 1944 that Turkey stopped selling chromite, a vital war materiel, to Germany and on

August 2 broke off all commercial relations with the Axis powers. She declared war on February 23, 1945, to become effective as of midnight on February 28.

But prior to 1944, Turkey signed treaties of friendship, neutrality, or nonaggression with the Soviet Union, Afghanistan, Iran, Iraq, the United Kingdom, France, and Germany. During the interwar period, power became fairly evenly balanced between the Axis and the Allies and between the Soviet Union and Continental Europe. To a certain extent Turkey was able to use her position to bargain advantageously with both sides — for loans, for control of the Straits, for munitions, for the Hatay region. But she could bargain only so long as she refused irrevocable commitment to any cause. The rise of Soviet power during and after World War II weakened the Turkish bargaining position, for the Turks dared not move at all in the direction of the Soviet Union, in view of the demonstrated hostility and power of the Russians.

We, therefore, derive a fourth pillar of Turkish policy, *friendship with the West.* Despite Turkey's tradition of diplomatic bargaining, the rise of hostile Soviet power forced the Turks into a firm commitment with the Western allies. Not only did the Turks need the military support of the West, but also its economic aid, for thoughtful Turks realized full well that their first line of defense against communist penetration was not the army, but rather sustained economic and social development. In the absence of such development, or in event of a serious slowdown, Turkey would become vulnerable, its traditional anti-Russian stance notwithstanding. The danger would mount as increasing numbers of people left the stable village environment and joined the urban proletariat. Membership in NATO, participation in the Korean War, and support of the Eisenhower Doctrine in the Middle East all followed from this necessity of identifying Turkey with the West.

A fifth and final pillar of Turkish foreign policy is *active support of efforts toward genuine international cooperation.* The Turks, as many of the smaller powers, would much prefer *multilateral* sponsorship and financial support for moves toward economic and military integration with the other non-Soviet nations, rather than a situation dominated by the United States. Dependence upon United States makes Turkey vulnerable to political leverage by the United States. The Turks would prefer not to be levered. Witness the Turkish press explosion in mid-1955 when it was suggested that the United States was laying down conditions for a large loan to Turkey. A highly placed Turkish official told the author in April 1955 that Turkey would accept Soviet aid rather than accept conditions imposed from without. "We do not beg," he added. "We never ask for help. We are proud." [13] The military regime under Gürsel was perhaps even more sensitive to foreign leverage than the preceding civilian administration.

It has also become apparent to the Turkish leaders that as the nation's economy becomes more modern, Turkey becomes increasingly dependent upon foreign markets, not less so. Only a primitive agrarian economy can approach self-containment. Therefore, by reason of historically generated attitudes and the pressure of external and internal events, republican Turkey moved from an initial policy of near isolation, through a decade of attempted self-sufficiency, to vigorous participation in international economic and financial institutions in the postwar era, for example, membership in the Organization for European Economic Cooperation, the International Cooperation Administration, the International Bank for Reconstruction and Development, the European Payments Union, and a large number of bilateral commercial arrangements with individual countries. In 1959, Turkey began an active effort to relate herself to the European Common Market in some way which would lead to full membership within ten or fifteen years. Internal economic development and the pressure of Soviet power has had much to do with this international orientation of postwar Turkey. Ideological aspects of the Cold War have been much less important.

CURRENT ISSUES

Thus far, we have been discussing major policies, several of which flow directly from important internal policies. We turn now to Turkish reactions to specific issues that have arisen, reactions which are completely rational within the context of Turkish national power, the decision-making process, and vital national interests.

Overshadowing all else is the fact of the *Cold War.*[14] Historically, Turkey has blocked Russian ambitions to control the Black Sea Straits and to possess a warm water port on the Mediterranean. As a device to extend its power, Czarist Russia tried at various times to establish a protectorate over the Christian minorities within the Ottoman Empire and to induce them to rebel against Turkish rule. Hence, the use of an ideology as a political weapon is nothing new to the Turks. The Turkish leaders see Soviet-led communism as simply one more effort to extend Russian power. Following World War II, the Russian threat became real and immediate by reason of two demands leveled against the Turks — the cession of Turkey's northeasternmost provinces of Kars and Artvin and revision of the 1936 Montreux Convention under which the Turks had been administering the Black Sea Straits. The Montreux Convention recognized the international status of the Straits in that the rules governing its use, and enforced by the Turks, were subscribed to by all of the leading maritime powers, plus those fronting on the Black Sea. In 1946 the Soviet Union proposed to turn the Straits into a regional waterway over which only the Black Sea powers would have had authority to establish the rules of use. Inasmuch as the Soviet Union was the major Black Sea power, Turkey would then have been subjected directly to Soviet influence. The Russians also desired bases in the Straits zone. With U.S. support, the Turks refused to consider a change in the status of the Straits, though they were willing to reconvene a meeting of the powers which had signed the Montreux Convention for a possible revision, if such seemed useful. The Russians were not interested, thereby exposing their intent. To this day, the Straits remain under Turkish control, and there has been no important deviation by the Turks from the rules laid down by the Montreux Convention.

In time of peace all merchant ships and naval vessels (up to a certain tonnage) including those flying the Soviet flag, may pass through freely, and they have. Black Sea powers, under certain conditions, may send through the Straits naval vessels up to any tonnage. Non-Black Sea powers are limited in the amount of naval tonnage they may have in the Black Sea at any one time. In event of war in which Turkey is not a belligerent, more or less the same rules apply. During a war in which Turkey is a belligerent, Turkey may close the Straits to unfriendly vessels. Even if Turkey is not actually at war but feels itself immediately threatened, the Turks have the right to control the movement of naval vessels. The Montreux Convention also gave the Turks the right to fortify the Straits and to administer the waterway in respect to such items as pilot services, navigational aids, and inspection. Signatories of the Convention: Bulgaria, France, Great Britain, Greece, Japan, Romania, Turkey, the Soviet Union, and Yugoslavia.[15]

Turkish resistance to the postwar Soviet claims was bolstered at the time by a show of American naval power in the Eastern Mediterranean, and Turkey moved in the direction of a closer Western alliance. The Russians had misjudged the Turkish reaction, and in 1953 they withdrew their claims on Turkish territory and also their demands for a more direct hand in control of the Straits.[16]

The Truman Doctrine of 1947 followed an unilateral American offer of support to any free nation threatened by the Soviet Union and wishing to build its defenses. The Doctrine was induced directly by the Soviet threat against Turkey and Greece, the latter being engaged in civil war with communist-oriented rebels. The Greek-Turkish Aid Program implemented the Doctrine. In that a military build-up in such countries constitutes a severe economic strain, and because Turkey was envisioned as a substitute for Eastern Europe as a source of food and raw materials for Western Europe, Turkey became a participant in the Marshall Plan. Conceived as a device for channeling U.S. aid to Europe for its reconstruction, the Plan was ill conceived as a device for assisting the long-run economic development of Turkey. After much pushing and hauling, the Agency for International Development emerged in Washington, an institution designed specifically to channel U.S. aid into long-run development in countries such as Turkey.

In 1952, despite an initial rebuff, the Turks were admitted to full membership in the North Atlantic Treaty Organization, thereby securing an American and European commitment to come to their defense if attacked. It was only after the valiant Turkish effort in the Korean War and much argument that the Western allies were willing to consider an attack against Turkey as an attack against themselves.[17] And on March 5, 1959, the United States signed separate defense pacts with Turkey, Iran, and Pakistan — the Middle Eastern members of the ill-starred Baghdad Pact, now the Central Treaty Organization. The pacts provide that the United States "will take such appropriate action, including the use of armed forces, as may be mutually agreed upon" in event of aggression against the three powers. The Turks had long sought a bilateral defense arrangement with the United States. Clearly, U.S. support and aid to Turkey has been a function of the Soviet threat to American interests. In the absence of that threat, would the United States support Turkey militarily and economically to the same extent? One doubts it. Hence, the Turkish interest in a continuing tense international situation is substantial. They gain by the Cold War so long as the situation does not erupt into war and so long as we justify our economic aid on military and political grounds rather than for its intrinsic value.

But why has Turkey been deemed so important to the United States as to justify 3.8 billion dollars ($1.6 billion economic; $2.2 billion military through 1962) worth of assistance and a defense commitment? Surely one reason has been the desire to deny the Soviet Union access to the Mediterranean. We have also been interested in building and protecting Turkish air bases for possible retaliatory action against Soviet industrial targets. There is too the moral boost the Western cause receives when a small nation such as Turkey stands fast against Soviet power and contributes significantly to collective action — such as in the defense of South Korea. For these several reasons we have bolstered Turkish power, thereby augmenting our own power position in the Cold War. The Turks are realistic enough to realize that American aid is forthcoming because such aid is in the interest of the United States. One Turkish editorialist wrote:[18]

> There is a mathematical necessity [for U.S. aid to Turkey]. The cost of maintaining one American soldier overseas is $6500. The cost of a Turkish soldier is $235. If Turkey became weak, and if a large number of American soldiers thus had to be sent to this area to defend the Middle East, it would be very much more expensive for America.

A further advantage gained by the United States, and one not really appreciated when the Turkish aid program began, was the support of Turkish diplomacy. The result? The Balkan and Baghdad Pacts. (That they proved of little real value in the end is irrelevant.)

Therefore, the Cold War has brought about a coincidence of interest between Turkey and the United States. But one cannot reasonably expect that such will always be the case. For instance, what if the Turkish leaders came to feel that the following conditions prevailed?

(1) Turkey does not block the realization of any vital Soviet interest. (There is reason to believe that it does not. Possession of the Straits is no longer of vital concern; they can be closed too easily in time of war from the air, and it is clear that Soviet

vessels may move through freely in time of peace, whatever the relations between Ankara and Moscow.)

(2) Turkey would not be an initial target of Soviet aggression. (There seems little reason why it would if it did not become a major missile-launching platform.)

(3) The participation of Turkish forces in a third world war would have little influence on its outcome. (Considering the nature of modern warfare, such an assumption is becoming increasingly realistic.)

Responsible Turkish leaders realize full well that if war comes to Turkey, much of the material development in which the Turks take such pride will be destroyed. Even if the war were won, Turkey would have to be rebuilt. This reconstruction would require massive foreign aid. But if the Russian menace were removed for the time being through defeat in war, would the United States or any other power spend billions putting Turkey back on her feet, particularly if the United States herself were badly damaged as undoubtedly would be the case? One may well doubt it. Wherein do Turkey's vital interests lie when these sobering thoughts are weighed? [19] As Prime Minister of Turkey, what should one do? It may be significant that during 1953 the Soviet Union dropped its claims against Turkey and began talking of bettering relations. Perhaps the Russians hoped eventually to maneuver into a position in which a swap with the Turks of nonintervention for neutrality might become possible. Admittedly, such will be very difficult so long as Soviet-controlled Communists appear to be a serious internal threat in the Arab states. Turkey dare not be isolated for reasons we have already stressed. Machines, oil, and skills she must have if her national power is to be sustained. Hence, she cannot tolerate communist regimes to the south.

Against this backdrop we consider the lesser or more specific regional issues — the Israeli-Arab conflict, the northern tier concept, Cyprus, and the rise of Nasser-led Arab nationalism.

On November 29, 1947, over the negative vote of Turkey and others, the United National General Assembly voted to partition Palestine. On May 15, 1948, the state of Israel was proclaimed. Ten months later, Turkey granted de facto recognition to the new nation. Meanwhile, the Turks carried on substantial commercial relations with Israel and permitted the emigration of Turkish Jews. Turkey's sole contributions to the Arab effort against Israel were the dispatch of a small military training cadre to Syria and the gift of some tents and other supplies to provide shelter for Arab refugees forced out of Israel. The Arabs charged that the Turks were two-faced.

It was true that any significant military contribution by Turkey to the Arab cause might have led to the destruction of Israel. There were possibly two reasons why the Turks desisted. Keenly aware of the much more ominous threat in the north, the Turks did not wish to quarrel in any substantial way with Western policy vis-à-vis Israel, which country constituted a very remote threat to Turkey. Turkey wanted a Western defense commitment, which she did not yet have. (Turkey did not become a member of NATO until February 1952.) First things first. Secondly, one suspects that the Turkish leaders did not look with complete displeasure upon the appearance of Israel, for its existence gave Turkey the opportunity to play the role of power balancer in the Middle East. As much as the

Arabs distrusted the Turks, they could not afford to offend too deeply. On the other hand, a completely secure Arab Middle East might be closed entirely to the Turks, because of the Turks' close identification with the hated Western imperialists — France, Great Britain, and the United States — in the greater struggle, the Cold War.

This identification grew as Turkey used her diplomatic skills to forge the famous "northern tier," and Arab affection for the Turks cooled accordingly. The first step in creating the northern tier was a mutual defense arrangement with Yugoslavia and Greece, the so-called Balkan Pact. Though the United States might support President Tito's regime with economic and military assistance, American public opinion probably would not have permitted a direct American defense commitment to this communist regime, even though it be vigorously anti-Soviet. The Turks — and the Greeks — were more realistic. Also, by this arrangement, the Turks rendered more secure their vulnerable Western frontier with Bulgaria, which lay only about 100 miles from Istanbul, Turkey's principal city and historic capital and seat of culture.[20]

Turkish diplomacy was then focused eastward. With Western encouragement, the Turks constructed the Baghdad Pact — a mutual defense arrangement between Pakistan, Iran, Iraq, Turkey, and Great Britain. The United States desisted from full membership.[21] A defensive alliance of this sort would have been embarrassing politically to the Truman administration, for it might then have become vulnerable to the charge that it was aiding the Arabs against Israel. Turkey and the West hoped initially that Arab states other than Nuri Said Pasha's Iraq would enter the Pact. Perhaps Lebanon, Jordan, Egypt. But all refused, as they followed Egypt's lead in condemning the Pact as a device of Western imperialism for dividing the Arab states. If Britain had permitted Turkey to move alone, the Pact membership might have been extended. But the British had bases in Iraq to protect (which, of course, are of little value now).

As events evolved, the Pact did become a divisive influence and was a contributing factor in bringing about the 1958 revolution in Iraq and Nuri Said Pasha's murder. One could well have taken a rather dim view of the northern tier concept right from the start. The real value of these paper pacts was questionable. An effective military pact must rest upon mutual interest and mutual confidence. Details relating to defensive strategy, codes, unit strengths, supply, disposition of men and equipment — information of a highly secret nature — must be exchanged. If not, a military pact has little value. Before a free exchange takes place, those responsible must assure themselves of the continued friendship of the other government, as well as its political security. One cannot believe that the Turks felt such confidence in either Greece or Yugoslavia, or Iran or Iraq. And for very good reasons. As it turned out, of course, the Balkan Pact became inoperative by reason of the rupture between Greece and Turkey on the issue of Cyprus. The various economic and political arrangements written into the pact have yet to be implemented. The Baghdad Pact foundered on the wave of the July 1958 revolution in Iraq, which the pact helped bring about. Insofar as the remaining members are concerned, it is the pact's economic commission which seems to hold most promise for positive achievement. Indeed, if the Baghdad Pact had been conceived right at the start as simply a regional economic development program devoid of all military implications, it might have introduced an element of unity and stability into the Middle East. Other Arab states might have been pulled in and constructive work started, about which a certain amount of regional enthusiasm might have been generated. As it stands, the pact has thoroughly tarred Turkey with the imperialist brush and *no* Arab state is a member.[22]

Curiously, the Baghdad Pact represented a Turkish departure from traditional policy of not committing itself irrevocably to any particular position in the Middle East. In taking the initiative in forming the Baghdad Pact, it incurred the enmity of Nasser-led Arab nationalism, for which Iraq's Nuri Said Pasha was a prime target.

One wonders why the Turks were moved to break with tradition. We go back to a point made earlier; Turkish power is in large measure dependent upon external supply. The supply routes must be kept open. In event of war, Turkey's only channels of supply would lie either through the eastern Mediterranean to the ports of Izmir and Iskenderun or overland across Iraq from the Persian Gulf. It follows that gaining maximum security for these communication lines constitutes an important Turkish objective. The Baghdad Pact was an effort on the part of Turkey to shore up the security of the Persian Gulf area. Coincidentally, the Turks stepped up improvement of their highway and rail lines in the direction of the Iraqi frontier and began talking of an oil pipeline to Iran's Qum field.[23]

It also follows that Turkey dare not permit itself to be cut off by communist take-overs in Syria and Iraq. In view of the disdain with which the Turks regard the Arabs, there is no mental bloc holding the Turks back from direct intervention in such eventuality. In 1957, when the Communists appeared to threaten Syria, there was a great deal of talk about Turkish military intervention. Turkish troops maneuvered on the Syrian frontier. "A routine maneuver," Turkish authorities explained. But the fact was that it was far from a routine maneuver. Again, at the time of the July 1958 revolution in Iraq, the Turkish army moved southward ominously. It is now known that Prime Minister Menderes had decided to intervene militarily in Iraq, and it was only by the most vigorous American arguments that he was dissuaded from doing so.[24] (By strange coincidence, immediately thereafter a large, long-sought loan from Turkey's Western allies was forthcoming, which did much to shore up the country's economy and to improve Prime Minister Menderes' political stature.) Some thoughtful Turks feel that Menderes should not have weakened in his determination to move into Iraq. (The author heard some Iraqi Arabs express the same view three years later.) Not only would the Turks have secured their line of communications to the Persian Gulf, but they would have gained control of a vital raw material — oil. The rich Mosul area, which the Turks relinquished to Britain and Iraq in 1926 after much resistance and which includes a large Turkish-speaking population, lies just south of the Turko-Iraqi frontier.[25] A clear-cut communist take-over in Iraq could very well make intervention irresistible to the Turks. In fact, the likelihood of such a Turkish move might have been a major deterrent to an outright grab of power by Iraqi communists in 1958.

As the United States attitude toward President Nasser of Egypt softens, one can perhaps anticipate a similar softening of the Turkish attitude. It would seem to be in the Turkish interest to have Nasser-oriented nationalist regimes securely in power in Iraq and Syria if the alternative be Soviet-oriented communist regimes.

The Cyprus problem brings to mind the whole matter of the relationship of the Turkish republic to the Turkish-speaking peoples outside its frontiers. The Turkish government appears to feel both obligated and justified in representing the interests of these groups in international gatherings. The Greek-Turkish conflict over Cyprus, which kept relations between the two countries at fever pitch from mid-1955 to early 1959, was resolved by an agreement signed on February 19, 1959, of such nature as to give both the Greek ethnic majority and the Turkish minority special status within an independent Republic of Cyprus. Greece, Turkey, and Britain have all guaranteed the independence of the island.[26] It is significant to note that the Cyprus conflict did not relate to vital interests of either Greece or Turkey. It was more in the nature of a convenient diversion of attention from pressing domestic problems for both governments. And when the time became propitious, the disagreement was resolved with surprising facility.*

But this Turkish interest in the welfare of the "overseas Turks" leads one to eye Turkish relationships with the Turkish-speaking people in the Soviet colonies of Central Asia (plus those along the Volga and in the Caucasus), an estimated 20 million; with those in western China, perhaps 10 million; with the Azerbaijani's of western Iran, about 6 million; and with 1.5 million Turks in Afghanistan.[27] In 1952, a spokesman for the Turkish General Staff told the author that in order to win Middle Eastern support, "We" (referring to Turkey and the Western Allies) should take more active measures to support the aspirations of the Middle Eastern peoples. "Take Azerbaijan, for instance," said he. "The people there are Turks. Aid to the Iranian Government helps them not at all. They want to be separate from Iran. We could help them achieve that independence." The unmentioned next step might be amalgamation with Turkey. This thread of Pan-Turanian feeling still pervades the thinking of Turkish leaders, though under present circumstances they almost never make public reference to it. It seems likely, however, that at one time the United States government suggested to Turkey that it pursue a more active Pan-Turanian policy, thereby causing the Turkish minority in the Soviet Union to become more restive and embarrassing to the Soviet Government. Apparently, the Turks refused. But one wonders what the Turkish position would be vis-à-vis these "overseas Turks" if for one reason or another Soviet power were to weaken appreciably relative to the West, or if Soviet power were to collapse altogether in Central Asia. Would we see another Turkish drive for empire? There is now a dynamism about Turkey that may, in the long run, be hard to contain.

* More recent communal violence on Cyprus has been a function of the growing lack of influence of the Greek Government over that of Archbishop Makarios plus the ambivalent policy of the Soviet Union in respect to Cyprus. One might argue that Soviet ambivalence has prevented Turkey and Greece from being pushed into a direct armed confrontation.

Chapter VIII

THE EVE OF REVOLUTION

COURSE OF EVENTS

TURKISH leaders, despite commendable attempts to make democratic political and liberal economic institutions work, apparently felt compelled by 1954 to start tightening their control over economic and political affairs. Observers became increasingly critical of events in Turkey — the oppressive press laws, the unfortunate anti-Greek riot in Istanbul (September 1955), the Cabinet crisis two months later and the emergence of Prime Minister Menderes as the strong man of Turkey, the spiraling upward of prices and costs of living, and the government's seeming inability or unwillingness to contain the deteriorating economic and financial position. In mid-1957 came an economic clamp-down. A new Menderes cabinet introduced drastic legislation against hoarders, profiteers, and speculators. Official agencies were empowered to set the price of almost every sort of commodity and service, from that of steel to a massage. News or public statements calculated to undermine the economic or financial stability of the state were no longer tolerated, and opposition spokesmen and newspapers were prosecuted to the full measure of the law.

Nonetheless, immediately before the October 1957 general elections, the Menderes government increased crop subsidies, declared a moratorium on farm debts, and discounted all thought of taxing the agricultural sector as heavily as others. These moves were hardly in line with the anti-inflationary effort in the cities and were tantamount to "buying" the vote. The Democrats likewise revised the election law so as to outlaw political coalitions. The upshot was that the Democratic Party — and Prime Minister Menderes — were returned to office, but with a popularity plurality of only 48 per cent and a substantially reduced, though still heavy, majority in the Grand National Assembly. The government refused to give out detailed returns, and there were charges of flagrant dishonesty in the count.[1] Others expressed doubt that there would be another honest, contested election so long as the Menderes administration held office.

During 1958, the exchange of political fire between Government and Opposition became even more acrimonious. Several cabinet ministers resigned, apparently in protest against the Prime Minister's personal authoritarian tendencies, and rumors of corruption in high places gained currency. A number of newspaper editors and writers were jailed and their publications suspended. On several occasions the government ordered the press not to publish news of specific events — particularly those involving reactionary religious activities.

From March 17, 1954, to May 14, 1958, 1,161 persons were interrogated under the Press Law. Of these, 288 were convicted, 366 were acquitted, 101 were freed (charges dropped), 11 were bound over, and 402 were released for lack of evidence. An additional 43 persons were still before the courts. Sentences meted out to the 288 totaled 683 months' imprisonment and fines adding up to 323,000 lira. Nine papers and journals were closed for limited periods of time by official court order. The most heavily prosecuted paper was the major opposition sheet *Ulus* (232 cases netting sentences totaling 11 years and four months, plus fines of 73,,830 lira). The paper was also closed twice by official act for a total of 63 days. *Zafer*, the Democratic Party organ in Ankara, was likewise closed down for a month.[2]

During 1959, the government issued 23 no-publication orders to the press, which were ignored only four times. Fifty journalists were sentenced 48 years and 10 months imprisonment and fined a total of 210,000 lira. Various papers were closed down by official order for a total of 14 months.[3] The alleged bases for most of the charges were: publication of articles was found to undermine the authority of government, the financial stability of the country, or the prestige or character of high government functionaries or those of a malicious or libelous character. Proof of the truth of allegations made was not admissible evidence for the defense.

In addition to these limitations on the press, university autonomy was seriously undermined by government-inspired action against certain of the more politically minded faculty members. And judicial independence was challenged by forced retirement or transfer of judges handing down decisions not to the liking of the regime. Meanwhile, religious reaction again became a leading issue as the *Nur* sect gained national notoriety. The Opposition claimed that the Democrats were using religion for political purposes, a penal offense in republican, secular Turkey.

During 1959 there were two attacks on Ismet Inönü, the Opposition leader, with apparent intent to kill. Until after the 1960 revolution, no one was indicted for involvement in these attacks. Though some Democrats seem to be implicated, it would appear unlikely that the incidents were instigated — or perhaps even approved — by Prime Minister Menderes. Being an extraordinarily astute politician if nothing else, the Prime Minister must have realized that the one thing that would again make Ismet Inönü a national hero was a direct, physical attack against his person. It was widely believed in Turkey at the time that President Celal Bayar was involved and that he and Menderes had had bitter words on the subject. The Prime Minister, it was said, dared not split openly with Bayar, for the Party (and hence, himself) probably could not have survived such a row politically. Some speculated that the curious mass, "nonpolitical, organization" *Vatan Cephesi* (Fatherland Front) had been created by Menderes so that he would have an organizational home in the event he finally felt compelled to bolt the Democratic Party. Otherwise, the Front seemed to have no function and no purpose. Even high ranking Democratic Party members spoke very bitterly to the author in September 1959 against President Bayar and in off-the-record conversations blamed him for a number of the excesses for which the Party, and Menderes in particular, were identified. On the other hand, perhaps this was all part of a campaign to save Menderes at the expense of Bayar. The postrevolutionary trial of Bayar and Menderes did not clarify the issue.

What did all this mean? In seeking an answer one must turn to the vast changes that had been taking place in Turkish society and in the structure of the nation's economy. Though personal ambition on the part of politicians might have been a factor, closer scrutiny of Turkish problems indicates that the drift back toward authoritarianism was much deeper than Prime Minister Menderes' alleged belief in himself as the "indispensable man." With or without Menderes, the crisis of Turkey remained, for it was bedded in structural defects of an economic and social nature. This last was what Opposition leaders in Turkey, and many foreign observers, failed to recognize as they condemned all governmental moves — good, bad, and indifferent. They were by no means all bad. This fanaticism on the part of the Opposition drove the Menderes' administration to further extremes in its attempt to prevent the Opposition from exploiting unpopular moves and dislodging the Democrats from power. In the field of education and religion, the Democrats gave ground, thereby gaining some favor with the electorate and perhaps making the economic measures somewhat easier to take, for in the economic area the Democrats pressed on remorselessly. Those who stood in the way or criticized too loudly were cut down by intimidation or imprisonment. A $359 million foreign credit announced in August 1958 had so eased the economic pressures by the end of 1959 that the Democrats even began to talk about another election. Meanwhile, Opposition leaders became bitterly critical of Turkey's Western allies for bailing the Menderes administration out economically in this fashion when it had seemed to be teetering precariously on the brink of political collapse. Intentional or not, foreign aid could be an important political crutch for a regime that was losing the confidence of key groups and exhausting its economic resources.

MAJOR PROBLEMS

The compass of Turkey's critical problems can be boxed in terms of the following problem areas: education, religion, economic change, land, urbanization, investment, inflation, and statism. In all of these areas, the basic dilemmas were of a structural nature, and no amount of administrative or financial juggling could resolve them. In general, Turkey's experience seemed to cast doubt on the efficacy of liberal political and economic institutions.

The Problem of Education[4]

Other than gross totals, there had been remarkably few educational statistics published in Turkey since 1955, which fact alone drew attention. In the 1958–1959 school year, something like 2.4 million students were reported attending 21,464 primary schools (grades 1 to 5), of which 19,379 were located in villages.[5] Of the total enrollment in the urban schools, 42 per cent were girls, and in the rural schools, 35 per cent.[6] Over the 1933–1949 period, the number of children of primary school age reported to be in school increased gradually from 30.9 to 58.3 per cent, although the growth during the last five years of this period (1945–1949) was exceedingly slow.[7] In 1955, a comparable figure was possibly 72 per cent. But curiously, in June 1958, only 140,318 students graduated from grade 5, or not more than 35 to 40 per cent of the children of appropriate age.[8] Undoubtedly, the percentage in the village schools was substantially lower. The rate of attrition was obviously high in the first five grades. At the same time some 262,297 students were in the secondary schools (grades 6 to 11), which meant that for every eight primary students only one entered secondary education, probably about the ratio that had obtained in 1949.[9] Clearly, the big hurdle in the Turkish educational system lay between the primary and secondary schools. If a student reached grade 6, there was an excellent chance that he would continue into a lycee (grades 9 to 11); perhaps as many as one out of three did so. Once he was in a lycee, there was a four-out-of-five chance that he would go on into higher education of some sort.

The relative number of girls and boys in the primary schools was revealing as a measure of what had happened to woman's place in Turkish society. Clearly, the percentage of girls in village schools had not been increasing, a fact which was confirmed by personal observation in Anatolian villages since 1950 (Table 3).

Table 3

Student Registration in Turkey's Primary Schools

	1936–1937		1945–1950		1958–1959	
	Boys	*Girls*	*Boys*	*Girls*	*Boys*	*Girls*
Type of School	*(per cent)*		*(per cent)*		*(per cent)*	
Village	69	31	65	35	65	35
Urban	66	34	59	41	58	42
Totals	67	33	63	37	62	38

Source: *Istatistik Yilliği, 1952,* (Ankara, Istatistik Umum Müdürlüğü, 1953), p. 159.

These statistics point up some rather serious problems. First, with the politically motivated release since 1950 of police pressure in enforcing the compulsory school law, the proportion of village girls in schools failed to increase and the rate of drop-out for all students continued to be very large. It is revealing that in a 1952 study, an American education consultant found indications that in perhaps half of the villages studied the villagers seemed either to stand in opposition to the village school or were indifferent to it.[10] Although the degree of support for secular education had surely grown somewhat on the village level, there was still much popular resistance. Across the country, village schoolteachers complained of official indifference to truancy and of inadequate funds with which to equip, staff, and maintain existing schools. The morale of village teachers was unquestionably lower than in 1950, and the problem of keeping teachers in the villages remained an awkward one.[11] A certain element of dedication and idealism was a prerequisite for a successful village teacher; he faced a difficult job at best. But if he felt that he were unsupported and unappreciated by his nation's leaders, as now seemed the case, there was an inclination for his dedication and idealism to deteriorate into cynicism and self-seeking — and ultimately, to resignation from the profession. The result was that not a few village schools stood empty.

A specially appointed National Education Commission, on which a number of outstanding Turkish educators sat, submitted its report to the Ministry of Education early in 1959. Although classified secret by the Turkish government, it became known that the Commission had made several of these same points. In addition to vigorous criticism of religious education, the commission cast doubt on the social and economic value of five years of primary education which had no follow-up. As already noted, relatively few village children were finding their way into a secondary school, virtually all of which were located in the towns, and few village parents seemed to see the value of secondary education, particularly for girls, nor could they spare their children's labor at the times of peak load (harvest, seeding, cultivation). Neither did they feel that they had the cash to provide board and room while their children attended a town school, only a fortunate few having town-dwelling relatives willing to assume responsibility. Also in the usual village there was virtually no juvenile literature which would encourage children to continue reading after graduation from fifth grade. Under these conditions, it was suspected that effective literacy was lost by most children within three to five years after primary school graduation.

By 1960, the army was lending its enormous prestige to basic education, thereby increasing popular acceptance of, if not demand for, education. The army began by setting up 16 basic education centers at which all illiterate draftees, an estimated 50 per cent, would be required to attend an eight-week course. It was expected that something like 100,000 men would move through these courses each year. Their study would focus on acquiring literacy, basic arithmetic skills, and the concept of measuring. For illiterates, the normal two-year period of compulsory military service was lengthened by two months to accommodate this new training. Special books, deemed to be of interest to soldiers, were printed for free distribution, the purpose of which was to stimulate the habit of reading and to develop reading skills. But this program did not touch the female population, and the problem of the secondary school remained.

The National Education Commission recommended a slow-up in the construction of new village primary schools (about half of the villages had one by 1960) and more emphasis on secondary schools to service rural areas. One problem was that the village communities were too small to justify separate secondary schools, and the cost and the difficulty of transportation rendered regional schools unrealistic in most areas. The Commission also urged that differences between rural and city schools be narrowed so as to avoid the creation of two distinct educational systems within the country. Under the Village Institute System, which was modified subsequent to the 1950 change of regime, the type of education offered in the villages had been quite different from that given in the towns, which fact made it even more difficult for the village children to move on into the secondary school system. As other forms of practical education were extended into the village via the agricultural extension service, mobile units teaching practical skills, the farm machinery schools, and military technical training, the type of practical training formerly stimulated by the Village Institute system was perhaps no longer necessary. There began to be more emphasis on turning out village teachers better equipped to teach basic cultural subjects. For several years, the Village Institutes had been called simply "Primary Teachers Training Schools," and there was an attempt to enroll in them at least a minimum of teacher trainees of city or town origin. The authorities felt that by mixing village and town youth in this fashion, the enormous difference between country and city mentality might be narrowed. But in practice, it proved virtually impossible to attract any significant number of town and city youth into the village teaching program.

Because the desire for education was one force pulling the more enlightened and progressive villagers into urban centers, the problem of providing better and higher level *rural* education became compelling, for the cost of settling new urban settlers was great, a subject upon which we shall dwell at some length in a later section. Furthermore, the leadership wished to reverse the tendency for most of the dynamic elements in the population to gravitate from village to town; from town to provincial seat; and from provincial seat to Ankara, Izmir, or Istanbul.

One of the most disturbing aspects of 1960 Turkey was

the apparently weakening support for education. Relatively speaking, a somewhat smaller share of Turkey's available resources had been invested in education in recent years, a tendency which had become apparent even in the 1948–1950 period.[12]

Investment in education has, of course, much to do with a people's ability to use, productively, investment in material forms of wealth, the so-called "absorptive capacity." In a rapidly developing country such as Turkey this concept is a very slippery one indeed, for the level of absorptive capacity is always changing. In reality, the term "investment" should be used to include investment in people as well as in things. The problem lies in striking an appropriate balance between these two forms of investment, not in determining a nation's absorptive capacity. Economist Theodore W. Schultz has written:

> People are, also, an important part of the wealth of nations. Moreover, as people invest in themselves they can augment the amount of human wealth: in many countries this form of wealth, measured by what it renders to production, is now vastly larger than all other forms taken together.
>
> * * * *
>
> Nevertheless, the main stream of modern economics has bypassed undertaking any systematic analysis of human wealth . . . Economists have found it all too convenient to think of labor as a homogeneous input free of any capital components.[13]

One suspects that the return on investment in education, within the Turkish context, was very much higher than was true for many projects under construction by 1960.

The findings of Bradburn's 1959 research in Turkey "indicated that cultural value-orientations centering around concern with the present to the exclusion of planning for the future and a non-activist approach to the environment and a consequent low need for achievement (were) . . . the major non-economic forces retarding economic development in Turkey." [14] Though he felt that the overwhelmingly dominant role of the father in the Turkish family tended to block rapid increase in achievement motivation, still he found some evidence of change. He speculated that this increase in achievement motivation was possibly a product of the Primary Teachers Training Schools (the former Village Institutes), various adult training programs, the rapid growth of cities and consequent geographical separation of families, and even the primary and secondary schools themselves. He reported that in a world sample of stories from third and fourth grade readers, those from Turkey contained "the highest degree of achievement imagery," which was taken as indicating that Turkish educators were concerned with "instilling achievement values." [15] Bradburn might have added to his list of forces corroding the dominance of the father two more: (1) the impact of two years of military training in a modern army, and (2) the weakening of religious justification for the traditional pattern of family relations.

The Problem of Religion

Not unrelated to the matter of balanced investment and absorptive capacity is the problem of religious reorientation, for traditionally religion has seriously weakened both the desire for secular education and skills and the push of economic incentive.[16]

It was under the Republican People's Party regime in 1949 and early 1950 that the first moves were made in the direction of greater religious liberalism. Religious lessons were introduced into the primary schools, a faculty of theology authorized at the University of Ankara, and ten worship leaders' and preachers' schools inaugurated.[17] The latter institutions were designed to train men for careers as village religious leaders (*hoca*). Significantly, these educational moves were made under the direction of the secular-oriented Ministry of Education, not under the Presidency of Religious Affairs, the government office administering the religious hierarchy. Undermining any political capital the People's Party might have generated out of these moves, however, was the fact that just prior to the 1950 election the government had been forced to arrest and try a popular religious leader, one Kemal Pilavoğlu, who was known as the sheikh of the Ticani sect. The Turkish secret police estimated at the time that he had some 300,000 followers.[18] In 1951, statues of Atatürk in various parts of the country were smashed, apparently by unhappy Ticani's in support of Islam's prohibition of graven images. The new Democratic regime had reacted by arresting scores of persons, most of whom were members of various of the outlawed religious sects — Nakşibendi, Nur, Bektaşi, Bahâi, and Kadiri, as well as Ticani. Sentences had been generally light, three to six months each, though Pilavoğlu himself remained behind bars for seven and one-half years.[19] From 1950 to mid-1960, some 500 persons had been arrested in Turkey for religious offenses and held for varying periods of time (admittedly a rough estimate constructed from a sampling of daily press reports, but believed to be not too far in error).

It remained a criminal offense in Turkey to use religion for political purposes, to establish an organization on a religious basis, to proselytize, or to defame the memory of Kemal. The legal problem was to prove that members of the various religious groups had in fact conducted themselves in an illegal fashion. Of course, the mere fact of their existence as organized groups was contrary to the law, but particularly since 1950 the authorities had been inclined to overlook them so long as they desisted from direct political involvement, from preaching disloyalty to secular government, and from openly attacking the memory of Kemal.

Shortly after coming to power, the Democratic Party administration had lifted the ban against giving the call to prayer in Arabic, extended the religious lessons offered in the public schools, improved the maintenance of town and city mosques, reinaugurated courses to train *hufaz* (plural of *hafiz,* one who has committed the Koran to memory), and increased the number of worship leaders' and preachers' schools to nineteen. In 1960, the administration boasted of its accomplishments in the field of religion. Since 1950, the number of professional teachers of the Koran had been increased from 131 to 702 (plus 1,500 part-time instructors), 2,055 *hufaz* had been trained, and some 30,000 students were reported to be attending the courses on the Koran.[20] The government was also, by 1960, donating money to the villages (1,000 to 5,000 lira each) for the construction and maintenance of local mosques.[21]

The leaders saw that with the relaxation of police power in the villages and small towns, the older, more conservative village religious leaders might well gain pre-eminence over the young village schoolteachers in terms of village influence. To reintroduce police surveillance and pressure in the pre-1950 style was politically unwise in a bipartisan state. The way out was to train, as fast as possible, a new generation of village religious leaders who would be oriented very differently from their elders. It was no coincidence that the curriculum in these training schools was heavily weighted (two-thirds) on the side of nonreligious subjects — history, science, foreign language. It seemed likely that licenses to practice as village religious leaders would be limited to graduates of these schools as they became available in significant numbers, which by 1960 was just beginning to happen. Gradually, it was hoped, the elderly, black-frocked, turbaned *hocas,* who represented the old mentality, would fade away.

Indeed, a new generation of enlightened religious leaders at the grass roots level could be a significant force in Turkish development. A provincial governor once commented to me about the great influence men of religious standing might have, particularly in the villages and small towns. "I once had a veterinary on my staff," he recalled, "who had been a *hafiz.* When he went into a village, he first delivered a sermon and then spoke of the benefits of raising Merino sheep [an improved breed that the government was trying to induce the people to raise]. Use of religious leaders in all fields can be very useful," he concluded.

To many opponents of the Menderes regime — particularly the city-bred intellectual — there was real doubt that, given the drift of events, a secular Turkey could survive the next ten to fifteen years without serious subversion from its religious conservatives. Menderes, it was charged, was buying votes by relaxing control over religious activity. In evaluating this indictment, one should recognize that whatever the party in power the authorities faced a delicate choice whenever there was a religious eruption of a subversive nature. Should the police power be used or not? If "yes," the victims might be martyred and their popular following strengthened. And, the party might lose precious votes. So long as popular support was fairly evenly balanced between the major parties, as was the case in the last few years before 1960, the administration might be understandably reluctant to use force against conservative religious groups. Yet, there might come times when no progressively minded leadership could afford to remain inactive. The hope was that the suppression of reactionary religious activities would continue to have support from the leaders of all major parties. But as tempers mounted and interparty frictions grew hotter, in 1959 and 1960, it became increasingly difficult to maintain this statesmanlike poise. Votes counted.

My own feeling is that by 1960, despite a religiously conservative element of politically significant size, it no longer endangered the secular republican state. Islam itself had been undergoing a subtle transformation even on the village level. Economic incentive, material well-being, innovation, the machine, commerce, and social change no longer appeared as challenges to religion. A village in the process of building a 100,000-lira mosque was, I found, likewise proud of its neat, well-attended secular school, of its twelve shops, of its two coffeehouses, of its skilled workmen, of its tractors. The new mosque did not, in this community at least, represent religious reaction, for the villagers talked incessantly of the material improvements in their lives and of those soon to come. And yet the casual observer might have seen only the new mosque and automatically equated this with renewed interest in traditional folk Islam. But he would have been wrong. An accommodation between folk Islam and modern life was in fact taking place.

It would perhaps be a mistake to overintellectualize the process at this point. As W. C. Smith observed,

One thing seems sure, if a Luther — to borrow their own metaphor — were to appear, he would get a ready hearing amongst the educated class of Turkey. Emotionally and intellectually, sociologically and religiously, they seem ready to follow new ventures of Islamic development. However, whether such a reform will indeed appear is another matter. Can one generate a Reformation by fiat? — even when providing the milieu? [22]

Almost unconsciously — without realizing the theological conflict the intellectual might feel — the Anatolian was beginning to reposition his religion so as to be relevant to the modern world. This process was a matter of enormous consequence in economic terms as well as social. The prestige and motivation provided by traditional folk Islam was being identified with new skills and incentives. It should be recalled that even in purely traditional terms, Islamic predestination could be a force for both resignation to an apparently inevitable fate and for enormous effort to achieve one's manifest destiny.

The Problem of Economic Change

In 1960 Turkey was still overwhelmingly agricultural; 70 per cent of its population was concerned primarily with farming, and 40 to 45 per cent of its national income was derived from this sector. The leaders realized that these figures had to shift substantially in the near future if Turkey were to forge ahead economically. Indeed, a shift was discernible — in 1938, agriculture yielded 50.3 per cent of the national product, in 1960, about 42 per cent. In other words, roughly 70 per cent of the total labor force produced less than half of the national product. Industry generated 12.6 per cent in 1938 and 13.7 per cent in 1960.[23] All in all, though, the shift was remarkably slight.

An increasing national standard of living might be

founded either on (1) gains from conquests, (2) decrease in population without comparable decrease in production, (3) natural windfall such as oil, (4) foreign subsidy, and/or (5) increasingly efficient production. In the long haul, the latter alternative is the only feasible and solid basis for national economic growth. But efficient production, even in most agriculture — the picking of fruit being perhaps the notable exception — rests on mechanization. For a grain, sugar beet, and cotton producing country such as Turkey, production costs of farm produce could be brought into a competitive range with those of the more advanced states only through large-scale mechanization. Better seeds, more adequate fertilizer, more extensive irrigation could help, but these alone were not enough. Hence, efficient agriculture — that is, low-cost, competitive agriculture — meant heavy capital investment and a vastly decreased farm labor requirement. Alternative employment opportunities must then be provided for the displaced farmer and farm hand; if not, social, economic, and political turmoil would surely follow.

A further compelling reason for trying to shift the basis of the Turkish economy from agriculture to a more diversified structure lay in the fact that so long as the economy rested predominantly on farming, it was profoundly effected by slight, chance variations in weather, thereby ruling out any effective long-run economic planning or stability. Particularly was this true of an agricultural economy resting upon dry grain farming, as in Turkey. In 1953, Turkey was the world's fourth largest exporter of grain. In 1955, it was a net importer of grain. Meanwhile, per capita real income apparently failed to move ahead. It was estimated to have been 556 Turkish lira in 1953 and 531 in 1956.[24] Such could be the impact of weather.

The need for Turkey to compete with the mechanized countries in the world market was compelling. If it failed to do so, it could not earn the foreign exchange with which to buy machines — a product of the mechanized or hard currency countries. Without those machines, Turkey would be unable to raise its standard of living by increasing the efficiency of production. By exploiting short-run market advantages, Turkey had been able to sell a substantial quantity of high-cost, low-quality produce on the world market in the decade of the 1950's, but only in inadequate amounts. Turkey had, by 1960, been running a trade deficit for fifteen years without interruption, the average annual deficit of the last five years having been about $150 million. Due to this running trade deficit, Turkey had been compelled to amass a foreign debt well over a $1.5 billion (about a quarter of its annual gross national product).

The choice of whether to improve the nation's standard of living or not was no longer in the hands of Turkey's leaders, thanks to 25 years of grass roots education and social reform, vast improvement in communications (including exposure to the Hollywood-produced motion picture, which the ordinary villagers and town bourgeoisie were viewing in increased numbers),[25] and a deliberate channeling of an undue share of the national income into the pockets of village farmers. The result was that economic incentive began working with tremendous force at town and village level. The single most important political issue in Turkey became the availability of such key consumer goods as coffee, tea, sugar, kerosene, radios, batteries, lamps, glass, textiles and shoes. This massive popular demand for rapid improvement in the standard of living existed in part because the ordinary folk were now conscious of the vast difference between their own standard of material well-being and that of Western Europe and North America. The demand for economic improvement, it was safe to say, took easy precedence over interest in maintaining democratic political institutions. And, so long as democratic government continued, there seemed to be no method available to the leaders to curtail this enormous economic incentive. Long dormant in Turkish society, economic incentives now threatened to move well ahead of the available tools with which its targets could be achieved. The masters of Turkey were, in reality, the political slaves of the village farming masses and the new lower class urban group.

Despite the $359 million loan in Turkey's favor announced in August 1958, many realized that this aid provided but a temporary release of pressure, for the Turkish economic problem was fundamentally a structural one, not fiscal or administrative. Nonetheless, at the insistence of its foreign creditors, the Turkish government pledged itself to issue no more new money, to restrict domestic commercial credits by freezing bank credits at preloan levels, to put state controlled industries on a self-supporting basis insofar as capital resources were concerned, and to establish a system of premium rates for foreign exchange transactions which amounted to a devaluation of the lira from $0.36 to $0.09 for most purposes. Clearly, the creditors had seen the Turkish economic crisis essentially as a financial, fiscal, and administrative problem. A 1959 OEEC mission to Turkey observed, "The difficulties in which the Turkish economy finds itself today stem basically from an attempt to do too much too quickly." [26]

But the Turkish economic problem could not be resolved by financial, fiscal, and administrative reforms alone. Nor, one suspected, were the Turks attempting to do too much too quickly. The reverse might have been more accurate. One internationally recognized authority declared, with a volume of evidence behind his arguments, that the Turkish economic crisis was due essentially to structural weaknesses and an overly conservative attack. To sustain Turkey's growth, he declared, a number of moves were required, the most important ones being:[27]

1. A stop to overexploitation of the land, which meant a substantial reduction in the amount of land under cultivation
2. A rapid reduction of the animal population to halt disastrous overgrazing
3. A dramatic increase in land and animal productivity by means of irrigation, fertilization, improved feed, scientific breeding, better tools, and improved traction power — all on a massive scale
4. The full-time productive employment of the now underemployed rural population, which might require compulsory labor service and heavy investment in public works and industry.

In the absence of such moves, Turkey could anticipate recurring balance of payments difficulties, inflation, and unemployment — whatever fiscal or financial policies were followed and however wise and efficient the administration. But politically, these moves were exceedingly difficult; little was done.

The Problem of Land

Land reform in the Turkish sense had not resolved the economic problem. Turkish land reform had been equated with the carving up of large state-owned tracts and a few unused private estates and distributing them at a nominal cost to landless or near landless villagers. Up to the end of 1959, a total of some 6,200,000 acres of tillable land and 3,000,000 acres of communal grazing land had been distributed to 365,000 families in 4,876 villages.[28] These totals would indicate that on the average each recipient family received 12.1 acres of crop land and 0.9 acres of grazing land. However commendable this program might have been from a sociopolitical point of view, it had made the rapid introduction of modern, mechanized agriculture doubly difficult. Land holdings already suffered from fragmentation due to observance of traditional Islamic law by most rural folk in the matter of land inheritance. The distribution of land caused further fragmentation, thereby reducing both the size of average farm plots and farm income below that which would sustain mechanization. Land reform also had had the effect of holding marginal or submarginal farmers back on the land, people whose labor could be more profitably utilized in industry.[29]

Adding further pressure on the marginal or submarginal farmer to stay on the land had been the deliberate policy of channeling to the farm sector more of the national income than was economically justified in terms of production, the major devices for which — as noted — were easy credit, tax exemption, public investment, and crop subsidy. Inherent in these programs was encouragement for inefficient agriculture, a situation very much at odds with national development.

On the other hand, if agriculture had been freed of these artificial stimulants, the human flood which would have swept into the cities would have far exceeded the already serious proportions of the rural-urban movement. The resulting political restlessness might have been disastrous. In short, a large number of people must be held back on the land. But was this the way to do it?

The Problem of Urbanization

A product of the effort to launch self-sustained growth in Turkey had been the partial industrialization (mechanization) of the country's economy. As already noted, the share of national income contributed by agriculture was dropping, albeit slowly. Coincidentally, a mass rural-urban movement of people was well under way by 1960. The large cities of Turkey were growing at a rate of 10 per cent or more each year. Average annual population growth lay between 2.5 and 3 per cent, probably closer to the upper limit. If Turkey succeeded in placing agriculture on a wholly modern, efficient basis within the next generation, it meant that within the next 20 years the majority of Turkey's population would have to be rehoused in an urban environment and provided with at least minimum urban services. The 70 per cent of the population living in the villages and deriving its livelihood from the land would be cut back to something like 40 or 50 per cent. During this time, Istanbul would probably become a city of perhaps some 4.5 million persons and Ankara, 1.5 million, in a nation of 40 million. (In 1960 the populations of Istanbul and Ankara were 1.7 and 0.6 million, respectively.) These estimates were based on a simple projection of contemporary trends, trends that apparently could be modified only by government intervention.

The sheer size of investment required to effect satisfactory urbanization on this scale and speed, not to mention the enormous organizational difficulties in providing adequate urban services and the investment required to employ these millions in nonfarm occupations, made it almost mandatory that Turkey find alternatives. Since 1950, in fact, roughly 1 million persons had apparently moved from village to city, and the larger cities were ringed by squalid shack towns.[30] There was every reason to believe that the movement was accelerating. A very conservative estimate was that the rural labor force (1958) still contained an unutilized two million man-years of labor which could be diverted from agriculture without deleterious effect on farm production. There might easily be twice that amount or more. Much of this underemployment arose from the highly seasonal nature of Anatolian agriculture; it did not mean that two million workers could be removed from the villages on a year-round basis without impairing farm production. But, it did mean that there were at least two million man-years of labor available for nonagricultural enterprise. To utilize this labor required that either nonagricultural enterprise be brought to the village or the labor to town- or city-based enterprise. In either event, a substantial proportion of the labor would be of a seasonal or temporary nature.

Some sociologists and others suggested that the alternative to urbanization was the industrialized village, perhaps a consolidation of the nonfarm sectors of several villages, the economy of which would be based on dispersed industrial units. Such industrial organization required rural electrification and good transport, but it would have the enormous social economy of not requiring the transport, the rehousing and provision of urban services for most of the Turkish population within the next generation. Many millions could then continue to live within their traditional social structure in their own homes and protected by their traditional informal, family-oriented, social security system. Admittedly, the social structure would change, as it was already doing, but the change would be less revolutionary and less costly in terms of both money and social and personal disintegration. Turkish leaders were seriously considering the problem, but the Menderes regime had not developed a program prior to its collapse in 1960.[31]

As we have seen, despite the movement of perhaps a million persons off the land since 1947, there were, as of 1960, between 2.0 and 5 million persons living on the land whose full-time labor was not required to maintain farm production, and many thousands were not required at all. For Turkey to forge ahead economically, these people had to be employed productively on a full-time basis — preferably outside the urban centers — either in industry, commerce, and/or public works. Some concluded that the only way out was a compulsory labor service, the man power thus recruited to be used in water resources development, soil conservation, forestry development, and accelerated industrial development. The political consequences of such a move would indeed be sobering, for democratic political institutions would be exceedingly difficult to sustain under these circumstances. But there was no doubt that responsible Turkish leaders felt compelled by 1960 to think in these directions, for Turkey's greatest untapped capital resource was the 2 to 5 million man-years of unused labor in rural Turkey. Some of the authoritarian tendencies of the Menderes regime may be explained — if not excused — in these terms.

The Problem of Investment

The problem of investment alone required that Turkey pursue a policy of avoiding urbanization. Its full resources had to go into development of better tools, machines, and social services (such as education and health), not to mention the maintenance of a modern military force. If, in addition, Turkey were to build enormous cities, the task would become impossible. It might be so in any event. Some observers claimed that even if the cost of urbanization were not counted, the targets toward which the Menderes regime was driving the country were unrealistic. But government leaders, admitting the economic difficulties, argued that the targets were dictated by irresistible political forces, namely the unrelenting and irresistible pressure exerted by the people for rapid improvement in living conditions, plus the not inconsiderable attractions of the Soviet Union which seemed, at least from a distance, to be one place where "operation bootstrap" had enjoyed sustained success without foreign intervention. Even the anti-Russianism of the Turk might eventually break under the pressure if the Turkish system failed to satisfy the requirements. So went the argument.

The economic target of the Menderes administration could be defined quite clearly; it was to bring the country within the range of the industrial states of the West in terms of productivity and standard of living within a meaningful time. It would buy no economic development program that committed Turkey to perpetual economic inferiority with the industrial West. As the immortal Kemal once said, "Economics means everything. To live, to be happy, whatever is necessary for civilized man; it means all of these. It means agriculture, it means industry, it means everything." [32] Prime Minister Adnan Menderes referred in public speeches time and again to the great future ahead for Turkey, a future he defined in terms of improved living standards. In 1957, Celal Bayar, the Turkish President declared,

We must work even harder, create even greater works . . . I want to present an idea. In Greece, for example, according to national income statistics for 1955, each citizen received [the equivalent of] 644 lira. Here, it was 868 lira. That means that we are surpassing their standard of living. But for us, this result is not enough. Our real aim is not only to surpass our neighbors; it is to reach the standard of the most advanced nations. The Turkish nation is equal to this and capable [of accomplishing it].[33]

And again, on October 20, 1957, President Bayar said, "We in our country, are working to follow the example of American development. We hope that thirty years from now when our blessed country will have a population of 50 million, it will be a little America." [34] The implication of approaching equality was always there, even as the Soviet leaders were always comparing Soviet production with that of the West, and with that of the United States in particular (and we with the USSR in respect to space technology).

One could calculate that for Turkey to catch up with the West in 60 to 90 years, an average annual growth of national product of something like 7 per cent had to be sustained. Relationships obtaining within the Turkish economy were such that this rate of growth would require an annual investment in capital goods equal to about 20 per cent of the national product — or close to $1 billion in 1958 (of which about $300 million would have to be in foreign exchange). By straining every economic fiber — and by massing a foreign debt at the rate $150 to $200 million a year — Menderes' Turkey managed to approach these levels in certain years. If Turkey could count on an uninterrupted series of bumper crops, plus continued large-scale American economic assistance, it might pull this rate of development off on a sustained basis. But obviously, it could not count on either of these. One demanded continued favorable acts of God, the other favorable acts of Congress; neither was completely dependable.

Estimates would lead one to believe that over the 1950–1958 period the average annual increase in both real per capita product and real per capita income was +4.1. But one could anticipate that incremental capital-output ratios (the ratio of net investment to increases in national income) had already begun to grow. That is, it would take substantially more investment in the future to generate the same rate of return as before. During the pre-1950 era of development, the capital-output ratio in Turkey was probably in the neighborhood of 1:1, though the basic figures were admittedly no more than informed guesses. But as Higgins points out, "If good land is exhausted [as was now true in Turkey], the capital-output ratio may rise sharply as the amount of capital per head is increased." [35] Over the 1950–1958 period, the Turkish capital-output ratio was probably close to 2:1. To assume a ratio between 3:1 and 4:1 for the 1960–1975 period was surely not unreasonable, which was what Professor Baade did in his penetrating 1959 report for the United Nations Food and Agriculture Organization.[36] He estimated that in order to shove real per capita income ahead by 2 or 3 per cent per annum — and the Turkish leaders would accept no lesser target — a total investment on the order of $16 to $19 billion between 1959 and 1975 was required, which meant that annual gross investment should increase from about $700 million (6,300 million lira) in 1959 to between $1.8 and $2.1 billion (16,200 and 18,900 million lira) by 1975, figures well over 1950–1960 investment levels. Furthermore, there was no hope, in Baade's opinion, of Turkey's repaying further international loans unless it received, "over a considerable number of years, gift subsidies which annually total approximately the same amount as these credits." He observed,

> It is completely illusory to imagine that Turkey, through this credit could increase its productivity and, particularly, its exports in relation to import requirements to such an extent that, in the future, the balance of payments would not only equalize, but would provide surplus funds for the payment of the credit. Since the crisis is structural, it can only be overcome by removing the imbalance in Turkey's economic crisis.[37]

There was little doubt that responsible Turkish leaders were beginning to think along these lines in 1959 and 1960. They knew perfectly well that the $359 million credit extended in 1958 by the United States and various of Turkey's European trading partners provided only a brief respite. The investment problem remained. But Menderes, weakened politically by the closeness of the 1957 election, did not dare undertake the politically unpopular moves required in the interests of sustained economic development at the pace that he himself deemed necessary. Rather, he struck out viciously at the opposition.

The Problem of Inflation

Obviously characteristic of an erupting, underdeveloped economy such as that of Turkey is chronic inflation; levels of expectation rise above the ability of the economy to deliver. Many American economists, businessmen, and government experts criticized the Menderes government severely for its unwillingness and/or inability to hold down the lid. Other observers, perhaps more versed in the peculiar problems facing such countries as Turkey, were inclined to the view that a chronic inflationary situation was perhaps the only environment within which these countries could secure the capital goods they required. Economist Sumner Slichter wrote that one of the four principal influences making for world-wide inflation was "the eager desire of many so-called 'underdeveloped' countries to raise their standard of consumption and their willingness — *and their need* — to use inflationary methods to acquire capital goods" (italics added). He went on to point out that "a further world-wide influence is the Cold War itself — a great technological competition such as the world has never seen before." [38] It was perhaps well not to heap too much blame for a local inflationary situation on the shoulders of the Turkish leaders. No one suggested how they might have effectively controlled the inflationary movement — given the political situation facing them and the administrative apparatus at their disposal — and at the same time maintain the necessary economic growth.

It was estimated by Turkish economists that consumer demand in 1954 was in the neighborhood of 12.6 billion Turkish lira and the supply of consumer goods, roughly 12.1 billion Turkish lira, thereby leaving an excessive demand of about one-half billion Turkish lira. A comparable 1955 figure was estimated to have been about 700 million Turkish lira.[39] This excessive demand and the pressure it generated were a function of low national income, low personal saving, and high investment, a share of which was from external sources. It was clear then why the cost of living index in Ankara, for instance, which had been showing an average annual increase of between 2 and 5 per cent for the period immediately preceding 1954, reached 9 per cent in 1954 and 13 per cent in 1955 and remained at that level of increase (15 per cent in 1958). Likewise, the money supply rose from 2.5 billion lira in

1953 to 4.1 billion toward the end of 1955, to 5.0 billion at the beginning of 1958.[40]

The rapid growth of domestic prices and money supply undermined confidence in the currency and caused a contraction in the volume of cash savings. Personal incomes were channeled increasingly into current consumption or into real estate. Real estate prices in cities such as Izmir, Ankara, and Istanbul increased markedly. A square meter of land in an upper-class residential section of Ankara valued at 10 Turkish lira in 1952 was sold for 20 Turkish lira in 1953, 30 Turkish lira in 1954, and 80 to 100 Turkish lira in 1955. It was substantially higher by 1960. Resulting speculation in real estate diverted savings from economically productive investment. Instability of prices and wages, plus uncertainty of securing imported materials and machines, combined to induce this overinvestment in real estate at the expense of productive capacity.

The increase in urban land values further increased the difficulty of providing adequate housing and urban services to the new city dwellers, who were now pouring in from the farms. One reaction of the Menderes' government was the condemnation of much urban property for more rational development, particularly in Istanbul and Ankara. The ousted landlords, who quite naturally did not receive for their property what they had originally anticipated (often being given what they had declared property values to be for tax purposes!) swelled the ranks of the political dissidents, thereby making the maintenance of democratic institutions still more difficult. The fact that the face-lifting job begun in Istanbul and Ankara in 1957 was accompanied by obvious inefficiency and perhaps some dishonesty fueled the fires of criticism. But the fact remained that drastic measures were necessary if future generations were to live in these ancient, rabbit-warren cities — and we speak here particularly of Istanbul. The Minister of Construction and Settlement declared at the time, "If the reconstruction of Istanbul had not been undertaken, the density of the population and the congestion of economic activity would be such today that the city would be paralyzed." [41] But the fact remained that confiscation and demolition of property without prior payment was unconstitutional. Many property owners were still awaiting payment as of mid-1962.

Several moves might have been made to control the corrosive inflation, but the most effective were clearly impossible within a political democracy. Taxation of agriculture either through extension of the income tax to farm income or by raising the land tax was one method. Farm income was largely tax-exempt. With 70 per cent of the population identifying itself with the land and with agriculture, it was doubtful that any Turkish government could have survived an election if it attempted either measure. Indiscriminate taxation of farm income would have alienated the mass of voters, 70 per cent of whom identified themselves with agriculture. A tax levied only against the larger landowners would have undermined party organization, particularly the Democratic which rested heavily on landowners for middle-echelon leadership. When an increased land tax had been proposed several years before, there was much head-shaking by village elders about a government which would even propose such a project.[42] Parliament, acting wisely in its own interest, quickly shelved this embarrassing proposal. As one MP declared at the time, "If the land tax is increased, I shall never be able to face my constituents again." The farm bloc held a solid majority in every electoral district of the country, with but two possible exceptions (out of 67).

Another anti-inflationary measure proposed from time to time had been the curtailment of agriculture credit. But the government had not dared act, so popular was the rural credit program. In fact, as a pre-election measure to influence the village vote in its favor, the Democratic Party regime had introduced a general moratorium on farm debt in September 1957. Elimination or substantial reduction of present crop subsidies was likewise difficult politically under conditions then prevailing. Another pre-election Democratic move had been to increase subsidies, not decrease them.

An increased sales tax on key consumer goods would also have brought the condemnation of a majority of the population, although some cautious moves had been made in this direction. With a people newly awakened to economic incentive, the government hesitated to move too fast or far in the direction of limiting consumer goods or decreasing the public's ability to purchase. It had permitted a general price rise, although with a careful eye on the prices of those commodities popular among villager-farmers. Much of the rural economy was still on a barter basis, which meant that the effect of a monetary inflation was small in the countryside as compared with what had happened in the cities — another argument for holding back urban growth.

An outgrowth of the effort to hold the line price- and wage-wise had been a reneging on the part of the Menderes government on its oft-repeated promise to grant the right to strike to labor. It not only feared the political use of the strike, but also its possible impact on wages and prices. On the other hand, in the absence of constant and really effective pressure for higher wages and improved working conditions by an organized labor, management lacked this powerful stimulus for improving efficiency of production. Higher wages required better machines and more rational management. If there were little pressure for higher wages, there would be that much less inducement to plow earnings back into an enterprise to increase its efficiency. An important dynamic element was thus absent from Turkish industrial management. At the same time the relatively low productive efficiency in agriculture, the mass of floating seasonal male labor bent on augmenting farm incomes, and the urban-bound move of many thousands of ex-villagers made it exceedingly difficult for the unions of lesser-skilled labor to operate effectively at any level without the protection of a benevolent, paternalistic government. The reverse side of the coin of benevolence was control. Labor-management relations continued to be a matter of direct concern to the state.

The Problem of Étatism

A characteristic of Turkish development subject to widespread Western criticism had been the tendency of the Democratic government — despite early promises to the contrary — to continue control over economic activity and, indeed, in a number of sectors to participate directly in production.[43] Quite apart from the historical causes, there were many compelling reasons for such a state of affairs even though divorced from ideological rationalization.

It was important to recognize that in Turkey one encountered seven essentially different — though not entirely mutually exclusive — categories of state enterprise. The fate of each must be considered separately.

First, the Turkish government maintained certain *legal state monopolies, primarily for revenue-begetting purposes,* such monopolies being limited to specific, general-use products — for example, salt, tobacco products, alcoholic beverages (other than wine and beer), and matches. Between 1950 and 1960, all of these monopolies were legally abolished, though the state remained the principal producer in each case. A second class of state monopoly enterprise related to certain *public services* — for example, rail transport, farm credit, maritime passenger service, the postal-telegraph-telephone organization, radio broadcasting, and various port facilities. The theory was that the public interest was so inextricably wound up in these activities as to demand either rigorous state control and/or state ownership. The political architects of Turkey had chosen the latter and there existed no political pressure to change the ownership of these politically vulnerable, notoriously low-return activities.

The third type of Turkish state enterprise had *developed historically* out of (1) earlier, Ottoman, state enterprise and (2) the efforts of the new self-conscious republic to break the hold of foreign interest on industries and services deemed to be essential and in which a high degree of public interest was involved. In some instances during the 1920's and 1930's, the Turkish leaders had felt compelled to buy out foreign interests so as to nationalize (or Turkify) such basic industries and services as the railroads, port facilities, urban power and gas companies, and coal mining. Local private enterprise was not then available on a large enough scale to accomplish the task. The *tradition of state activity* in these fields had thus become strong, and it continued to be so.

A fourth type of state enterprise was that set up in

order *to control potentially dangerous industries* — dangerous from the point of view of either public health or security — such as trade in opium and the manufacture of firearms and explosives. Again, there had been no tendency to change. A fifth category had been created *to conserve certain scarce natural resources,* forests and minerals being the principal examples. In these cases, private exploitation was possible — indeed encouraged — but only under license. Although ownership remained with the state, private mining activity had accelerated greatly during the Democratic years. Sixth were those *de facto state monopolies,* industries theoretically open to private enterprise but in which private enterprise had not participated for a variety of reasons (such as nonavailability of adequate capital, low relative rate of return, head start by the state). Most notable of these had been the iron and steel, paper, and the coal and iron ore mining industries. Only very recently (1956) had private capital gone into regional power development, and only then in response to considerable government pressure.

Related to this last category, but distinct from it, was a relatively new type of state economic interest arising out of *the limited size of the effective Turkish market* for certain products. For any industry in which "economies of scale" and "interplant economies" were a significant factor — or in which the level of indivisibility demanded high volume — a competitor within such a limited national market as Turkey might well force production per plant below the economic minimum. Both the individual Turkish customer, as well as the Turkish economy as a whole, would have been adversely affected. Certain of these industries, including some in which foreign capital had been participating, could probably have produced specific products in sufficient volume to supply the entire Turkish market adequately. A competitor might simply reduce production below the optimum level for all participants.

The Turks had desisted from actually awarding legal monopolies to such enterprises, even though in some instances agencies of the Turkish government were major stockholders. In fact, the Turkish "Law for the Encouragement of Foreign Investment" [44] specifically stated in its first article: "This law shall apply to foreign investment that . . . will entail no monopoly or special privileges." On the other hand, it was doubtful that the Turkish government would have permitted additional foreign entrants in certain industries if such would have meant — and it did — the guaranteeing of further "hard" [45] foreign exchange for the repatriation of profits, not to mention the additional claims created on such exchange by new plants for the import of parts and industrial supplies. Turkish authorities became determined to get the largest possible quantity of machines and industrial materials per unit of hard currency by utilizing local resources (including labor) whenever possible.

Similar limitations began to be applied in the case of Turkish-owned industry. An important source of industrial credit for private development and expansion purposes was the Industrial Development Bank of Turkey, the resources of which had been derived chiefly from the Turkish government, foreign-aid-generated counterpart funds, the bank's own earnings, and dollar loans from the World Bank. Inasmuch as demand for industrial credit exceeded supply, and because each project required roughly a third of its cost to be in hard currency, the bank was understandably disinclined to extend credit to an industry in which it deemed the saturation point had been reached. In other words, the bank management, being conscious of the national interest, tried to match investment and essential product requirements; even though a given investment project gave promise of high return, it might be rejected as nonessential. The process of business failure, bankruptcy, foreclosure, and reinvestment was believed too uncertain, costly, and time-consuming. In some instances, control over credit led to the award of a *de facto* monopoly to one firm for a certain period of time.

It should be recognized that the very size of a market such as that of Turkey may thus lead to near monopoly in some industries, thereby giving rise to state regulation to a degree unnecessary in larger markets where competition is possible. A company investing under such circumstances cannot reasonably expect freedom from direct government interest and control in respect to such matters as services, prices, and profits. One suspects that all of this adds up to one further pressure toward sustained state control of economic enterprise, and there were others.

It was quite apparent in Turkey that in a number of industrial areas, private enterprise could not be depended upon to generate the initial development. During this early period either the supply of raw material and/or a demand for the final product was inadequate to permit operation at a financially profitable level. However, the long-run impact of an enterprise might be such as to make a substantial net contribution to the national product even though suffering financial losses for several years. In such cases, public investment was used to finance the enterprise through its developmental period. The point was that public capital could be related to long-run, net contribution to national produce (or "social return") but private capital had to be related to short-term, financial return.[46] In Turkey there could be wide differences between these two measures of return, not only in respect to the "social overhead" type of investment, but in respect to industrial enterprises as well. Therefore, the appearance of private enterprise was not simply a matter of creating the appropriate "climate."

Inasmuch as the Turkish government was not irrevocably committed to a socialist ideology, public capital could be withdrawn from profitable enterprises after the developmental period was over. Private interests could then move in. In the textile, sugar, meat packing, cement, and power industries — to cite several examples — the Turkish government of the Menderes era had used various devices for thus attracting private capital. Though the casual observer might have listed these enterprises as wholly state-owned, in fact a number of them were by 1960 mixed enterprises involving both public and private investment funds. Some observers believed it possible that the new financial and organizational relationships worked out in Turkey between public and private interests were more relevant to the accelerated developmental situation found there than were the more traditional public-or-private enterprise dichotomy on which so many of us base our economic convictions.[47]

Additional forces sustaining state enterprise and economic control in Turkey during the 1950's could be summarized:

> At the start of industrialization and concurrent social change, the effectiveness of commercial law was far from assured, thereby ruling out the large-scale formation of private corporations and banking institutions.

Basically agriculturally oriented at the start of industrialization and mechanization, the mass of the people clung stubbornly to the land, thereby making necessary the creation of attractive working conditions in the new industry in order to pull in adequate labor (conditions up to and including an elaborate social security system to replace the informal security of rural-village life).

The largest accumulation of capital was in the hands of the government, the result of tax collection, public borrowing, *and growth in the reserves of social insurance funds.*

The disinclination of responsible leadership to permit private banking institutions to service the village-farm population (due to past history of usury and exploitation), thereby creating the necessity for a state agricultural bank and greater economic control in government hands — and further adding to the capital resources available to the state.

The need for some control over the rate of city growth, and hence the eventual forced dispersion of industry and the use of factories as levers for regional development.

Despite government efforts to hold back the process, rapid urbanization had been associated with industrialization and farm mechanization, a process which had driven up urban real estate prices and attracted an unduly large portion of the country's scarce capital resources, thereby necessitating control over the flow of private funds if maximum use was to be made of them in the national interest. (For example, government leadership had felt politically compelled to move into the field of cheap housing.)

The desirability of using industrial enterprises as educational devices as well as for production.

The necessity of holding down levels of consumption — either through rationing or inflation — so as to generate a high enough level of capital to sustain basic development. In either case, vigorous government intervention was required — in the first, to administer, and in the second, to contain.

The conviction on the part of responsible leaders that scarce factors of production (capital, machines, skilled labor, competent management) had to be channeled into those developments of highest priority from the point of view of long-run national development, thereby avoiding the allegedly more wasteful process of bankruptcy, reinvestment, et cetera. (In many instances, the rate of financial return and of social or national return did not coincide.) That is, a growth calculus was used, not a financial calculus.

All in all, it was remarkable that the Turkey of Menderes had been able to restrain public enterprise from being all-pervasive. According to one study,[48] private investment in industry (mining included) fell from 57 per cent of the total in 1950 to 54 per cent in 1958. In some fields, such as textiles, private production actually increased relative to state enterprise. So, likewise, had private mining activity. But virtually all of the large-scale, newer industrial enterprises remained in public hands.

AN EVALUATION

This entire battery of problems quite naturally tempts a regime that is at all responsive to national interests to exercise greater and greater control — first over foreign trade and foreign exchange, then over prices and distribution of critical commodities, then over the direction of capital flow, then over the sale of urban real estate, and finally over the movement of people from country to city. Each of these controls tends to antagonize large groups of the population, particularly those which have the effect of holding down levels of consumption and of controlling the movement of people. The Menderes administration, one might add, did not attempt to effect this latter control, but it would have been a logical next move — and it was being considered. If attempted, a corollary move would have been the selection of factory and commercial sites by centralized authority so as to force dispersion of nonfarm employment opportunities even at the risk of higher immediate cost. The resulting conservation of housing and social services might well have outweighed the higher financial costs, but it was doubtful that private enterprise would have looked at such investment in this light.

Perhaps corollary to this entire pattern of change was regional planning and development. Turkish leadership by 1959 was moving quietly in this direction. The Antalya scheme, by which the Baade study[49] had been motivated, was now reaching the action stage. Although there had been no public pronouncements on this point, Turkish authorities were thinking by late 1959 in terms of blanketing the country with 12 regional authorities. The first moves toward this end were to be made in the Antalya,

Marmara, Izmir, and Çukurova regions. Simultaneously, there was to have been an effort to make the administrative zones of those government activities already organized on a regional basis coincide — the forestry service, the postal-telegraph-telephone service, the national highway administration, the agricultural extension service, the power and irrigation agencies, and others. Little by little, without causing the politicians undue alarm, governmental authority was to have been elevated from provincial to regional level. Meanwhile, perhaps even more provinces would have been created, always a popular move with the electorate. But in time, the province would have been the equivalent of the present *kaza* or county, and the chief administrators of the central government would have been the twelve *umūmî valî's* — or general governors — each of whom was to have administered a region. If the government had attacked the problem of administrative conflict and expansionism more directly by simply melting the present sixty-seven provinces down into twelve regions, the political opposition would have been enormous. Fifty-five cities would no longer have been provincial capitals. But even so, regional development was difficult in an underdeveloped, poor, multiparty state. While attention and investment were concentrated in the Antalya region, it was doubtful that the rest of Turkey would have taken a sufficiently generous view to desist from clamoring "me too." Further pressure toward central control might thus have been generated.

Everything seemed to be a closed circuit from bad to worse. Whatever one attempted, the impact seemed to be either economically bad, administratively difficult, or politically impossible. Little wonder that the state felt compelled to continue to intervene directly in economic matters and, in so doing, foreclose on certain political freedoms. The political climate worsened as a frustrated, overworked Menderes thrashed around desperately. In the spring of 1960 the Menderes regime called upon the army to enforce certain politically inspired moves. Some began to wonder how long the army would remain loyal.

Chapter IX

THE ARMY TAKES OVER

On May 27, 1960, civilian government came to an abrupt end. On that day, General Cemal Gürsel and his Committee of National Union captured the government by suddenly arresting all important political leaders and neutralizing superior military commanders suspected of loyalty to the ousted regime. The group that thus came to power was surprisingly young. Among the 38 members of the Committee — all regular Army officers — the average age was forty-one, including twenty-one men under forty. Only five of the thirty-seven were generals. Twenty more were mere captains or majors. An informed guess would have placed the Turkish army officer corps (excluding reservists) at about 10,000 as of this time, including 48 generals, 562 colonels, 876 lieutenant colonels, and 1,608 majors.[1]

THE TURKISH ARMY IN HISTORY

The Army take-over ended thirty-seven years of uninterrupted civilian administration. Deliberately fashioned by Kemal as one of the basic principles of the Turkish republic, civilian supremacy had almost become a tradition. The idea of a military coup, though considered possible if not likely by some independent observers, had been held unthinkable among most knowledgeable Turks and apparently among American diplomats in Ankara as well. The United States Embassy in Ankara is reliably reported to have assured Washington just prior to the coup that Turkish civilian administration had everything under control. A precedent of thirty-seven years standing was on their side.

But there was a much longer precedent of military intervention in government, the most recent examples of which being the 1908–1909 and the 1919–1921 upheavals. Historian Lybyer wrote, "the Ottoman Government had been an army before it was anything else . . . in fact, Army and Government were one. War was the external purpose, Government the internal purpose, of one institution, composed of one body of men." [2] H. A. R. Gibb quotes el-Gazali, at the end of the 11th century: "Government in these days is a consequence solely of military power, and whosoever he may be to whom the holder of military power gives his allegiance, that person is the caliph." [3] Although one should note the striking difference between the roles played by the old Ottoman Janissary forces and that of the New Army, which dated from 1826, still a long record of military intervention in politics is hard to erase.

It was also true, as we have seen, that under the Ottoman Empire, while the vigor of the ruling institution waned, the military corps had taken a large hand in modernization of knowledge and institutional innovation.

These themes were still resonant at the time of the founding of the Turkish republic. The body of men who seized and shaped the new Republican power was essentially a military body. The loyalty of this elite, as of the larger populace, was given to Kemal — the triumphant military commander. It was the military corps that named, and military prestige that sustained, the leader — once a sultan-caliph, then a president. But curiously, Kemal did not use the army as a major innovating force after achieving personal power.

CIVILIANIZATION

Once installed, he had moved in a radically new direction. Shortly after the peace was signed in 1923, he obliged the leaders of the revolutionary government to divest themselves of military office. His own official portrait was taken in white tie and tails, rather than military regalia. This move revealed the man's uncanny feel for the vivid symbol.

Kemal's position on this point had been made abundantly clear as early as 1909 when he, along with Ismet Inönü (Kemal's successor as President and chief assistant and confidant throughout) argued vigorously in the councils of the Committee of Union and Progress against the direct participation of army officers in political affairs. At the annual party meeting in Salonica in the summer of 1909, Kemal declared,

> As long as officers remain in the Party [i.e., Party of Union and Progress] we shall neither build a strong Party nor a strong Army. In the 3rd Army most of the officers are also members of the Party and the 3rd Army cannot be called first class. Furthermore, the Party receiving its strength from the Army will never appeal to the nation. Let us resolve here and now that all officers wishing to remain in the Party must resign from the Army. We must also adopt a law forbidding all future officers having political affiliations . . .[4]

Later, on another occasion that year, Kemal commented publicly, "To be victorious in the internal affairs of a country is due less to an army than to the successful offices of a government."[5] Late in 1909, Kemal himself resigned from the party. So, likewise, did Inönü. And, from 1908 to 1919, both men devoted themselves exclusively to military activity. In 1923 Kemal observed that the great victory won by Turkish arms was not enough to achieve real liberation; the victory had only provided a strong foundation for future victories, victories in science and economics.[6] Again and again he reiterated this thesis.

This policy of "civilianization" of administration, though not proclaimed explicitly as one of the six cardinal principles of the republic, was nonetheless firmly imbedded in the Turkish Constitution, article 40 of which clearly gave command of the army to the Grand National Assembly and, as its representative, to the President. Also made unconstitutional was the holding of a second government office by Assembly members. Presumably included was an army assignment. Likewise, the Constitution forbade the government to declare marshal law for a period longer than a month without specific Assembly approval. The chief architects of the 1924 Constitution? Kemal and Inönü.

It was not by mere chance that of the 35 men who served in the Nationalist cabinets from 1920 to 1923, only nine were professional military officers, either active or retired (excluding those who had separated from the services and taken up civilian careers).[7] Even that part of the military forces used for rural policing purposes, the gendarmery, was placed under direct civilian control within the Ministry of Interior. Officers and personnel of this special corps, although still wearing the Turkish army uniform, were under general staff command only for routine administrative purposes. Within the municipalities, law and order was maintained by a civilian police force which had no direct relationship with the army and was commanded by a separate branch of the Ministry of Interior. Later, a general law was enacted which forbade all private societies based on common religion, race, family identification, region, or social and economic class. Undoubtedly, a military political organization would have been illegal under the general terms of this legislation, although this type of association was not specifically named.

In October 1924, in anticipation of an alleged military plot against his political authority, Kemal requested all of his chief military commanders to resign their Assembly seats. He observed at the time, "I have come to the conclusion that, for the maintenance of discipline in the required measure in the army for the exercise of command, it is incompatible the commanders should at the same time be deputies." [8] Although the chief of the general staff was excluded in 1924 from the cabinet, on which he had been sitting since its inception in 1920, he was nonetheless still answerable only to the President of the republic. This situation continued up to the end of 1943 when, apparently in anticipation of the retirement of the much revered Marshal Fevzi Çakmak, the army was placed more directly under full civilian control by making the general staff chief answerable to the cabinet and prime minister. In 1949, a Supreme Council of National Defense was formed, on which sat several civilian cabinet ministers. This organ in part balanced the power of the general staff.[9] The election laws of Turkey later went so far as to disenfranchise all military officers, soldiers, military students, and police personnel.[10]

In retrospect, it becomes evident that Kemal deliberately attempted to fence the military off from active political life as soon as its political support was no longer essential to his power.

On only two occasions prior to 1960 were there reports

of military plots directed against the civilian government of republican Turkey. On both occasions the picture was unclear. First, there was the 1926 plot against Kemal's life, a conspiracy in which at least some military officers were implicated. Several high ranking officers were arrested, including the two generals who had refused in 1924 to resign from the National Assembly as Kemal had demanded and instead chose to resign from their military duties. Both generals were released shortly after their arrest but not before their political ruin. Was this merely a clever attempt to discredit these politically ambitious officers still further? A third officer, a colonel who had been a military aide-de-camp to Kemal, went to the gallows. It was not until 1957 that there was again any hint of a military plot against the civilian government. Late in that year it was alleged that an attempt had been made to establish a secret organization within the army to incite revolt against the Menderes regime. Nine army officers were arrested — three colonels, three majors, and three captains. All, however, were either released or acquitted with the exception of one major, who was given a two-year prison sentence. Quite obviously, the authorities did not take the matter very seriously.[11]

Realizing that the independence and national power of Turkey was based primarily on a sustained social, political, and economic evolution, and that the country was not immediately threatened from without, Kemal's regime had diverted relatively little of its total effort to a revamping and modernizing of the military forces during the early years of the republic. That portion of the general budget allocated to national defense fell from roughly 40 per cent in 1926 to about 28 per cent in the early 1930's. It was not until 1939, when the threat of World War II became a reality, that the military budgets were again stepped up. The national defense portion then rose to 46 per cent and in 1940, to 56 per cent, at which high level it remained during the war years. Following the war, in 1946, the percentage was cut back to about 33. But by this time the promise of large-scale American military assistance was very much in the air.[12] It has been estimated that even as late as 1932 the size of the Turkish army was little greater than that existing in 1922 (78,000 men). It was not until 1939 and 1940 that the Turks mobilized a substantially greater force, possibly something in the neighborhood of 800,000. And throughout, the army rested upon nonprofessional soldiers drafted for a limited time from civilian life. Only the officers and some noncommissioned officers were professional.

Though the military was thus isolated from partisan politics and generally de-emphasized, the case should not be overstated. Economic development plans, especially during the 1930's, were shaped in part by military factors. In times of emergency, military commanders occasionally took over civilian administrative functions, the most notable examples being in the Kurdish area after the uprisings in 1925 and 1930 and in Istanbul during World War II and following the anti-Greek riot of 1955. Many retired army officers stood for, and were elected to, the Assembly or were named to high administrative posts, although, as Dankwart Rustow points out, "the proportion of them in public life has diminished steadily since the War of Independence." About one-sixth of the Assembly in 1920 was of military origin, about one-eighth in 1943, one-ninth in 1946, one-twentieth in 1950 and 1954, one-twenty-fifth in 1958.[13]

According to Rustow's calculations, since the founding

of the Republic up to 1955, "men of military background have served as President of the Republic (27 years),[14] Prime Minister (16½ years), Minister of Defense (16½ years), of Public Works (15 years), of Communications (9 years), and other cabinet posts." Rustow observes that the first ministry including no officers was that of Hasan Saka in 1948.[15] In addition, many of the provincial governors — the vali's — were men of professional military origin. The civilian government did not hesitate to tap the administrative talents developed by the military, but only after the individuals concerned had divested themselves of their military identities.

Nonetheless, as the first Cold War decade opened in 1948, the innovating function which had characterized the 19th century Ottoman officer corp had all but disappeared from the Turkish military. This change was a product of (1) the lack of any serious external or internal challenge to the army, (2) the deliberate isolation of the military organization from political activity, (3) successful innovation by the civilian elements, (4) a conscious de-emphasis of military development by the political leadership, and (5) the growth of a military elite based on seniority rather than demonstrated ability. By 1948, the army was still horse drawn, equipped with World War I weapons, ill-trained, poorly fed, and inadequately clothed. The military no longer represented the avant-garde of modernization that it had in Ottoman times. Nor was it any longer a channel of upward mobility around a frozen civilian elite. Civilians were clearly in a position of unchallenged supremacy, politically and technologically, and it was in the civilian hierarchy that mobility was most clearly recognized as a basis for promotion and power. Kemal had appealed deliberately to young men, thereby building an identification between the careers of the more dynamic younger elements and his civilian administration. Meanwhile, the military hierarchy froze and went into suspended animation; the civilian hierarchy opened up and led the way to innovation. This was apparently part of Kemal's grand design. Otherwise, it becomes inexplicable why Kemal, a military man himself, permitted his army to petrify.

By 1948 the Turkish military forces were so steeped in tradition that any change was difficult to introduce without reorganizing and remanning the officer corps. Organized along rigid, Prussian-like caste lines, the forces had no personnel policy; rarely were men assigned to tasks on the basis of ability. All high school and college graduates, other than members of certain ethnic minority groups, could become officers without difficulty, but enlisted men, regardless of proven capacity, could not. Many thousands of soldiers were used as family servants by the officer corps. All in all, a vast amount of military man power potential was wasted.[16] During the 1923–1948 period, the young men of Kemal's ambition and competence were not attracted to the army.

AMERICAN MILITARY ASSISTANCE

Only with the advent of large-scale American military and economic assistance to Turkey in 1948 did the Turkish army begin its transformation into a modern, technically trained, mechanized force. In order to clear the way after its rise to power in 1950, the new Democratic Party administration retired a number of the senior military officers and replaced them with younger, more progressively minded men. Subsequently, promotion within the Turkish army was related increasingly to demonstrated ability rather than sheer seniority.

Absence of intellectual mobility is often associated with the lack of social mobility.[17] In a social structure whose performance standards are relatively low, recruitment and promotion can afford to be on the basis of status rather than merit. As performance standards are raised, traditional social barriers break down and the key functions go to the men who can do them best, regardless of their social stigmata. In this sense, the American aid program provided a stimulus needed for the revival of the Turkish military corps. With American military aid came a new mission for the Turkish army, and the new concepts and methods needed to fulfill this mission. This new mission was formulated on the operational level by an American military adviser, who reported in 1949,

> The difficulty is that the men are conscriptees, and the most complicated piece of machinery they may have seen before coming into the service is a wooden stick plough. They hardly know the difference between a hammer and a screwdriver . . . The Turkish Army will have a tough time keeping the equipment going which we have given it.[18]

He might have added that a further difficulty was the hard-headed opposition by the older officers to the reorganization and retraining of the military establishment. These officers may have been familiar with modern military machines from a distance, but few were competent in their use. Hence, modern technical training implied a threat to their leadership.

With the institution of American military aid in 1948 designed to implement the Truman Doctrine, the Turkish army found itself in the awkward position of having its generals receive instruction from American noncommissioned officers, who were, on the whole, as well or better paid and privileged.

The main mission of the Turkish army was, of course, to provide an efficient force for national defense. To do this, the army had to undertake the modernization of the most substantial and significant sector of the population — the young, healthy males from the rural hinterlands, 700,000 of them. These men had to be taught the difference between a hammer and a screwdriver. They had to be taught how to use equipment of a type which they had never seen or heard of before. They had to learn how to participate in a modern military formation. Fortunately, the appearance of this new mission coincided with a change in the Turkish political regime (resulting from the 1950 general election), which made possible a shake-up in the general staff and the consequent elimination of some of the older and more conservative officers. The new regime owed no personal debts to the older senior officers. Turkey's participation in the Korean War also added to the general pressure for reorganization and new types of training — in short, modernization.

Following the arrival of the American Military Aid Mission in 1948, a number of technical schools were established or greatly expanded, including schools designed to train technicians in naval electronics, naval ordnance and gunnery, mine warfare and sweeping, naval damage control and fire fighting, naval shipyard and industry, submarine, antiaircraft, army signal, army medicine, army ordnance, infantry, artillery, army motor transport, army engineer, pilot training, radio aeronautical mechanicians, meteorology, aeronautical supply, and the operation of heavy highway equipment.

By 1952, under the Joint American Military Aid Mission to Turkey (JAMMAT) were a bevy of "field training teams," one for each of the three Turkish army headquarters and for each aid-supported division, brigade, and regiment. Such teams were essentially advisory units, the word "inspection" being avoided. Their need had arisen out of a potentially dangerous situation: 40 to 50 per cent of all American Aid supplied vehicles in Turkey were out of order. The reason was bad maintenance. ("Out of order" in this case did not mean merely "dead lined" in the American sense; it meant literally that the wheels would not turn.) By mid-1952, perhaps 90 per cent of the vehicles were again in operating condition. How was the situation redressed? In part by the direct intervention of the American field teams. Standing operating procedure required that if a team found something amiss in a Turkish unit — either in respect to its equipment or its training — the unit commanding officer was "advised" on the spot what should be done. If he refused to conform, the officer was then informed that the matter would be reported to Ankara. If he still stood adamant, a report went to the Military Aid Mission headquarters in Ankara, where the matter was taken up with the interested members of the Turkish General Staff. At the time, one American field team member declared, "Then, we almost invariably get action." Turkish unit commanders knew this to be true, and as a result, cooperation on the unit level was reported to be excellent. The point was that by 1952 the change in political regime had made possible the replacement of a number of the older senior officers by younger, more progressively minded men who responded positively to efforts to conserve the machines being supplied Turkey under the aid program, even if it meant the active intervention of foreigners on the operational level. This maintenance crisis, plus the support of the Turkish General Staff, gave considerable impetus to the Turkish military technical training program generally.[19] The need for vastly improved technical training had been made dramatically clear.

Out of these events — and others — had emerged widespread recognition that Turkey's primary need was the rapid and steady increase of its "capacity for absorption" — this involving nothing less than the reshaping of the Turkish people and their perspectives on the world. The thousands of young Turkish farm lads who went through the military technical training programs had acquired more than a skill in the maintenance and operation of modern machinery. Many had also acquired some degree of literacy, and along with it, the historic widening of outlook that comes with the acquisition of the three R's. They had acquired new personal habits of dress, of cleanliness, of teamwork. In the most profound sense, they had acquired a new personality.[20] Along with the physical and social mobility opened to them through the military training program, they had acquired also the habits of *psychic mobility*. The military corps became, in this decade, a major agency of social change precisely because it spread among this key sector of the population under its control a new sense of identity, an identity with the new skills and concepts — with the machine. Young Turks from isolated villages now suddenly felt themselves to be part of a larger society. The connection between their private lives and public roles became vivid to them — and this sense of their new personality they diffused around them when they returned to their villages.

In 1951, anthropologist Paul Stirling reported as follows:

> The villagers today are conscious of their membership in the Turkish nation . . . Under the Ottoman empire, the villagers thought not in terms of a nation, with a national territory, but of themselves as a group distinct from their neighbors on grounds of language or religion, or both. To what extent the villagers of those days identified themselves to the rulers of the empire as against the subject peoples I cannot say. According to the authorities, Turkish nationalism was the last to develop and did so mainly under the stimulus of the 1918 defeat, and the allied attempts at dismemberment in the years immediately following. Whatever its origin, the present villagers are decidedly nationalistic; *proud of Turkey's military prowess, interested in her mechanical achievements,* touchy about unfavorable comparisons with European countries. No European invention seems to spread more rapidly than nationalism, and if Turkey was a late starter, she has proved no exception in the long run. *Undoubtedly, consciousness of being part of the whole nation is greatly strengthened by the compulsory term of military service which all the young men seem vastly to enjoy, and by the migrant labor which wanders about all over the country.*[21]

By the mid-1950's, one could list eleven major changes that had been accomplished or at least incorporated into the thinking of the Turkish general staff:

1. Reduction of the Turkish army from an estimated 700,000 to 400,000
2. Inauguration of service training schools and great expansion of technical training generally
3. The training abroad of a significant number of officers and noncommissioned officers, many of whom would later become instructors[22]
4. Institution of a testing and classification system as a basis for assignments

5. Organization of a personnel section in the general staff and assignment of separate personnel officers to each major unit headquarters
6. Reorganization of the Reserve Officers Training School
7. Requirement of a year's troop duty before admission to the Military Academy
8. Reduction of the initial stint for noncommissioned officers
9. A new noncommissioned officers law, making possible officer status for qualified NCO's
10. Elimination of the use of soldiers as personal servants by officers
11. Much improved living conditions for enlisted men.[23]

The first three items indicated a major and realistic reconsideration of Turkey's "capacity to absorb." Cutting the size of the army almost in half, while simultaneously improving and expanding technical training, bespoke a determination to do better by each man who passed through military training — to make him a qualified modern soldier and, upon his return to civilian life, a qualified modern man. The third item likewise implied an accelerated transmission to Turkey of not only Western military and technical skills but also of Western political and social concepts, which would be passed on to the ordinary soldier during the course of his training. The next four items were clearly designed to make superior training reach its payoff points by adequate methods of personnel selection and job classification. The last four items were important measures of democratization. While these changes were occurring, a couple of million men passed through their military training.

IMPACT OF MILITARY MODERNIZATION

Consider the impact upon these young men of their first exposure to the wider world outside their village, as they underwent training in this rapidly modernizing and democratizing army. At least 50 per cent of the recruits were rural illiterates gaining their first exposure to a social institution operating in the modern style. Not only was this an army in which enlisted men might become officers, but even the members of ethnic minorities were accepted as candidates for officer status, and in the fall of 1955 several women were admitted to Turkey's War Academy as cadets. All of this new egalitarianism took place within the context of an overpowering — to illiterate and impoverished boys from the village — "materialism."

Army living standards began to edge beyond those obtaining for a large part of the surrounding civilian society. Many young discharged soldiers found their traditional society inadequate to sustain their new level of expectations. Out of that frustration one could expect pressure for innovation and "progress." The young man had been exposed to the machine concept and to the advantages accruing to the mastery of certain mechanical skills. Furthermore, the enormous prestige of the military had become identified in his mind with the new technology. Hence, it was likely that upon his return to his native village he resisted falling back into the premechanical era.[24]

This resistance could — and often did — lead to a falling-out between father and son. Contemporary observation in selected Turkish village communities led me to believe that the very rapid spreading out into primary family households, which was apparent in some villages by the late 1950's, was caused in part by this friction. That is, young men were breaking away physically from their father's households prior to the death of the father and setting up their own homes perhaps a few hundred yards away. This practice was a distinct break with tradition. In addition, one had the impression that a substantial number of these younger men were leaving the villages permanently and seeking a new life in the market town or big city. In 1959, a high ranking Turkish government planner speculated in a private conversation that one of the driving forces behind the accelerating urbanization in Turkey was the desire by many of the younger generation for an element of primary family privacy that was not available to them within the traditionally highly compact small, and semi-isolated rural communities. It was also true that the separation of son from father, due to compulsory military service, while the former was in his late teens or early twenties, might lead to a higher level of "need for achievement" or motivation.[25] If the young man returning from the army — even though breaking away from his father's household — remained within the village, he might be the driving force behind both technical and social innovation, such as the purchase of modern agricultural equipment and the organization of a local youth society. He might also possess the necessary skills to operate the tractor. At the very least he possessed the technical background that rendered him a likely candidate for a short training course in the operation and maintenance of modern agricultural equipment. In other words, the absorptive capacity of Turkey had increased by reason of the military development program. Furthermore, as the number of such young men grew, the prestige of the military became identified increasingly in the public mind with technical competency. In Turkey particularly this identification was of prime importance, for the military ranked high in Turkish eyes.

Turkish society has long been oriented toward military power. This orientation has been indicated in the foreign policy of Turkey, both Ottoman and Republican, as well as in the prestige patterns of Anatolian village societies. Early nomadic existence on the Asiatic Steppe, where boundaries were not stabilized and every change of feeding ground meant possible conflict, created within those very early Turkish tribes a closer personal reliance upon military force than was generally the case of more settled communities elsewhere. Later, the militaristic theme of Islam provided this tradition with religious fervor and theological rationalization. It was thus inevitable perhaps that the Ottoman Empire should have lived by conquest. Wealth hence became associated with the rise and fall of military power. A strong militaristic attitude continued to permeate Turkish society, and the more recent threat of the Soviet Union did much to perpetuate the prestige of the military. On the basis of systematic field work in Turkey, sociologist George Helling concluded that the dominating image for modern Turkish rural youth of 1955 was still the soldier.[26]

Therefore, identification of technical skills with military competence was perhaps of greater significance in Turkey than in some other national societies. And, as noted in the last chapter, the army had entered the field of basic education as well. Student motivation was quite obvious. One journalist reported his visit to the first pilot class in April 1959, as follows:

> Visitors to a classroom were welcomed by this rehearsed teacher-pupil exchange in Turkish:

"What will you be if you do not learn to read and write?" asked the teacher.

"Privates," chorused the class.

"And what will you become if you study hard and learn your lessons?" pursued the teacher.

"Corporals and sergeants," the class answered enthusiastically.[27]

By 1960, something in the neighborhood of two billion dollars' worth of American and European equipment and technical assistance had gone into the shoring up of Turkish military strength. Meanwhile increasing attention had been directed to the build-up of morale within the army and a more careful consideration given to the total impact the army might have on economic and social development. In a long statement in February 1958,[28] the Turkish Minister of National Defense explained the manner in which a new law was being applied laying down the guide lines of personnel assignment policy, the purpose being to broaden the geographical experience of army personnel. In essence, the country was divided into three districts — western, central, and eastern — and within each various military posts were classified into five categories depending upon their general environment — economic, social, climatic, cultural, and medical. Before an officer could be assigned a second time to the first district he must serve out an assignment in either the second or third. Likewise, the classification of his specific post must change from assignment to assignment. (For some time, a general policy had been followed to the effect that draftees from the cities should be assigned to the more rural areas and whenever possible the rural draftees, to duty in the larger cities.)[29] The Minister also reported improvement in military housing and health conditions. It was significant that he made reference to army and navy efforts to produce in their military factories machine and vehicular parts required by the civilian economy. He used the phrase, "in order to make possible the participation of the military industrial establishments in our general development."

In a number of ways, then, the Turkish army had been nourished by, and in turn had nourished, that type of modern materialism which placed a high, even a supreme, value upon material well-being. This was the "rising tide of expectations" which had been sweeping the underdeveloped areas around the world. In many areas, this process had turned out to be extremely treacherous. Expectations were raised long before they could be satisfied. The result was, quite often, a rising tide of frustrations. In one underdeveloped area after another, the inadequately satisfied or inhibited aspirations of the new literates had cumulated into a persistent discontent that made stable governance impossible. This had led, in a sobering number of cases, to military take-over and the imposition of stability by coercion.

Until May 1960, the Turkish case was exceptional. The army, while adding its bit to the rising tide of expectations, had moved rapidly to provide the perspectives, the skills, and the roles which could satisfy these expectations. In so doing, it had moved further and faster than the army (or the civilian sector) had been able to do in many other underdeveloped countries. The evidence seemed clear; the Turks had used the army successfully as a lever for general development, while maintaining republican institutions and civilian supremacy.

The Turkish army seemingly had, almost uniquely, abandoned the military prerogative of standing aloof and watching civilian institutions crumble and then taking over after the civilian elites had been brought to a complete impasse. It had, rather, committed itself to the firm and efficient support of a rapidly modernizing and democratizing society under the rule of civilian supremacy. This was exemplified by its commitment to recruit, train, assign, promote, and release the 400,000 men under its charge on the democratic basis of merit and the efficient basis of ability. Such commitment, in any military corps, acknowledges civilian supremacy in defining the goals and regulating the larger processes of the society as a whole.

But there was an ominous warning in all this, for precisely the same reasoning that suggested continuing military-generated pressure in Turkey for innovation — and hence increased absorptive capacity — put the principle of civilian supremacy squarely to the test. If Turkish leadership, under conditions prevailing by 1960, failed to sustain a satisfying pace of development, a frustrated military leadership might very well feel compelled — and fully competent — to assume political control. And as military promotion again opened to young men on the basis of ability, the civilian sector no longer held a monopoly on appeal to the growth elements in the population — the ambitious technicians and innovators. Indeed, the political deterioration that had set in since 1955 had rendered the civilian agencies of government decreasingly attractive to these same elements. Something had to give. Among underdeveloped countries, then, the Turkey of 1960 was not only a test case for the efficacy of liberal government, but — perhaps more fundamentally — for the supremacy of civilian authority itself.

THE 1960 REVOLUTION

The immediate events that propelled General Gürsel and his colleagues into political activism in May 1960 are still not entirely clear. The general's own explanation was simply that Prime Minister Adnan Menderes' regime (elected by popular vote in 1950, 1954, and 1957) had been flouting the Constitution, using political power for personal profit, involving the army in politics, oppressing the people, and dividing the nation. In the absence of any constitutionally defined power to limit unconstitutional act, the army had been obliged to oust the regime in order to protect the Constitution and the public.

One of the first acts of the military junta was to assemble a group of law professors in order to prepare a statement legitimatizing the new regime. On the second day of the new order, May 28, this learned group issued a statement including these paragraphs:[30]

> The legitimacy of a government is not derived solely from the time that it comes to power; it is possible to maintain legitimacy only by the manner in which it respects while in office the Constitution that brought it to that elevated position, by the manner in which it cooperates with public opinion and the Army, with the legislature and the judiciary, with institutions of learning, and by its ability to continue to exist in a rule of law.
>
> Instead, the government and political power kept formulating new laws wholly contrary to the Constitution and then proceeded to utilize these laws to violate the Constitution. It also engaged in activities without benefit of any law.
>
> Then again, it behooves the government to be a factor of peace and tranquility but this one forfeited any claim to legitimacy by the manner in which it set State, political and State institutions and their staffs at each other's throats, by the manner in which it vilified each of them at home and abroad and transformed each into a factor of anarchy.
>
> The political power also caused the Grand National Assembly (whose function is to represent the nation) to lose its attributes of a legislative organ; by transforming the Assembly into a political party group serving personal and class

interests, it brought it to a state of actual and effective disintegration.

Side-stepped by the authors were several very relevant points. *First,* article 102 of the Turkish Constitution declared that it might be amended by a simple two-thirds vote of all National Assembly members. For virtually its entire term in office, the ousted Democrats had held well over that proportion of Assembly seats, and most of the more controversial measures had been passed by at least a two-thirds vote. Hence, it could be claimed that these laws had been, in effect, constitutional amendments. Had they been so labeled, there could have been no legal argument. *Second,* the Turkish Constitution was very vague on the subject of basic human rights. For instance, article 77 stated simply, "The press is free *within the limits of the law* and shall not be submitted to any censorship *previous to publication*" (italics added). All depended upon what the law might be, and certainly the right of postpublication censorship (and hence seizure after publications) was implied. Though the Democrats had been restraining forcibly the more violent opposition press, one has difficulty in pointing to situations in which censorship previous to publication had occurred — except in matters clearly relating to military and national security. In other words, the Constitution guaranteed certain basic rights — such as press, religion, and assembly — but always as defined in law. This vagueness proved, of course, a serious flaw. *Third,* if one uses the same criteria as proposed here for measuring legitimacy of government, the preceding administration headed by Ismet Inönü (1938–1959) was unquestioningly illegitimate. It had flouted the Constitution perhaps even more flagrantly than did the Menderes regime. *No* opposition was permitted during much of its tenure in office, specifically from 1938 to 1946. During the Menderes regime an active, organized opposition was always tolerated, even though harassed. Even a national opposition press continued to appear. *Fourth,* the Democrats had been brought to office and retained in office as a result of generally honest, hotly contested general elections. Admittedly, there had been attempts to buy votes by promises of economic reward (crop subsidy or local improvement projects) and by gerrymandering. There had also been some restrictions on whose name might appear on the ballot. But such practices were not unknown among the older democracies. Although in the last Turkish election the combined opposition drew a 52 per cent majority, the Democrat Party had won a 48 per cent plurality. The Republican People's Party secured but 41 per cent of the popular vote. Because of the provincial system of representation instituted and maintained under the previous People's Party administration, the Democrats ended up with 424 seats in the National Assembly (70 per cent of the total), and the opposition with only 182.

Personal observation in various parts of Turkey in the fall of 1959 convinced me that the Democrats had picked up grass roots strength since the 1957 election. Even local People's Party workers agreed. The reasons were several: (1) good crops, (2) higher crop subsidies and easy farm credit, (3) an easing of consumer commodity shortages due to the receipt of large foreign credits a year previous, (4) the many village development projects undertaken by the Democrats, and (5) the easing by the Democrats of restrictions on religious activity. It could be argued that the first was an act of God; the second, an act of vote-hungry politicians contrary to national interest; the third, the temporary result of external forces; the fourth, a crude attempt to buy votes; and the fifth, a dangerous appeal to reactionary religious elements. Often overlooked was the fact that many arrests of politically ambitious religious leaders had taken place under the Democrats. Also, it was probably true that the earlier repressive police measures against religious organization were no longer required in the same degree in order to maintain secular political authority. The Turks, even in the villages, had come a long way in the past 40 years.

A further point should be made. In the statement legitimatizing the new regime, no explanation was offered as to why the army — the defender of the Constitution — had not felt a similar compulsion to oust the Inönü regime (1938–1950) which, as we have pointed out, contravened the Constitution much more openly and obviously than had the Menderes' regime. Nor was it explained why the coup came just as the country seemed to be on the verge of a national election. Was it that those instituting the move against the Menderes administration feared that it would be returned to office by popular vote?

There were early statements to the effect that overthrow of the government had been directed against no particular group, that it had been designed merely to uphold the Constitution and assure free elections. But in fact, *all* Democratic members of parliament were arrested and confined (except 17 who were either out of the country or could not be found), the partisan Democratic press was closed, all political organization outside provincial and county seats was forbidden (which move in effect prevented the 70 per cent of the population living in villages and small towns from participating in the political life of the country), several hundred persons were arrested apparently for merely speaking against the regime, a revolutionary tribunal was created to try the disenchanted, military leadership and martial law were instituted, and new elections were postponed for well over a year.

Some of the arrests reported in a single Turkish paper, *Cumhuriyet*: an undisclosed number arrested for speaking against the government (June 3); arrests in Nazilli and Diyarbakir (June 17); arrests in Edirne (June 16), three persons arrested in an Aydin village (June 28); twenty-six persons arrested in Izmir (July 1); forty-one persons arrested in Diyarbakir (July 15); pitched battle between partisans in some Kayseri villages (August 12); arrests in Kocaeli (August 14). These arrests were apart from the arrest of political leaders and outstanding personalities — 613 by June 21.[31] During a two-week period in May 1961, 140 arrests were reported officially.[32]

Meanwhile members of the ousted government were brought to trial by a regime not enjoying an explicit mandate from the people and clearly not constitutional. The number of political arrests reported from the villages and small towns indicated that the Democrats even by late 1961 would have had a very good chance in another election were the party organization and leaders permitted freedom to operate. They had been winning local elections for the past year or two preceding the 1960 coup.

During 1959 and through April 1960, there had been press reports of 296 village elections. The Democrats reportedly won in 256 of these contests. (Many of these reports were carried by *Cumhuriyet*, an independent paper which had become highly critical of the Menderes regime.) The Democrats were also reported as having won in three municipal elections, the only ones reported by the press as having taken place. The *New York Times* correspondent in Turkey, Jay Walz, reported a "roaring welcome" by an estimated 60,000 persons in Izmir for Menderes on May 15.[33] The almost complete absence of any Turkish reporting of public reaction to the coup outside Ankara and Istanbul was in itself suggestive. Even well after the coup, on July 9, 1961, pro-Menderes forces were able to muster a 39.6 per cent "nay" vote on the constitutional referendum submitted at that time despite the absence of leaders or organization.

Why, then, did the army group move when it did? One may suggest at least four reasons: (1) the opportunity for maximum public support in Ankara, Istanbul, and Izmir — the big cities — by reason of the student uprising and violent government reaction, (2) the knowledge that Menderes was aware of the young officer conspiracy and was about to move against those involved, (3) fear that if a general election were held the Democrats would be returned to office by their village and small town supporters who constitute 70 to 75 per cent of the electorate, and (4) the announcement by Menderes on May 25 (two days before the coup) that the Special Parliamentary Committee appointed a month before to investigate charges of alleged conspiracy by the Republican People's Party to subvert the authority of the state was about to report. Let us consider the first reason cited — government excesses in quelling the student riots: Though many extravagant charges were made against the Menderes administration at the time as to the number of students killed in suppressing the disorders, it seems clear that the Prime Minister was telling the truth when he admitted on May 15 the death of two, both in Istanbul.[34] One was killed when police fired on students on April 28 and the other, when he fell under a tank in the same Istanbul disorders.

Three others were killed, but their cases were very different — a second lieutenant who was shot by guards during the Army coup on May 27, a boy who was shot when the car in which he was riding with his father failed to stop on command during the same action, and a War College cadet who was shot during rifle practice.[35] Exhaustive searches failed to produce any further bodies or the names of those allegedly murdered. But despite the facts, Menderes had lost much political ground in Ankara, Istanbul, and Izmir because of the riots and alleged brutality in containing them. The army group struck at what was possibly a low point in Menderes' urban popularity.

Let us now consider the fourth reason cited above — the naming of the special investigatory commission: One is struck by the omission of any mention of this report by the military junta after the coup. If the charges that initiated the investigation were ridiculous and unproven, one should have thought that the commission's report might have been published as yet a further example of the ousted regime's irresponsibility and as evidence of its intent to establish a one-party state. In his letter of May 3 to the Defense Minister, made public after the May 27 take-over,[36] General Gürsel demanded that the law authorizing the investigatory commission be rescinded. One wonders why? Of what concern was that to a general in the army, even if he were Commander of the Land Forces? Did he have certain knowledge of the falseness of the charges? To a disinterested bystander, the Menderes regime seemed to have had at least some grounds on which to justify the investigation, perhaps even for the suspension of partisan political activity during the course of that investigation. The contrary argument was that the commission was such a powerful Menderes symbol that, given the tense political situation, it was intolerable and, hence, dangerous to the security of the state.

On March 21, the government announced that it had intercepted orders from headquarters of the Republican People's Party to all party branches directing in effect that the party should prepare to go underground. Secret couriers were to be appointed and an "ear newspaper" established.[37] These reports were not refuted and, given the tenor of the time, were plausible.

On April 3, Opposition leader Inönü set off for Kayseri in central Turkey to participate in a local party meeting — to be held indoors, and restricted to party members. Authorities detained him on the way, charging that he intended to contravene the law on assembly, one of the allegedly unconstitutional acts passed by the Menderes-dominated Assembly. This law forbade outdoor, public political meetings or demonstrations except during a 90-day period prior to elections. Admittedly, the law was enacted to harass the Opposition, but not until the Opposition had demonstrated every intent of keeping the country in a constant turmoil by continuing an uninterrupted antigovernment campaign at pre-election intensity. In so doing, every government policy and program was vigorously condemned, and respect for the authority of government was in fact being undermined — just as it would be in the United States were the American Republicans maintaining an *uninterrupted* campaign at a pre-presidential election pitch against the Kennedy administration. An angry Menderes administration finally passed this restrictive, and perhaps ill-considered, law. Article 79 of the Constitution simply stated, "Limitations upon . . .

association . . . shall be determined by law." They had been.

In any event, after some hours of argument, Inönü was permitted to continue on his way to Kayseri where, contrary to law, he did address a public gathering from the balcony of the People's Party headquarters. The next day, while on his way to attend another party meeting in a small town west of Kayseri, he was stopped by an army detachment and forcibly returned to Ankara. In rural Turkey, police authority lay with the gendarmery, which was in a sense a branch of the army though under special assignment to the Ministry of Interior, a civilian agency, for law enforcement purposes. Until then, regular army personnel had not been used for law enforcement except in emergency. In any event, the use of the army for political purposes was now an issue, although Menderes argued that it had been used merely to enforce a law that had been duly enacted by Parliament. And it seemed to some observers that Inönü had almost gone out of his way to bring the issue to a head.

On April 16, Ismet Inönü, ex-general, ex-president, and leader of the Opposition People's Party, was visited in his home by fourteen retired generals and admirals. A public statement was issued the next day in which it was reported that he had told the group that retired military officers composed an able group who could protect the ideals of national progress.[38] By now, suspecting a conspiracy between the Opposition and certain military groups (among which there were long-standing personal ties), the Menderes government on April 28 acted to suspend all political activity for three months, and to appoint a parliamentary commission with extraordinary powers to investigate. On May 25, Menderes announced that the commission had finished its study in only one month and would report very shortly to the Assembly.[39] Within thirty-six hours he was under arrest.

The point is that the Opposition must share the blame for the violent partisan feelings that had developed and divided the nation into hostile camps. There is much evidence that the opposition was deliberately needling the administration and, by its constant public condemnation of everything the government attempted was trying to make the orderly process of government difficult. There was also reason to believe that there was afoot a deliberate move to destroy the Menderes administration by ways other than by defeating it at the polls, which was precisely what Menderes had charged. This observation does not, of course, absolve the administration of responsibility for its repressive policies and ill-considered action against the demonstrating students, but it does suggest that Menderes was not completely unjustified in demanding an investigation. Why then did General Gürsel demand that the investigation stop? Some have said that his demand arose out of the apparent fact that it was the appointment of the special investigatory commission that had touched off the student riots in the first place.

It was also curious that in his letter of May 3 General Gürsel demanded the resignation of President Bayar "since the conviction is general throughout the country that every evil emanates from this person." He said nothing of Menderes. Yet it was Menderes who was later hanged, not Bayar. (Granted, Bayar was condemned to death, but he was then found too old to hang.) This observation about Bayar coincided with my own findings. There was reason to believe that Menderes had been willing to consider creating a bipartisan coalition cabinet even after the student uprisings, but that Bayar had prevented this move.[40] Some believed that it was Bayar who had been responsible primarily for the 1955 anti-Greek riots in Istanbul and for recent physical attacks against Inönü. The two men were known to be personal enemies. Gürsel and his associates may also have toyed with the idea of using Menderes — if he would cooperate. (It is quite clear now [1962] that Menderes' popular support was not equaled by any other leader.) With him gone, a disastrous leadership vacuum could develop. Whether or not Gürsel considered using Menderes in a new coalition effort is not clear, but whatever was in his mind or discussed in secret committee sessions, the idea was not acted upon. Perhaps it was clear that the nation's elite would not have worked with Menderes, even in a coalition government. Gürsel had to move against Menderes as well as Bayar.

Initially, Gürsel's committee decreed that the Constitution would be redrafted, and elections held immediately to select a new Assembly which would, as its first order of business, consider the new version. Meanwhile, leaders of the former government would be held in custody to be turned over to the new civilian government. It then developed that a new Constitution would become operative on the basis of a popular referendum, that elections would not be held at least until the fall of 1961 (18 months after the coup), and that the Democratic Party leaders would be tried under the authority of the provisional military government although before a civilian tribunal.

The new constitution, drafted by a Constitutional Committee and passed by a constituent assembly chosen by the new regime, called for these major changes:[41]

1. A full and unqualified guarantee of a full roster of personal rights including complete freedom of religion, the right to strike, the right of *habeas corpus*, the right to travel in and out of the country, the right of absolving liability for published statements by introducing proof of their accuracy
2. A Senate to be comprised of 150 elected members and 15 chosen by the President, one-third of which are to be selected every two years
3. An Assembly to be elected on the basis of proportional representation every four years
4. The requirement that all laws must pass both houses of the Grand National Assembly, or, lacking the approval of a senate majority, an absolute majority vote of all Assembly members or, if rejected by a two-thirds vote of all Senate members, the vote of two-thirds of all Assembly members
5. Elimination of the requirement that Cabinet members, other than the President and Prime Minister, be members of the Grand National Assembly
6. A seven-year term for the President (formerly 4 years) and prohibition against re-election
7. Election of the President by a joint session of the two houses
8. Establishment of a Constitutional Court empowered to judge the constitutionality of legislative acts
9. Guarantees of absolute autonomy to universities and to the judiciary
10. Establishment of a State planning organization
11. Provision for constitutional amendment by two-thirds vote of all members of each house of the Grand National Assembly.

The new constitution was submitted to a popular referendum on July 9, 1961. With a turnout of 83 per cent of the electorate, 60.4 per cent (6,348,191) voted "yes" and 39.6 per cent (3,934,370) voted "no."[42] It became law on July 20, 1961, and the Second Republic was born. Observers found the size of the negative vote surprising in view of the massive government and People's Party-sponsored campaign in favor and the absence of any organized opposition. Seven out of 67 provinces had in fact returned a negative majority. It was apparent that Adnan Menderes, though on trial for his life, still enjoyed massive support in some quarters. General elections were scheduled for October 15 as martial law was extended through that date.

The new constitution was probably an improvement over that which it replaced. The unlimited guarantees of personal freedom and the many checks on the political leadership would make reinstitution of arbitrary authoritarian rule difficult. On the other hand, these same provisions could make it virtually impossible for any Turkish government to proceed with a consistent and realistic economic program over an appreciable period of time. Short of a powerful personality as president or prime minister, it was not likely that a government would have the necessary working majorities to maintain necessary party discipline in order to pursue policies and programs many observers felt necessary but which would be exceedingly unpopular with a broad strata of the electorate.

Events proved the substance of these fears. The general elections of October 15, 1961, introduced a prolonged political stalemate. Results of the elections: for the Senate, the Republican People's Party (37.2 per cent of the popular vote, 36 seats), Justice Party (35.4 per cent and 70 seats), New Turkey Party (13.9 per cent and 28 seats), Republican Villager's Nations Party (13.4 per cent and 16 seats); for the Assembly, RPP (36.7 per cent and 173 seats), JP (34.7 per cent and 158 seats), RVNP (13.9 per cent and 54 seats). The Senate, in addition, included 15 persons appointed by the president, plus the 22 members of the former Committee of National Unity, the latter holding life tenure. (Twenty-two because one of the original 37 had died and 14 had been ousted because of deviationist political views, and dispatched to foreign diplomatic posts.) The Justice Party was identified in the popular mind as the successor to the now banned Democrat Party. No group had a working majority in either house.

After some delay, a coalition government was formed at the bidding of President Gürsel by Ismet Inönü, now prime minister. Because of Justice Party insistence on an amnesty for the still imprisoned Democrats (the former members of Parliament) and the refusal by others to accede to this demand, little legislation could pass the Senate and Assembly. As of mid-1962, no laws had been enacted by the new government other than the budget and an act reinstating 147 university professors who had been ousted by the military junta in 1960. The leadership vacuum was becoming increasingly serious.[43]

Meanwhile life had run out for Adnan Menderes that frantic, hard-living, well-meaning little man who had worked so hard — albeit mistakenly at times — to put Turkey's development over the top. Denied, if not corrupted, by his friends and allies, he was found guilty in August 1961 of unconstitutional acts by all nine members of the clearly unconstitutional, military-empowered tribunal sitting in judgment on the ousted Democrats. Condemned to death and refused mercy by the Committee of National Union, Menderes was hanged on September 16, 1961, the day after former Foreign Minister Fatin Rüştü Zorlu and ex-Finance Minister Hasan Polatkan met a similar fate, Menderes' execution being delayed by an alleged suicide attempt. The military junta carried out these executions over the protest of several of Turkey's Western allies — including the United States — and that of the leaders of the Republican People's Party.[43a]

In all, 601 members of the regime had stood trial, which started in October 1960 before a special tribunal on Yassi Island in the Sea of Marmara. The court sat on 220 days and heard 1,068 witnesses. Of the original 601 defendants, nine died during the trial and 128 were acquitted, leaving 464 declared guilty of charges running from corruption, misuse of public office, unconstitutional act, to personal immorality. Fifteen were condemned to death, including former President Celal Bayar, but twelve of these sentences were commuted to life imprisonment. (The nine-man tribunal had been unanimous only in respect to the three.) Thirty-one others received life imprisonment and 418 terms of from one to fifteen years.

Menderes, in addition to the death sentence, was given eleven years for alleged misuse of public funds and directed to repay $546,000, six years' hard labor and a fine for organizing the Istanbul riots of September 1955, and one year's hard labor and a fine for involvement in illegal shipping deals. He was acquitted of charges of having had an abortion undertaken and of killing his illegitimate child. Proof of Menderes' personal responsibility for the violence that erupted in the 1955 riots was inconclusive, so likewise was the alleged "proof" of personal corruption, except in the sense of sheer carelessness. (Apparently he was guilty of not prosecuting close personal associates known to him to be dishonest.) Being an extremely wealthy man in his own right, and a very generous man (witness his very substantial gifts of personally-owned land to peasants in his Aydin area), Menderes seemed to lack motive for deliberate appropriation of public funds for personal gain. If he is charged with use of public funds for *political* purposes, it is necessary to differentiate political from governmental — a distinction that the earlier Inönü regime had blurred by its use of public funds for such Party-supported activities as the People's Houses, various partisan publications, et cetera. And how a tribunal lacking any semblance of constitutional power could have found anyone guilty of an unconstitutional act was difficult to understand. The consensus of informed observers seemed to be that the military junta dared not spare Menderes for fear of his possible return to power if anything resembling an honest, contested election were held. The 40 per cent vote against the new constitution — which was a measure of the solid core of popular Menderes support — probably sealed his fate. If the percentage had been trivial, the authorities might have commuted his sentence. If it had been a majority, the regime might not have dared act.

That Turkey's leaders as of mid-1961 had not forsaken the economic goals of the Menderes regime was made clear by the State Planning Organization in July. Three five-year development plans were to be devised. It was stipulated that the over-all economic objective was a sustained annual national income increase of 7 per cent. With an annual population increase of about 3 per cent, the annual per capita income increase would be 4 per cent. To achieve this rate of development, it was estimated that about 18 per cent of the gross national product would have to be invested in productive enterprise. Of this amount, approximately 4 per cent, it was anticipated, would come from external sources. The Menderes regime had never achieved this level of investment.

A similar rate of growth and implied level of investment had been suggested initially as a reasonable national objective by the author eight years before over vigorous American official objection.[44] At that time I had urged a 6 per cent annual growth rate, a figure based on the assumption that annual population growth would be in the neighborhood of 2 per cent and that the capital-output ratio was roughly 3 to 1. Shortly thereafter, it became apparent that the population increase would amount to 3 per cent, hence the 4 per cent national growth rate in real product terms.

Further jolts were in store for the conservatives. Land distribution was to be stepped up. A central planning agency was established. A new building and land tax was to be levied which would raise assessed values on land from three to nine times and on buildings from one to four times. The officially supported price of wheat was increased 10 per cent. The right to strike was drafted into law. Meanwhile, the country was called upon to make new sacrifices as the triple-headed monster — trade deficits, inflation, underemployment — continued to ravish the best laid development plans. Curiously, over the three or four years preceding the coup, the opposition People's Party had made political capital by jumping on the Democrats for even suggesting these same moves, which fact was among the reasons for the extreme sensitivity of Prime Minister Menderes to opposition tactics. Surely the Turks needed more enlightened, more consistent, more careful economic planning than had existed prior to May 1960. But did anyone really know how to do the job better? At the heart of the matter were decisions as to how to best allocate the resources available to the country, "best" in terms of (1) present popular welfare, (2) national power, and (3) future production. As was well known to students of development, these decisions would not easily resolve themselves into a set of mathematical-financial formulas, even if we lived in a political and emotional vacuum. Sometimes the *ad hoc* judgments of politicians might be as valid as those of economists, businessmen, or bankers.

The best *postrevolutionary* estimates of Turkish national income indicated a steady upward trend which carried right through to 1960. The average annual increase in real per capita income over the Menderes decade was something like 3.6 per cent,[45] and there was no real indication by 1960 of any serious faltering in the rate of growth despite the friction in the economic machinery. Even given some obvious waste and corruption, the investment and economic policies of the Menderes regime could not have been too far off the mark. Otherwise, this growth would not have been recorded.

A FINAL WORD

The lesson to be derived from the failure of civilian leadership in Turkey is that such leadership can survive only as long as it continues to lead. The Turkish army could be entrusted with major programs that shaped national development — basic education, technical training, industrial production — as long as the civilian leadership generated the ideas and shaped the institutions which made these service programs functional for society as a whole. The government made policy; the army served it. But when civilian leadership seemed to falter — (1) by leaning upon the army for political support, (2) by clogging channels of promotion for young men of ability and subjecting them to partisan pressures, (3) by alienating the national intellectual elite, which was closely identified with the junior officer corps and (4) by giving priority to local interests over the national — the situation changed. The last two were of special importance. Since 1954 the civilian administration had been losing its former appeal to the growth elements in the population — the modern intellectuals, the ambitious technicians and managers, the innovators and entrepreneurs, which together formed the elite in a modern context. As the civilian administration became a closed society (with clique values more important than ability and achievement in pushing men ahead), opportunities in the military establishment were becoming increasingly available to men of ability regardless of their origin, family, party, or age. The army's dynamism was not matched by the civilian sector. This tended to make the army's programs dysfunctional; its satisfactions turned into frustrations. When the tightly closed regime then apparently tried to use the army for its own partisan political purposes — thereby violating the basic Atatürk doctrine of an apolitical army — it subverted the principle of civilian supremacy. The only way to save civilian supremacy under these conditions was, some thought, a military coup to install a caretaker regime that would re-establish the conditions of democratic civil government. But would it?

There was admittedly an appeal and a validity to the idea of temporarily setting aside popular government in Turkey and constructing in its place a military-intellectual oligarchy. Within the emerging nations there seems to be a tendency for these two groups to move together and, in terms of membership, to overlap. In Turkey, the nonmilitary intellectual, however, has kept pretty largely to the big cities and has had little direct knowledge or understanding of grass roots society within his own country. It is significant that General Gürsel saw fit to declare publicly that the gap between the masses and the intellectuals must be closed. By mid-1961, a serious disenchantment between the two groups was apparent.

The general and his Committee of National Union had declared the number one issue in the country to be that of education, and they spoke of reconstituting the Village Institutes (training centers for village teachers) and People's Houses (local cultural centers), of using army officers as teachers, and of much increased emphasis on education and rural development generally, including a land reform program that would be much more extensive than that previously undertaken, presumably using in part confiscated *private* properties.

A 1952 study, updated in 1960 and used in the planning process in 1963, reported the landownership pattern shown in Table 4.[46] Plotted against a perfectly equal distribution of land among the farm population, which is represented by the diagonal line in Fig. 1, the ownership pattern was clearly one in which the few owned most of the cultivated area. The new planners hoped to cut the unequal distribution of farm land among Turkey's rural population by roughly one-third through accelerated land distribution.

Many of the city folk had become unhappy with the Menderes regime precisely because it had diverted so much money and attention from urban business to rural development. It had upset the existing social and eco-

Table 4

Ownership of Farm Land by Size of Area Cultivated

Area cultivated (decares)	*Number of families by size of area*	*Percentage of families by size of area*	*Total area cultivated (hectares)*	*Percentage of total area in each category*
1 to 20	773,000	30.6	836,000	4.3
21 to 50	797,000	31.5	2,790,000	14.3
51 to 75	336,000	13.3	2,097,000	10.8
76 to 100	216,000	8.6	1,915,000	9.9
101 to 150	168,000	6.7	2,108,000	10.8
151 to 200	92,000	3.6	1,648,000	8.5
201 to 300	68,000	2.7	1,712,000	8.8
301 to 500	39,000	1.5	1,520,000	7.8
501 to 700	17,000	0.7	1,015,000	5.2
701 and more	21,000	0.8	3,811,000	19.6
	2,527,000	100.0	19,452,000	100.0

nomic order too much too rapidly, and in the end Menderes' Democratic Party represented essentially agrarian interests. The new military regime seemed ready to push even more rapidly in this direction.

Because of the sustained popularity of Menderes among the common folk, the growing rancor even among Menderes' liberal-minded adversaries against the harshness of Gürsel's military regime, and the new bitterness arising out of Menderes' execution, it was difficult to see how the military junta would dare hold an honest, contested election as promised unless the electoral and legislative systems were such as to breed political stalemate, which was precisely what the introduction of proportional representation and a bicameral legislature had guaranteed. The

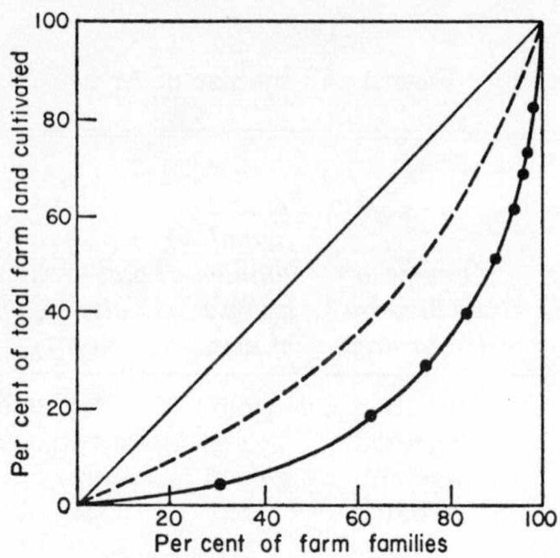

Fig. 1. Present and planned distribution of landownership compared with equal distribution: *solid curve,* actual distribution; *broken curve,* target distribution of present plans; *straight line,* equal distribution.

point was that a very dangerous precedent had been set and ex-Democrats, disguised now as the Justice Party, could conceivably sweep back into parliamentary control (which they came within a shade of doing in the October 1961 election). It would then require extraordinary benevolence and self-control to refrain from seeking vengeance in a new series of hangings. Some wondered how closely General Gürsel could control the army in such eventuality for affairs had not been entirely harmonious within the Committee of National Union itself. One faction had insisted all along on much more radical economic reform, another on certain racist views. As a result, fourteen members had been ousted. Also, one needed to bear in mind that thus far only the officer corps had been involved. The noncommissioned officer corps — the link between officer and recruit — remained inarticulate.

With the tragedy of Menderes, Turkey seemed to have come full circle through four decades of increasing and then decreasing liberalism, from the authoritarian rule of a caliph-sultan to the authoritarian rule of an army general. (And by early 1963, in the postjunta era of the second republic, politics seemed to have the same instability of the Young Turk era which followed the authoritarian rule of Sultan Abdul Hamid II. Weakness follows strength.) But there were important differences, for much had happened to Turkey and to the Turks in the interim.

The caliph-sultan had attempted to contain a political change impelled only by a relatively small intellectual-military elite against the backdrop of a largely lethargic population. The conflict, which the sultan tried to resolve by appeal to religious and traditional authority and finally to tyranny, was largely that between rival political concepts. Relatively few persons were immediately concerned. But now, the conflict revolved about the priority of effort as between political and economic development, and large numbers of people were emotionally and materially involved beyond recall. Turkey was, in fact, in the painful throes of accommodating political liberalization and economic acceleration. The new authoritarianism was designed to force this accommodation, which in personal terms could be equated to an accommodation between the *political hopes* and aspirations of the city- and town-bred intellectual and business-professional class on the one hand and the *economic demands* of the agrarian-village masses on the other. The army was perhaps the most appropriate vehicle to use for this purpose, for reasons already explained.

Nonetheless, Gürsel's military junta appeared by the Fall of 1961 to have jeopardized seriously its chance of success in affecting this accommodation for exactly the same reasons that Menderes had fallen short of success. The reasons were these: dependence upon personal authoritarian leadership, unwillingness to live within a rule of law, use of vengeance as a political policy, restriction of political participation, use of political criteria for administrative appointment, inability to recruit the most talented of the country for public service. Like Menderes, Gürsel had begun catering to the economically motivated masses perhaps because of the army's popular base. But in so doing he had recreated the very conditions which had made it impossible for Menderes to fulfill his promises of economic development. Those who had the necessary talents — that is, the politically motivated and liberal-minded of town and city — were again largely in the Opposition, if not in jail. One very vociferous — and highly educated — Menderes opponent of the past declared in retrospect that the Democratic era had been a golden age. Inönü's coalition government was, by early 1963, doing little better. Although the regime was more liberal, politically it was on dead center; it could not act. And always in the offing was the threat of new military intervention in politics. (In fact, two attempts were made during 1963 as the political standoff continued.)

The issue had become very clear: were political or economic values going to determine the allocation of Turkey's limited physical and human resources and energy? In view of the dichotomy between the village-based masses and urban-based talents, how did one resolve the conflict? The institutions of political liberalism appeared unable to effect the difficult structural changes required for self-sustaining economic growth because political power lay in the agrarian villages where promise of immediate material gain without change in social relationships determined the vote. But the apparent political precondition (authoritarian rule) for the necessary structural changes was such as to deny to the government the services of those very individuals carrying the skills required to effect the structural changes, for in large part these skills were possessed by the educated, town- and city-dwelling, politically sensitive liberals, many of whom had been trained in the west in both technology and political philosophy. Many would not tolerate authoritarian rule.

Perhaps of all the many vicious circles in which an emerging nation is caught, this is the most vicious of all. The breakthrough must wait upon the simultaneous appearance of propitious historical circumstances and individual genius cloaked in a powerful political personality.

Turkey awaits its second Mustafa Kemal.

CHRONOLOGY OF IMPORTANT EVENTS IN TURKEY 1919–1961

CHRONOLOGIES CONSULTED:

John K. Birge, *A Guide to Turkish Area Study* (Washington: American Council of Learned Societies, 1949). Jan. 1, 1919 — Feb. 23, 1945 (pp. 233–240).

Cumhuriyet Gazetesi, October 16, 1961. May 27, 1960 — October 15, 1961.

Cumhuriyet Halk Partisi, *On Beşinci Yĭl Kitabĭ* (Ankara: Cumhuriyet Halk Partisi, 1938). May 19, 1919 — October 29, 138 (pp. ix–xv).

Tahsin Demiray (ed.), *Türkiye Yĭllĭgĭ 1947* (Istanbul: Türkiye Basĭmevi, 1948). Jan. 1, 1919–Dec. 30, 1947 (pp. 592–622).

———, *Türkiye Yĭllĭğĭ 1948* (Istanbul, Türkiye Basĭmevi, 1949). Jan. 1, 1947 — Dec. 31, 1947 (pp. 416–450).

Gotthard Jäsche, *Die Türkei in den Jahren 1942–1951* (Wiesbaden: Otto Harrassowitz, 1955). Jan. 1, 1942 — Dec. 31, 1951.

Richard D. Robinson, *Developments Respecting Turkey* (New York: American Universities Field Staff, 1954–1957). July 1, 1953 — October 15, 1954 (vol. 1); October 16, 1953 — August 30, 1954 (vol. 2); Sept. 1, 1954 — Sept. 5, 1955 (vol. 3); Sept. 6, 1955 — Sept. 20, 1956 (vol. 4).

Arnold J. Toynbee, *The Western Question in Greece and Turkey* (London: Constable and Company Ltd., 1922). 1919 — March 22, 1922 (pp. 365–370).

CHRONOLOGY OF EVENTS

1919

Jan. 1	Ayntab occupied by the British (Maraş on Feb. 22, Urfa on Mar. 24).
Feb. ?	Greek Premier Venizelos presents to the Peace Conference in Paris a formal claim to the possession of Izmir.
Mar. 3	Society for the Defense of the Rights of Eastern Anatolia is founded in Erzurum.
Mar. 7	Cabinet of Damad Ferid Pasha comes to power with a policy of cooperation with the victorious powers.
Mar. 29	Italians land at Antalya as the first step in taking over southwestern Anatolia in accord with secret Allied wartime agreements. (In Fethiye, Bodrum, and Marmarĭş on May 11, Burdur on June 28.)
Apr. 30	*Mustafa Kemal [Atatürk]* is appointed Inspector-General of the 3rd Army,*† which is commanded by Kâzim Karabekir and headquartered in Erzurum.
May 15	*The Greeks land at Izmir* (Smyrna) with the approval of the Allies and under British, French, and U.S. naval protection.
May 16	Kemal leaves Istanbul.
May 19	Kemal arrives at Samsun. With him are 18 carefully chosen officers. Contrary to orders, which are to restore order in Anatolia, he begins organization of further resistance to Allied demands on Turkey.
May 23	The Greeks order the occupation of Aydĭn, and two-thirds of the city is destroyed by fire.
May 28	First armed clash between the Turks and Greeks at Ödemiş, west of Aydĭn.
June 6	The War Minister requests Kemal's immediate return to Istanbul.
June 12	Kemal arrives in Amasya and dispatches circulars to all commanding officers and higher civil officials, urging them to proceed with the formation of national resistance organizations throughout the country.

* Brackets are used to indicate surnames adopted after the passage of the law on family names (June 21, 1934).

† Italics throughout signify the most important developments.

June 22 Kemal, at Amasya, addresses a circular letter to all military and civilian authorities whom he considers trustworthy. He declares that the national independence is being threatened, that the government in Istanbul is no longer capable of carrying out its responsibilities, and that a national congress will soon be convened in Sivas to which every province will be asked to send delegates. The letter is signed by Kemal, Ali Fuat Pasha [Cebesoy] (Commander of the XXth Army Corps in Ankara), Hüseyin Rauf [Orbay], and Colonel Refet [Bele] (an army colonel stationed at Samsun).

June 23 The Istanbul government orders Kemal's return.

June ? Kemal meets with a Russian general who offers military aid. Kemal accepts materiel but not troops.

July 8 Kemal is dismissed by the sultan. Simultaneously, he resigns from all official duties and from his army commission.

July 11 Kemal is declared an outlaw by the sultan.

July 23 *A Nationalist Congress is convened at Erzurum* by the Society for the Defense of the Rights of the Eastern Provinces. Kemal is elected chairman. The Congress writes the original version of what later becomes known as the National Pact.

Aug. 6 The Erzurum Congress adjourns.

Aug. 12 Inter-Allied Commission of Inquiry on the Greek Occupation of Smyrna and Adjacent Territories begins study (Gr. Br., Fr., Italy, U.S.).

Sept. 4 *The Nationalist Congress at Sivas convenes.* Kemal is elected chairman.

Sept. 7 Society for Defense of the Rights of Anatolia and Rumelia is founded, an amalgamation of regional groups formed earlier.

Sept. 9 The Congress issues the Declaration of Sivas, which affirms the territorial integrity of Turkey and declares against the Allied occupation and the formation of an Armenian state.

Sept. 11 *Kemal is named chairman of a permanent Representative Committee of the Society for the Defense of the Rights of Anatolia and Rumelia.* An Istanbul government delegation to the Peace Conference in Paris is declared illegal by Kemal. Sivas congress adjourns.

Sept. 12 Telegraphic communications with Istanbul severed by the Nationalists.

Sept. 13 *The National Pact is promulgated.* Six principles are enunciated: self-determination; a plebescite for Kars, Ardahan, and Batum; security of Istanbul; opening of the Straits; rights of minorities; abolition of capitulations.

Sept. ? Kemal sends a mission to Baku to negotiate Russian aid.

Oct. 5 Damad Ferid Pasha's cabinet resigns and Ali Riza Pasha succeeds him. Kemal demands that Ismet [Inönü] be named Undersecretary to the Minister of War and Fevzi [Çakmak] as Chief of Staff, which is done. (Fevzi soon becomes Minister of War.)

Oct. 7 Kemal telegraphs to the Ottoman government the peace terms formulated at the Congresses of Erzurum and Sivas.

Oct. 17 The Inter-Allied Commission (see Aug. 12) reports that the safety of the Greek population of Izmir and Aydĭn had not been threatened since the Armistice, that the alleged proclamation calling Moslems to massacre Greeks was a forgery, and that the Greek forces were responsible for the ensuing disorders and outrages against the Turkish population. It recommends that all or part of the Greek troops be relieved by Allied troops much fewer in number. (No action follows.)

Oct. 22 A representative of the Ottoman government confers with Kemal in Amasya. Agreement is reached on five points: territorial integrity of Turkey is to be preserved, no special privileges are to be granted minorities, the Istanbul government is to recognize the Nationalist organization, Turkish delegates to the peace conference are to be approved by the Nationalists, and the new Chamber of Deputies is not to meet in Istanbul. (This so-called Amasya protocol is ignored by the Istanbul government.)

Oct.–Nov. The Nationalists are victorious in elections to the new Chamber of Deputies. (Kemal is elected a member from Erzurum.)

Nov. 1 French forces replace British in Ayntab, Maraş, and Urfa.

Dec. 27 Kemal arrives in Ankara, where the Representative Committee is established.

1920

Jan. 12 The newly elected Chamber of Deputies convenes in Istanbul. (Kemal remains in Ankara.)

Jan. 21 Nationalists attack the French garrison in Maraş.

Jan. 27 Nationalists successfully raid a munition dump on the Gallipoli Peninsula.

Jan. 28 *The National Pact is enacted by the Chamber of Deputies.*

Feb. 9 The French garrison is evacuated from Maraş and many Armenian civilians are killed by the Turks. A general Armenian exodus from southern Turkey begins as the French withdraw.

Mar. 3 Ali Riza's cabinet resigns under Allied pressure and replaced by Salih Pasha (Mar. 8), who negotiated the Amasya Protocol.

Mar. 15 Many prominent Turks are arrested in Istanbul by the British and deported to Malta, including Rauf [Orbay], Ziya [Gökalp], and Fethi [Okyar].

Mar. 16 Istanbul is declared to be under Allied military control.

Mar. 18 Ottoman Parliament holds its final session in Istanbul (is formally dissolved by the sultan on Apr. 11).

Mar. 19 Kemal calls for a meeting of an emergency assembly in Ankara.

Apr. 1 Mandate over Armenia offered to League of Nations by Supreme Allied Council. Decision is to establish a free and independent republic.

Apr. 2–5 Salih Pasha's cabinet resigns and is replaced by Damad Ferid Pasha when the former resists Allied demands to disavow the Nationalists.

Apr. 9 Ismet [Inönü] and Fevzi [Çakmak] arrive in Ankara, having evaded the Istanbul authorities.

Apr. 11 French forces driven out of Urfa by the Nationalists.

Apr. 11 The Sheik-ul-Islam issues a *fetva* (Moslem juridical ruling) declaring the Nationalists rebels against the sultan and that it is permissible to kill them.

Apr. 11 Ottoman Parliament is dissolved.

Apr. 20 U.S. gives *de facto* recognition to the Armenian Republic.

Apr. 23 The necessity for a provisional government is declared by the Nationalists in Ankara as the Grand National Assembly meets in Ankara for the first time.

Apr. 24 Kemal is elected president of the Assembly.

Apr. 28 The Nationalists conclude a military understanding with the USSR, by which the Turks are to secure necessary supplies.

Apr. 29 Law concerning treason against the nation is passed.

May 1 The Assembly adopts a plan for governmental organization in which the Assembly, after being urged to do so by Kemal, retains complete responsibility. The Assembly is to elect and dismiss individual ministers by majority vote.

May 3 Council of Ministers is elected by the Assembly, including Dr. Adnan [Adivar] as Minister of Health, Fevzi [Çakmak] as Minister of National Defense, and Ismet [Inönü] as Chief of Staff.

May 11 A Nationalist mission leaves for Moscow under leadership of the Minister of Foreign Affairs. Among the members is the Minister of Economy.

May 11 Kemal is condemned to death by the government in Istanbul (which sentence is approved by the sultan on May 24).

May 19 The Assembly in Ankara declares Damad Ferid Pasha a traitor.

May 28 An independent Armenian government proclaims the annexation of Turkish Armenia.

May ? Turkish Communist Party is founded under Kemal's orders (not a member of the Third International), apparently in order to appease the USSR, to placate those Turkish politicians committed to the "Eastern Ideal" see Sept. 1–9 below), and to assure that all communist activity is controlled by Turkish Nationalists.

May 30 Armistice between the Turks and French.

June 10 *The Treaty of Sèvres* is presented to the Turkish government at Istanbul, by which treaty the sultan's government is required to renounce all claims to non-Turkish territory. The Kingdom of the Hijaz is to be recognized as independent. Syria is to become a mandate of France, and Mesopotamia (with Mosul) and Palestine, mandates of Britain. Izmir and its hinterland are to be administered by Greece for five years, after which a plebiscite is to be held. The Dodecanese and Rhodes are to go to Italy, and Thrace and the remainder of the Turkish islands in the Aegean are to be assigned to Greece. Armenia is to be recognized as independent, and is ceded the provinces of Erzurum, Trabzon, Van, and Bitlis. The exact frontier is to be defined by the President of the United States. The Straits are to be internationalized and the adjoining territory demilitarized. Istanbul and a strip of territory on the European side are to remain Turkish, as will the remainder of Anatolia. The sultan protests vigorously, and the Nationalists will have nothing to do with the Treaty.

June 22 The Greek army begins to advance against the Nationalists into Anatolia. (The Greeks are strongly encouraged by Lloyd George, who is attempting by this device to force the peace terms on the Turks.)

June 24 The Greeks defeat the Turks at Akşehir.

June ? A secret and illegal communist party is formed in Turkey and associates with the Third International.

July 9 The Greeks take Bursa.

July 25 The Greeks take Edirne (Adrianople).

Aug. 10 The Istanbul government signs the Treaty of Sèvres, which causes a definite break between the sultan's government and the Nationalists.

Aug. 24 The USSR and the Ankara government agree to establish diplomatic relations and a draft treaty is initiated.

Sept. 1–9 A Grand National Assembly delegate participates in the Baku Congress of Eastern Nations, at which it is proposed to create an Eastern Federation of nations including Turkey and ultimately to be associated with the USSR. Enver Pasha is present in a private capacity but with apparent Soviet support as a possible force against the Turkish Nationalists committed to the "Western Ideal."

Sept. 18 First Tribunal of Independence organized.

Sept. 22 First Soviet military supplies received at Trabzon.

Sept. 28 Turkish troops, under General Kâzim Karabekir attack Armenia.

Oct. 19 Russia demands that Armenia accord free passage to the Turks, denounce the Treaty of Sèvres, and break all relations with the Allies. Armenia refuses and calls upon the West for help.

Oct. 20 Damad Ferid Pasha's cabinet resigns and is succeeded by Tevfik Pasha, the last Grand Vezir of the Ottoman Empire.

Nov. 2 Turkish Nationalist forces take Kars.

Nov. 21 Turkey's first ambassador to the USSR leaves for Moscow.

Nov. 22 President Wilson announces that Trabzon, Erzurum, and virtually all of eastern Anatolia are to be given to Armenia. Meanwhile, Soviet forces enter Armenia from Azerbaijan and declare Armenia a Soviet Republic, thus completing the Sovietization of Transcaucasia.

Dec. 2 A Soviet government is established at Erivan, capital of the Armenian Republic.

Dec. 3 Turco-Armenian peace treaty is signed, by which Turkey gets Kars and Ardahan, and Armenia (now a Soviet Republic) is reduced to the province of Erivan.

Dec. 4 Soviet ultimatum to the Turkish Nationalists forbidding them to advance farther into Armenia.

Dec. 29 Ethem and his guerrilla forces attack and disarm a regiment of regular Nationalist soldiers at Kütahya (following his refusal to comply with Kemal's orders to place himself under the orders of Ismet.)

1921

Jan. 6–10 Turkish Nationalists under Ismet defeat the guerrilla leader Ethem and his forces, which had joined the Greeks at Inönü, a small village northeast of Eskişehir — known as the First Battle of Inönü.

Jan. 20 The Constitutional Act is adopted by the Grand National Assembly in Ankara providing for popular sovereignty, a parliament elected by manhood suffrage, a collectively responsible ministry, and a president with extensive power.

Jan. 28 Turkish delegate to the Baku Congress of Eastern Nations assassinated in Trabzon, possibly at Kemal's direction.

Feb. 23–Mar. 12 London Conference in which representatives of the sultan, the Nationalists, Great Britain, France, Italy, and Greece participate. The purpose is to modify the Treaty of Sèvres. Proposed modifications fall far short of the Nationalists' demands, and no agreement is reached. Also, the Nationalists object to the presence of the sultan's delegation.

Mar. 11 Batum occupied by Turkish forces.

Mar. 13 Kemal and the Italians reach agreement, by which the latter agree to evacuate Anatolia in return for promises of extensive economic concessions. (The last Italian forces leave in June.)

Mar. 16 Treaty of Moscow between Kemal's government and the Soviet Union. Turkey gives up Batum, and Russia recognizes Turkey's right to Kars and Ardahan. (Ratified by Turkey on Oct. 2.)

Mar. 23 A new Greek offensive is launched in western Anatolia.

Mar. 30 The Greeks take Eskişehir.

Mar. 31–Apr. 1 The Greeks are thrown back by the Nationalists in the "Second Battle of Inönü."

May 10 Kemal organizes, in the Assembly, the Defense of the National Rights of Anatolia and Rumelia group and is elected its president.

July 5 The Italians withdraw from the Antalya area.

July 10–19 The Greeks take Kütahya, Afyon, and again Eskişehir.

Aug. 5 Kemal is given extraordinary powers as commander-in-chief by the National Assembly and takes over command in the field from Ismet.

Aug. 23 Battle of Sakarya begins.

Sept. 13 Battle of Sakarya ends as a desperate defense by the Turks prevents a Greek breakthrough to Ankara.

Sept. 19 The title "Gazi" is bestowed on Kemal by the National Assembly, and he is given the rank of marshal.

Oct. 13 Agreement between Turkey and the Soviet republics of Armenia, Georgia, and Azerbaijan (Treaty of Kars).

Oct. 20 Agreement between Kemal and the French (the Franklin-Bouillon or Ankara Accord) after months of hostilities in southern Anatolia from Aintab on the east to Mersin on the west. The French agree to evacuate in return for economic concessions.

Oct. 30 Turkish exiles who had been held on Malta return to Turkey.

1922

June 26 Nationalist Government recognized by Persia.

July 8 An opposition group in the Assembly succeeds in getting a law passed providing for the election of cabinet ministers by the Assembly, not by the Prime Minister.

July 12 Rauf [Orbay] is elected by the Assembly as President of the Council of Ministers (Prime Minister), thereby replacing Kemal, who nonetheless remains as commander-in-chief and the real power.

July 31 The Law Establishing Tribunals of Independence is passed by the National Assembly. Crimes falling under the Law against Treason (see April 29, 1920) are henceforth to be tried before the special tribunals, members of which are to be chosen from among Assembly members.

Aug. 8 Enver Pasha, former strong man of Turkey, is killed in action in Turkistan by Soviet troops after an unsuccessful attempt to lead a Moslem resistance movement against Soviet authority in the Khiva-Bukhara area.

Aug. 26 The Turkish counteroffensive against the Greeks begins.

Aug. 30 The Turks take Afyon in the Battle of Dumlupĭnar.

Sept. 5 The Turks take Bursa. The Greek armies break and flee in confusion to the coast.

Sept. 11 The Turks secure Izmir, which is to a large extent destroyed by fire. Greek soldiers and civilians are evacuated in part by Allied vessels.

Sept. 15 Lloyd George appeals to the Allied Powers and the British Dominions to join in defense of the Straits against the Turks. The French and Italians refuse. Of the dominions, only Australia and New Zealand show interest.

Oct. 3–11 The Conference of Mudanya, between the Allies and the Turkish Nationalists. Ismet represents the latter. The Allies agree to return Eastern Thrace and Edirne to the Turks, including recognition of Turkish sovereignty over Istanbul, and the Turks accept the neutralization of the Straits under international control.

Oct. 14 The Greeks accede to the armistice.

Oct. 19 A Turkish Nationalist commission enters Istanbul.

Oct. 28 The Allies send invitations to a peace conference to be held at Lausanne to both the government of the Grand National Assembly and to the sultan.

Oct. ? Ismet, upon Kemal's insistence, resigns his army commission and becomes Minister of Foreign Affairs for the Nationalist government in Ankara.

Nov. 1 *Kemal proclaims the abolition of the Sultanate,* in part to prevent participation of the Istanbul government in the impending peace conference. (Initially, the majority of deputies simply wished to designate another sultan.)

Nov. 17 The deposed sultan, Mohammed VI (Vahidettin), flees from Istanbul on a British ship.

Nov. 18 Abdul Mejid, cousin of Mohammed VI, is proclaimed caliph (but not sultan).

Nov. 20 Lausanne Conference convenes. Ismet heads the Turkish delegation.

Nov. 25 The Turks secure Edirne.

1923

Feb. 4 The Lausanne Conference recesses without agreement after heated arguments over the abolition of capitulations, the status of Mosul, and the payment of reparations by Greece. In objection to Kemal's authoritarian tendencies, a so-called "Second Group" develops in the Assembly, including some of the more prominent deputies — Ali Fuat [Cebesoy], Rauf [Orbay], Refet [Bele], Kâzim Karabekir, Adnan [Adivar], Hüseyn Cahit [Yalcĭn], Ahmet Emin [Yalman].

Feb. 27–Mar. 6 Ismet is attacked in Parliament, for the breakdown at Lausanne and Kemal is obliged to take part in the debates. A unanimous vote of confidence is finally recorded.

Feb. 17 Kemal opens Turkey's first Economics Congress in Izmir. He speaks of the critical need for rapid economic development.

Apr. 16 The Grand National Assembly dissolves itself for an election.

Apr. 23 The Lausanne Conference reconvenes.

June National elections are held. Kemal's supporters win overwhelmingly.

July 24 *The Treaty of Lausanne is signed.* Turkey gives up all claim to the non-Turkish territories lost as a result of the World War, but recovers eastern Thrace to the Maritza River. Turkey receives the Aegean islands of Imbros and Tenedos, but loses the rest of the islands to Greece. Italy retains the Dodecanese, and England, Cyprus. Capitulations are abolished in return for a promise of judicial reform. Turkey accepts treaties to protect minorities. Turkey pays no reparations. The Straits are to be open to ships of all nations in time of peace, and in time of war if Turkey remains neutral. If Turkey is at war, enemy ships may be excluded. A separate Turkish-Greek agreement provides for the compulsory exchange of populations.

Aug. 4 Rauf [Orbay] resigns under pressure as President of the Council of Ministers and is replaced by Fethi [Okyar].

Aug. 9 *The People's Party is founded.*

Aug. 11 The second National Assembly convenes in Ankara. Kemal is re-elected Assembly Chairman. Fethi [Okyar] replaces Rauf [Orbay] as Prime Minister.

Aug. 23 Treaty of Lausanne is ratified by the Grand National Assembly.

Oct. 2 Istanbul is evacuated by the last Allied contingents.

Oct. 6 The Turks take formal possession of Istanbul.

Oct. 13 *Ankara is made the capital of the Turkish national state* upon a motion introduced by Ismet [Inönü].

Oct. 25 Ismet is elected vice-president of the Grand National Assembly.

Oct. 27 Fethi and his cabinet resign, apparently under Kemal's order, so as to precipitate a constitutional crisis. All agree not to participate in a new cabinet until the Grand National Assembly strengthens the Cabinet, thereby in effect creating a viable republican government.

Oct. 29 *The Turkish Republic is formally proclaimed,* with Kemal, President and Ismet, Prime Minister. (Ismet is also Minister of Foreign Affairs; Fevzi [Çakmak] is named Minister of National Defense.) A number of leaders question the haste of the move.

1924

Jan. 5 Law on Weekly Holidays is adopted, making Friday a compulsory holiday.

Jan. ? The editors of 7 daily papers meet in Izmit at Kemal's request. He convinces them of the necessity for eliminating the caliphate.

Mar. 1 Kemal announces to the Assembly the necessity for abolishing the caliphate and reorganizing religious administration.

Mar. 3 *The caliphate is abolished and Abdul Mecid is banished.* Leading figures opposing the move: Rauf [Orbay], Ali Fuat [Cebesoy], Kâzim Karabekir, Adnan [Adivar]. The Presidency of Religious Affairs, subor-

	dinate to the Prime Ministry, is created by law. *Legislation for a national secular education system is enacted.* Medresses (religious seminaries) are closed by law. The Ministry for *Vakif* property is abolished.
Mar. 17	The Village Law is enacted, providing for village administration.
Apr. 3	Electoral law amended to eliminate requirement that electors, candidates, and voters must be taxpayers and to extend the vote to all male Turks over 18.
Apr. 4	Law on rural credit organizations passed. (Not really effective until the 1930's.)
Apr. 8	*The courts of Sheri (religious) law are abolished* and their jurisdiction transferred to lay courts of the Western type.
Apr. 9	Law enacted exempting raw materials for export industries from duties.
Apr. 20	*A constitution, an elaboration of the Constitutional Act, is adopted.*
Aug. 4	Lausanne Treaty goes into force.
Aug. 6	The English-Turkish dispute over Mosul (left open at Lausanne) is submitted to the League of Nations.
Aug. 26	The Bank of Business is founded.
Oct. 31	Apparently in anticipation of an incipient plot against his leadership, Kemal declares that it is incompatible for army commanders to retain their military functions while sitting in the National Assembly. He requests them all to resign their seats. Those generals supporting Kemal resign their seats, but General Kâzim Karabekir, Ali Fuat [Cebesoy], and Refet [Bele] do not.
Oct.	A wave of resignations from the People's Party, including Rauf [Orbay].
Nov. 17	Opposition Assembly members organize the Progressive Republican Party. Among the leaders are Rauf [Orbay], Adnan [Adivar], and Generals Kâzim Karabekir, Ali Fuat [Cebesoy], and Refet [Bele].
Nov. 21	Allegedly because of ill health, Ismet [Inönü] resigns as Prime Minister and is replaced by Fethi [Okyar], president of the Assembly.
Nov. 10	The People's Party becomes the Republican People's Party.
Nov. ?	The Chief of the General Staff is excluded from cabinet rank.

1925

Feb. 11 Great insurrection in Kurdistan directed against the religious policy of the government and aiming at Kurdish autonomy.

Feb. 27 A tax equal to one-twelfth of gross product, often collected in kind, is abolished.

Mar. 3 Accused of weakness in pushing the campaign against the Kurds, Fethi [Okyar] resigns as Prime Minister.

Mar. 4 Nearly dictatorial powers are given to the government for two years. Subsequently, "independence tribunals" are set up in the eastern provinces and in Ankara with power to impose death sentences. (Not terminated until Mar. 1929.) Organized communist activity becomes illegal. (Most Turkish communist leaders are arrested in August.)

Mar. 6 Ismet [Inönü] again named Prime Minister.

Mar. 7 The Kurds take the city of Diyarbakïr.

Apr. 19 The Bank for Industry and Mining is founded.

June 5 The Progressive Republican Party is dissolved by the government after the founders refuse to disband voluntarily.

June 29 The Kurdish revolt suppressed, 46 of its leaders are hanged.

Aug. 24 Kemal appears in public wearing a hat for the first time.

Sept. 7 *The number of Moslem "clergy" is drastically reduced* by decree. Only certain officially designated persons may wear religious garb.

Sept. 30 *Religious orders are suppressed.*

Oct. 8 The Temporal and Spiritual Council of the Jewish Rabbinate in Turkey notifies the Turkish government, in the name of the Jewish Community, that it renounces the special rights accorded to it under the Lausanne Treaty.

Oct. 29 The Armenian community likewise renounces the special rights accorded to it under the Lausanne Treaty.

Nov. 5 New School of Law is opened in Ankara.

Nov. 25 *Wearing of the fez is forbidden by law.* (The use of the veil by women is officially discouraged, but not banned.) The hat is proclaimed the national headdress.

Nov. 30 Tekke's (dervish meeting places) and turbe's (religiously significant tombs) are closed.

Dec. 16 League of Nations awards Mosul to Iraq.

Dec. 17 Treaty of Neutrality and Non-aggression signed with the Soviet Union.

Dec. 26 *International calendar and system of time adopted.*

1926

Jan. 1 The Gregorian calendar comes into effect.

Jan. 7 Greek community, after much debate, follows the Jews and Armenians, in renouncing the special rights accorded to it under the Lausanne Treaty.

Feb. 17 *New civil law code is adopted* (based on the Swiss code), effective October 4.

Mar. 1 *New criminal law code is adopted* (based on the Italian code), effective July 1.

Mar. 22 Law on educational organization enacted.

Apr. 4 Law enacted requiring all economic enterprises to use Turkish.

Apr. 22 Iranian-Turkish Treaty for amicable settlement of frontier problems.

June 5 Anglo-Turkish Treaty in which Turkey recognizes Mosul as part of Iraq, and the Turkish-Iraqi frontier is defined.

June 15 A plot against Kemal's life in Izmir is exposed, as a result of which a number of known reactionaries are hanged. Among those allegedly implicated are Generals Kâzim Karabekir, Refet [Bele], and Ali Fuat [Cebesoy], Adnan [Adivar], Halide Edip, and Colonel Arif (formerly Kemal's military aide), and several members of the National Assembly. Subsequently (Aug. 26) 13 persons are executed, including Colonel Arif and Cavid (Ottoman Finance Minister and a member of the Lausanne delegation).

June 28 *New commercial code is adopted* (based on those of Germany and Italy), effective Oct. 4.

Sept. 1 Civil marriage is made compulsory.

Oct. 3 First statue of Kemal in Istanbul is unveiled (thus breaking with Islamic tradition against the reproduction of living things).

1927

Jan. 18 U.S. Senate rejects the Turco-American Treaty of Lausanne, a result of strong Armenian and religious opposition based on the absence in the proposed treaty of any mention of minority rights in Turkey or of naturalization procedures.

Feb. 17 U.S. and Turkey re-establish diplomatic relations (broken off in 1917).

Mar. 7 A Kurdish revolt under Sheikh Said breaks out in southeastern Turkey. (Successfully put down in 1928, some 53 Kurdish intellectuals and military leaders are later condemned to death by a Tribunal of Independence sitting in Diyarbakir and publicly hanged there.)

May 28 Law for the encouragement of industry enacted to promote private enterprise by promising concessions and government support for enterprises.

May 29 Ankara-Kayseri railroad opened.

June 7 Law for the reform of rural instruction enacted. (Leads to opening of many 3-year rural schools.)

July 1 Kemal visits Istanbul for the first time as President.

Sept. 2 National elections. (Kemal is empowered to name all People's Party candidates.)

Oct. 15–20 Historic speech is given by Kemal to the Second Congress of the People's Party. In it, he reviews the course of the national revival and nationalist movement.

Oct. 28 First national census taken.

Oct. 28 The Kurdish National Society, the Hoyboon, proclaims the independence of Kurdistan as laid down in the Treaty of Sèvres, with Diyarbakir as its capital.

Nov. 1 Kemal unanimously elected president for four years by the Grand National Assembly, as the second assembly convenes.

1928

Jan. 1 Important part of the Anatolian railroad system is purchased by the Turkish government from foreign interests.

Apr. 10 Abolition of the article in the constitution declaring Islam the state religion. *The state is declared to be secular.*

May 24 International numbering system is adopted.

Aug. 9 Kemal announces publicly an impending change in the alphabet.

Nov. 3 *Decree introduces the Latin alphabet,* to be applied in all publications after December 1, 1928. All Turks under 40 are obliged to pass an examination in the new writing or attend school to learn it.

1929

Jan. 1 The national school system begins to function.

Jan. 19 Turkey is the second country to ratify the Kellogg-Briand pact renouncing war as an instrument of national policy.

Mar. 4 The law giving the government near-dictatorial powers in 1925 and subsequently renewed in 1927 is allowed to run out.

June Suppression of communist propaganda in Turkey, thereby making clear the limits placed by Kemal on friendship with Russia.

June 1 The law concerning agricultural cooperatives is passed.

June 8 The Law for the Protection of National Industries is passed, which imposes protective tariffs (effective Oct. 1). A Land Distribution Law is passed.

1930

Mar. 28 Foreigners are asked to use Turkish geographical names: Istanbul for Constantinople, Ankara for Angora, Izmir for Smyrna, Edirne for Adrianople, etc.

Mar. A Kurdish revolt breaks out in the Mount Ararat region. (Defeated by the Turks later in the year.)

Apr. 16 *Law enacted giving women the right to vote in municipal elections.*

June 11 The Central Bank of Turkey is established. (Begins operations on Oct. 3, 1931.)

June 15 Official approval is given for Turkey's first foreign loan — $10 million from the American-Turkish Investment Corporation in return for a match monopoly in Turkey.

Aug. 12 Formation of an opposition party, the Liberal Republican, is permitted in the effort to enliven political life and educate the people toward multiparty parliamentary government. The new party favors a more moderate nationalism and greater cooperation with the West. It is led by Fethi [Okyar], a former prime minister and, since 1925, Ambassador to Paris.

Aug. 30 The Ankara-Sivas railroad is opened.

Oct. 5–13 The Turks attend the first Balkan Conference, at Athens, and take an active part in the work of the

Greek-Bulgarian reconciliation and the formation of a Balkan Pact.

Oct. 30 The Treaty of Ankara between Greece and Turkey is signed following settlement of property claims of repatriated persons. The two parties recognize the territorial status quo and agree on naval equality in the eastern Mediterranean.

Nov. 15 Fethi, leader of the Liberal Republican Party, accuses the government of election irregularities.

Nov. 17 The Liberal Party leaders decide to dissolve the party, but a group of independent deputies continues to exist in the National Assembly.

Dec. 23 A dervish uprising near Izmir (Menemen). Twenty-eight leaders are executed, and other measures are taken to break Moslem opposition to the regime.

1931

Apr. 1 Decimal system of measurement is adopted, effective January 1, 1933.

Apr. 15 Turkish Historical Society is founded.

Apr. National elections. Candidates of the People's Party are unopposed.

Apr. 20 Kemal declares the People's Party to be republican, nationalist, populist, étatist, secular, and revolutionary. He defines the role of government in economic affairs.

May 4 Fourth National Assembly convenes and unanimously re-elects Kemal as President, his third term.

Oct. 30 Renewal of the Turco-Russian treaty of friendship for 5 years.

1932

Jan. 23 Frontier with Iran fixed by an agreement signed in Teheran.

Feb. 19 *First People's Houses are opened by the People's Party.*

May 8 Ismet, while on a visit to the USSR, signs an agreement for an $8 million loan from the Soviet Union.

July 5 State Office for Industry is created as a vehicle for establishing and managing state economic enterprises.

July 12 Turkish Language Society organized on directive from Kemal to institute a linguistic reform (i.e., Turkification of the language).

Aug. 12 Turkey joins the League of Nations.

1933

May 25 Soviet loan agreement is ratified by Turkey.

June 3 Law creating the Sümer Bank is enacted, thereby replacing the Industry and Mining Bank.

Sept. 14 Conclusion of a nonaggression pact for 10 years between Greece and Turkey.

1934

Jan. 9 First *Five-Year Plan for the development of industry is announced.*

Feb. 9 Conclusion of the Balkan Pact between Turkey, Greece, Romania, and Yugoslavia (Bulgaria refuses to come in). The four powers mutually guarantee security of their Balkan frontiers and agree to take no action with regard to any Balkan nonsignatory without previous discussion.

Mar. 27 New income tax law enacted. (A 1925 law had been largely ineffective.)

June 14 New law on land distribution is enacted.

June 21 *Law requiring all citizens to adopt family names is adopted,* effective January 1, 1935.

June 16 Riza Shah Pehlevi, hereditary ruler of Iran (since April 1926) visits Kemal in Ankara. He is obviously much influenced by Kemal's modernization program.

Nov. 26 National Assembly bestows the family name of "Atatürk" upon Kemal. (Ismet takes the name of Inönü, thereby commemorating his victories at Inönü.)

Nov. 27 Law passed abolishing all titles and hereditary positions.

Dec. 8 Women are made eligible to vote in national elections and to become members of the National Assembly.

1935

Jan. 1 Family names are required of all Turkish citizens as of this date.

Jan. National elections. Candidates of the People's Party are unopposed. Women participate for the first time, 18 being elected to the Assembly of 399.

Feb. 5 *Étatism is written into the Constitution as one of the six cardinal principles of the Republic.*

Mar. 1 Atatürk re-elected President for 4 years.

May ? By decree, all establishments are required to have a weekly holiday from 1 p.m. on Saturday until Monday morning, thereby making Sunday rather than Friday the day of rest.

June 14 Law enacted creating the Eti Bank for mining and power development.

Sept. 16 Kayseri textile plant, built with Soviet assistance, opens.

Oct. 21 Second national census is taken.

Oct. 23 Rail line to Diyarbakĭr opens.

1936

Apr. 11 The Turkish government appeals to the signatories of the Lausanne Treaty for permission to refortify the Straits (an effect of the Ethiopian crisis and Turkish support of League action against).

June 8 Turkey's basic labor law is enacted to regulate working conditions.

June 22 Great Britain, Australia, Bulgaria, France, Greece, Japan, Romania, the USSR, Yugoslavia, and Turkey meet at Montreux to consider Turkish demands re the Straits.

July 20 *The Montreux Convention on the Turkish Straits Regime* is signed, with Italy abstaining. Turkey is authorized to remilitarize the Straits. Traffic through the Straits is to be controlled by Turkey under regulations defined in the Convention.

Nov. 1 In an Assembly speech, Atatürk declares that Alexandretta, Antakya, and their environs are Turkish, that he intends to press the matter seriously.

Nov. 9 All signatories of the Montreux Convention, except Japan, deposit notices of ratification. (Japan does so on April 19, 1937, and Italy adheres to the Convention on May 2, 1938.)

1937

Jan. 7 Atatürk leaves Ankara to take command of Turkish forces massing on the Syrian frontier and threatening Alexandretta.

Feb. 5 The five principles espoused by the Republican People's Party — republicanism, nationalism, populism, étatism, secularism, and revolution (continued and

	rapid reform) — are written into the Constitution as the basis of the Republic.
May 11	Atatürk gives his farms to the National Treasury and all of his other real estate to Ankara municipality.
May 29	The League of Nations Council, after acceptance by France and Turkey, adopts a constitutional act for the province of Alexandretta (part of French-mandated Syria, now called Hatay) which had been drawn up in response to an appeal by Turkey. (Forty per cent of the population is said to be Turkish. Disorders in the province have been recurrent despite a guarantee of special rights for the Turkish population in the Franco-Turkish Agreement of October, 1921, and in the Franco-Syria Treaty of September, 1936.)
June 14	The Turkish Assembly recognizes the independence of Hatay.
Summer	After an unsuccessful effort to impose taxes and the draft on the Kurdish tribes of Dersin (now known as Tunceli), the Turkish army occupies strategic points and fighting ensues. (The Turks do not win complete victory until March 1938, when Sheikh Said and his chief followers surrender and are tried. Twelve are hanged, including Said and two Kurdish members of the Grand National Assembly, Said Abdul Kader and Hasan Khairi.)
July 9	Signature of a nonaggression pact (The Saadabad Pact) between Turkey, Iraq, Iran, and Afghanistan, securing Turkey on the east as the Balkan pact did in the west.
Oct. 25	Inönü, close collaborator of Atatürk and Prime Minister since 1925, resigns, apparently at Atatürk's insistence, seemingly a product of recurring personal differences of a minor character. He is succeeded by Celal Bayar, who since 1932 had been Minister of Economy.
Dec. 7	Turkish government denounces the treaty of friendship with Syria (May 30, 1926) after threatening to use force in Hatay. The French sent a military mission to Ankara.
Dec. 10	A three-year program for mining development announced.

1938

Jan. 14 The Saadabad Pact is ratified (see July 9, 1937).
Mar. 11 First official news relating to the illness of Atatürk.
Apr. 7 Additional law on land distribution is enacted (see June 14, 1934).
May 2 Italy adheres to the Montreux Convention (see July 20, 1936).
June 24 Law forbidding bargaining in shops and markets is adopted. The Office of Soil Products is established as a device to support grain prices and to collect grain for export and stockpiling.
June 28 *A revised Law on Societies is passed, which outlaws all formal organizations based on common religion, race, class, or kinship.*
July 3 The French and Turks come to agreement on the province of Alexandretta (Hatay); each is to send 2,500 troops into the province to supervise elections.
July 5 Turkish troops enter Alexandretta.
July 9 The cement industry is nationalized.
Sept. 2 The Republic of Hatay (Alexandretta), a new autonomous state, is voted into being by the newly elected Assembly, in which Turks hold 22 seats out of 40, by prior agreement with the French. (The Turks are in complete control, and the republic exists only *pro forma.*)
Sept. 18 *Second Five-Year plan for industrial development announced.*
Nov. 10 *Atatürk dies.*
Nov. 11 The Grand National Assembly unanimously elects Inönü President of the Republic. Celal Bayar continues as Prime Minister.
Dec. 27 Inönü is elected chairman of the Republic People's Party for life.

1939

Jan. 25 Celal Bayar resigns as Prime Minister and is replaced by Refik Saydam, Minister of Interior in the last Bayar cabinet and from 1923 to 1937 Minister of Health and Social Welfare.
Mar. 15 The Germans occupy Czechoslovakia.
Apr. 5 Turkish troops cross into the Hatay.

May 13	Terms of a defensive arrangement with Britain announced (see Treaty of Mutual Assistance, Oct. 19. Terms are the same).
May 17	Germany maintains that Turkey has broken her neutrality.
June 23	France and Turkey conclude a nonaggression pact, and France agrees to the incorporation of the Republic of Hatay into Turkey.
June 29	The Hatay Assembly votes for union with Turkey.
June 30	*Turkish troops take possession of the Hatay.*
Aug. 22	Soviet-German Pact greeted with surprise and consternation in Turkey.
Sept. 1	World War II begins.
Sept. 11	The Karabük Iron & Steel Works goes into operation.
Sept. 17	Soviet Union invades Poland.
Oct. 2	Soviet Union demands that Turkey close the Straits, sign a mutual assistance pact, and abandon obligations to France and Britain.
Oct. 17	Turkish-Soviet conversations in Moscow broken off.
Oct. 19	*Treaty of Mutual Assistance (Ankara Pact) signed with Great Britain and France.* It provides that Turkey will give the two powers every aid and support in its power in event of an act of aggression by a European power leading to a war in the Mediterranean area in which Britain and France are involved, or if they are forced into war in fulfillment of guarantees given to Greece and Rumania in April 1939. Britain and France agree that they will aid Turkey to the limit of their power if she becomes the victim of aggression by a European state, or if she becomes involved in a war in the Mediterranean area occasioned by any such aggression. (The agreement leads to French and British loans to Turkey totaling £43.5 million for armaments and commercial clearing.)
Dec. 30	Turks see rebirth of Russian imperialism in Russo-Finnish War. (By year-end, Turkish army is mobilized.)

1940

Jan. 8	Turkish-French-British financial and economic agreement is signed in Paris under which Turkey is given £25 million arms credit. In return, Turkey gives the

Allies right to purchase certain agricultural products for duration of the war and an exclusive right to buy Turkish chrome during the following two years.

Jan. 18 The "National Defense Law" is enacted which gives the government emergency powers, including the power to declare martial law (which is imposed on the easternmost and westernmost provinces) and to seize property.

Apr. 17 *Law on Village Institutes is enacted* to provide public education for village youth who agree to serve subsequently as rural schoolteachers.

May ? Moslem chaplains return to the army.

June 10 Italy declares war.

June 12 Turkey breaks off commercial relations with Italy.

June 14 Paris falls.

June 18 New Turkish-German trade agreement is signed, but chrome is excluded from goods to be sold to the Germans.

Oct. 28 Italy attacks Greece.

1941

Feb. 17 Germany occupies Bulgaria.

Mar. 25 Russian-Turkish proclamation to the effect that if either becomes subject to aggression, the other will remain neutral.

June 18 *German-Turkish Friendship and Non-aggression Pact is signed* as the Germans overrun the Balkans. (Ratified July 5.)

June 23 Germany launches attack on the USSR. (Turkey is greatly relieved and initiates pressure on the West to terminate the war.)

Oct. 9 Turkey agrees to sell Germany 90,000 tons of chrome annually.

Dec. 3 The U.S. extends Lend-Lease to Turkey.

1942

Jan. ? Electoral law changed so as to require party approval to place one's name on the ballot in elections for the National Assembly.

Feb. 24 Attempt to assassinate German Ambassador von Papen in Ankara. (Government suspects communist involvement. Leads to measures against Soviet activity in Turkey.)

June 17 — Severe penalties are imposed on Turks and Russians implicated in the von Papen incident.

June 27 — The Soviet Ambassador is withdrawn in protest.

July 9 — Şükrü Saraçoğlu, Minister of Foreign Affairs since November 1938, replaces Refik Saydam as Prime Minister following the latter's death.

Nov. 11 — A law imposing a wealth tax is enacted. (In its implementation, the law leads to a near-confiscatory levy on minority and foreign businessmen, particularly in Istanbul. Defaulters are placed in forced labor camps.)

1943

Jan. 30 — Prime Minister Winston Churchill and President Inönü meet in Adana. Turkey is left free to enter the war when it sees fit.

Feb. 2 — The Russians win the Battle of Stalingrad.

Feb. 28 — National elections for the seventh National Assembly. People's Party is unopposed.

Mar. 8 — Inönü is re-elected President, and Saraçoğlu is reappointed Prime Minister.

Oct. 30 — Major leak to Germans of Allied war secrets begins out of British Embassy in Ankara (operation Cicero).

Nov. 4–7 — Cairo Conference between Turkish and British foreign ministers in which Britain tries to gain use of Turkish airfields and to push Turkey into the war. Turkey refuses.

Dec. 4–6 — Conversations among Churchill, Roosevelt, and Inönü in Cairo, in which the Allied leaders try to get Turkey to declare war. Inönü requests additional assistance and argues that Turkey's belligerency would serve no useful purpose.

1944

Jan. 12 — Marshal Fevzi Çakmak resigns as Chief-of-Staff, ostensibly by reason of age but possibly because of his pro-German views. Replaced by Kâzim Orbay.

Mar. 15 — Defaulters under the wealth tax who had been impressed into forced labor are released, and unpaid amounts written off (see Nov. 11, 1942).

Apr. 6 — Flow of Allied war secrets to Germans terminated (see Oct. 30, 1943).

May 1 — Turkey stops the sale of chrome to Germany. (Up to

this date since the start of 1943, Turkey had sold 58,000 tons to the Allies, 62,000 tons to the Axis.

May 18 The Turkish cabinet decides to prosecute certain racialist leaders. Martial law is declared in Istanbul, and 23 alleged pro-Nazis are arrested (including leading pan-Turanists).

June 14 Turkey forbids the passage through the Straits into the Black Sea of several thinly disguised German naval auxiliaries.

Aug. 1 Turkey breaks off diplomatic and economic relations with Germany.

Sept. 7 The trial of 23 racialists begins before military court in Istanbul.

1945

Jan. 3 Turkey breaks off diplomatic and economic relations with Japan.

Feb. 23 Turkey declares war on Germany and Japan, effective at midnight Feb. 28, to become a charter member of the U.N.

Feb. 24 *Turkey signs the U.N. charter.*

Mar. 19 The USSR delivers a note to Turkey that the 1925 Turkish-Soviet Treaty of Friendship and Neutrality, which had been renewed ten years before, is not to be renewed again in November, when it is due to expire.

Apr. 7 Turkish reply is delivered to Moscow to the effect that Turkey is prepared to reconsider any reasonable changes in the treaty.

April Secret trial of 135 alleged communists by Turkish government leads to bitter denunciation from Moscow.

May 19 Inönü speaks publicly of land distribution and the institution of more democratic political procedures.

June 11 *A land distribution law is passed* authorizing the distribution of state lands and, under certain conditions, the seizure and distribution of large private holdings, to landless or near landless village farmers. Some Assembly members argue for a more restricted authorization. The debate leads to a political split leading to the formation of the Democratic Party.

June 12 Four Assembly members for the People's Party — Celal Bayar (former prime minister), Fuad Köprülü (distinguished historian), Adnan Menderes (lawyer and cotton grower), and Refik Koraltan (former provincial governor) — propose changes in the party program, which are rejected.

June 7 *The USSR declares that it is willing to negotiate a new treaty of friendship with Turkey if the latter will agree to return Kars and Ardahan to the Soviet Republic of Georgia and accept Soviet participation in the defense of the Straits.* (The Turks reject the demands.)

June 22 Law establishing the Ministry of Labor is passed.

June 27 Law enacted to establish industrial accident, maternity, and occupational disease benefits.

July 17–Aug. 2 At the Potsdam Conference, the USSR insists on increased participation in control of the Straits, also upon return of Kars and Ardahan. Allies ignore the latter issue, but on the matter of the Straits agree that the Montreux Convention might be revised.

Aug. 6 Turkey delivers to the USSR 195 Soviet refugees of Turkish ethnic origin.

Aug. 15 The U.N. charter is ratified by the National Assembly. In the discussion, Menderes declares that Turkey has committed itself to democratic principles by its act.

Sept. 21 Menderes and Köprülü are expelled from the People's Party.

Sept. 27 Celal Bayar resigns from his seat in the National Assembly.

Oct. 23 An earlier decision calling for jail sentences for 23 racialists (see Sept. 7, 1944) is reversed by higher court, and all are released.

Nov. 1 Inönü recommends to the National Assembly a single, direct, secret election (to replace the present two-stage electoral college system), also the repeal of a number of restrictive laws.

Dec. 3 Bayar resigns from the People's Party when the Party refuses to let him submit liberalizing amendments to the Press Law.

Dec. 4 Student mobs attack and destroy certain leftist publishing houses in Istanbul.

1946

Jan. 7 *The Democratic Party is officially founded by Bayar, Köprülü, Koraltan, and Menderes.*

Jan. 23 The Agricultural Produce Tax (a forced collection in kind, a wartime measure) is abolished.

Apr. 5 U.S. show of naval strength in the eastern Mediterranean as the battleship *Missouri* and cruiser *Providence,* plus other ships, arrive off Istanbul.

May 3 Democratic Party leaders decide not to enter the impending municipal elections because of the extra-legal pressures harassing the new party and lack of electoral reform.

May 7 Turkish-American agreement on the Lend-Lease debt is reached; the U.S. is to cancel $100 million debt. (Ratified by Turkey on May 20.)

May 31 *New electoral law is enacted providing for a direct, secret ballot* (replaces two-stage electoral system) and nomination either by party or petition.

June 7 *The Law on Societies is modified so as to permit the establishment of organizations based on class or economic interest.*

July 21 General elections held, the first under the direct electoral system. The Democrats put up candidates for 273 Assembly seats (out of 465), of which 61 are elected (also 6 independents). Many charges of electoral irregularities are made by the Democrats.

Aug. 5 The new Assembly re-elects Inönü to the presidency and Kâzim Karabekir to the presidency of the Assembly. Recep Peker is named Prime Minister.

Sept. 7 Trade liberalized by releasing prices, foreign currency accounts, etc. Lira devalued from $0.56 to $0.36.

Sept. 20 Press and penal law changes augment government control. Political bitterness mounts.

Sept. 22 Turkey receives a Soviet note insisting on a joint defense of the Straits.

Nov. 23 Another U.S. naval visit to Istanbul.

Dec. 16 Two political parties, six periodicals, and a number of other groups closed down by the government for political reasons.

Dec. 24 Assembly debate on religious education begins, the first in many years.

1947

Jan. 11 In its national congress, the Democratic Party accepts a "Freedom Charter" stipulating three conditions for democracy: abrogation of unconstitutional laws, elections controlled by the judiciary, separation of the presidency from party chairmanship.

Feb. 15 The Dodecanese Islands and Rhodes (seized by the

Italian fleet during the Tripolitanian War, 1912–1913) are ceded by Italy to Greece, with the signing of the Treaty of Paris.

Feb. 20 *Law enacted authorizing the organization of labor unions.*

Mar. 11 Turkey joins the International Bank for Reconstruction and Development and the International Monetary Fund.

Mar. 12 *President Truman announces a program of U.S. aid to Greece and Turkey* to implement the Truman Doctrine, which calls for U.S. aid to countries menaced by Soviet power.

May 19 U.S. military and naval missions arrive in Ankara to administer the forthcoming American assistance.

May 22 President Truman signs the Greek-Turkish Aid Bill.

June Inönü institutes a series of meetings between the government and Democratic Party leaders in an attempt to reconcile differences.

June 5 U.S. Secretary of State Marshall suggests U.S. aid for European recovery (which leads to the formation of the Committee for European Economic Cooperation, in which Turkey participates).

July 12 Inönü issues a declaration to the effect that the President should be a nonpartisan head of state, that charges against the Democrats of sedition and against the government of oppression are groundless.

Sept. 1 Turkey ratifies the Turkish-U.S. Agreement on Military Aid.

Sept. 10 Recep Peker is forced to resign as Prime Minister by opposition within his own party. Replaced by Hasan Saka (who subsequently heads four cabinets in succession.)

Nov. 29 The U.N. General Assembly votes for the partition of Palestine. (Turkey votes for partition, but desists from giving any military assistance to the Arabs in subsequent Israeli-Arab hostilities.)

Dec. 22 After seven years, martial law is lifted in Istanbul and nearby provinces.

1948

Jan. ? Turkey's application for Marshall Plan aid is rejected (subsequently accepted after resubmission).

Apr. 16 *The Organization for European Economic Cooperation is constituted, with Turkey participating.*

May 14 British mandate in Palestine ends, and Israel declares its independence.

May 20–25 The People's Party Assembly group decides to permit religious teaching in primary schools on an optional basis, to create special schools to train preachers and worship leaders, and to establish a faculty of Moslem theology.

July 8 Turkey ratifies the "Economic Cooperation Agreement" with the United States.

July 20 The Nation's Party is founded with Marshal Fevzi Çakmak its nominal leader. Rapidly becomes the center of religious conservatism and racialism.

Nov. 25 Government directs that religious lessons be given in 4th and 5th grades to those children whose parents desire them.

Dec. 5–7 People's Party liberalizes selection of party candidates to the National Assembly by authorizing provincial branches to select 70 per cent by secret ballot.

1949

Jan. 13 Hasan Saka resigns as Prime Minister. Is succeeded by Şemseddin Gunaltay, who forms a more liberally oriented cabinet.

Jan. 15 The first of the new preachers and worship leaders schools opens in Ankara.

Feb. 15 Voluntary religious instruction instituted in 4th and 5th grades.

Mar. 24 Turkey grants *de facto* recognition to Israel.

May 4 The "Independence Tribunals" are officially abolished. (Although long inactive, they were felt to be a political menace.)

May 30 Law is passed reorganizing the Ministry of National Defense. The chief of the general staff is now responsible to the prime minister rather than to the president.

June 3 A more progressive (15 to 45 per cent) income tax is passed.

June 6 The old age pension law is passed (effective Apr. 1, 1950).

July 1 Turkey's general staff is placed under the authority of the Ministry of National Defense.

Aug. 8 Turkey is admitted to the Council of Europe.

1950

Oct. 31 The Faculty of Theology opens in the University of Ankara.

Feb. 16 *New electoral law is enacted, in which the judiciary is given responsibility for administration.*

Mar. 1 Law passed reopening many tekke's and turbe's (see Nov. 30, 1925).

Mar. 15 An amendment to the 1945 law on land distribution virtually limits land to be seized and distributed to state and pious foundation (*vakif*) property.

Apr. 10 Fevzi Çakmak's funeral in Istanbul is the occasion for a reactionary outbreak, which alarms government leaders.

May 14 *National elections. With 89.3 per cent of the electorate participating, the Democrats win 396 Assembly seats out of 487;* the People's Party, 68; the Nation's Party, 1; independents, 7 (15 are vacant by reason of double candidacies).

May 19 The new Assembly meets. Bayar is elected President, and Menderes becomes Prime Minister. Koraltan is named President of the Assembly; Köprülü, Foreign Minister. The new government promises political and economic liberalization.

May 25 The Western powers offer to arm the Middle Eastern states for purposes of internal security and area defense on condition that recipients give an undertaking that no aggression is intended against any other state.

June The International Bank for Reconstruction and Development assists the Turks in establishing the Industrial Development Bank of Turkey to stimulate private enterprise.

June 8 A shake-up of top military personnel as many are relieved of their posts.

June 16 A law is passed (the Democrats' first) authorizing the call to prayer to be said in Arabic rather than Turkish, as had been required.

July 1 People's Party authorizes provincial branches to name all candidates to the National Assembly. (Formerly the Central Party Council named 30 per cent.)

July 4 Israel and Turkey sign a trade agreement.

July 7 — The ban on religious radio programs is lifted as the Koran is read on the air.

July 25 — Turkey offers the U.N. 4,500 armed troops with which to meet aggression in Korea (subsequently accepted and sent).

Aug. 1 — Turkey applies for membership in the North Atlantic Treaty Organization.

Aug. 12 — Bulgaria announces intent to deport immediately its 250,000 subjects of Turkish ethnic origin.

Aug. 31 — Turkey agrees to accept Bulgaria's Turkish minority.

1951

Aug. 7 — *Law for the Encouragement of Foreign Investment is enacted* authorizing the government to grant licenses permitting the transfer of profits up to 10 per cent per year.

Aug. 9 — Law on paid holidays is enacted.

Sept. 19 — Turkey is formally accepted in the North Atlantic Treaty Organization, but not in the Supreme Headquarters, Allied Powers in Europe (SHAPE).

Oct. 13 — Great Britain, France, the U.S., and Turkey invite Egypt to help found the Allied Middle East Command.

Oct. 14–20 — Democrat Party rules that provincial branches should select 80 per cent of the party's candidates to the National Assembly; the General Executive Committee, 20 per cent.

Oct. 15 — Egypt refuses to join a Middle East Command.

Nov. 3 — Soviet note received in Ankara to the effect that Turkey's membership in NATO is "an act of hostility against the Soviet Union."

1952

Feb. 18 — *Turkey (and Greece) become full-fledged members in NATO, including active participation in SHAPE.*

Aug. 18 — Announcement is made that the headquarters for SHAPE's Southeastern Europe Allied Land Forces will be in Izmir.

1953

Feb. 25 — *Non-Aggression and Friendship Pact signed with Greece and Yugoslavia — the Treaty of Ankara* (ratified by Turkey on May 18).

May 30 *Soviet Union announces that it is relinquishing all claims on Kars and Ardahan in northeast Turkey and for participation in the administration of the Straits.*

July 21 Law forbids university faculty members to engage in political activity.

Sept. 15 Soviet-Turkish agreement signed on the Serdarabat Dam on the frontier near Iğdir. A 15-year dispute over Turkey's share of the cost has prevented it from profiting from the dam.

Nov. 4 The Atatürk Mausoleum in Ankara is opened.

Nov. 7 Greece, Yugoslavia, and Turkey sign a supplement to the Treaty of Ankara (see Feb. 25) which calls for establishment of a permanent secretariat and regular meetings of the joint staffs to plan for mutual defense of the Balkans.

Dec. 14 *The government confiscates all property of the People's Party not indispensable to Party activities. This act leads to the closing of the People's Houses and to the seizure of the Party's newspaper presses in Ankara.*

1954

Jan. 23 New law on foreign investment cancels previous restrictions on repatriation of profits and capital.

Jan. 27 Nation's Party dissolved by court order on grounds that it seeks to use religion for political purposes.

Jan. 28 *Law is passed in effect terminating the Village Institutes* as the distinction between Teachers' Training Colleges and the Institutes is abolished.

Feb. 2 The Republican Nation's Party is founded as the successor to the Nation's Party (see Jan. 27).

Mar. 9 *Law is passed prescribing heavy punishment for newsmen* whose writing is deemed harmful to the political or financial prestige of the state or which invades private life.

Mar. 7 An oil law is enacted which permits private and foreign exploitation of Turkey's oil reserves.

Apr. 2 Treaty of mutual friendship is signed by Turkey and Pakistan. Adjoining nations are invited to join.

May 2 *National elections,* in which the Democrats win 503 Assembly seats out of 541, thereby increasing their majority.

May 14 New Assembly meets. Bayar is re-elected President, and Menderes is again named Prime Minister.

May 3	Greek Prime Minister Papagos announces that Britain must cede Cyprus to Greece or he will take the issue to the U.N.
June 6	Greece, Yugoslavia, and Turkey decide to set up a joint consultative assembly and to convert their treaty of friendship into a military alliance.
June 22	A law is enacted that makes all government officials (including professors and judges) subject to retirement when they have completed 25 years of service or become 60 years of age.
July 5	*A law is passed giving the government power to discharge civil servants (including professors and most judges) without right of appeal.*
July 21	A cabinet decree limiting profits on the sale of most goods goes into effect.
Aug. 9	*The Balkan Pact is signed* by Greece, Yugoslavia, and Turkey which binds the three countries in a mutual defense accord for 20 years.
Oct. 19	Britain agrees to evacuate the Suez base, although retaining the right of re-entry in event of an attack against Turkey or any of the Arab League states.
Nov.–Dec.	Political strife becomes bitter. A number of arrests occur for alleged slander of high government functionaries and for writing or speaking in such a way as to undermine the financial stability of the country. Issues: availability of consumer goods, press freedom, judicial freedom, adequacy of economic planning, constitutionality of law.

1955

Jan. 6–18	Menderes visits Iraq, Lebanon, and Syria to form a defense pact, apparently under Western urging.
Jan. 17	Egypt opens a campaign to prevent Arab countries from cooperating with Turkey. An impending visit to Egypt by Menderes is canceled.
Jan. 22	Arab League representatives assemble in Cairo, where Egyptian Prime Minister Nasser harshly criticizes impending Turkish-Iraqi pact.
Jan. 23	Iraq, Lebanon, Jordan, and Syria refuse to censure the impending Turkish-Iraqi pact.
Feb. 24	*Turkish-Iraqi mutual defense pact (Baghdad Pact) is signed* (ratified by Turkey on Feb. 26 and becomes operative Apr. 15).

Mar. 1 Moscow radio declares that the Baghdad Pact is a "stab in the back of all Arab nations."

Mar. 2 Yugoslavia, Greece, and Turkey agree to set up a consultative assembly consisting of 20 members of parliament from each of their national parliaments.

Apr. 1 Turkey and Iraq invite Pakistan to join the Baghdad Pact.

Apr. 4 Great Britain becomes the third member of the Baghdad Pact.

Apr. 17 Asian-African Conference opens in Bandung, Indonesia, with Turkey participating.

Apr. 20 U.S.-Turkish relations allegedly deteriorating due to unwillingness of the U.S. to provide more economic aid, U.S. demands for internal economic and fiscal reforms, and inept diplomacy.

Apr. 21 Cyprus issue is becoming explosive in Istanbul as a meeting of Turkish students erupts into a near riot.

June 21 U.S. rejects Turkey's request for a $300 million loan.

July 26 Greece asks U.N. to include Cyprus issue on its agenda.

Aug. 24 Menderes declares that Turkey will protect the Turkish minority on Cyprus in event local authorities are unable to do so. He declares Turkey's minimum position is that Cyprus continue as a British crown colony.

Aug. 29 London conference on Cyprus begins, with Britain, Turkey, and Greece participating.

Sept. 6 *News of the alleged bombing of Atatürk's birthplace in Salonica (Greece) sets off anti-Greek rioting in Istanbul, Izmir, and Ankara.* Extensive damage is done to non-Moslem property in Istanbul. Martial law is declared, and a curfew enforced. (Close to 3,000 persons are subsequently arrested, later to be released.)

Sept. 7 The London conference on Cyprus adjourns without agreement. The Greeks insist on union with Greece.

Sept. 12 The government blames the rioting on communists.

Sept. 23 Pakistan joins the Baghdad Pact.

Sept. 23 The U.N. rejects the Greek proposal to place the Cyprus issue on the agenda.

Sept. 27 Nasser announces that the USSR is offering arms to Egypt.

Sept. 28 Menderes promises assistance to those injured in the Sept. 6 rioting.

Oct. 11 Iran joins the Baghdad Pact over vigorous Soviet protest.

Oct. 12 After many newspapers have been suspended and newsmen jailed by government action, 19 Democratic Party members of the National Assembly demand that proof of the accuracy of a published statement be made relevant to defense in prosecutions under the Press Law. Rejected by the party. Subsequently 10 of the 19 resign from the party, and the other 9 are expelled.)

Nov. 26 State of emergency declared on Cyprus as violence breaks out between the Greek majority and Turkish minority.

Nov. 29 The number of Democratic Assembly members who have resigned from the Party grows to 22 as a revolt within the Assembly group flares up. The cabinet resigns, but Menderes calls for a vote of confidence in himself, which he receives. President Bayar directs Menderes to form a new cabinet (which he is unable to do until Dec. 9).

Dec. 19 Martial law is lifted in Ankara and Izmir.

Dec. 20 The Freedom Party is established by rebel Democratic Assembly members (now 28). Political relations continue to deteriorate.

1956

Mar. 10 Archbishop Makarios is exiled by the British from Cyprus.

May 18 A law is enacted giving the government increased power to regulate the distribution and pricing of goods and services. Many goods are in critically short supply.

June 6 Amendments to the Press Law are passed which increase the government's power over the press. Violently opposed by all opposition groups.

June 16 Coverage of the Labor Law is extended.

June 27 *A bill limiting the holding of public political meetings is enacted,* as opposition groups boycott the Assembly.

July 26 Egypt nationalizes the Suez Canal.

Aug. 14–17 London conference to discuss the seizure of the Suez, with Turkey participating. Turkey supports the U.S. position and insists on the recognition of Egyptian rights and sovereignty. (Favorable Arab reaction.)

Sept. 13	Decree is published approving the inclusion of religious lessons in middle schools (grades 6 and 7).
Sept. 27	Turkey joins the Suez Canal Users' Association.
Sept.	The razing of a part of Istanbul as a prelude to reconstruction becomes a major political issue.
Oct. 1	The People's Party rejects a Freedom Party proposal to form a united opposition.
Oct. 11	Turkey's participation in the International Finance Corporation is announced.
Oct. 23	Hungarian revolt begins.
Oct. 28	Turkey joins Western powers in protesting Soviet action in Hungary.
Oct. 29	Israeli forces attack Egypt.
Oct. 31	Anglo-French attack on Egypt begins.
Nov. 2	Turkey supports U.S.-sponsored motion in the U.N. for a cease-fire in Egypt (passed).
Nov. 6	French and British order a cease-fire.
Nov. 26	Turkey withdraws its ambassador to Israel until such time as Israel is willing to resolve its differences with the Arabs.
Dec. 1	The Dean of the Political Science Faculty of the University of Ankara is taken into custody because of alleged public, politically-inspired criticism of the government. (Other faculty resignations in protest follow, also a student boycott of classes.) The issue of university autonomy becomes important.
Dec. 1	Turkey holds army maneuvers on Syrian frontier as reports of a Soviet-sponsored communist buildup in Syria circulate.
Dec. 29	*President Eisenhower proclaims U.S. intent to guarantee the national integrity and independence of Middle Eastern states. — Eisenhower Doctrine.*

1957

Jan. 15	U.S.-Turkish agreement in which Turkey undertakes to guarantee the convertibility and transfer of capital and earnings of approved U.S. private investment in Turkey.
Feb. 26	U.N. General Assembly passes resolution to the effect that the Cyprus issue should be resolved by the interested parties.
Mar. 6	The schools for preachers and worship leaders given official status.

Mar. 9	U.S. Congress passes the Eisenhower Doctrine as a joint resolution. (See Dec. 29, 1956.)
Mar. 22	U.S. announces its intent to join the military committee of the Baghdad Pact.
Sept. 4	After a long discussion, the three major opposition parties issue a joint proclamation of principles.
Sept. 7	Fuat Köprülü, a Democratic Party founder, resigns from the party. (He had resigned as Foreign Minister on June 19, 1956.)
Sept. 11	*A law is enacted that makes political coalitions in elections illegal.*
Sept. 12	Ten-months' moratorium on all farmers' debts is enacted into law.
Oct. 27	*National elections.* With slightly less than a majority popular vote, the Democrats win 424 Assembly seats; the People's Party, 178; the Freedom Party, 4 seats; the Republican Nation's Party, 4 seats. Considerable disorder attends the election.
Nov. 1	The National Assembly re-elects Celal Bayar as President. Menderes is again named as Prime Minister.

1958

Jan. 16	Nine army officers arrested for plotting against the government.
July 14	Military coup d'état in Baghdad in which the monarchy is overthrown, and Nuri Said Pasha — pro-Turkish leader — is killed. Turkish army begins moving toward the Iraqi frontier.
July 10	Ministry of Coordination created for central economic planning.
July 15	U.S. Marines land in Lebanon upon the request of the Lebanese government currently under violent attack by Lebanese rebels who are allegedly receiving arms from Egypt. The U.S. move is approved by Turkey.
July 25	The USSR accuses Turkey of planning attack on Iraq. (U.S. officials dissuade Turks from invading Iraq.)
July 31	Turkey recognizes the new Iraqi state.
Aug. 3	A loan of $359 million is granted to Turkey ($234 million from the U.S., $25 million from the International Monetary Fund, and $100 million from OEEC countries). In return, Turkey promises financial reforms of an anti-inflationary nature. Lira devalued from $0.36 to $0.11 for most purposes.

Oct. 17 The Republican Nation's Party and the Villager's Party decide to unite to form the Republican Villager's Nations Party.

Nov. 24 The Freedom Party dissolves itself to merge with the People's Party.

1959

Feb. 17 Menderes is a survivor of an airplane crash outside of London in which a number of persons are killed. The incident makes a deep impression among the more conservative (religious) elements of the Turkish public.

Feb. 19 *Greek, Turkish, and British representatives agree to establish an independent Cypriot Republic* on a communal basis, with the president to be of Greek ethnic extraction and the vice-president, Turkish. Britain is to retain her military bases on the island. Cyprus, Turkey, and Greece are to cooperate for common defense.

Mar. 5 *Turkey and the U.S. sign a bilateral defense accord* in which it is stated that in accordance with the U.S. Constitution the U.S. government will, in the case of aggression against Turkey, "take such appropriate action, including the use of armed forces, as may be mutually agreed upon . . . in order to assist the Government of Turkey at its request."

Sept. Turkey applies for associate membership in the European Economic Community.

Oct. 10 Negotiations completed for construction of an IRBM base in Turkey.

Dec. 6 President Eisenhower arrives in Turkey for two-day visit.

1960

Mar. 19 Israel and Turkey sign a trade and payments agreement.

Apr. 3 *Army troops are used to stop a political tour of Inönü.*

Apr. 16 Cyprus becomes independent.

Apr. 18 *All party political activity is ordered suspended for three months* pending an investigation of the People's Party by an Assembly commission.

Apr. 28 University students demonstrate against the government, and martial law is imposed.

Apr. 30 Another student demonstration in Istanbul. The universities are closed.

May 2 Antigovernment riot, led by students, in Istanbul. Troops are used to suppress it.

May 3 Lt. Gen. Cemal Gürsel, Commander of the Land Forces, demands political reforms in a letter to Menderes (published later).

May 5 Gürsel resigns.

May 6 Inönü predicts "rejection" of the Menderes regime by the people.

May 9 Turkish-U.S. defense agreement ratified by the Assembly (see Mar. 5, 1959).

May 14 Large student demonstration in Ankara against the government.

May 21 Turkey Army War College cadets march in Ankara in support of the antigovernment demonstrations.

May 27 *An officer group led by General Gürsel seizes power. Menderes, Bayar, and other political leaders are arrested.* Free elections are promised.

May 28 Gürsel becomes acting President and Prime Minister, assisted by a 16-man cabinet, largely civilian. A 37-member Committee of National Union, entirely military, remains the real power.

May 28 A board of university professors and jurists is appointed to draft a new constitution.

June 1 All but 17 Democratic members of the Assembly are under arrest, plus many others.

June 12 A provisional constitution for the period until new elections are held is announced.

June 23 All political meetings are prohibited, and local branches of political parties are ordered closed.

June 30 The Press Law is abolished by decree.

July 7 All political activity is forbidden.

Aug. 18 Decree establishing revolutionary tribunals is proclaimed.

Sept. 24 The International Development Association is created with Turkey as a charter member.

Sept. 29 *The Democratic Party is abolished by court order.*

Sept. 30 The State Planning Organization is created (is later incorporated in the new constitution).

Oct. 6 The press laws of the Menderes Government are repealed by the ruling Committee of National Union.

Oct. 14 The leaders of the Menderes government go on trial for corruption and unconstitutional act.

Oct. 27 The government summarily dismisses 147 members of Turkish university faculties without explanation.

Nov. 13 Gürsel dismisses 14 of the 37 members of the Committee of National Union for their extremist views. (They are appointed to "advisory" posts abroad.)

1961

Jan. 6 A Constituent Assembly convenes under special law promulgated by the Committee of National Union. It consists of a 272-man lower house (selected by designated political, professional, and business groups) and an upper house consisting of the 23 members of the Committee.

Feb. 11 The Justice Party is established and is supported by many former Democrats; also the New Turkey Party, closely identified with the regime.

Feb. 24 The USSR protests Turkey's cooperation with NATO in permitting IRBM bases on its soil.

Apr. 1 Political parties are permitted to proceed with their regional organization and to hold indoor meetings.

May 22 The Constituent Assembly extends martial law for three more months.

May 27 The new constitution and a new electoral law embodying proportional representation are accepted by the Constituent Assembly.

July 9 The new constitution receives a majority vote (60 per cent) in a popular referendum in which 83 per cent of the electorate participates.

July 31 Martial law is extended to all of Turkey by decree of the Committee of National Union because of the activity of pro-Menderes groups.

Sept. 4 The Constituent Assembly adjourns for elections.

Sept. 15 Menderes, Bayar, Fatin Rüştü Zorlu (former Foreign Minister), Hasan Polatkan (former Finance Minister), and eleven other members of the Menderes regime are sentenced to death. The sentences of Bayar and the eleven are commuted to life imprisonment (Bayar, because of age; the eleven, because of lack of unanimity among members of the court).

Sept. 16 Zorlu and Polatkan are hanged.

Sept. 17 *Menderes is hanged* after a suicide attempt.

Oct. 15	National elections. No party wins a majority in the Assembly or Senate, but the People's and Justice Parties predominate.
Oct. 24	The four major parties (People's, Justice, New Turkey, Republican Villagers) agree to form a coalition government.
Oct. 25	The new, two-house Grand National Assembly convenes, with 450 deputies and 172 senators participating.
Oct. 26	Gürsel is elected President.
Nov. 20	A coalition cabinet is formed under the prime ministry of Inönü.
Dec. 1	Martial law is ended.

NOTES

Chapter I. The Young Turks

1. T. Z. Tunaya, *Türkiyede Siyasi Partiler* (Istanbul, 1952), p. 165.

2. *British Documents on the Origins of the War,* vol. V, "The Near East" (His Majesty's Stationery Office, London, 1928), p. 34.

3. A good general account of pre-republican reforms is Bernard Lewis, *The Emergence of Modern Turkey* (London: Oxford University Press, 1961), pp. 1–233, 317–480.

4. Most important were the Hatti-Şerif of 1839, the Hatti-Hamayun of 1856, and the Constitution of 1876. Texts of the first two are to be found in J. C. Hurewitz, *Diplomacy in the Near and Middle East* (Princeton: D. Van Nostrand Company, 1956), vol. 1, pp. 113 and 149, respectively, and of the 1876 Constitution in E. Hertslet, *The Map of Europe* (London: His Majesty's Stationery Office, 1891), vol. iv, pp. 2531–2540. A summary of the last appears in C. Brockelmann, *History of the Islamic Peoples* (New York: G. P. Putnam, 1947), p. 376. See also Şerif A. Mardin, "Some Explanatory Notes on the Origins of the Mecelle," *The Muslim World,* vol. LI, nos. 3 and 4, July and October 1961.

5. See. E. E. Ramsaur, *The Young Turks* (Princeton University Press, 1957); R. D. Robinson, "Main Currents in Turkish Literature" (New York: American Universities Field Staff, 1954); Halide Edib, *Conflict of East and West* (Delhi: Jamia Millia, 1936), pp. 189–194; and Şerif Mardin, *The Genesis of Young Ottoman Thought* (Princeton University Press, 1962).

6. *British Documents,* vol. V, "The Near East," p. 319. The English scholar and gentleman, Sir Charles Eliot, wrote an entire book about Turkey at the time without any mention of the Committee. The future of Turkey, according to Sir Charles, depended upon the character of the next sultan and the attitude of the Russians. See his *Turkey in Europe* (London: Edward Arnold, 1908).

7. See F. McCullagh, *The Fall of Abd-ul-Hamid* (London: Methuen & Company, Ltd., 1910); also I. Orga, *Phoenix Ascendant* (London: Robert Hale, 1958), pp. 37–38.

8. Ernest Jaeckh, *The Rising Crescent* (New York: Farrar & Reinhard, 1944), p. 96.

9. See A. E. Yalman, *Turkey in the World War* (New Haven, 1930) for the record of Turkey's wartime years. For decision to enter war, see Djemal Pasha, *Memories of a Turkish Statesman* (New York: George H. Doran Company, 1922), pp. 107ff.

10. Sarkis Atamian, *The Armenian Community* (New York: Philosophical Library, 1955), map facing p. 52. Percentage of Armenians in the so-called Armenian provinces: Sivas-Amasya, 37.9 per cent; Erzurum, 34.2 per cent; Van-Hakkâri, 52.8 per cent; Mus-Bitlis, 47.2 per cent; Diyarbakir, 35.5 per cent; Elaziğ-Malatya, 37.3 per cent.

11. See F. Kazemzadeh, *The Struggle for Transcaucasia* (New York: Philosophical Library, 1951), pp. 43–46, 85–86; also W. E. D. Allen and Paul Muratoff, *Caucasian Battlefields* (Cambridge: University Press, 1953), pp. 458ff.

12. See A. Moorehead, *Gallipoli* (New York: Harper & Brothers, 1956).

13. Orga, *Phoenix Ascendant*, p. 42.

14. For text of the Mudros Armistice, see J. C. Hurewitz, *Diplomacy*, vol. II, p. 36.

15. Estimated population of the Ottoman Empire in 1908 was 30 million, of which about 6 per cent was of Greek Orthodox faith, 3 per cent Gregorian, and 2 per cent Hebrew. The racial breakdown was reflected in the 275 members of the 1909 Parliament: 142 Turks, 60 Arabs, 25 Albanians, 23 Greeks, 12 Armenians, 5 Jews, 4 Bulgarians, 3 Serbs, 1 Walachian (Tunaya, *Türkiyede Siyasi Partiler*, pp. 164–165).

16. Z. Gökalp, *Turkish Nationalism and Western Civilization* (New York: Columbia University Press, 1959; tr. and ed. Niyazi Berkes), p. 137; see also Uriel Heyd, *Foundations of Turkish Nationalism* (London: Luzac & Company, 1950), pp. 62–63.

17. Gökalp, *Turkish Nationalism*, p. 138.

Chapter II. The New Turk

1. Orga, *Phoenix Ascendant*, pp. 38–39.
2. Moorehead, *Gallipoli*, p. 18.
3. *Ibid.*, p. 139.
4. *Ibid.*, pp. 139–140.
5. *Ibid.*, p. 290.
6. Allen and Muratoff, *Caucasian Battlefield*, p. 429.
7. A. E. Yalman, *Turkey in My Time* (Norman: University of Oklahoma Press, 1956), p. 50.

8. This aspect is discussed in Tevfik Bĭyĭkoğlu, *Atatürk Anadolu'da* (Ankara: Türk Tarĭhĭ Kurumu Basĭmevi, 1959), p. 11.

9. "The British had sent Mustapha Kemal," writes veteran Foreign Service Officer Robert Dunn in his *World Alive* (New York; Crown Publishers, 1956), p. 311.

10. M. Kemal, *Speech of October 1927* (Leipzig: K. F. Koehler, 1929), p. 15.

11. Robert Dunn, *World Alive*, pp. 412–413.

12. Zsa Zsa Gabor, "My Story," *McCall's*, August 1960, pp. 150–151.

13. *Ibid.*, p. 151.

14. H. C. Armstrong, *Grey Wolf* (London: Arthur Barker, Ltd., 1932), p. 333. See also D. von Mikusch, *Mustapha Kemal* (London: William Heinemann Ltd., 1931); H. Froembgen, *Kemal Ataturk* (New York: Hillman-Curl, Inc., 1937); and Irfan and Margarete Orga, *Atatürk* (London: Michael Joseph, 1962). There are also several biographies in Turkish, of which the most useful are perhaps E. B. Şapalyo, *Atatürk'ün Hayatĭ* (Ankara: Zafer Gazetesi, 1954) and "Atatürk," *Islam Ansiklopedisi*, fasc. 10 (Istanbul: Milli Eğitim Basĭmevi, 1949).

15. See Orga, *Phoenix Ascendant*, pp. 28–46.

16. For a theoretical discussion of this process, see Everett E. Hagen, *On the Theory of Social Change* (Homewood: Dorsey press, 1962), pp. 88ff. Kemal even went through a period of personal retreatism which is described by Hagen as generally intervening between the authoritarian personality (identified with traditional society) and the appearance of creative personality. Indeed, Hagen's description of the development of creative personality is, to an extraordinary extent, an outline of Kemal's own life and characteristics.

Chapter III. Kemal's Problem

1. M. Kemal, *Speech*, p. 9.

2. Sultan Mohammed VI.

3. Mohammed VI's Grand Vizier and brother-in-law.

4. Reported in the *Literary Digest*, March 20, 1920.

5. *Ibid.*

6. *Ibid.*

7. *Ibid.*, July 17, 1920.

8. H. W. Jessup, "Future of the Ottoman Empire," *Annals of the American Academy of Political Science.*

9. Gregory Mason, "Turkey in Decay," *Outlook*, 123:85–86 (September 17, 1919).

10. Adapted from H. A. R. Gibb, *Mohammedanism* (London, New York: Oxford University Press, 1949), pp. 121ff.

11. A recent estimate places the number of Alevis (Shiites) at 12 million. (Professor Bahrî Savci in a public statement reported in *Cumhuriyet*, April 29, 1963.)

12. For further analysis of village life, see John A. Morrison, "Alişar, a Unit of Land Occupance in the Kanak Su Basin of Central Anatolia" (unpublished Ph.D. dissertation, submitted at the University of Chicago, 1938); I. Yasa, *Hasanoğlan* (Ankara: Yeni Matbaa, 1957); P. A. Stirling, *The Social Structure of Turkish Peasant Communities* (unpublished Ph.D. dissertation, submitted at Oxford University, 1951); M. Makal, *A Village in Anatolia* (London: Valentine, Mitchell & Co., Ltd., 1954); I. Orga, *The Caravan Moves On* (London: Secker and Warburg, 1958); P. A. Stirling, "A Death and a Youth Club: Feuding in a Turkish Village," *Anthropological Quarterly*, January 1960, p. 51; I. Yasa, *Problems of Outlying Rural Administration in Turkey* (Ankara: Public Administration Institute for Turkey and the Middle East, 1956); *1949 Village Census* (Ankara: Central Statistical Office, 1952); G. Helling and B. Helling, *Rural Turkey, a New Socio-Statistical Appraisal* (Istanbul: University of Istanbul, Faculty of Economics, 1958); N. Helburn, "A Stereotype of Agriculture in Semiarid Turkey," *The Geographical Review*, vol. XLV, no. 3, 1955. See also R. D. Robinson, Letters to the Institute of Current World Affairs, New York 1949–50; no. 10 (Village Statistics), no. 24 (Village Law), no. 25 (Village Housing), no. 26 (Village Clothing), no. 27 (Village Food), no. 28 (Village Tools), no. 34 (Village Institutions), no. 35 (Village Communications), no. 36 (Village Economics), no. 40 (Alişar Revisited); Paul Stirling, "Social Ranking in a Turkish Village," *British Journal of Sociology*, vol. IV, no. 1, March 1953, p. 31. A recent authentic account of village life in fictional form is Yashar Kemal, *Memed My Hawk* (New York: Pantheon, 1961). An older, somewhat romanticized fictional account of rural Anatolian life is Reşat Nuri Güntekin, *The Autobiography of a Turkish Girl* (London: George Allen & Unwin, 1949).

13. The "warrior virtues" still rate high in Turkey. See G. Helling, "A Study of Turkish Values" (paper delivered at the Conference on Turkey, Harvard University, June 1959).

14. See D. Lerner and R. D. Robinson, "Swords and Ploughshares: The Turkish Army as a Modernizing Force," *World Politics*, vol. XIII, no. 1, October 1960, p. 19.

15. See C. W. Ryan, "Preliminary Report on Fuel Supplies of East Turkey" (Ankara: Foreign Operations Administration, 1954).

16. The function of the *kabile* is described in detail by Stirling, *Social Structure.*

17. L. M. J. Garnett, *The Women of Turkey and Their Folklore* (vol. 2, London: David Nutt, 1891), p. 115.

18. Aneurin Bevin, *In Place of Fear* (New York: Simon and Schuster, 1952), p. 37.

19. D. Lerner, *The Passing of Traditional Society* (Glencoe: Free Press, 1958), pp. 143ff.

20. *Ibid.*, pp. 49ff.

21. *Ibid.*, p. 70.

22. See A. H. Lybyer, *The Government of the Ottoman Empire in the Time of Suleiman the Magnificent* (Cambridge, Mass.: Harvard University Press, 1913), pp. 101–103; H. A. R. Gibb and Harold Bowen, *Islamic Society and the West* (vol. 1, London: Oxford University Press, 1950), pp. 235ff.

23. Reported in "Minstrel Veysel" (New York: Institute of Current World Affairs, 1952).

24. London School of Oriental and African Studies, 1953.

25. See Albert H. Lybyer, *Government of the Ottoman Empire* and Barrette Miller, *The Palace School of Muhammed the Conqueror* (Cambridge, Mass.: Harvard University Press, 1941).

26. There is no good sociological study of traditional life in the provincial towns of Anatolia. Although written much later, it may be useful to refer to R. D. Robinson, "Gaziantep, General Description" (New York: Letters to the Institute of Current World Affairs, December 1948) and "Gaziantep After Five Years" (New York: American Universities Field Staff, May 10, 1955).

27. Kemal H. Karpat, "Social Themes in Contemporary Turkish Literature," part II, *Middle East Journal,* vol. 14, no. 2, Spring 1960, p. 160.

28. *Ibid.*, p. 159.

Chapter IV. The Atatürk Revolution

1. See M. Kemal, *Speech,* pp. 19–20.

2. *Ibid.*, pp. 16–17.

3. Bĭyĭkoğlu, *Atatürk Anadolu'da,* p. 12.

4. See D. A. Rustow, "The Army and the Founding of the Turkish Republic," *World Politics,* vol. XI, July 1959, pp. 533, 539ff.

5. *Ibid.*, pp. 524–525.

6. M. Kemal, *Speech*, p. 167.

7. *Ibid.*, p. 58.

8. *Ibid.*, p. 119.

9. For text, see H. M. Davis, *Constitutions, Electoral Laws and Treaties of States in the Near and Middle East* (Duke University Press, 1947), pp. 354–356.

10. For the text, see *ibid.*, pp. 357–358.

11. For a good summary account, see Elaine D. Smith, *Turkey: Origins of the Kemalist Movement* (Washington, D.C., 1959), pp. 1–29.

12. For text, see *ibid.*, pp. 38–39.

13. M. Kemal, *Speech*, p. 380.

14. For the text, see Hurewitz, *Diplomacy*, vol. II, pp. 81–89.

15. In the end 12 of the 17 army commanders of World War I were committed to the resistance movement. Rustow, *World Politics*, July 1959, p. 533.

16. Listed in Smith, *Turkey*, p. 35.

17. E. B. Şapolyo, *Kuvayi Milliye Tarihi: Gerilla* (Ankara: Ayyĭldĭz matbaacĭlĭk ve Gazetecilik, 1957), pp. 200–201; also A. F. Cebesoy, *Milli Mücadele Hatĭralarĭ* (Istanbul: Vatan Neşriyatĭ, 1958), pp. 344–345.

18. Cevat Üstün, retired Turkish Ambassador, in a personal interview, August 1959.

19. A. Karaev, *Iz Nedavnego Proshlogo* (Baku, 1926), p. 60, quoted in G. S. Harris, "The Rise and Fall of Communism in Turkey, 1919–121" (paper submitted to the Department of Oriental Languages, Princeton University, 1953).

20. See also Dunn, *World Alive*, p. 414.

21. See A. J. Toynbee, *The Western Question in Greece and Turkey* (London: Constable & Company Ltd., 1922) and H. Armstrong, *Turkey in Travail* (London: John Lane The Bodley Head Ltd., 1925).

22. J. Degras, *Soviet Documents on Foreign Policy* (London, 1951), p. 15, quoted in H. Dinerstein, "Soviet Policy in the Near and Middle East, 1917–1923" (Ph.D. dissertation, Harvard University, 1942), p. 195.

23. See M. Kemal, *Speech*, pp. 568–569 and Armstrong, *Turkey in Travail*, pp. 240–247.

24. For text of the Lausanne Treaty, see Hurewitz, *Diplomacy*, p. 119.

25. A useful account of the reforms is to be found in G. Lewis, *Turkey* (New York: Frederick A. Praeger, 1955), pp. 61–111; also in A. J. Toynbee, *Survey of International Affairs, 1925* (London:

Oxford University Press, 1927). See also D. A. Rustow, "Politics and Islam in Turkey, 1920–1955" in Frye (ed.), *Islam and the West* (The Hague: Mouton and Company, 1957).

26. Described by Mardin, *Some Explanatory Notes.*

27. A widely believed fiction is that the title caliph had been borne by the Ottoman sovereigns since 1517 when Selim I conquered Egypt and induced the titular Abbasid Caliph to cede his rights and office. But, in fact, long before this the title "had been applied in relation to a number of Moslem rulers (including the Ottoman Sultans)." See Gibb and Bowen, *Islamic Society,* vol. I, part 1, p. 34. It had been concluded by Islamic jurists that "every righteous ruler who governs with justice and enforces the *Şeria* is entitled to the style and prerogatives of the Caliphate . . . Caliphate and Sultanate were to all intents and purposes synonymous terms" (*ibid.*). The title initially carried the connotation of a successor or deputy to the Prophet. "That the Ottoman Sultan was the universal Caliph of Islam, after the Caliphs of Medina, Damascus, and Baghdad, was an idea entertained by no responsible jurist" (*ibid.*). However, there seems little doubt that to millions of Sunni Turkish Moslems the sultan in Constantinople was the universal caliph. Hence, in the Turkey of which we speak here, there was no real distinction between Church and State, and the sultan, as caliph, was considered the religious leader as well as emperor. The *Skeikh-ul-Islam,* who could be appointed and dismissed by Imperial order, assisted the sultan-caliph in the discharge of his religious duties and acted as the supreme court of appeal for cases over which the *sheria,* or religious law, had jurisdiction. Decisions of the *Sheikh-ul-Islam* were known as *fetvas* and might, if the sultan did not act first to prevent their issuance, even go so far as to justify the deposition or death of the sultan.

28. For text, see M. Kemal, *Speech,* p. 477.

29. *Ibid.,* p. 481.

30. For detailed historical account, see Toynbee, *Survey,* vol. I, pp. 25–29.

31. In his *Istiklal Harbĭmĭz* (Istanbul: Türkiye Yayĭnevi, 1960), pp. 978n, 1058n, 1065, 1137.

32. M. Kemal, *Speech,* p. 685.

33. Yalman, *Turkey in My Time,* pp. 141–142. He errs on the date of the law abolishing the Caliphate; that likewise was March 3.

34. *Ibid.,* pp. 142–143.

35. See L. Ostorog, *The Angora Reform* (London: University of London Press, Ltd., 1927); "The Reception of Foreign Law in Turkey," *International Social Science Bulletin* (United Nations

Economic and Social Council, vol. IX, no. 1, 1957), pp. 13–81; W. C. Smith, *Islam in Modern Society* (London: Oxford University Press, 1957), pp. 161–205; P. Stirling, "Religious Change in Republican Turkey," *Middle East Journal*, Autumn 1958, pp. 395ff.; H. A. Reed, "The Religious Life of the Modern Turkish Muslem" in Frye (ed.), *Islam and the West.*

36. See chapter V, p. 131.

37. For an account of the Armenian problem, see Atamian, *The Armenian Community;* also Dunn, *World Alive.*

38. J. K. Birge, personal conversation, 1948.

39. See H. Edip, *Conflict of East and West in Turkey* (Lahore: Shaikh Muhammed Ashraf, 1935).

40. See U. Heyd, *Language Reform in Modern Turkey* (Jerusalem: The Israel Oriental Society, 1954).

41. Prior to this move, the government had exercised a more general authority to reject applications for the formation of societies.

42. E. Bisbee, *The New Turks* (University of Pennsylvania Press, 1951), p. 281, n. 4.

43. Evidence for various interpretations is given in Karpat, *Turkey's Politics*, pp. 64–68. Karpat is surely wrong, however, in including, among the reasons for growing opposition in 1930, a commitment by the government to build a "state-owned economy." And his explanation for the inadequate pace of economic growth up to this time is clearly oversimplified. (See chapter V.)

44. See Frederick W. Frey, "The Turkish Elite" (to be published by the Massachusetts Institute of Technology Press, 1964), especially Chapter III.

45. There are two rather good books in English which provide a useful account of how the Atatürk Revolution affected personal and family life. The two are: I. Orga, *Portrait of a Turkish Family* (New York: Macmillan Company, 1950) and A. Bridge, *Dark Moment* (London: Chatto & Winders, 1952). The first is autobiographical, the second is a novel.

Chapter V. Economic Development to 1945

1. For a systematic study of Turkish values, see G. Helling, "A Study of Turkish Values" (paper presented to the Conference on Turkey, Harvard University, June 1959); also G. Helling, *A Study of Turkish Values by Means of National Stereotypes* (Ph.D. dissertation, University of Minnesota, 1959).

2. N. M. Bradburn, *The Managerial Role in Turkey: A Psychological Study* (Ph.D. dissertation, Harvard University, 1960), pp. 139–141. Bradburn defines need for achievement as "a disposition to engage in activities in which doing well or competing with a standard of excellence are important" (p. 10).

3. *The Capitulations* ("Memorandum submitted on behalf of the nonofficial British community in Constantinople," Istanbul, undated but probably published in late 1922), p. 4.

4. See P. M. Brown, *Foreigners in Turkey, Their Juridical Status* (Princeton University Press, 1914); also Eliot G. Mears, *Modern Turkey* (New York: Macmillan, 1924), pp. 354–383.

5. See D. C. Blaisdell, *European Financial Control in the Ottoman Empire* (New York: Columbia University Press, 1929).

6. *Turkey's External Public Debt History* (Washington: International Bank for Reconstruction and Development, Economic Department, May 1949), pp. 1–3.

7. James R. Mood, *Turkish Foreign Debt* (Washington: U.S. Department of Commerce, Supplement to Commerce Reports, Trade Information Bulletin no. 268, 8 September 1925), pp. 2 and 7.

8. See Stephen P. Ladis, *The Exchange of Minorities, Bulgaria, Greece and Turkey* (New York: Macmillan, 1932), pp. 441–442.

9. *Ibid.*, p. 438.

10. *Ibid.*, p. 439.

11. F. A. Ross, C. L. Fry, and E. Sibley, *The Near East and American Philanthropy* (New York: Columbia University Press, 1929), p. 30.

12. I. H. Tokin, *Türkiyede Sanayi* (Ankara: Istatistik Müdürlüğü, 1946), p. 34.

13. Mears, *Modern Turkey*, p. 312.

14. Reprinted in *ibid.*, pp. 356–357, from a French publication entitled *Les Intérêts financiers de la France dans l'Empire Ottoman* (July 1919).

15. Mears, *Modern Turkey*, p. 357.

16. *Ibid.*

17. Mood, *Turkish Foreign Debt*, p. 6; also "Railways in Turkey," *Levant Trade Review* (vol. XVII, no. 10, November 1929), pp. 361–368.

18. Tokin, *Türkiyede Sanayi*, p. 13.

19. Quoted in "Syndicates in Turkey," an official document prepared by the Ministry of Labor, Ankara (undated and unsigned,

but presumably written in mid-1949, typewritten, unpublished), p. 2. See also S. Rosen, *Labor in Turkey's Economic Development* (Ph.D. dissertation, Massachusetts Institute of Technology, August 1959).

20. Tokin, *Türkiyede Sanayi*, p. 10.

21. *Ibid.*, p. 12; see also Leigh-Ashton, "The Economy of Turkey" (Press Office, British Embassy, Ankara, January 1942, unpublished, typewritten), section V.

22. Adnan Halit Taşpinar, "Supplementary Notes to Industrial Organization" (Robert College, Istanbul, 1949, mimeographed only), pp. 3–5.

23. *Ulus*, December 12, 1956 (quoting Ismail Rüştü Aksal, former Minister of Finance).

24. *Bayindirlik Dergisi* (Istanbul: Bayindirlik Bakanliği, December 1948), chart following p. 6.

25. *Supra*, n. 12.

26. Enver Ziya Karal, *Türkiye Cumhuriyeti Tarihi, 1918–1953* (Istanbul, 1954), p. 182.

27. For further discussion, see Z. Y. Hershlag, *Turkey, An Economy in Transition* (The Hague: Uitgeverij van Keulen N.V., 1958), pp. 75–176; also Robert W. Kerwin, *Étatism and the Industrialization of Turkey: a Study of Turkish National Economic Policies and Attitudes (1933–1950)* (unpublished Ph.D. dissertation, School of Advanced International Studies, Johns Hopkins University, 1956).

28. *Islam Anisklopedisi* (Istanbul: Milli Eğitim Basimevi, 1949, "Atatürk"), Fasc. 10, pp. 789–791. A complete text of the speech appears in *Atatürk'ün Söylev ve Demeçleri* (Istanbul: Maarif Matbaasi, 1945), pp. 215ff.

29. *K. Atatürk Diyorki* (Istanbul: Varlik Yayinevi, 1951), p. 85.

30. For further details, see Tokin, *Türkiyede Sanayi*, p. 42.

31. "Petition Addressed to the Ministry of Economy by Private Textile Industrialists" (Ankara, October 1949, unpublished, typewritten).

32. Tokin, *Türkiyede Sanayi*, pp. 40, 43, 79.

33. *K. Atatürk Diyorki*, p. 85.

34. See H. V. Cooke, *Challenge and Response in the Middle East* (New York: Harper & Brothers, 1952), pp. 256–285; also *The Economy of Turkey* (Washington, D.C.: International Bank for Reconstruction and Development, 1951), pp. 3–9.

35. See Cooke, *Challenge and Response*, p. 269; also R. D.

Robinson, "Foreign Investment in Turkey" (New York: Letters to the Institute of Current World Affairs, December 1949).

36. For analysis of the structure of Turkish state enterprise see R. D. Robinson, *Investment in Turkey* (Washington: United States Department of Commerce, 1956) and A. H. Hanson, *The Structure and Control of State Enterprises in Turkey* (Ankara: Public Administration Institute for Turkey and the Middle East, 1954).

37. Subsequently, two other industrialization plans, 1937–1942, 1946–1950 were instituted. See *Ikinci 5 Yĭllĭk Sanayi Planĭ* (Ankara: Başvekâlet Matabaasĭ, 1936) for details of the first two plans; also Taşpĭnar, "Supplementary Notes." A good English language source is Hershlag, *Turkey*, pp. 103–124.

38. *The Development of National Banking in Turkey* (Ankara: Press Department, Ministry of Interior, 1938).

39. See *Labor Problems in Turkey* (Geneva: International Labor Office, 1950).

40. *K. Atatürk Diyorki*, p. 87.

41. Reported in *Vatan* (Istanbul, 14 March 1950), from remarks made by Cemil Sait Barlas, then Minister of State, to the Grand National Assembly.

42. Reference is to Max Thornburg, *Turkey, an Economic Appraisal* (New York: Twentieth Century Fund, 1949).

43. Hanson, *Structure and Control of State Enterprises*, pp. 10–11.

44. In 1927 204 Turkish lira as against 307 Turkish lira in 1945, according to Şefik Bilkur, *National Income of Turkey* (Ankara: Central Statistical Office, 1949), p. 40. See also Royaumont, France, *National Income Estimates of Turkey and New Measures to Improve Reliability* (Ankara: Central Statistical Office, 1951). A more recent study estimates a 1929 per capita real income index of 87 (1938 = 100) and a comparable figure for 1945 of 78 (H. B. Chenery, G. E. Brandow, and E. J. Cohn, "Turkish Investment and Economic Development" [Ankara: Foreign Operations Administration, Special Mission to Turkey, December 1953, mimeographed]), Table I-1. Certain aspects of the Chenery study are summarized in R. D. Robinson, "Turkish Investment and Foreign Exchange Problems" (New York: American Universities Field Staff, December 1954).

45. See Fay K. Berkes, *The Village Institute Movement of Turkey; an Educational Mobilization for Society Change* (unpublished Ph.D. dissertation, Teachers College, Columbia University, 1960); also R. D. Robinson, "Village Institutes" from Letters to the Institute of Current World Affairs (no. 34).

Chapter VI. The Postwar Decade, 1946–1956

1. For further statistical comparisons, see R. D. Robinson, *Developments Respecting Turkey* (New York: American Universities Field Staff, 1954–1957), vols. I, II, III, IV.

2. Observations are those made on a visit to this village by the author in 1949, as compared with the description of the same village by John A. Morrison in his *Alisar, A Unit of Land Occupance,* based on field work in the summer of 1932. See Robinson, "Alişar Revisited" from Letters to the Institute of Current World Affairs (no. 40).

3. See Robinson, "Village Economics" from *ibid.* (no. 36).

4. *Economic Report on Turkey, 1949* (Washington, D.C.: International Bank for Reconstruction and Development, 1950).

5. "Petition Addressed to the Ministry of Economy by Private Textile Industrialists" (unpublished, typewritten, October 1949).

6. Calculated from statistics published in *British Chamber of Commerce of Turkey Monthly Trade Journal* (Istanbul, December 1953), p. 877.

7. Figures given in special report prepared for the author by the Turkish Ministry of Labor, December 1949.

8. See R. D. Robinson, "Turkish Labor" (New York: Letters to the Institute of Current World Affairs, March 5, 1950).

9. O. Tuna, *Grev Hakkĭ* (Istanbul: Ismail Akgun Matbassĭ, 1951).

10. See R. D. Robinson, "Turkish Coal" (New York: Letters to Institute of Current World Affairs, March 3, 1950).

11. S. Rosen, *Labor in Turkey's Economic Development*, p. 230. Of the 492 disputes reaching the Supreme Arbitration Board up to March 1955, two-thirds were resolved in favor of labor (excluding 75 rejected for reasons of form).

12. A very useful analysis of organized Turkish labor as of mid-1951 was written by Irving Brown of the AFL-CIO in "A Trade Union Mission to Turkey" (New York: typewritten manuscript, April 17, 1951). See also *Labor Problems in Turkey,* note 39, chapter V.

13. "Survey of Answers" (Ministry of Commerce and Economics, Research Council, Spring 1950, unpublished, typewritten). The questionnaire was circulated in 10 October 1949.

14. Cemil Sait Barlas, Minister of State, on 13 March 1950, as reported in *Ulus* (Ankara, 14 March 1950). A useful account of The Industrial Development Bank of Turkey is contained in "Public

International Development Financing in Turkey" (New York: Columbia University School of Law, mimeo. 1962), pp. 71–100.

15. A point also made by Hershlag, *Turkey*, p. 184.

16. *1950 Sanayi ve İş Yerleri Sayimi* (Ankara: T. C. Istatistik Genel Müdürlüğü, press release, 20 March 1952).

17. *Vatan* (Istanbul), 3 February 1948.

18. *Cumhuriyet* (Istanbul), 9 July 1948.

19. *Son Posta* (Istanbul), 3 May 1949.

20. Reports dated November 13, 1949, and January 1, 1950, secured by the author from the Ministry of Agriculture, Ankara.

21. See R. D. Robinson, "The Operation of the Economic Cooperation Administration in Turkey" (New York: Letters to the Institute of Current World Affairs, February 1950).

22. See Karpat, *Turkey's Politics;* also R. B. Strassler, *Ismet Inönü: Turkish Leader* (a senior honors thesis, Department of History, Harvard College, 1959).

23. See Frey, "The Turkish Elite," Chapter VI.

24. As reported in *Ulus* (Ankara), 30 May 1950.

25. *Ibid.*

26. Per capita real income in 1953 was 556 Turkish lira, in 1956, 531 Turkish lira (at 1948 prices).

27. Reported in *Ulus* (Ankara), 14 February 1950.

28. See R. D. Robinson, "Tractors in the Village—A Study in Turkey," *Journal of Farm Economics,* vol. XXXIV, no. 4, November 1952, and *Economic and Social Aspects of Farm Mechanization in Turkey* (Faculty of Political Science, University of Ankara, 1953). The former article is based on a longer study, "Tractors in the Village" (New York: Letters to the Institute of Current World Affairs, 1952).

29. For a somewhat higher estimate, made in 1953, see Chenery *et al., Turkish Investments,* p. 116.

30. C. H. Wilson, *A Settlement Plan for Turkey* (Ankara: Economic Cooperation Administration, 1951).

31. M. D. Hansmeier, *Report Covering Crops and Conservation Work in Turkey* (Ankara: Foreign Operations Administration, 1954).

32. See *Proceedings of the Ankara Symposium on Arid Zone Hydrology* (Paris: UNESCO, 1953).

33. See C. W. Ryan, *A Guide to the Known Minerals of Turkey* (Ankara: United States Foreign Operations Administration, 1954).

34. See K. V. Wofford, "Report on Rural and Primary Education and related Teacher Training in Turkey" (Ankara: Ministry of Education, 1952, mimeographed).

35. See A. H. K. Sassani, *Education in Turkey* (Washington: Federal Security Administration, Office of Education, 1952); and T. Oğuzkan, *Adult Education in Turkey* (Paris: UNESCO, 1955).

36. See *Labor in Turkey* (Washington, D.C.: United States Department of Labor, February 1959), p. 8.

37. An interesting eyewitness account of the rioting is Frederic Dondern, "Istanbul's Night of Terror" (*Reader's Digest,* May 1956, pp. 185–192).

38. See R. D. Robinson, "Turkish Democracy Under Strain" (New York: Letters to the Institute of Current World Affairs, June 15, 1952), "Turkey's Undemocratic Laws" (July 10, 1953), "The Opposition and the Press" (May 1954), and "Economics and Democracy" (New York: American Universities Field Staff, March 1955).

Chapter VII. Turkey in Global Politics

1. H. Morgenthau, *Politics Among Nations* (New York: Alfred A. Knopf, 1950).

2. *Iktisat Gazetesi,* January 29, 1959; see also R. D. Robinson, "Turkish Oil" (New York: Letters to the Institute of Current World Affairs, November 1, 1950). 1962 figures from *Aylĭk İnstatistik Bülten,* June–July 1962; and *Aylĭk Bülten* (Merkez Bankasĭ), Nos. 1–12, 1963.

3. *U.S. News & World Report,* February 24, 1956, p. 58.

4. Morgenthau, *Politics,* p. 100.

5. *Cumhuriyet,* December 18, 1958.

6. See Z. N. Zeine, *Arab-Turkish Relations and the Emergence of Arab Nationalism* (Beirut: Khayat, 1958); L. S. Stavrianos, *The Balkans Since 1453* (New York: Rinehart & Company, 1958); and H. Saab, *The Arab Federalists of the Ottoman Empire* (Amsterdam: Djambatan, 1958).

7. See R. D. Robinson, "Turkey and Pan-Islamism" (New York: Letters to the Institute of Current World Affairs, 1949).

8. M. Kemal, *Speech,* pp. 378 and 591ff.; see also Lewis, *Turkey,* pp. 81–82.

9. C. J. Edmonds, *Kurds, Turks and Arabs* (New York: Oxford University Press, 1957), p. 383. Edmonds gives a useful personal account of the Mosul issue.

10. E. F. Rivinus, *Turkey and Her Near Eastern Neighbors* (Washington: Foreign Service Institute Monograph, Department of State, 1950), pp. 86ff. See also Toynbee, *Survey of International Affairs, 1925,* pp. 440–457.

11. *Cumhuriyet,* February 16, 1960.

12. For details on Turkey's World War II record see G. Kirk, *The Middle East in the War* (London: Oxford University Press, 1952), pp. 443ff.; A. Kilic, *Turkey and the World* (Washington: World Affairs Press, 1959), pp. 73ff.; Franz von Papen, *Memoirs* (London: Andre Deutsch, 1952); and L. C. Moyzisch, *Operation Cicero* (London: Alan Wingate, 1950).

13. See also R. D. Robinson, "Deterioration of Turkish-American Relations?" (New York: American Universities Field Staff, January 24, 1955). For cases of attempted leverage by Americans, see R. D. Robinson, "Americans in Turkey" (New York: Letters to the Institute of Current World Affairs, July 1, 1952).

14. See Walter Z. Laqueur, *Communism and Nationalism in the Middle East* (New York: Praeger, 1956).

15. See J. T. Shotwell and F. Deak, *Turkey at the Straits* (New York: Macmillan Company, 1940); *The Problem of the Turkish Straits* (Washington: U.S. Government Printing Office, 1947); and Kilic, *Turkey and the World,* pp. 114ff.

16. See R. D. Robinson, "Turkish-Soviet Relations, Mid-1953) (New York: Letters to the Institute of Current World Affairs, July 1, 1953).

17. See R. D. Robinson, "Turkey Looks at Egypt and the West" (New York: Letters to the Institute of Current World Affairs, November 15, 1951).

18. *Cumhuriyet,* August 12, 1958.

19. See R. D. Robinson, "Turkey's Strategic Position" (New York: Letters to the Institute of Current World Affairs, February 1, 1952).

20. For a more detailed account of the background and provisions of the Balkan Pact, see R. D. Robinson, "The Turks, the Greeks, and the Yugoslavs" (New York: Letters to the Institute of Current World Affairs, March 22, 1952) and R. D. Robinson, "Trieste, Yugoslavia, and Turkey" (New York: American Universities Field Staff, 1954).

21. The United States affiliated itself with the Pact's Economic and Anti-Subversion Committees in November 1955, and formally joined its Military Committee in June 1957.

22. In August 1959, the name of the Baghdad Pact was changed to the Central Treaty Organization. Its permanent headquarters is now in Ankara.

23. See G. Lenczowski, *Oil and State in the Middle East* (Ithaca: Cornell University Press, 1960), pp. 34–35.

24. On May 24, 1961, evidence was introduced at the trial of

Adnan Menderes before a revolutionary tribunal substantiating this account (*Cumhuriyet*, 25 May 1961).

25. An excellent historical account of the Mosul dispute is Toynbee, *Survey of International Affairs*, pp. 471ff.

26. Text of agreement appeared in the *New York Times*, February 24, 1959. See also Frank Tachau, "The Face of Turkish Nationalism," *Middle East Journal*, Summer 1959.

27. See C. W. Hostler, *Turkism and the Soviets* (London: George Allen and Unwin Ltd., 1957); O. Caroe, *Soviet Empire, the Turks of Central Asia and Stalinism* (London: Macmillan & Co., Ltd., 1953); S. A. Zenkowsky, *Pan-Turkism and Islam in Russia* (Cambridge, Mass.: Harvard University Press, 1960); and I. Spector, *The Soviet Union and the Muslim World* (Seattle: University of Washington, 1956).

Chapter VIII. The Eve of Revolution

1. The opposition Republican People's Party published an unofficial tally; *Secim Neticerleri Üzerinde Bir İnceleme* (C. H. P. Araştĭrma Bürösü, Yayĭn, no. 7, 1959). For an informed commentary on the 1957 elections see K. Karpat, "The Turkish Elections of 1957," *Western Political Science Quarterly*, 14:436–459 (June 1961).

2. *Cumhuriyet*, December 16, 1958, and *Ulus*, December 19, 1958.

3. *Cumhuriyet*, January 1, 1960; see also *Monthly Bulletin of the International Press Institute*, 1958–1959.

4. This section is substantially the same as part II of the author's article "Mosque and School in Turkey" in *The Muslim World*, vol. 51, no. 3, July 1961. It is reprinted here by permission.

5. E. Hekingil, *Education in Turkey* (Geneva: 22nd International Conference on Public Education, 1959), p. 7.

6. Ibid., p. 7.

7. R. D. Robinson, "An Analysis of Turkish Education" (Ankara: International Bank for Reconstruction and Development, a working paper for the 1950 Economic Survey Mission to Turkey, 1950, typewritten).

8. R. D. Robinson, *Developments Respecting Turkey*, vol. IV, p. 278; *Aylĭk Ististik Bülten* (Ankara: Istatistik Umum Müdürlüğü, November 1956, no. 33), p. 122; and Hekimgil, *Education in Turkey*.

9. Robinson, "Analysis of Turkish Education," p. 21.

10. K. Wofford, "Report on Rural and Primary Education and Related Teacher Training in Turkey" (Ankara: Ministry of Education, 1952, mimeographed), p. 30.

11. Substantiated by personal investigation by the author.

12. Robinson, "Analysis of Turkish Education."

13. See T. W. Schultz, "Investment in Man: An Economist's View," *The Social Service Review*, 32:109 (June 1959); and his "Human Wealth and Economic Growth," *The Humanist*, 1959, no. 2, p. 71.

14. Bradburn, *The Managerial Role in Turkey*, p. 139.

15. *Ibid.*, pp. 141–142.

16. This section is substantially the same as part I of the author's article "Mosque and School in Turkey" in *The Muslim World*, vol. 51, no. 2, April 1961. It is reprinted here by permission.

17. See H. A. Reed, "Turkey's New Imam-Hatip Schools," *The World of Islam*, n.s., vol. IV, nos. 2–3, 1955; H. L. Morgan, "A Turkish Textbook on Islam," *The Muslim World*, vol. 46, no. 4, October 1956 (for pt.1), vol. 47, no. 1, January 1957 (for pt.2).

18. Source of estimate is confidential but is believed to be reliable. See R. D. Robinson, "Official Religion in Turkey" (New York: Letters to the Institute of Current World Affairs, May 1, 1952).

19. For a description of religious events of this period, see B. Lewis, "Islamic Revival in Turkey," *International Affairs*, vol. XXVIII, 1952; H. A. Reed, "Revival of Islam in Secular Turkey," *Middle East Journal*, vol. 8, no. 3, Summer 1954; and Dankwart A. Rustow, "Politics and Islam" in Frye (ed.), *Islam and the West* (The Hague: Mouten and Company, 1957), pp. 90–107.

20. *Zafer*, February 25, 1960.

21. *Zafer*, March 1, 1960.

22. W. C. Smith, *Islam in Modern History* (Princeton University Press, 1957), p. 205.

23. The figures used here represent percentage distribution according to industrial origin of total national product at constant (1948) prices. See *Aylĭk İstatistik Bülten* (Ankara: Istatistik Umum Müdürlüğü, August 1956, no. 30), p. 120 and October 1962, no. 92), p. 148.

24. *Iktisadî Rapor*, 1959 (Ankara: Union of Chambers of Commerce, Chambers of Industry and Commercial Markets of Turkey, 1956), p. 7.

25. The first village cinema is reported to have opened in 1960 (*Cumhuriyet*, February 5, 1960).

26. Quoted in Fritz Baade, *Turkey-Country Report* (Rome:

Food & Agriculture Organization of the United Nations, 1959), p. V-3.

27. *Ibid.*, pp. V-Iff.; see also R. D. Robinson, "Turkish Investment and Foreign Exchange Problems" (New York: American Universities Field Staff, December 6, 1954); and "Report on Turkey," *Middle East Report, 1959* (Washington: Middle East Institute, 1959).

28. Official report in *Zafer*, February 4, 1960.

29. For details regarding Turkey's land distribution program, see A. J. Meyer, *Middle East Capitalism* (Cambridge, Mass.: Harvard University Press, 1959), pp. 65ff.; also R. D. Robinson, "Land Reform in Turkey" (New York: Letters to the Institute of Current World Affairs, July 15, 1952).

30. See R. D. Robinson, "Turkey's Agrarian Revolution and the Problem of Urbanization," *Public Opinion Quarterly*, vol. XXII, no. 3, Fall 1958.

31. A recent approach to this problem has been the attempt to set up industrial districts which would have the effect of pulling industry out of congested urban areas. For example, see the study prepared for the governments of Turkey and the United States by Checchi and Company of Washington, D.C., *Industrial Districts for Turkey: Proposed Plans for Pilot Project At Bursa* (Washington: Checchi and Company, 1962).

32. *Islam Ansiklopedisi*, p. 791.

33. Reported in *Zafer*, October 12, 1957, p. 4.

34. Reported in *Cumhuriyet*, October 21, 1957, p. 1. Used as major page 1 headline.

35. B. Higgins, *Economic Development* (New York: W. W. Norton, 1959), p. 418.

36. Baade, *Turkey-Country Report*, pp. V-3, V-16.

37. *Ibid.*, p. V-3. For an excellent account of foreign resources made available to Turkey over the 1950–1960 decade, see "Public International Development Financing in Turkey" (New York: Columbia University School of Law, mimeo, 1962).

38. In the *Harvard Business Review*, 35:32 (September-October 1957).

39. *Iktisadî Rapor, 1956*.

40. Extracted from various recent issues of *Aylı̆k Bülten* (Ankara: Central Bank of Turkey, monthly).

41. Hayrettin Erkman, as quoted in *Zafer* (February 5, 160). For further discussion of the inflationary factor in Turkey, see Robinson, "Report on Turkey," pp. 67ff.

42. Based on personal observation in Turkey at the time.

43. This section is substantially the same as the author's article "State Enterprise in Turkey" in the *New Outlook* (vol. IV, no. 4, February 1961). It is reprinted here by permission.

44. Law no. 6224, January 18, 1954. A text may be found in R. D. Robinson, *Investment in Turkey,* pp. 173–175.

45. In the case of Turkey, a "hard" currency or exchange is that of any machine or oil exporting country.

46. For a discussion of the measurement of "social return" in Turkey, see Chenery, Brandow, and Cohn, *Turkish Investment and Economic Development.*

47. For further details on the emerging pattern of public-private relationships in Turkey, see R. D. Robinson, "Kayseri and Adana, Pattern of Industrial Development" and "Gaziantep After Five Years" (New York: American Universities Field Staff, April 25 and May 10, 1955); also "Joint International Business Ventures in Turkey" (New York: Columbia University, July 1959), which was the basis for Chapter III, part II, in W. G. Friedman and G. Kalmanoff, *Joint International Business Ventures* (New York: Columbia University Press, 1961), pp. 481–499; and Richard D. Robinson, *Cases in International Business* (New York: Holt, Rinehart, and Winston, 1962), pp. 78–99.

48. *Turkey 1958* (Paris: Organization for European Economic Cooperation, 1959), p. 9.

49. Baade, *Turkey-Country Report.*

Chapter IX. The Army Takes Over

1. Much of this chapter is adapted from Lerner and Robinson, "Swords and Ploughshares." The material is used here by permission of *World Politics* and Professor Lerner. A useful descriptive account of the 1960 coup and subsequent events is Walter F. Weiker, *The Turkish Revolution, 1960–1961* (Washington: The Brookings Institution, 1963).

2. Lybyer, *Government of the Ottoman Empire,* pp. 90–91.

3. Gibb and Bowen, *Islamic Society and the West,* I, i, p. 31.

4. Quoted in Orga, *Phoenix Ascendant,* p. 38; see also "Atatürk," *Islam Ansiklopedisi* (Istanbul: Ministry of Education Publishing House, 1940), p. 271.

5. Orga, *Phoenix Ascendant,* p. 39.

6. *Atatürk Diyor Ki* (Istanbul: Varlĭk Yayĭnlarĭ, 1951), p. 86.

7. Rustow, "The Army and the Founding of the Turkish Republic," p. 535.

8. M. Kemal, *Speech,* p. 692.

9. See Law no. 5398, May 30, 1949.

10. Article 8, Election Law of 1946; Article 9, Election Law of 1950.

11. *Cumhuriyet*, November 26, 1958.

12. Figures are taken from *Maliye Istatistikler* (Ankara: Başbakanlik İstatistik Genel Müdürlüğü, 1947), and *Commentary on the 1950 National Budget by the Ministry of Finance* (Ankara: translated from the Turkish by the Economic Cooperation Administration Special Mission to Turkey, 1950).

13. Rustow, "The Army and the Founding of the Turkish Republic," *World Politics*, vol. XI, p. 550; see also the *Album* (1950, 1954, and 1958) published by the Grand National Assembly in Ankara. (In an article entitled "Military Deputies in the Assembly," *Halkçi* of February 3, 1955, gives short biographies of the 15 retired military men sitting in the Tenth Assembly. Two of these had also pursued civilian careers in law and government administration.)

14. In Rustow, 17 years, which is an admitted typographical error. Kemal was president from 1923 to 1938; Ismet, from 1938 to 1950.

15. Rustow, "The Army and the Founding of the Turkish Republic," p. 530.

16. See R. D. Robinson, "American Military Aid Program," (New York: Letters to the Institute of Current World Affairs, November 15, 1948); also "Impact of American Military and Economic Assistance Programs in Turkey" (New York: American Universities Field Staff, 1956). For a graphic account of the relative low level to which the Army had fallen by World War II, see A. Humbaracî, *Middle East Indictment* (London: Robert Hale, 1958), pp. 36–40.

17. For further development of this concept, see Daniel Lerner, *Passing of Traditional Society: Modernizing the Middle East* (Glencoe: Free Press, 1958), particularly chapters II, IV, and V.

18. R. D. Robinson, "American Military Aid Program."

19. R. D. Robinson, "Americans in Turkey."

20. Based on interviews with Lt. Col. Leon D. Marsh, Classification Officer and Assistant G-1, TUSAG, Ankara, during January 1952.

21. P. Stirling, *The Structure of Turkish Peasant Communities* (Ph.D. dissertation, Oxford University, 1951, reproduced in Ankara by R. D. Robinson, mimeographed), p. 165. Italics added.

22. No exact figures are available as to the number sent abroad, but as of early 1951, over 1,000 Turkish military personnel had been trained in American methods either in the United States or Germany. (R. T. Hartman, *Uncle Sam in Turkey* [New York:

Turkish Information Office, 1952, p. 14]—a reprint of articles published in the *Los Angeles Times* during September 1951). Early in 1958, the Turkish Minister of Foreign Affairs announced that 300 Turkish jet pilots had been trained in Canada alone (*Zafer*, February 26, 1958).

23. Humbaracî, *Middle East Indictment*, p. 39 (n), attributes the improvement of conditions in the Turkish Army during the early 1950's to a short spell of political liberalism, the experience of several thousand soldiers in Korea where they had seen armies with very different standards, as well as the influence of the U.S. Military Mission.

24. It is useful to examine these developments against the "withdrawal-of-status-respect" theory developed in Hagen, *On the Theory of Social Change*, particularly chapter 9, pp. 185ff.

25. A concept developed by David C. McClelland in his *The Achieving Society* (New York: D. Van Nostrand Company, 1961) and further explored by Hagen, *On the Theory of Social Change*.

26. Helling, "A Study of Turkish Values." In a mimeographed paper, "Changing Attitudes Toward Occupational Status and Prestige in Turkey" (University of Omaha, 1962), Helling reports that of the four groups of respondents used ("rural transitionals," "rural-urban transitionals," "urban middle class," and "cosmopolitans") only the first two placed the "colonel" as first in occupational respect ratings, which was eleven places (out of 63 occupations) above that given by the "cosmopolitans." Helling observed, "The precipitous decline in prestige of religious leaders and almost equally impressive decline in respect for the professional soldier with increasing sophistication is obvious. Equally interesting is the much more variegated collection of occupations (private, artistic, professional, business, etc.) that receive higher degrees of respect among Cosmopolitans than among Rural Transitionals." (*Ibid.*, p. 8).

27. Jay Walz in *The New York Times*, April 17, 1959.

28. Reported in *Zafer*, February 25, 1958.

29. Reported in *Cumhuriyet*, July 16, 1957.

30. Reported in *News from Turkey*, May 30, 1960.

31. *Cumhuriyet*, June 21, 1960.

32. *News from Turkey*, May 18, 1961.

33. *New York Times*, May 16, 1960.

34. *News from Turkey*, May 19, 1960.

35. *News from Turkey*, June 16, 1960.

36. See *News from Turkey*, June 16, 1960, for text of the letter.

37. Reported in *Zafer*, April 6 and 7, 1960.

38. *Cumhuriyet*, April 17, 1960.

39. *Cumhuriyet,* May 26, 1960.

40. An account by Istanbul University Professor Ali Fuat Başgil of a private conversation with the government leaders on April 28 (*Cumhuriyet,* June 5 and 6, 1960).

41. A useful account of the framing and adoption of the new constitution is Ismet Giritli, "Some Aspects of the New Turkish Constitution" (*The Middle East Journal,* vol. 16, no. 1, Winter 1962, pp. 1–17).

42. *Cumhuriyet,* July 12, 1961. For text of 1961 constitution, see *Middle East Journal,* vol. 16, no. 2, Spring 1962, pp. 215–235.

43. For annual summaries of ensuing events in Turkey see the author's reports in the *Americana Annuals* (New York: Americana Corporation, 1956 on).

43a. There is fairly substantial evidence that Menderes' very poor showing at his trial was occasioned by the administration of drugs by the authorities prior to his public appearances.

44. In articles published in *Cumhuriyet,* January 12, 1955; and *Istanbul,* December 31, 1954; also Robinson, *Turkish Investment and Foreign Exchange Problems,* p. 301.

45. Reported in *Türkiye Iktisat Gazetesi,* no. 431, July 29, 1961. The highest rates achieved had been 16.7 per cent in 1954 and 15.2 per cent in 1955. The average between 1950 and 1958 had been about 12 per cent.

46. Özgen Acar, "Toprak Reformu Kaçi̇lmaz bir Sonuçtur," (*Cumhuriyet,* May 8, 1963, p. 4).

INDEX

HARVARD MIDDLE EASTERN STUDIES

1. *Desert Enterprise: The Middle East Oil Industry in its Local Environment.* By David H. Finnie. 1958.
2. *Middle Eastern Capitalism: Nine Essays.* By A. J. Meyer. 1959.
3. *The Idea of the Jewish State.* By Ben Halpern. 1961.
4. *The Agricultural Policy of Muhammad 'Alī in Egypt.* By Helen Anne B. Rivlin. 1961.
5. *Egypt in Search of Political Community: An Analysis of the Intellectual and Political Evolution of Egypt, 1804–1952.* By Nadav Safran. 1961 (also a Harvard Political Study).
6. *The Economy of Cyprus.* By A. J. Meyer, with Simos Vassiliou. 1962.*
7. *Entrepreneurs of Lebanon: The Role of the Business Leader in a Developing Economy.* Yusif A. Sayigh. 1962.*
8. *The Opening of South Lebanon, 1788–1840: A Study of the Impact of the West on the Middle East.* By William R. Polk. 1963.
9. *The First Turkish Republic: A Case Study in National Development.* By Richard D. Robinson. 1963.
10. *The Armenian Communities in Syria under Ottoman Dominion.* By Avedis K. Sanjian. 1965.

* Published jointly by the Center for International Affairs and the Center for Middle Eastern Studies.